American Child Bride

American Child Bride

A History of Minors and Marriage in the United States

Nicholas L. Syrett

THE UNIVERSITY OF NORTH CAROLINA PRESS

Chapel Hill

This book was published with the assistance of the Thornton H. Brooks
Fund of the University of North Carolina Press.

Designed by Jamison Cockerham
Set in Arno Pro
by codeMantra
Manufactured in the United States of America

The University of North Carolina Press has been a member
of the Green Press Initiative since 2003.

Cover illustration: Mr. and Mrs. Browning Taking a Stroll, © Bettmann/CORBIS.

Library of Congress Cataloging-in-Publication Data
Names: Syrett, Nicholas L., author.
Title: American child bride : a history of minors and
marriage in the United States / Nicholas L. Syrett.
Description: Chapel Hill : The University of North Carolina Press, [2016] |
Includes bibliographical references and index.
Identifiers: LCCN 2015042775 | ISBN 9781469629537 (cloth : alk. paper) |
ISBN 9781469645551 (pbk. : alk. paper) | ISBN 9781469629544 (ebook)
Subjects: LCSH: Age of consent—United States—History. | Child marriage—
Social aspects—United States—History. | Child marriage—Law and
legislation—United States—History. | Marriage customs and rites—
United States—History. | Marriage law—United States—History.
Classification: LCC HQ535 .S97 2016 | DDC 306.8/10973—dc23
LC record available at http://lccn.loc.gov/2015042775

TO MICHAEL

Contents

Figures and Tables

Acknowledgments

Although the final product might be similar, writing a book that did not begin as a dissertation feels like another kind of undertaking, almost like a different species of document. No longer are people obligated to help you: no institutionalized prodding and deadlines and helpful suggestions on draft after draft, no stern looks and veiled threats about funding (or the lack thereof). Because of that I am struck by just how generous so many people have been as I wrote this book. It gives me great pleasure to acknowledge them here.

First and foremost I must thank the libraries and archives, as well as the librarians and archivists, who helped me find the documents that allowed me to answer my questions. Thanks to the staff of the Social Welfare History Archives at the University of Minnesota (especially Linnea Anderson); the Bancroft Library at UC-Berkeley; the San Francisco Public Library (especially the staff of the Government Documents Reference Desk); the Denver Public Library; the James Michener Library at the University of Northern Colorado (Jay Trask, in particular); the Sophia Smith Collection at Smith College (particularly Maida Goodwin); the Brooklyn Collection at the Brooklyn Public Library (Alla Roylance); the Columbia University Rare Books and Manuscripts Library; the American Antiquarian Society; the Rockefeller Archives Center (Monica Blank); the New York Public Library; the New-York Historical Society; the Boston Public Library; the California Historical Society Library; the Robbins Rare Book Room in the Law Library at UC-Berkeley; Patty Heard and the staff of the Law Library at Berkeley's Boalt Hall School of Law, who uncomplainingly searched out state statutes and session laws for me for more than a month; the Huntington Library; the Library of Congress; John Gartrell and Sarah Carrier at the Duke University Library and Archives; the New York County Clerk's Office; Heather Potter at the Filson Historical Society; and Carol Myers at the San Diego Historical Society. Thanks also to the staff of the following state libraries, archives, and research centers: New York (especially Nancy Horan); Tennessee (the always enthusiastic Allison DeFriese); North Carolina (Debra Blake); Texas (Megan Cooney); Maine (Nicole Dyszlewski and Anthony Douin); New Hampshire (Benoit Pelletier Shoja); Massachusetts (Jennifer Fauxsmith); California (Jessica Herrin); New Mexico (Felicia Lujan and Sibel Melik); Colorado; Ohio (Connie Connor); Washington (Erin Whitesel-Jones and Lupita Lopez); and Elizabeth Bouvier at the Massachusetts Supreme Judicial Court Archives.

I could not have completed this research without the generous support of a sabbatical leave, research monies from the Provost's Fund and the AVP for Research summer fund, and a course release from the RSCW program, all at the University of Northern Colorado. Also at UNC the Pilot Fund for Faculty Publications paid for the cost of reproducing the illustrations herein. I am grateful for a Clarke Chambers Travel Grant from the Social Welfare History Archives at the University of Minnesota and a travel grant to the John Hope Franklin Research Center in African and African American History and Culture at Duke University.

Thanks to a number of people who went out of their way to send me leads, point me in the direction of sources, or answer my questions: Corinne Field, Amanda Hendrix-Komoto, Holly Jackson, Lindsay Keiter, Jan Ellen Lewis, Katie Parkin, Renée Sentilles, Tavia Simmons at the U.S. Census Bureau, Rose Stremlau, and Chris Talbot. Sarah Arnusch and Cyrus Fernandez were excellent research assistants in the first stages of this project, and I'm grateful for their help.

I was fortunate to be able to give talks about this material at a number of schools: the Bentley School, Case Western Reserve University, the University of Cincinnati, Indiana University, and the University of Michigan. Thanks to Jason Chang, Renée Sentilles, Mackenzie Keys, Erika Gasser, Colin Johnson, Kristin Hass, and Mary Kelley for inviting me. Thanks also to all of the chairs, commentators, and fellow conference panelists at meetings of the AHA, ASA, ASLH, Berks, NWSA, OAH, SAWH, SHA, and SHCY from whom I learned so much: Kristin Celello, Beth Clement, Tim Cole, Brian Connolly, Rebecca Davis, Rebecca de Schweinitz, Sari Edelstein, Corinne Field, Richard Godbeer, Michael Grossberg, Melissa Hayes, Tera Hunter, Holly Jackson, Colin

Johnson, Will Kuby, Greta LaFleur, Adam Golub, Anna Krome-Lukens, Alison Lefkovitz, Sarah Levine-Gronningsater, Amanda Littauer, Jen Manion, Susan McKinnon, Allison Miller, Alexis Broderick Neumann, Rebecca Onion, Ishita Pande, Leslie Paris, Elizabeth Pleck, Johanna Rickman, Renée Romano, Don Romesburg, Lynn Sacco, Honor Sachs, Jim Schmidt, Bethany Schneider, Renée Sentilles, Julia Shatz, Rebecca Thaler Sherman, Christina Simmons, LaKisha Simmons, Stephen Vider, Barbara Young Welke, Barbara Bennett Woodhouse, and Karin Zipf. And for making those conferences so much fun: Dolores Inés Casillas, Jim Downs, Erika Gasser, Brian Halley, Colin Johnson, Will Kuby, Aaron Lecklider, Will Mackintosh, Jen Manion, Lucia McMahon, La Shonda Mims, Heather Murray, and Phil Tiemeyer.

Mike Grossberg, Jan Lewis, and Steve Mintz have been unfailingly generous even when they were under absolutely no obligation to be so. I am deeply grateful for their support. Likewise Mary Kelley remains a true mentor and friend. At the University of Northern Colorado, my colleagues have been supportive, reading drafts of a number of these chapters. Thanks especially to Joan Clinefelter, who has been chair of the department, as well as Emily Brownell, Fritz Fischer, Aaron Haberman, Diana Kelly, T. J. Tomlin, and Robbie Weis.

A number of people have read all or part of the manuscript. Thanks to Tom Bredehoft, Rebecca Davis, Jim Downs, Colin Johnson, Erin Jordan, Ned Kane, Aaron Lecklider, Ann Little, Renée Sentilles, and Malena Watrous for their insights and suggestions. Thanks also to Robin Bernstein and Stephanie Coontz, who took the time to read the book as it neared time to go to press. Two anonymous readers for UNC Press, one of whom turned out to be Kristin Celello, read the whole manuscript and improved it in all kinds of ways, for which I am grateful. Dolores Inés Casillas and I have been trading writing for more than fifteen years now, and I can always count on her for encouragement and to tell me when I'm not making any sense. I'm planning on at least fifteen more. Beginning with our collaboration on *Age in America*, no one has helped to shape this book more than Corinne T. Field. Cori has sent me sources, loaned me her notes, and generously read drafts of papers and chapters and articles and applications and, of course, the entire manuscript. I'm grateful for all her help and excited about our next intellectual collaboration.

At the University of North Carolina Press, I have been lucky to work with Mark Simpson-Vos, Lucas Church, Laura Dooley, and, for the second time, Jay Mazzocchi and Gina Mahalek. Thanks to all of them for their attention to detail, for their enthusiasm, and for answering all of my questions. Portions of this book have appeared, in different forms, in the *Journal of the History of*

Childhood and Youth, Children and Youth during the Gilded Age and Progressive Era, edited by James Marten (New York University Press, 2014), and *Age in America: The Colonial Era to the Present*, edited by Corinne T. Field and Nicholas L. Syrett (New York University Press, 2015). Thanks to Johns Hopkins University Press and NYU Press for allowing me to republish them here and Laura Lovett, Jim Marten, and Karen Sánchez-Eppler, and all the anonymous readers for their comments and suggestions.

Many friends and relatives have helped along the way. For putting me up when I was in town to visit archives, thanks to Michael Bond and Sarah Tahamont; Angela Brooks and Tim Syrett; Chris Hardin; and Tom Meyers and Guillaume Normand. I was fortunate that Amanda Ford agreed to venture with me up through the mountains of Hancock County to visit Sneedville and Treadway. For asking about the book and providing encouragement, I thank my friends, from Maine to California, and lots of places in between: Darrin Alfred, Geoffrey Bateman and Mark Thrun, Michael Bond and Sarah Tahamont, the members of the Brown Velvet Book Club, Jason Chang and Erin Pipkin, Tony Chicotel and Lynn Wu, Holly Dugan and Paul Lamade, Erik Flatmo, Amanda Ford, Emily Ford, Erika Gasser and Jon Barber, Chris Hardin and Andy Vázquez, Megan Hudacky and David Larrabee, Erin Jordan and Todd Fantz, Ned Kane, Alana Ketchel, Natalie Kittner, Amy LaCour, Brian Lam and Will Mackintosh, Ann Little and Chris Moore, Mauricio Mena, Tom Meyers and Guillaume Normand, Nancy Schwartzman, Michele Sutton, Malena Watrous and Matt Schumaker, Carl Watson and Zhenya Pelepey, and Dana Wooley. Thanks also to Blanchards, Cadigans, Syretts, Pahrs, Partsches, and a Bagley. My brother and sister-in-law, Tim Syrett and Angela Brooks, answered my legal questions, and my mother, Katie Syrett, is generous in ways too numerous to count.

Finally, thanks to Michael Pahr for letting me have the office when I needed to write, for putting up with many years of commuting between Colorado and San Francisco, for making so many meals (and pies), and for truly having best quality heart. For sharing his life with me outside the bonds of matrimony, I dedicate this book to him.

Introduction

When Susie King Taylor published her 1902 memoir, *Reminiscences of My Life in Camp*, narrating the story of her escape from slavery and subsequent service as a nurse during the Civil War, the book made little mention of her 1862 marriage. Susie Baker, as she was then called, had been fourteen when she wed Edward King, a soldier in the unit alongside which she served on Saint Simon's Island, Georgia, then occupied by Union forces. Taylor's age readers must intuit for themselves by reading forward from the year of her birth, provided at the beginning of the book. And perhaps it is unsurprising that Taylor does not focus on her marriage or her age at the time of that marriage; the autobiography's chief purpose was to highlight the service of African Americans at a time when many were celebrating memories of the Civil War and erasing the history of slavery (and of black Union soldiers). Her marriage was incidental to this story. But it is also the case that marrying at the age of fourteen was not at all uncommon for a newly freed girl like Susie Baker, or indeed for many others throughout the nation in the middle of the nineteenth century. Susie King Taylor may well have glossed over her youthful marriage because it simply was not noteworthy in 1862 or in 1902.[1]

By contrast, when country star Loretta Lynn published her autobiography, *Coalminer's Daughter*, in 1976, the story of her marriage at thirteen was one of the book's central episodes, as it was in the narrative of her life in country music. Indeed, in Lynn's own words, her early marriage was part of what characterized her home, Butcher Holler, Kentucky, as being in "the most backward part of the United States." The early marriage would also feature prominently in the subsequent 1980 film, for which Sissy Spacek won an Academy Award.

By the late twentieth century many Americans perceived early marriage as being both uncommon and backward, something that might have happened long ago in the wilds of Appalachia, but surely not elsewhere in the United States. Lynn capitalized on her early marriage to appear as "country" as possible. The autobiography is written in a folksy, down-home dialect; it was how she marketed herself as genuine. In fact, it turns out that in talking about her marriage (in the autobiography and elsewhere), Lynn had misrepresented her age. Reporters for the Associated Press revealed in 2012 that Lynn had lied about the date of her marriage and thus her age at the time of that marriage: she had been fifteen, not thirteen. Contemporary readers may think the difference inconsequential (she was still plenty young, after all), and Lynn may well have lied in order to appear younger now (not then), necessitating a backdating of the marriage. The fact remains, however, that her early marriage was remarkable and in many people's minds characteristic of a particular place: the poor and rural South. This was not inaccurate, but neither was it the whole story.[2]

This book tells two interrelated narratives: the first is about people in the United States, most of them far more ordinary than Susie King Taylor and Loretta Lynn, who married as minors, which is to say below the age of eighteen. And the second is of Americans' perceptions of how and when marriage at early ages is appropriate or inappropriate. That latter story also means looking at when some adults have taken it upon themselves to regulate the marriage of young people by changing laws to prevent their marriages, reforming families to try to discourage the practice, or trying to annul their children's marriages because of their age. Broadly speaking, then, this is a history of child marriage in the United States, a phenomenon that Americans tend to associate with other countries, places we usually perceive as backward or "third world" in part because they allow children to marry.

The marriage of legal children, in fact, has been relatively common throughout U.S. history. The U.S. Census Bureau did not link age with marital status till 1880, which makes national figures unavailable before that time. But in that year 11.7 percent of fifteen-to-nineteen-year-old girls were wives (the census did not specify exact age and marital status till 1910). That number dipped in 1890 and then increased incrementally through the 1920s to 12.6 percent in 1930. Youthful marriage decreased, as did the overall marriage rate, during the Great Depression. It then rose again dramatically after World War II but has been declining since the early 1960s. That said, people below the age of eighteen continue to marry to this day. A 2011 study published in the journal of the American Academy of Pediatrics estimates that about 9 percent of contemporary American women were married before they turned eighteen. Many of those women are now older, having married in the 1950s or 1960s, but they are not women of the distant past; they live among us today. The Centers for Disease Control estimates that the probability of marrying by age eighteen in the contemporary United States is 6 percent for women and 2 percent for men.[3]

If early marriage has been a part of everyday life for millions of Americans, why have we have come to think about it as a bizarre exception to the rule? The answer lies within the history of childhood itself. In order to think it strange for a child to marry, we must see "childhood" as a stage of life separate from adulthood, cordoned off from adult rights and responsibilities. Although earlier Americans did recognize this, the precise line of when childhood ended and adulthood began was much fuzzier for them, emerging in something close to its current form only by the end of the nineteenth century. In part this was because both chronological age and our own ages—the numbers we call ourselves—were far less important to early Americans. Many people in the seventeenth, eighteenth, and indeed nineteenth and early twentieth centuries did not know when they were born and had only vague understandings of how old they were. For many, precise ages were not an important part of their self-understanding. Marrying at younger ages in such a world would be far less noteworthy than it would be for us. But earlier Americans also reckoned age differently than we do. They did not believe, for instance, that there were particular ages at which a person should go to school (especially if there were no schools), start working, or get married. These things happened when a person was large enough or able enough or financially prepared enough, and those moments might come at different times for different people.[4]

For most of American history there was no distinction between the marriage of two minors or that between one party who was older (sometimes considerably so) and one who was younger. Once contracted, marriage has been, and largely remains, a one-size-fits-all institution. Culturally and socially, however, observers may react very differently to these phenomena, understanding the former as perhaps foolhardy, whereas the latter could be dangerous or exploitative. Contemporary observers may recoil when an older man marries a girl below the age of eighteen because they suspect him of pedophilia. Marriage, in this analysis, is simply a back door to that which is illegal outside of it, especially when divorce is widely available; the man can simply divorce the underage girl when he tires of her (or when she ages). These concerns are not invalid, but they were usually not shared by Americans before the twentieth century, who were far more concerned that premarital sex led to the ruin of girls who would be unable to marry and might thus be destined for lives of prostitution. Before the 1920s, most people also did not share our understanding of pedophilia, the sexual predilection of some adults for children. Because of this, most objections to the marriage of girls (or boys) would not have been framed around the issue of sex or sexual exploitation. Instead, early critics of youthful marriage worried that it robbed girls of girlhood or that it might lead to divorce. Although I never dismiss the very real imbalance in power that characterized marriages with great age disparities, in this book I also explain why earlier Americans did not necessarily see this as a problem and offer historical context for how and when Americans came to see man-girl marriage as sexually suspect.

The phrase from the title of this book—"child bride"—is useful because it binds together two nouns that many think should be incompatible. It neatly conveys discomfort and disbelief rather than having to articulate those feelings explicitly. In the United States a child should not be a bride because we reserve the institution of marriage for adults, indeed demand adulthood for its fulfillment. Children who marry sacrifice their childhood and make a mockery of our understanding of marriage. But that has not always been the case. The *Oxford English Dictionary* records the first printed instance of the phrase "child bride" in 1843; a search of American newspapers from the nineteenth century reveals its regular use beginning only in the 1870s and 1880s (the same is true of "child wife" and "boy husband," two other phrases that once enjoyed some popularity). This was not because there were no children marrying before 1843. Rather, the practice was just not particularly remarkable.

The phrase "child bride" also perversely expresses the legal power of the institution of marriage, which really *can* transform a child into something adultlike, a bride. This was because earlier Americans had a functional, rather than a chronological, understanding of childhood. Before the middle of the nineteenth century, many Americans believed that marriage could transform a child into a wife who was legally and socially an adult because of marriage. Her marital status trumped her chronological age.[5]

In order for the phrase "child bride" to generate the reaction it implicitly demands, we need to believe two things. The first, as we have seen, is that children, defined through chronological age, are fundamentally ill-suited to marriage—that they are too young for what marriage requires of them, not just sex but also the emotional maturity to be spouses and perhaps parents. The second belief is that marriage, if not always a union of equals, is at the very least a partnership between people who can both be presumed to contribute to its health in similar and complementary ways. Stephanie Coontz has memorably described the historical change in understanding the marital relationship as being a transition from "obedience to intimacy." Both beliefs—about childhood as a stage of life and about marriage as a particular love relationship—developed relatively recently, beginning in the eighteenth century, starting first among the nascent middle class, and gaining widespread adherence by a majority of Americans only in the early twentieth century. Before the eighteenth century, children as young as eight or nine married in America, and children in their teenage years have been marrying in the United States since then. The practice is most common today in rural areas, where it remains hidden from most urban and suburban dwellers, who tend to assume that teenage marriage is a relic of the past.[6]

So why focus on child *brides*? In the vast majority of marriages where one party is a legal minor, that minor is a girl. The reasons for this have remained relatively consistent over time and reflect Americans' concerns about female fertility and their belief that marriage is a gendered institution where females are dependent on males; youthful brides facilitate both ends. This remains the case today, when most marriages (between parties of any age) involve a man who is older than his bride, even if only by a couple of years. The marriage of girls became objectionable only when some Americans (at first only a small minority) began to believe that girls, like boys, deserved the opportunity to grow up and make the choice of a marital partner only after achieving adulthood. And when some came to believe that marriage was supposed to be a union of equals. Both changes in belief occurred haltingly over the nineteenth century. Without those beliefs, girl marriage is not particularly objectionable, largely because it so closely resembled the marriage of adult women throughout much of American history. The beliefs that make us see child marriage as repugnant (to girls *and* to marriage) themselves have a history, one that I tell in this book.[7]

It is also the case, however, that throughout American history, boys have generally had far fewer reasons to marry young than girls. Unlike men, women were largely defined through their marriages; opting for an appropriate mate early on in life might be the best chance a girl would have. With employment options for women few and pay generally dismal, marriage was often a way out of the natal home when no other escape existed. Boys and men experienced few of these advantages precisely because they were the ones expected to work for pay on reaching adulthood (or as a means of proving adulthood itself). For men, marriage represented an extra responsibility: the support of a wife and, in an era before reliable birth control, children. The imbalance between child brides and boy husbands is thus a reflection of cultural expectations for girls *and* boys.

Wives were expected to be dependents, husbands to be breadwinners. The first status has no age qualification; the latter generally does, because men needed either to inherit their father's estate or to establish themselves in some sort of job.

The growing revulsion over time against child marriage is also partially a story of perceived American exceptionalism and a belief in the onward march of "civilization." Since the early nineteenth century many Americans have believed that child marriage is practiced only in other places—India, Afghanistan, various African nations—or, if in the United States, only by religious sects where multiple girls are married to one older man against their will. These versions of child marriage—forced unions arranged by parents, sometimes the exchange of a dowry, brides below the age of twelve—are indeed different from what usually happens in the United States, where marrying girls have tended to be in their teens and have usually themselves made the decision to marry. But characterizing child marriage as foreign (whether nationally or religiously or both) also allows Americans to ignore youthful marriage in their midst. From early nineteenth-century reports by Christian missionaries in India to contemporary scandals over fundamentalist Latter-Day Saints in Colorado and Utah, Americans have represented youthful marriage as something practiced only by backward people who live elsewhere or deliberately flout the law if they live here.[8]

The truth is that many thousands of girls below the age of eighteen will marry legally in the United States this year. Almost all states have minimum marriageable ages below eighteen (with parental consent); many have various exceptions to their minimum marriageable ages that allow girls as young as fourteen to marry. In 2010, the U.S. Congress failed to pass the "International Protecting Girls by Preventing Child Marriage Act," and as of this writing the United States remains one of only two nations (Somalia is the other) not to ratify the United Nations Convention on the Rights of the Child and one of seven not to have ratified the 1979 Convention on the Elimination of All Forms of Discrimination against Women, one plank of which explains that the marriage of a child below eighteen shall have no legal effect. If child marriage is a problem, it is our problem as well.[9]

And much of American resistance to outlawing youthful marriage altogether stems from attitudes toward sex. Throughout U.S. history Americans have supported a legal regime that codifies the belief that sex and childbirth belong within marriage, no matter the ages of the couple contracting it, even if, especially if, they have already had sex. Even as the United States has decriminalized sex outside of marriage (what used to be called fornication) and made illegitimacy largely meaningless as a legal category, American laws continue to promote the notion that sex and childbirth should occur within marriage, even if those having sex are teenagers. Americans' acceptance of early marriage demonstrates their great faith, however misguided at times, in the powers of marriage, another consistent theme of this book. Throughout most of American history, marriage was seen as transformative. It made illicit sex licit. It legitimized offspring. Actions performed outside of marriage that were dangerous, debasing, or immoral were transformed into safe, respectable, and moral within marriage. But marriage exists only because human beings invented it and continue to believe in it. As Havelock Ellis observed in the early twentieth century, sexual intercourse "cannot become good and bad according as it is performed in or out of marriage. There is no magic efficacy in a few words pronounced by a priest or a government official." Yet for those who believe in it, this is *exactly* what marriage provides. I am not arguing that marriage is not real—clearly it is—but rather that its realness depends on continued belief in its existence, which is codified in the law. For people to be transformed by marriage, for sex to be legitimate in marriage, for women to be protected in marriage, one must believe that marriage does these things. Legal scholar Ariela Dubler refers to this constellation of beliefs as "the marriage cure." The marriage of legal minors strains those beliefs, and yet it remains legally valid. At key moments in the past when children married, it forced those around them to rethink what marriage could really do to and for the people who entered it. It made them confront the differences between their idea of marriage and the lived reality of actual husbands and wives. Almost everyone in these debates agreed that children were deserving of protection; how to ensure it was at issue.[10]

And for every person like Havelock Ellis who doubted the powers of marriage, there were many more who hoped to rehabilitate it. Reformers in the past who sought to combat the scourge of child marriage that they discovered in their midst were, as this book demonstrates, often at least as invested in "protecting" the institution of marriage as they were in advancing the cause of women or saving children from supposed harm. Campaigns about child marriage in the United States are inextricably bound up in fears about the fate of marriage as a supposed building block of society. As a group of social reformers from Cleveland who professed to be especially worried about children put it in 1926, allowing children to marry would "weaken and cheapen the institution of marriage itself." Amid the controversy over same-sex marriage, a look at the history of child marriage in the United States reveals much about our investment in marriage as an institution that we believe transforms the individuals who enter it, bestowing on them the mantle of full adult citizenship. Today's opponents of same-sex marriage may well be less distressed at what married gay people actually gain through marriage (tax breaks and so forth) as what their married status symbolically grants them: the respect accorded to adult citizens. Historical struggles over child marriage reveal that marriage has always been about the privileges of adulthood, demonstrating the ways that the symbolic power of marriage continues to be a vehicle for discrimination against those who are unable, or choose not, to enter it.[11]

The narrative of this book could be read as a triumphal march forward from a moment when children married because no one valued childhood and adult wives were treated like children anyway to one where we do not allow children to marry because we protect them and we understand the institution of marriage differently than early Americans did. There is some truth to this account, in part because the incidence of youthful marriage declined over the twentieth century (the 1950s excepted). Nevertheless, I hope to complicate this arc in a number of significant ways.

The first and most obvious fact obscured by such a narrative is that large numbers of American girls have married before turning eighteen well into the twenty-first century. Those who would congratulate themselves on successfully protecting American youth from marriage should think again. In the history of child protection that began with the early modern legal recognition that children were incapable of rational consent and should thus be protected from adult decisions and responsibilities, marriage remained an enormous exception to the rule. For most of American history, girls have been able to consent to the one contract that, for most of its history, was presumed to last a lifetime. This is because in most cases where a belief in a protected childhood has run up against fears of nonmarital sex, preventing illegitimacy and sex by single girls has trumped childhood. State law has codified the belief that the institution of marriage can "solve" the problem of teenage sex and pregnancy.[12]

Second, the long and varied history of children marrying, indeed the explicit sanctions for the practice throughout most of American history, demonstrate that it is difficult to find just one "traditional" marriage to which nostalgic defenders of the institution would have us return. It is not just that girls as young as twelve could marry within the bounds of the law in the recent past, a practice to which most of us would not want to return. It is also that the incidence of youthful marriage has itself *not* been on a slow and steady decline from the colonial era to the present. Indeed, it saw one of its great revitalizations during the 1950s. Although there are real and persistent changes in marriage over time, there are also variations that defy our expectations. So not only are those who espouse the triumphal story of marital progress partially incorrect, so too are those who embrace a narrative of marital declension: it is simply not the case that marriage once existed in only one form that has now been adulterated by feminism and interracial and same-sex marriage.

Last, although readers may find it difficult to think about youthful marriage as anything other than exploitation, historically many children saw real advantages in the institution. It was one of the few ways that they could escape their parents' homes if they so desired. Most state law and most judges in those states held that it legally emancipated them from their parents. Marriage also legalized the sex that young people might want to have with each other or that young girls might have with their older husbands, exempting those husbands from prosecution for statutory rape. Marriage went a long way toward legally turning children into adults, and depending on the situation they found themselves in, this was an appealing prospect for many youth. None of these claims is without its counterargument, of course (all of which I explore), but seen from the perspective of children themselves, marriage could offer distinct benefits.[13]

Absent specific evidence to the contrary (and I do detail instances of coercion herein), I have taken children at their word when they have consented to become married. This is not to say that I think the decisions sound, but as childhood studies scholars have argued for some time, the history of children was long written in a way that discounted the choices—good, bad, and otherwise—that they made. Children themselves had agency, even when they made terrible decisions. Readers may occasionally balk at the notion that a child of twelve or fourteen really could "choose" to get married. Indeed, one way that we define childhood is that, by virtue of their age, children are incapable of making such choices. Most of these children, however, with some notable exceptions, believed that *they* were making choices. Exploring how and why they did so—often in the face of pressure and coercion and circumscribed options—helps us to understand the history of American childhood and the ways that children have been at the center of debates about marriage, sexuality, and the regulation of both.[14]

In earlier eras the marriage of girl children was also less problematic than it is today because waiting longer to marry would not have enlarged most girls' opportunities in any significant way. Marrying early has circumscribed children's lives in direct relation to the degree to which children actually *were* protected and women's autonomy *was* promoted. Both of these are trends that have increased over the course of the nineteenth and twentieth centuries, however haltingly and unevenly. When neither existed—that is, when children were expected to take on adult responsibilities early in their lives and when women had few opportunities aside from wifehood—marrying early did not make a bride's life significantly different from her peers who married later. What she began at fifteen her sister would, almost inevitably, begin at nineteen or twenty. Either way it was unlikely to be a life of self-determination or autonomy.

There is an exception to this argument, and it has to do with the physical obligations of marriage and the physiological harm they may cause to girls. Even historical critics of youthful marriage rarely framed their arguments explicitly in opposition to the sex that young wives would be expected to have and the children they would bear before they had reached physical maturity. They sometimes hinted obliquely at these aspects of youthful marriage, and because historians have demonstrated that girls actually reached menarche later in the past than they do today, these were, and are, valid concerns. But because they were so rarely the focus of early marriage's critics, I have found almost no evidence of young wives of the past who wrote about the sexual burdens they faced.[15]

If early marriage largely resembled later marriage for many women in the past, at least in the realm of the law, in a world transformed by feminism, this is no longer the case. Today contemporary American women can postpone marriage as long as they like and enter into (relatively) egalitarian marriages with supportive husbands (or wives). Because of this, for anyone who favors contemporary women's autonomy and independence, marrying as a minor looks like a terrible idea. At best, it limits women's opportunities, tethering them to the home before they have gained a sense of whether that is what they want out of life. But the disadvantages of marrying as a minor in earlier eras were far less pronounced than they are now, in part because before the mid-twentieth century, marriage, by definition, limited women's opportunities no matter their ages. Until relatively recently, it simply made less difference whether a woman married young or quite young; her role in life would be similar. The only real "out" was not to marry at all, and that was an option generally available to a minority of women.[16]

Today, by contrast, when women have far more opportunities for meaningful autonomy, marrying early cuts short almost all of those options. But, crucially, that is predominantly true for women who are in a position to take advantage of those opportunities. Where marriage as a minor remains most common today— among poor and rural Americans—many girls believe that marriage at some age is their lot in life, regardless. Postponing it may have little overall consequence. Marriage itself has undergone a remarkable transformation in the past two hundred years, becoming much more egalitarian for many spouses. Because of who marries as a minor today and why they do so, most young wives are unable to take advantage either of this new marital equality or of the option of not having marriage define one's life chances. Studies show that those who marry today as legal minors are much more likely to suffer adverse health consequences, including depression, than those who marry as adults (effects that might have been found among young brides in the past if anyone had asked). What the studies do not show is whether these health risks are associated with the early marriage itself or the circumstances that led to it. Either way, we should note that poverty (and its consequences: shoddy education, including sex education, and lack of access to contraception) and unequal opportunities make early marriage a symptom of much larger problems rather than the primary issue.[17]

This book proceeds chronologically from the founding of the United States in the late eighteenth century through the very recent past, each chapter taking up a different subject or issue related to the marriage of minors. Some chapters focus on the laws that allowed or prevented children from marrying or the way the courts interpreted those laws; others document reform efforts to curb the practice; still others explore particular marriages or the nationwide reaction to them. Most combine the methods and sources of legal, social, and cultural history to demonstrate how and why young people married, as well as the ways that adults (who made the laws) sought to regulate the practice. Four chapters are dedicated to the antebellum period, two to the turn of the nineteenth into the twentieth century, and four to the twentieth century.

To tell this story, I must explain some terminology. I use the word "marriage" to refer to the legal institution where two people make a contract with the state (and sometimes a church) to remain united until death or divorce. I do include some marriages that did not exist as a matter of civil law but were treated as marriages by all around them: Indian marriage, slave marriage, and polygamous marriage. By and large, however, this is a history of civil marriage. Although religion factors into this story at times—priests authorizing marriages, ministers performing them; religious organizations opposing early marriage and the divorce they feared sprang from it—because marriage is regulated by state governments, this is not primarily a religious history. Even when religious officials performed marriages, they were doing so "by the power vested in them" by the state, and all the major religious denominations performed marriages within the bounds set by the state (the exception being polygamous Mormons, who usually did marry according to the laws of *their* state). The states allowed or prevented children from marrying, and reformers primarily called on the states when they wanted to curb the practice.[18]

The use of the word "child" is more complicated, in part because it has different definitions in the realm of the law, medicine, and culture, and of course those definitions have changed over time. Legally anyone below the age of eighteen is a child today in the United States (except in Alabama and Nebraska, where the age of majority is nineteen, and Mississippi, where it is twenty-one).[19] The word "minor" is a synonym for child in this instance. The law defines minors (or "infants" in the law) as being legally dependent on their parents. Although historically they have been subject to certain duties or entitled to certain privileges that precede legal majority (like the duty to serve in the military, for instance, or the right to marry), only majority brings with it full legal personhood. I have chosen to focus this book on those below the age of eighteen, because that is our current legal definition for childhood, but I recognize that that number is arbitrary. It could have been seventeen or twenty or twenty-one, which was the age of majority for most of American history. Though the age of eighteen might be arbitrary, it has become meaningful to Americans, not just legally, but also culturally. Contemporary Americans *believe* that the age of eighteen is special and that those below it are not yet adults. That process is itself, of course, historical; codifying the age of eighteen in the law is what has made us think that those below it are children. The law itself does not simply recognize that which already exists, it creates certain kinds of subjects, including children. Marriage law has been integral to this process.[20]

The word "child" has meanings aside from those in the law; the fields of medicine and psychology have contributed to these understandings in meaningful ways. When not quoting from sources (which sometimes use the word in other ways), I employ the word "child" to speak of those who have not yet reached their teens. I reserve the words "adolescent" and "teenager" for those past age twelve when I write about the twentieth century, when the words themselves were first coined and entered the vernacular ("adolescent" in the early 1900s and "teenager" in the mid-twentieth century). Before those moments I use the words "youth" or "young people" to refer to similarly aged people. At all moments I have attempted to be as specific as possible about a young person's age. Although I frequently reference the average age of first marriage and document statistics demonstrating marriages of those in certain ranges provided by various authorities (fifteen to nineteen, for instance), at all other times this a book about those who married below the age of eighteen.[21]

It is also helpful to recognize that the word "child" has two meanings in the English language: a person below a certain age, and the offspring of another. One is defined by age, the other by filiation. As historian Nara Milanich has pointed out, in Spanish there are two separate words for these two meanings (*niño/a* and *hijo/a*), which allow a specificity that sometimes gets blurred in English. In the realm of the law this is particularly evident. Does a child require consent to marry because she is fourteen and thus ineligible for marriage or because she is still legally under the control of parents who may not want her to leave their home? The answer depends on the context and the particular law. Although a father's right to his children is dependent on their ages (it ends at their majority), children also have duties and obligations because they are *his* children, not just children by definition of age. I have tried, in the pages that follow, to identify which version of the "child" was being regulated because that has changed over time. In the nineteenth century the state was more likely to regulate the child as a person who belonged to his or her parents. Around the turn of the century states more often saw themselves as having a vested interest in children as defined by chronological age: children could claim some rights on their own behalf, but they were also increasingly regulated as a class of people based on that status. By the middle of the twentieth century, a liberationist notion of "children's rights," which pushed back against those regulations of children-as-minors, had fully come into its own. These are different versions of "the child," however, so paying attention to which child was being regulated can tell us much about the anxiety that produced the regulation.[22]

I have called this book *American Child Bride* even though we would today likely describe most of the brides we will meet in these pages as teenagers or adolescents. Yet from the moment that it entered Americans' vocabulary, the phrase "child bride" has regularly been applied to those in their teens and even twenties. Priscilla Beaulieu Presley's biographer called her book *Child Bride*, for instance, even though Priscilla married Elvis Presley when she was twenty-one (she had begun dating him at fourteen). The phrase encompasses the discomfort that Americans feel about young people marrying, even when those young people may not be, by one definition or another, "children." This book is a history of how and when that discomfort developed and how the practice continued nevertheless.[23]

One final caveat: this is largely a book about marital beginnings. It is not a study of what happened to the marriages of those who contracted them while still legally children. Marriage is mostly regulated at its beginning; we do not issue licenses and do not have ceremonies (at least until recently) for the continuation of marriages solemnized years earlier. There is much more discussion about who is fit to *enter* a marriage and when, but not who is fit to continue it (though there has been, admittedly, a lot of discussion about who might exit a marriage and why). Marital beginnings therefore present an opportune moment to see what Americans have thought marriage was for and what Americans believed it could do for those who contracted it.[24]

That said, each chapter does begin and end with one marriage that I take to be in some way representative of the issue or the era discussed in that chapter; readers will learn at the end of the chapter what happened to the couple they met at the beginning. In the spirit of this before-and-after approach, and before we meet our next couple, let me recount that Susie and Edward King remained married until Edward's untimely death only four years after they wed, just before Susie gave birth to a son. Susie King moved north to Boston in the 1870s and remarried, to Russell Taylor, in 1879. Taylor died in 1901, leaving Susie King Taylor a widow again at the age of fifty-three. Following a trip to the South in the 1890s to nurse her dying son, where she witnessed injustices perpetrated against southern blacks, Taylor became an eloquent spokeswoman against segregation and on behalf of memorializing African American service during the Civil War. She died in 1912, and today her memoir is taught in classrooms across the country.[25]

Loretta and her husband, Oliver "Doolittle" Lynn, had six children and remained married for more than fifty years, until his death in 1996. He was an enormous supporter of her early career. But the marriage was not without its problems, Doolittle's cheating among them. Loretta documented much marital strife in her songs, including the classic "You Ain't Woman Enough (To Take My Man)." Loretta Lynn's recording career now spans more than five decades, embodying a working-class feminist sensibility that continues to resonate with listeners. She was inducted into the Country Music Hall of Fame in 1988 and awarded the Presidential Medal of Freedom in 2013.[26]

The stories of Taylor and Lynn were far more celebrated than most marriages contracted by young people. In addition to being relatively common throughout U.S. history, the marriage of minors has usually been far more ordinary. And it is by no means a thing of the past. Just as I was finishing this book, the *New York Times* published an op-ed entitled "America's Child-Marriage Problem," documenting the many thousands of girls, and more than a handful of boys, who were married in the twenty-first century, largely thanks to exceptions in state marriage laws that allow judges to consent to such marriages, as well as parents who force or coerce their children into wedlock. Our shock that this phenomenon continues today, however, has everything to do with the changed ideals of childhood and marriage that have made it seem as if child brides should be, must be, a thing of the past. It is to that past that we now turn.[27]

ONE

Any Maid or Woman Child

A New Nation and Its Marriage Laws

In 1762, Arthur Dobbs, the sixth governor of the royal colony of North Carolina, took a second wife, his first having predeceased him in their native Ireland. Dobbs's second wife, Justina Davis, was fifteen, and Dobbs was then seventy-three. One critic, attempting to bring shame on Dobbs, painted the scene like this: "Our Old Silenus of the Envigorated age of seventy eight [*sic*] who still damns this province with his Baneful Influence grew stupidly enamoured with Miss Davis, a lovely lady of sprightly fifteen of a good family and some fortune." The letter continued, describing Dobbs as "the Old Fellow, old [in] every Human Characteristic but sense and virtue," and as having "old teeth of Enormous length, that for many years despised to be cloathed with gums." At no point does the anonymous critic, clearly no fan of Dobbs's politics, describe Justina Davis as being too young for marriage; indeed, he claims (though there is no evidence to support it) that she was planning to marry someone of similar age when Dobbs decided he was interested in her. The problem here was not Davis's youth but rather Dobbs's age (as well as his politics). He was a fool for allowing himself to fall for someone so youthful, but that she might be suitable for marriage at the age of fifteen was certainly not in doubt.[1]

There was nothing in the law of North Carolina that forbade the marriage of a fifteen-year-old girl (or boy, for that matter). Even though Justina presumably had her parents' (perhaps enthusiastic) permission to marry the governor, the law did not require it. No English colony kept systematic marriage records, so we do not know how common it was for girls and boys in their teens to marry in colonial America, but historians have demonstrated that in some seventeenth- and eighteenth-century communities, early marriage was not unusual. This was particularly so in southern colonies, where men outnumbered women, and where some wealthy parents had a vested interest in selecting their daughters' husbands. Some children married as young as eight or nine.[2]

Although North Carolina did not have a statute that set the age at which a child could contract marriage (or the age at which it required parental permission to do so), a number of other colonies did. Following the American Revolution, some of the remaining original thirteen colonies passed such laws, and others amended or updated their marriage statutes. New states in the Midwest and Deep South frequently entered the Union with marriage statutes they had passed during their time as territories. These laws had a number of things in common, though they also varied regionally. The early statutes, in particular, demonstrate that the desire to regulate when a child might marry had less to do with the child's youth than that the child was somebody's son or daughter. This was a kin-based understanding of childhood rather than one focused on age, with parents preserving the right to decide when *their* children might marry, rather than states forbidding all people below a certain age from doing so. The thirteen colonies, which became the first states, demonstrate this trend most. The newly admitted states of the Midwest tended toward statutes that emphasized the chronological age of children as well as their relationships to parents, indicating the growing importance of chronological age in the nineteenth century and a divergence from precedents in English common law. Second, many of the statutes (and this was especially true for the South) were concerned more with regulating access to the inherited wealth of daughters than they were of protecting those daughters from marriage. In these statutes there is less a belief that girls below a certain age are ineligible for marriage than a commitment to allowing parents to control which men might have access to a daughter and her fortune. Third and last, almost all statutes from the colonial period through the antebellum years—the subject of this chapter—allowed girls to marry earlier than boys. This was, of course, because lawmakers believed and expected that girls *should* marry earlier than boys.

But there is something telling in that belief. Although historian Holly Brewer has argued that children were increasingly protected from adult rights and responsibilities over the seventeenth and eighteenth centuries—because lawmakers and philosophers now presumed that they lacked the capacity for reason necessary for informed consent—in the realm of marriage this was most true for male children. Or, put another way, the law already treated adult women like minor children in so many ways (especially if they were married) that the transition between girlhood and wifehood was not as significant legally as was the transition between boyhood and manhood. When Justina Davis became Justina Dobbs, the law of coverture erased her legal existence in a way that was consistent with what she had experienced in her natal home; she moved seamlessly from dependent in one household to dependent in another. That she could consent to this transition meant that the legal protections afforded children did not apply to girls in the realm of marriage. Paternalist lawmakers might have seen girls and wives as being *protected* in both circumstances, yet from our perspective they were decidedly not protected from the ability (which could look like compulsion) to marry as teens (or sometimes younger). The decision to wed was one that many thousands of girls made (or had made for them) from the colonial era through the antebellum period. It was also the one contract that was difficult to reverse in many states. Whatever lawmakers may have intended in crafting new laws demarcating childhood from adulthood—and I argue here that in the realm of marriage they did not really intend all that much, at least not for girls—many children bound themselves to marriage nevertheless.[3]

This distinction between girls and boys at the intersection of age and the law is also evident in the antebellum trend among most western and midwestern states to lower the female age of majority by three years, effectively making girls into adults three years below their brothers. This kept girls' majority in line with the age at which they were capable of marrying, and although some girls saw advantages in their premature legal adulthood, in the aggregate it served to move girls more smoothly as dependents between different men's households and to ensure that a male head of household always governed their property.

One caveat: this chapter details codified law, not practice (the subject of the next chapter). The law, written primarily by the English and Spanish, tells us much more about what lawmakers believed children and adults should and should not do than it does what people actually did. The law also did not apply to four groups of people who married outside the bounds of codified law, all of whom were nevertheless married. These were Native Americans, African Americans (most of whom were enslaved), those Mormons who practiced polygamy, and anyone who entered marriage simply by living together (what came to be called common-law marriage). Native Americans married according to their own customs and rituals, which were

not codified in the written laws I discuss here. Slaves, because they were property owned by others, were unable to marry legally, even though many did
wed in community-sanctioned rituals that were marriages in all but the legal
sense. Mormon men who practiced polygyny (by no means the majority)
were legally married only to their first wives, but they and their second and
subsequent wives were no less married in the eyes of their communities. And
last, those who married through cohabiting and claiming to be married were
the norm in many rural or isolated communities, but also at the margins of
these laws. This was because marriage law—especially related to age, consent,
ceremony, registration, and so forth—was designed to regulate the *entrance*
into marriage, which common-law married couples largely bypassed by simply moving in together. We will meet couples in all of these groups in the next
chapter; for now my goal is to explore how lawmakers envisaged the law as
it regulated children's capacity to enter the institution of marriage. Doing so
helps us see how lawmakers understood the roles of parents and children, the
institution of marriage, and the varied fears they had about all three. It also
demonstrates the regional variation of these concerns, even as lawmakers
across the growing nation agreed that girls could (and should) become wives
earlier than boys, regardless of whether they were legal minors.[4]

ENGLISH COMMON LAW AND THE ORIGINS
OF TWELVE AND FOURTEEN

As the United States came into being, the thirteen states did not reject wholly
the laws that had been in place before they united to become a new nation.
In the case of marriage law, in fact, they retained most of what had preceded
their being states. This was done, however, in two different ways. As English
colonies, they had used the common law, a set of legal principles that guided
English jurisprudence, most accessible to us through the *Commentaries on the
Laws of England*, compiled (and in some sense codified) by William Blackstone in the middle of the eighteenth century. All the colonies had also passed
individual laws of their own to regulate marriage in an environment that was
clearly not England. Those laws were often guided by common-law principles,
but many augmented or abrogated the common law in important ways. Once
each state joined the United States, it retained its own colonial statutes unless
it passed new laws explicitly repealing them. Where statutory law did not exist
on certain subjects—and age of marriage was one of these issues for some
colonies—the common law governed marriage practice, including marriage

age. This remained the case for some states (both original colonies and states formed after independence) well into the nineteenth century and, in some cases, the twentieth. In order to understand the laws that states passed related to marriage, and age of marriage specifically, we thus must first understand what English common law said about marriage, as well as how the original thirteen colonies modified that law.

The common law's understanding of marriage is most famous in regard to coverture, the doctrine that held that a man and a woman became one person at marriage and that person was legally him. Anything a wife earned belonged to her husband. She could not enter a contract with him or sue him, because legally she would be contracting with or suing herself. Her husband could not rape her because her marriage to him presumed ongoing sexual consent. She was also obligated to serve him, as were their children until they reached the age of majority, which was twenty-one. In return, a husband was obligated to support his wife financially. English common law also stipulated who was eligible to marry. The common-law ages of marriage were twelve for girls and fourteen for boys. Either could actually marry at the age of seven, but between the ages of seven and twelve/fourteen, the marriage would be considered imperfect or inchoate, almost like a trial run for a real marriage. A girl or boy could opt to leave an inchoate marriage, but only on reaching the age of twelve or fourteen and only if the couple had not consummated the marriage. If, however, a wife or husband stayed in the marriage past those critical years, or if they consummated the marriage at any time, then the marriage stood. No second marriage ceremony was required on reaching those ages; the couple just continued to be married, as they were before reaching the magical ages of twelve and fourteen. So, for instance, a girl of ten could marry a boy of fifteen. On reaching the age of twelve, she could then choose to remain married or to have her marriage declared void. These ages may sound far-fetched, but there is plentiful evidence, both from England and the early colonies, to indicate that children as young as eight, nine, and ten did marry. Some of them remained married, and some sought an end to their early unions. But that they were legally able to enter into marriage was not in dispute. Also key here is that parental consent was not required for marriage at these young ages. Though the common law held that the age of majority was twenty-one for both girls and boys, a child between the ages of seven and twenty-one could marry without his or her parents' permission even though still legally a minor and under those parents' control. In the end, this was what most colonial legislatures changed about their marriage laws, enshrining filial obedience in statutes.[5]

So where did these ages—seven, twelve, and fourteen—come from? Setting aside for now the fact that they are quite low, they are worth investigating because they play such an important part in the rest of the story. The ages are especially confusing because many people in early modern England or in the American colonies did not know how old they were. Some did not know on which day they had been born, and this made it difficult to calculate precisely how old they might be. (Birthdays were not regularly celebrated in the United States until well into the nineteenth century.) Age-consciousness—the belief that one's age is a fundamental part of one's personal and social identity—did not exist as it does now. The common law itself made many distinctions based on age, and some people did know their dates of birth—recorded in family Bibles—and thus their ages. But with large numbers of people unable to read and little schooling available, age was not as meaningful to the early modern English as it is to us. Of course people were aware of differences between very young and very old people and between children and adults, but these were stages of life more than they were precise age markers. Age was in some sense functional rather than purely chronological. In the key stage that is the subject of this book—what we would call adolescence, youth, or later childhood—a boy or girl would be old enough to work when he or she could perform certain tasks. This stands in contrast to our focus on precise ages as calculated by month and year of birth, how we determine when children are eligible to begin kindergarten, for instance, or whether a child is meeting particular growth and development projections as determined by pediatricians. These did not exist for the early modern English, some of whom became colonists in the Americas.[6]

So if age did not matter to them as it does to us, why fixate on the particular ages of seven, twelve, and fourteen? There are two ways to address this question. The first is to say that the common law is riddled with precise ages because framers of laws needed to devise some way of dictating who was entitled to do various things. In particular they wanted to make sure that people who were too young for certain rights and privileges were barred from them. The age of majority, for instance, was twenty-one, but that is clearly an arbitrary number. A man of twenty-one is not necessarily any more able to manage property than a man of twenty years, eleven months, and twenty-nine days. But most believed that there had to be some cut-off below which young people were incapable of managing property or writing their own wills or inheriting in their own names. So they settled on twenty-one. Even Blackstone, in recording the age of majority, acknowledged that the number selected was "merely arbitrary," noting that other countries chose other numbers for this crucial age. Explaining that in England a father's power over his children (and to command their labor) ceased at twenty-one, he told readers why: "for they are then enfranchised by arriving at years of discretion, or that point which the law has established (as some must necessarily be established) when the empire of the father, or other guardian, gives place to the empire of reason."[7]

A variety of other ages were meant to slowly allow young people the privileges of adulthood. These ages were also somewhat arbitrary, but they were understood to be necessary. They tended to matter only in certain circumstances. That is, especially if most people did not know how old they were, many would not have experienced an important legal shift once they met these particular age thresholds, but some would, especially those who had inherited property or wanted to escape an abusive father or were orphaned at young ages and wished to pick their own guardian. Because this had happened to some young people and would no doubt happen again, ages had to be chosen at which children could be entitled to do these things. And although most would never experience firsthand the legal repercussions of arriving at those ages at those precise moments, a significant enough minority in each generation would do so, and for them ages had to be set.

So this accounts for such precision even in a world that largely had little concern for precise ages. But what of these ages: seven, twelve, and fourteen? The ages have their roots in religious canon law—they were sometimes called canon ages—but theorists also advanced secular explanations for their significance. Blackstone explained that before the ages of twelve and fourteen, young people would possess "imbecility of judgment," but that does little to clarify how these specific ages had been chosen, and further, why they differed for boys and girls. Henry Swinburne's 1686 *Treatise of Spousals or Matrimonial Contracts* sets out in as clear language as we are likely to find why these ages were selected, and it is largely a biological explanation. He explained that below seven years of age, "these young Infants want Reason and Judgment to judge these affairs," by which he means marriage or promises of marriage. This age was the same for both boys and girls and, in Swinburne's view, linked a lack of intellectual capacity with tender years: infants below seven were not old enough to make sound decisions. Above that age they were capable of sound reason and judgment, though not as much as when they reached the ages of twelve, fourteen, or indeed twenty-one.[8]

Swinburne acknowledged that ages of marriage—twelve and fourteen—were indicative of the age when young people were "presumed to be of discretion, and able to discern betwixt good and evil, and what is for their profit and disprofit," but he emphasized the young people's biological capacity for marriage. He explained that these ages conformed to the time at which girls and boys have the "Natural and Corporal Ability to perform the duty of Marriage, and in that respect are termed *Puberes*, as it were plants, now sending forth Buds and Flowers, apparent Testimonies of inward Sap, and immediate Messengers of approaching Fruit." Swinburne was referencing the onset of puberty and sexual capacity, and even though he acknowledged that these ages might seem "over-tender," he believed that girls and boys generally arrived at puberty at these ages and thus experienced sexual desire, which needed to be contained within marriage. In other words, marriage was allowed at these early ages to provide a proper site for sex and the reproduction of children. This was also why the age of marriage was not the same as the age of majority, why children were allowed to make this incredibly important decision at twelve or fourteen but not a decision about any property they might own till they reached twenty-one. No one wanted to encourage sex or pregnancy out of wedlock, and most did not want to shorten the time during which a couple might produce legitimate children.[9]

Like most people at the time and biologists today, Swinburne understood that girls experienced puberty sooner than boys, and this accounted for why they could marry two years before boys. He gave readers a number of possible explanations for why women arrive at puberty earlier than men; the best was that the female body is "more *tender* and *moister* than the Male," whose body is "harder and drier." Because of this, men are "more slow in ripening; and Women's Bodies, because they are softer and moister, are more quickly ripe; like as it is to be seen in Plants and fruits." Although Swinburne's biological expertise is surely questionable, his explanation for the ages and their differences may be taken as representative of early modern English thought. He also explained that precisely because women "ripened" earlier than men, so they "doth sooner decay." Because of this, "women as they are sooner able, so they sooner become unable to bring forth Men to beget." Women's reproductive capacities ceased before men's did, and so they must be allowed to marry earlier so that they might beget children sooner. So the ages of seven, twelve, and fourteen have roots in presumptions about both intellectual and biological capacity, with the difference between girls and boys lodged firmly in the latter. Even though historians can demonstrate that the onset of puberty for girls and boys was higher in the past than it is today, Swinburne and others believed that enough girls and boys arrived at biological adulthood at twelve and fourteen to warrant these ages.[10]

COLONIAL ANTECEDENTS TO STATE STATUTES

Although the common law set the groundwork for marriage in the North American colonies, some colonial legislatures passed laws of their own to govern the marriage contract, most notably in New England by making marriage a civil contract unregulated by the Church of England and by making divorce available. Colonial assemblies were also attuned to adapting the English law for decidedly un-English environments. Some of these colonial laws were related to children's ability to marry with or without their parents' consent. These laws demonstrate the concerns (or lack of them) that colonists of different regions possessed about property, inheritance, filial obedience, and the regulation of the young. Of those that did pass laws on the subject, northern colonies tended to emphasize parental control, whereas southern colonies focused on the regulation of property through marriage. Neither of these is surprising, given the origins of the two regions: the South had been founded with commercial aims and the North as a haven for families fleeing religious persecution. The middle colonies were settled for more mixed reasons, and their laws were the most likely to emphasize set ages above which children no longer required parental consent.

In the New England colonies, Plymouth Bay passed a statute in 1636 mandating that "none be allowed to marry that are under the covert of parent but by their consent and approbation." Two years later, in 1638, because "diuers persons vnfitt for marriage both in regard of their yeong yeares as also in regard of their weake estate," and because some men practiced the "enveaglement of mens daughters" and "mayde servants wthout leaue and likeing of their masters," the General Court passed a law mandating that men needed to acquire the consent of fathers and masters before they might marry daughters and maidservants. Punishment could be monetary or corporal. Plymouth also provided a means for those who wished to marry and were prevented by a master or guardian from so doing "through any sinistre end or couetous desire" to plead their case before a magistrate. The colony updated its statutes in 1658 and 1672, and though the language changed somewhat, the basic stipulations remained the same. Like all the colonies, Massachusetts had elaborate procedures for the posting of banns (or announcements) of engagements that would give any parent ample time to halt a marriage to which he (or less likely, she) objected. In 1647, Massachusetts made clear that parents had the right to dispose "their children in marriage" and that suitors must obtain permission from parents in order to pursue marriage with young women. That said, in

1641, Massachusetts included among its "Body of Liberties" a provision (like that of Plymouth) for children whose parents "shall wilfullie and unreasonably deny any childe timely or convenient marriage"; that child could "complain to Authoritie for redresse." With a clear religious mandate to replenish the new colony, Massachusetts lawmakers might want children to obey their parents, but they also wanted them to marry and reproduce in a timely fashion. Soon after joining with Plymouth, Massachusetts passed a statute for the "orderly consummating of marriages" in the second session of the 1692–93 legislative meeting stipulating that officials were empowered to marry people but that they must have "the consent of those whose immediate care and government they are under." This might be parents, but it could be masters in the case of indentured servants, indicating the degree to which both colonies were concerned primarily that dependents in households paid proper deference.[11]

Connecticut passed a similar statute in 1650 barring children and servants from marrying without the permission of a master, guardian, or parent. The colony of New Haven mandated in 1656 that it was a crime for any man to attempt to "indeavour to inveagle, or draw the affections of any Maide or Maideservant" without the consent of her father, guardian, or whoever might have control of her. The statute, though it mentioned marriage, also implied that a man might "inveagle" a girl into something other than marriage, for various punishments are laid out for first, second, and third offenses, which would be unlikely if the end result of the crime were always marriage. Connecticut passed a similar law in 1672. Rhode Island also passed a statute in 1647 (which the legislature amended a number of times) requiring all "children" to obtain parental consent before marriage; any man who married a girl without her parents' consent shall "forfeit five pounds to the parents of the maid"; all accessories to the marriage also forfeited five pounds, half paid to the parents, half to the town. New Hampshire passed no law regulating age of marriage or parental consent until after the American Revolution and the founding of the United States.[12]

Colonial New Englanders, long famous for their concern with the maintenance of orderly households, were attempting to ensure that children did not marry unless their parents or guardians or masters approved both of their prospective spouses and of when they wished to marry. Noteworthy in most of the statutes is a focus on regulating girls who were clearly servants in others' homes (not just living in their natal homes); lawmakers sought to bar those under another's control (not just daughters) from marrying without permission. The issue here was about respect for authority and the orderly succession of the generations, as well as claims to girls' and boys' labor, not with the protection of childhood as a stage of life, or with property, at least not directly. The statutes named no ages at all.[13]

Of the middle colonies, New York and Delaware did not regulate children's capacity to marry, meaning that they abided by the English common law. By contrast, in 1676, Pennsylvania prescribed eighteen and twenty-one as the minimum marriage ages for girls and boys, respectively. Then, in 1700, Pennsylvania, in an act to prevent clandestine marriages, mandated that consent of parents or guardians should be obtained before children married. The law was updated in 1730 to stipulate that anyone under the age of twenty-one required consent of parents, guardian, or master/mistress. In its 1719 "Act to prevent Clandestine Marriages," New Jersey explained that the act was being passed because "several Young Persons have been by the Wicked Practices of evil disposed Persons, and their Confederates, inticed, inveigled and deluded, led away and Clandestinely Marryed." This had led to the "Ruin of the Parties so marryed" and the "Grief of their Parents and Relations." The law stipulated that no one below the age of twenty-one could be married without permission of parent or guardian. It also included punishments for those officials who issued marriage licenses contrary to the act's stipulations and a mechanism whereby a parent could recover damages if his or her child managed to marry despite its provisions. Although two of the middle colonies had no age stipulations at all, it is clear that in Pennsylvania and New Jersey, lawmakers were worried, not so much that children might defy their parents' authority, but that they might be coerced into marriages that parents would see as detrimental to their well-being and perhaps their property.[14]

A focus on property animates the statutes of the two southern English colonies that passed laws regulating age of marriage. Of the five, Georgia, Maryland, and North Carolina passed no law on the subject. In 1632, Virginia stipulated that the parents or guardians of those "beinge under the age of twenty and one years" must give consent to the marriage of minors. In 1657, the colony reiterated this stipulation, though with less emphasis on the precise age and more on the fact of parental consent. The Virginia House of Burgesses tinkered with its marriage law with some regularity throughout the seventeenth century, indicating that colonists must have been working their way around the rules. In 1662, the burgesses had passed a law against the "secrett marriage" of servants, and in 1670, they noted that "diverse persons" were "defrauding parents and guardians of that naturall right and just priviledge in disposing of their children or orphans in marriage" by gaining marriage licenses from clerks in counties where they did not reside and were not known. "And soe the parents of the inequality of the match dishonoured, the child ruynated in her fortunes," they thus enacted a law mandating that the license had to be issued in the county in which the girl lived. This, however, seemed not to be enough. In 1696, noting too many secret and clandestine marriages that resulted in the "utter ruin of many heirs and heiresses to the great greif [sic] of all their relations," Virginia passed a law stipulating more complicated instructions for the announcement of marriage banns, mandating a fine of five hundred pounds and a year's imprisonment for anyone who broke the law. Following in English tradition Virginia also established that any girl between the ages of twelve and sixteen who married without parental or guardian permission forfeited her inheritance to her next of kin. She could reclaim the inheritance only if her husband died. This removed any incentive for men to marry a young woman of means without her parents' or guardian's permission because the means themselves would disappear at the moment of marriage. In updating its marriage laws Virginia reiterated this act in 1705 and 1748. Virginia had, far and away, the most complicated architecture for the solemnization of marriage in the original colonies, and one of its primary concerns was making sure that young girls (not boys), especially if they had inherited property, did not marry without their parents' permission.[15]

South Carolina explicitly adopted English statutes in order to govern itself. Among these were a statute enacted in 1712 making it illegal to take any "unmarried maid or woman child" under the age of sixteen for the purposes of matrimony without her parents' or guardian's permission. South Carolina also enforced a law similar to that of Virginia that disinherited a woman (and therefore her husband) if she was married between the ages of twelve and sixteen without permission. Noteworthy here again is the notion that legislators were less concerned with children marrying than they were with rich girls marrying without their parents' permission; preservation of fortunes seems to be a higher priority than the protection of children per se. Also noteworthy is the use of the phrase "unmarried maid or woman child," which echoed language used in English law. "Woman child" should be a contradiction in terms, and yet legally it was not. Marriage legally turned a girl into a woman and emancipated her from parental control. Traditionally it would also have given her access to any inheritance she possessed; this was what the law was attempting to forestall in certain cases. Because marriage was a termination of childhood and effected emancipation from natal homes, many of these statutes, and not just the southern ones, mandated that a child gain permission of his or her parents in order to cease being a child, becoming someone who no longer required parental consent. The evolution of the law toward a conception of childhood as a separate stage of life did not protect them; it simply allowed their fathers to consent to their legal transformation into adults. For boys, this could have meaningful legal and social implications; gender blunted the consequences of this for girls. They moved from one household to the other, continuing their dependence and taking on many new responsibilities, sex among them.[16]

In the French and Spanish colonies of New France and New Spain in the era before the United States came into being, the Catholic Church, not civil authorities, controlled marriage, which was a sacrament. The minimum ages for marriage were eleven for girls and thirteen for boys. Each prospective couple completed a matrimonial investigation administered by a local priest to determine if the parties were fit for marriage. The priest was concerned primarily with whether the parties were already married or betrothed or in any way related to each other, either by blood (consanguinity) or through having had sexual relations with each other's relatives (a relationship of affinity or spirituality). Although both of these were forbidden, in the more remote regions of what would later become the United States, the population of Spaniards and French was sparse enough that priests often gave dispensations and allowed the marriages of those who were already related. This church-based regulation of marriage would remain in place in large parts of the future southern and western United States so long as they remained French, Spanish, or Mexican territories. This meant that the minimum ages of eleven and thirteen applied to any Catholics in what would eventually become Louisiana, California, New Mexico, Texas, Arizona, Nevada, and parts of Colorado, Wyoming, Utah, and Oklahoma so long as the territories were controlled by France, Spain, or Mexico (1853 at the latest with the completion of the Gadsden Purchase).[17]

REVOLUTIONARY AND ANTEBELLUM MODIFICATIONS

A number of states modified their marriage laws either soon after becoming states or during the Revolution itself. In the states that had already adopted statutory law, the timing of the Revolution may have been coincidental; in those that had previously retained English common law, these new laws can be seen as an assertion of newfound independence. In 1777, Maryland mandated parental consent for girls and boys below the ages of sixteen and twenty-one, respectively, whereas Massachusetts (1786) and Delaware (1790) chose the more typical ages of eighteen and twenty-one. These states were continuing the common tradition in the northern states of emphasizing parental consent

rather than absolute ages at which children might make these decisions themselves. In the 1820s, both New Jersey (1829) and North Carolina (1820) modified their laws to specify fifteen as the minimum marriageable age for girls.
New Jersey made the marriage of a "woman child" below that age a high misdemeanor, and North Carolina made it a crime to marry a girl under that age
unless she had parental permission. Echoing its neighbors to the immediate
north and south, North Carolina set up elaborate procedures to deny the man
who married such a girl access to her estate. In the case of the North Carolina
bill, one sponsor made it clear that he had designed the bill not just to ward off
mercenary suitors but also to "secure female infant wards against being drawn
into premature marriage by the interested views of unprincipled Guardians."
In either case, however, the concern was not so much that a girl below the age
of fifteen was incapable of *being married* but rather that her parents were those
who should make that decision and that she (and her fortune) might be vulnerable. In the mid-1850s, North Carolina again modified its marriage statute,
mandating fourteen and sixteen as minimum marriageable ages and increasing
the penalty on a clerk who married a girl below the age of fifteen without consent. Virginia also made changes in the antebellum era, in 1792 augmenting
(but retaining) stipulations about punishments for clandestine marriages. The
legislature later amended the divorce code to stipulate that twelve and fourteen (the common-law ages) were in fact the ages of consent to marriage.[18]

New York State provides an interesting example of what could go wrong with
new laws around the age of marriage. Throughout the colonial era, New York
stipulated no minimum marriageable ages, nor did it have a law pertaining to
when a child required parental consent to marry. In 1825, the legislature passed
a law mandating an overhaul of all its revised statutes. As part of this project a
number of lawmakers reviewed the existing statutes and made recommendations for updates. Among them were changes to the law of marriage. With the
exception of divorce, the common law governed marriage. The revisers, however, believed that "rules of the common law are insufficient to meet all the exi-
gencies of this important relation" and so proposed a new statute on marriage.
They noted that the common law allowed boys and girls of fourteen and twelve,
respectively, to contract marriage, and then wrote: "But it may well be enquired,
whether these ages are not too young, and whether it would not be better to sub-
stitute 17 and 14?" The new statute responded to this question affirmatively and
laid out fourteen and seventeen as the ages at which girls and boys, respectively,
were capable of contracting marriage. By 1827, when these ages were proposed,
many states in the Midwest had already adopted them, and although the revisers

acknowledged their debts to other states and nations in framing the law overall, they gave no justification for selecting these particular ages.[19]

The legislature repealed them the very next year, along with all stipulations that the minister or magistrate who performed the marriage should record the ages of the parties married at all. Determining why is a challenge. The new marriage law was widely publicized; newspapers throughout the state published the statutes as the legislature debated and adopted them. One newspaper even called attention to the new marriageable ages as being among the principle departures from the common law. This much publicity surrounding the new ages may have led to objections from the public. At the time of the repeal a number of newspapers focused on the requirement of recording the ages of *all parties*, explaining that "to the more *ancient maidens* particularly, this must have been a provision altogether unpleasant, and we congratulate them right heartily on its abolishment. 'Twill save many a precious blush." Another explained, with apparent sarcasm, that the new bill "repeals that odious portion of the revised statutes which requires the person solemnizing the marriage to ascertain and record the ages of the parties. Mr. Vanderpoel [the bill's sponsor] deserves a medal for his gallantry. What more impertinent question can be asked a bride about to receive the nuptial ring than, 'how old are you madam?' " This newspaper clearly thought that the repeal was foolish. In revising Kent's *Commentaries on American Law* for its thirteenth edition, the editor simply noted that the "provision was so disrelished, that it was repealed within four months thereafter." An 1887 commentator on that year's new marriage law explained of the 1829 revisal that "so deep rooted had the common law rule become that [the new law was repealed], the Legislature of that year having arrived at the conclusion that owing to the delicate nature of the marital relation and the complications growing out of it, the common law rule had better be allowed to stand." Although New York had reverted to the common-law ages of twelve and fourteen, it did retain another related law, also passed in 1829, that criminalized the act of clandestinely marrying a girl below the age of fourteen without her parents' permission. In 1841, legislators also passed a law that allowed such a girl's parents to sue for annulment of the marriage.[20]

Two others of the first thirteen colonies passed marriage age legislation in the antebellum era, one of which (New Hampshire in 1842) simply legislated the common-law ages of twelve and fourteen by statute, and the other (Connecticut in 1854) stipulated that consent was necessary for minors. Connecticut already had a statute mandating consent for those under control of their parents, so the law simply spelled out an age that was already indicated by the statute passed in the seventeenth century. Georgia, Pennsylvania, Rhode Island, and South Carolina did not change their laws at all. In the case of Georgia and Rhode Island, this meant that the common law continued to govern marriage. Pennsylvania continued to mandate consent below twenty-one, and South Carolina remained intent on punishing men who married underage girls for their fortunes. Taken together, a few patterns emerge. The original states modified common law for two reasons: to mandate parental consent or to make it difficult for men to marry girls for their money. These were clear changes, yet these states were much less likely than any of the states that entered the union post-Revolution to adhere to absolute minimum marriageable ages. Along the East Coast, parental consent reigned supreme.[21]

NEW STATES ENTER THE UNION

By the 1850s, when a host of new states had entered the union, regional distinctions were more sharply drawn: the Northeast and South continued to emphasize parental consent, with the South also placing a premium on protecting a girl's fortune. In new states of the West and Midwest, those that had little connection to common-law legal precedents, age minimums were much more common, even if these states also mandated parental consent below certain ages. This was most true for states in the Midwest, but the trend is evident in other regions as well. In part, this was a result of states modeling their statutes upon one another; some states also derived from the same original territory, and they carried identical territorial statutes with them when they divided into multiple states. The minimum marriageable age trend is evident, for instance, in Ohio, Indiana, and Illinois, all of which derived from the Northwest Territory and took fourteen and seventeen as their minimum marriageable ages, retaining also parental consent below eighteen and twenty-one. As a territory, Indiana imported wholesale Virginia's statute punishing a man who married a girl between twelve and sixteen without her parents' permission. Wisconsin, Iowa, Minnesota, Michigan, Kansas, Oregon, Nevada, and Missouri followed similar trends (see table 1.1, below, for specific ages). Noticeable here is the importance of regional similarity, as well as the degree to which states could be influenced by the statutes on which they modeled themselves.[22]

These minimums varied a good deal, of course, with Kansas being the lowest (twelve and fifteen, consent below eighteen and twenty-one) and states of the Old Northwest Territory being the highest (fourteen and seventeen, consent below eighteen and twenty-one). All of these states also mandated

Table 1.1. Minimum Marriageable and Consent Ages in the Antebellum United States

State (Year Joined U.S.)	Marriage Ages at Time of Joining U.S.—Girls/Boys Marriageable Minimums; *Age below which Consent Required*	Marriage Ages in 1865—Girls/Boys Marriageable Minimums; *Age below which Consent Required*
Massachusetts (1788)	*18/21*	*18/21**
New Hampshire (1788)	–	12/14
Connecticut (1788)	*Children living at home*	*21/21*
Rhode Island (1790)	–	–
Vermont (1791)	–	*18/21*
Maine (1820)	*18/21*	*18/21*
Delaware (1787)	–	*18/21*
New Jersey (1787)	*21/21*	*21/21**
Pennsylvania (1787)	*21/21*	*21/21*
New York (1788)	–	–*
Virginia (1788)	*21/21**	*21/21**
Maryland (1788)	*16/21*	*16/21*
Georgia (1788)	–	–
South Carolina (1788)	–*	–*
North Carolina (1789)	–	14/16*
Kentucky (1792)	–	12/14; *21/21**
Tennessee (1796)	–	–
Louisiana (1812)	*21/21*	12/14; *21/21*
Mississippi (1817)	*18/21*	*18/21**
Alabama (1819)	*18/21*	14/17; *18/21**
Missouri (1821)	–	*18/21*
Arkansas (1836)	*18/–*	14/17; *18/21*
Florida (1845)	*21/21*	*21/21**
Texas (1845)	12/14; *18/21*	12/14; *18/21*
West Virginia (1863)	12/14; *21/21**	12/14; *21/21**
Ohio (1803)	14/17; *18/21*	14/18; *18/21*

Cont. on page 32

Indiana (1816)	14/17; *18/21**	14/17; *18/21**
Illinois (1818)	14/17; *18/21*	14/17; *18/21*
Michigan (1837)	14/18; *18/21**	16/18
Iowa (1846)	14/18; *18/21*	14/16; *18/21*
Wisconsin (1848)	14/18; *18/21*	15/18; *18/21*
Minnesota (1858)	15/18; *18/21*	15/18; *18/21*
Kansas (1861)	12/15; *18/21*	12/15; *18/21*
California (1850)	*18/21*	*18/21*
Oregon (1859)	15/18; *18/21*	15/18; *18/21*
Nevada (1864)	16/18; *18/21*	16/18; *18/21*

* Denotes some sort of punishment for marrying a girl without parents' permission.
Sources: statutes and codes in chapter 1, notes 11, 12, 14–16, 18–24.

both minimum ages *and* parental consent below certain ages. What this meant, in theory, was that children could not marry below certain ages, but between those ages and eighteen and twenty-one, they could marry with their parents' permission. Above the ages of eighteen and twenty-one, for girls and boys, respectively, they could do as they pleased. These laws were stricter than the older states on the East Coast, which relied on the common-law ages of twelve and fourteen as their minimums. There are a couple reasons for this. First, because these states came into being after English rule, they were less wedded to the common law as a system of governance, and some relied on the civil law traditions inherited from the Spanish and French. Second, for those states that entered the Union later in the antebellum period, chronological age had become more meaningful in determining reason and capacity; the adoption of precise ages might have made more sense to legislators by the 1820s and 1830s.

The second trend, common in states in the Northeast and the South, was simply to mandate parental consent below certain ages. This was the case in Vermont, which mandated consent for minors in 1797 and then changed its law in 1839 to stipulate consent below eighteen and twenty-one. When Maine separated from Massachusetts in 1820 to become its own state, it chose these ages as well. Southern states, including Florida, Kentucky, Louisiana, Mississippi, and Texas, did the same thing (though some mandated twenty-one for both sexes). West Virginia simply borrowed Virginia's code; it also retained punishments for men marrying girls below the age of fourteen. Arkansas and Alabama initially did something similar before also adopting minimum marriageable ages; they thus joined North Carolina in being the only states in the South in the antebellum years to maintain minimum marriage ages higher than the common-law ages. California was the lone western state that mandated only parental consent ages and no minimum ages just after becoming a state in 1850.[23]

Unlike states in the North, however, a number of southern states also modified their laws specifically to protect the assets of minor girls and discourage men from marrying them without their parents' permission. In 1798, Kentucky, for instance, passed a statute stripping a man of access to his wife's estate (and conveying it to her next of kin) if she was between the ages of twelve and sixteen and he married her without parental permission; it reads as strikingly similar to Virginia's statute. In 1832, Florida made it a crime to "fraudulently and deceitfully entice or take away" any unmarried female below the age of sixteen and marry her clandestinely without her father's permission. The punishment was as much as a year in a penitentiary, a thousand-dollar fine, or both. Alabama and Mississippi passed similar laws. The final trend was simply to do nothing, which was what Tennessee did, joining Georgia and Rhode Island (whose statute about permission for girls seems to have disappeared postindependence) in refusing to set minimum marriage or consent ages at all. By contrast, the nation's capital set a minimum of twelve (for girls and boys) in 1857 and mandated consent below eighteen and twenty-one.[24]

The regional differences then were that states in the Midwest were more likely to have minimum marriageable ages as well as ages below which consent was necessary (table 1.1). States in the South and Northeast were more apt simply to mandate consent below certain ages, thus relying on the common-law ages of twelve and fourteen as their minimums. The best explanation for this is that the older states were those that had relied on common law from their inception as colonies; modifying it, as New York did in 1829, did not sit well with citizens. The exception to this rule was in some southern states (and New York and New Jersey), where various kinds of penalties attached to marrying girls below certain ages without their parents' permission. The southern states were explicitly focused on preventing ne'er-do-well men from gaining access to girls' property. New York and New Jersey simply criminalized the same act. Though both were attempting to prevent clandestine marriage, the southern states were more focused on the protection of property. Importantly, however, every single state allowed legal minors to marry, and almost all allowed girls to do so before boys, either with or without their parents' permission.

The children of the new United States were protected from the responsibilities of marriage, to a degree, but not if their parents decided that it was in their best interests to marry.

THE AGES OF MAJORITY AND DIFFERENTLY GENDERED ADULTHOOD

Some states went one step further and lowered the female age of majority by three years—to eighteen, the same age as that when they could consent to their own marriages—making girls adult women three years earlier than their brothers. Under the common law the age of majority was twenty-one for both sexes: below that age, girls and boys were minors; above it, they were adults. Although state and federal statutes regulated many things based on other ages—apprenticeships, indentures, military service, and obviously marriage—the age of majority not only was important as a symbol of adulthood (especially for men, who voted at twenty-one) but also marked the moment when people could convey real estate, make wills (for men and single women), inherit property and control it in their own name, and enter into contracts. Its practical effects were thus chiefly related to property. Most states had retained the common-law age of majority, but during the mid- to late nineteenth century, twenty states and territories—almost half the total—modified it to make women legally adults at the age of eighteen; they retained age twenty-one for men. Almost all of these states were in the Midwest and West (the exceptions were Vermont and Arkansas), and most were settled after the colonial period, meaning that their attachment to the common law was more tenuous than the original colonies' bond. None of the original thirteen colonies, for instance, modified the age of majority.[25]

This reduced age of majority was not simply an anomaly in the law unrelated to marriage ages; it seems to have been a consequence of girls' lower ages of marriage. In other words, the lower age of majority followed from the lower age of marriage, not the other way around. In most states where the age of majority was lower, it matched the age below which a girl required her parents' consent to marriage, usually eighteen. The same was true for boys, of course, but boys remained minors till they were twenty-one, three years longer than girls. At the first meeting of its legislature in 1850, for instance, California passed marriage legislation declaring eighteen and twenty-one the ages of consent to marriage for girls and boys, respectively; below those ages, they required parental consent. Four years later in May 1854, legislators decided that "males shall be deemed of full and legal age when they shall be twenty-one years old, and females when they shall be eighteen years old." This meant that "males and females of legal age, as fixed by this Act, shall be competent to make contracts, convey real estate, and do all other acts and things that persons of full age may legally do." The marriage statute preceded the age-of-majority statute, the one seemingly changing because of the other.[26]

Although not all states spelled out quite as clearly as California what the lower age of majority was meant to do, many did echo the California statute's ties to property. These statutes were passed in three main ways: (1) in bills that simply declared a legal age of majority; (2) in bills that spelled out what a minor might or might not do, especially in regard to property and contracts; and (3) in bills regulating guardianship, where the girls' minority ending at eighteen also meant the end of their guardianship, the former stemming from the latter. Although the first set of bills makes determining the legislators' intent difficult—especially regarding their understanding of what minority and majority meant in practical terms—there are clear links in both of the other categories that allow us to see what the younger age of majority would do for women (and men). In Ohio's 1834 "Act for fixing the age of majority," for instance, the legislators spelled out that men of at least twenty-one years and women of at least eighteen "shall be capable of contracting respecting goods, chattels, lands, tenements and any other matter or thing which may be the legitimate subject of a contract." The second part of the act repealed any law in the state that would "restrain any unmarried female person, of the age of eighteen years and upward," from doing the same things. Like California and Ohio, the states and territories of Idaho, Montana, Nevada, Oklahoma, Utah, and Oregon also emphasized that women of the age of eighteen had the right to contract, with Oregon specifying that adult women had not just the rights but also "the liabilities of citizens of full age."[27]

A similar focus on property animates the laws where differential minority is spelled out through guardianship statutes. In Arkansas, Minnesota, and Nebraska, the statutes begin by declaring what constituted a minor and follow by detailing the responsibilities of guardians. Fathers were children's "natural guardians" under common law, and whereas these statutes sometimes reiterated this, their main purpose was to set down law in cases where fathers (and sometimes mothers) were deceased: who appointed the guardian, when a minor might choose his or her own guardian, when guardianship ceased, and what constituted the guardian's responsibilities. This is where the age of majority mattered; one of the primary responsibilities of a guardian was the management of property, along with care and education. All of this ceased for minor girls three years earlier than it did for minor boys. The statutes of Colorado, Illinois, and Iowa spell this out even more explicitly. In these states, the stipulation about girls' minority ending at eighteen is tacked on at the end of a section addressing financial arrangements. After explaining that guardians shall have the power to sue and receive all moneys on behalf of their wards; to put the interest from any money "upon mortgage security"; and to lease any real estate of the ward, all four end by explaining that "such leasing shall never be for a longer time than during the minority of the ward; and the minority of females shall cease at the age of 18 years." Given the subject of the clause itself, this reads as something of an afterthought, but its placement is crucial in revealing the lawmakers' intent: the management of girls' property by their guardians ceased at eighteen, when they were legally adults. This was the true meaning of girls' different age of majority in these states.[28]

There is a bizarre contradiction here: girls who, once married, would largely be incapable of contracting or making decisions about property at all were empowered to do so as single people three years earlier than their male counterparts. They were legal adults for three years more than their brothers so long as they didn't marry. The reason for lowering the age of majority was both to allow for the movement of property with greater ease and because it was presumed from the outset that girls would marry sooner than boys: this was why the age of majority and the age of marriage without parental consent matched in all but two of these states.[29] Although men were presumed to be the rightful owners of property, in the case of women who might inherit property through the death of a father or other relative—not at all uncommon in frontier states—this lower age of majority allowed them to sell it at an earlier age instead of having it languish under a guardian's care until a girl reached her majority. If that majority were lowered, she would be empowered to contract a sale of the property in her own right. Or, of course, she could marry at a younger age without her parents' or guardian's consent and the property would pass into the control of her new husband. Although some young women could take advantage of these laws to their own benefit, the point of the law was not to empower women; it seems to have been about facilitating property transactions.

Taken together with the laws regulating marriage, the lower age of majority for women is another instance in which age, which ostensibly regulated both women and men, was less meaningful for women. Girls enjoyed the protections that were supposed to inhere in minority for less time than boys did. Men's arrival at the age of twenty-one marked a transition to manhood; women's arrival at twenty-one had always been less momentous because their adulthood was circumscribed by gender—what did they get by becoming adults, after all?—but reducing their age of majority for the sake of property conveyance only made this clearer. It was not women's best interests that were served by the law but rather men's. And throughout the antebellum period both marriage laws and those governing age of majority were all geared toward encouraging the early marriage of girls.[30]

Later in the year of their marriage, 1762, Governor Arthur Dobbs suffered a stroke that paralyzed one side of his body and left his lower limbs virtually useless. For two years he continued as governor but began to plan a leave of absence from his duties and a return to his native Ireland for convalescence. In preparation for their visit, his wife, Justina, sent her stepchildren in Ireland a barrel of rice and "a small box of New England spermaceti candles." Arthur and Justina planned to stay in North Carolina through Christmas of 1764, leaving in the spring. On March 25, 1765, while packing, Dobbs suffered a seizure and took to his bed. He never got out, dying two days later. Justina wrote to her stepson Conway, "Alas I have loste my ever Dear Mr. Dobbs which makes me almost Inconsolable. . . . I have lost one of the best and tenderest of husbands and you a kind and most affectionate father." Justina signed the letter to a man she had never met, "yrs affectionate Mother, Justina Dobbs." She soon remarried Abner Nash, a former member of the Virginia House of Burgesses who had moved to New Bern, North Carolina, where he also became active in politics. Nash was only five years her senior, and together they had three children before Justina died in 1771 at the age of twenty-six. Abner Nash (who himself remarried) would become the second governor of the new state of North Carolina in the 1780s.[31]

Aside from the extreme age difference between Davis and Dobbs—and the fact that she married two governors, which is why her marriage was so well publicized—there is little to distinguish Justina Davis Dobbs Nash's story from thousands of other marriages in colonial America or, indeed, the antebellum United States. Davis was younger than both of her husbands, only fifteen when she married her first. But this was not uncommon. Because wives were always meant to be dependent on their husbands, marrying while still legal minors actually moved them between what were, in the end, reasonably similar legal statuses: daughter and wife. What bears noting is that her childhood did not protect her from this marriage, and this lack of protection was much more common for girl than for boy children. Many laws had changed to demarcate childhood as a separate and protected stage of life in the early modern period. But the law of marriage still allowed—indeed usually encouraged—girls to marry well before they reached legal adulthood, thus making the most important and binding decision of their lives before they were legally capable of bearing witness, managing property, or legally much of anything else. Marriage was a giant exception to the legal protections afforded to minors, and as we have seen, girls' minority itself did not extend as long as boys' did in most midwestern and western states. When lawmakers wrote many of the laws I have detailed here, especially those in the Northeast and South, they wrote them not so much to protect children as *youthful people* but to safeguard the rights of parents over *their children*, at times a very different undertaking.

TWO

The Child Was to Be His Wife

Patterns of Youthful Marriage in Antebellum America

Born in 1798 in Lunenberg, Massachusetts, Abel Stearns went to sea at age twelve following the death of his parents. Rising to the position of supercargo in the South American and China trade, he set out for Mexico in 1827 to make his fortune and became a naturalized Mexican citizen the next year. Making his way north from central Mexico to Alta California, he first settled at Monterey, the region's capital, before making the pueblo of Los Angeles his home. There he went into business, indeed multiple businesses, and soon became one of the region's richest and most important merchants, ranchers, and landowners, joining the ranks of men like Juan Bandini, who had been born of Spanish parents in Peru and come to Alta California about ten years before Stearns's arrival.[1]

Bandini and his first wife, Dolores Estudillo, had three daughters in San Diego, Arcadia, Ysidora, and Josefa, known as the most beautiful girls in Alta California. Having known the Bandini family for many years and now past his fortieth birthday, in 1841 Abel Stearns set his sights on Arcadia, Don Juan's eldest daughter, who was fourteen. He, Arcadia, and Don Juan must have come to an agreement (Doña Dolores had died when Arcadia was eight), because in 1841, Don Abel Stearns petitioned both the civil government in Los Angeles and the ecclesiastical authorities for permission to marry María Arcadia Bandini. The dispensation from the Catholic Church was necessary for all couples

San Diego History Center

Abel Stearns and Arcadia Bandini de Stearns (opposite). Abel Stearns, a native of
Massachusetts and a naturalized Mexican citizen, was forty-three when he married
fourteen-year-old Arcadia Bandini in Alta California. The couple wed with the
blessing of her parents, as well as the permission of the Catholic Church and the
territorial government. Both gained through the marriage: Arcadia a wealthy husband
of indisputable whiteness, and Abel connections to one of the wealthiest landowning
families in the territory. Both images courtesy of the San Diego History Center.

because the authorities needed to investigate their suitability for marriage: the betrothed's ages, the circumstances of their births, possible betrothals to others, and the key issue of whether they were related to each other. Stearns also had to petition the civil authorities (the Prefect of the Second District of Alta California) because he was not Mexican by birth. Stearns, "wishing to avoid the ridicule which might arise among the idle young because of the disparity in years, she being 14 years old and I being 40," and because he was busy with important business matters in other places, requested of Fray Narciso Duran "to please exempt me the three banns, or at least two, I pledging myself to satisfy the alms which may be thereby imposed on me." Stearns lied about his age in this letter and in the marital investigation conducted by the church; he was actually forty-three. Although the difference in their ages— twenty-nine years—and the fact that he was marrying at this late age both seemed to embarrass him, it does not appear that Arcadia's own youthfulness was the issue here. Indeed, the Catholic Church, as we saw in the previous chapter, set eleven as the age below which a girl was ineligible for marriage, and by the time of Stearns's proposal, many other pubescent *Californianas* had married older Euro-Americans in Alta California. In any event, Duran granted the permission to marry on the first of May 1841, and also dispensed with the banns, as Stearns had requested. Abel and Arcadia were married in June. Immediately thereafter they moved into what locals called *El Palacio de Don Abel* at the corner of Main and Arcadia Streets, the handsomest house in Los Angeles, known for years as the center of Californio socializing in the pueblo.[2]

The story of Don Abel and Doña Arcadia is unrepresentative of youthful marriage in the antebellum era only in the bureaucratic hoops through which the couple had to jump in order to wed. But the fact of a fourteen-year-old girl marrying, or the difference in ages between the two, appears to have been common during this era and in a wide variety of locations across the United States and the lands that would be annexed into it by the end of the era. The explanations for its prevalence, however, vary by region. Reliable figures exist only for a handful of states, and generally only for the end of this period, so determining with any precision the number of minor brides and grooms is impossible. But reading the sources with an eye toward the phenomenon reveals not only that early marriage was everywhere but also that most observers at the time did not find it unusual. Youthful marriage was common because, even though states had passed laws regulating when children might marry, many of those states' residents had not yet embraced the notion that young people in their teenage years really were unfit for marriage. Common

Table 2.1. Percentage of Males and Females Who Married
under the Age of Twenty in Various Locations, 1850s

Sex	Massachusetts 1857	Massachusetts 1853–57	Rhode Island 1854–57	South Carolina 1857	Kentucky 1856
Males	1.62	1.72	3.59	4.85	6.50
Females	22.23	22.50	24.09	38.97	42.03

Source: *Sixteenth Report to the Legislature of Massachusetts Relating to the Registry and Return of Births, Marriages, and Deaths, in the Commonwealth of Massachusetts for the Year Ending December 31, 1857* (Boston: William White, 1858), 187, Massachusetts Archives.

practice, especially among those people for whom age itself had yet to become an important marker of identity, was at odds with the law. And in a country where many laws of marriage were sporadically and haphazardly enforced, youthful marriage could continue unchecked.

To the degree that it is possible to tell, the marriage of young people was least common in the industrializing Northeast, and most common in the South, Midwest, and West. In table 2.1, drawn from Massachusetts's 1857 compendium of vital statistics, we see a limited comparison between four states in an assemblage of years in the 1850s: Massachusetts (in 1857 and for a five-year period, 1853–57), Rhode Island (1854–57), South Carolina (1857), and Kentucky (1856).

These statistics demonstrate, first, that it was far more common for girls to marry below the age of twenty than it was for boys, and second, that there were distinct regional variations. In the two northeastern states, between 22 and 24 percent of all marriages contracted in the given years were by girls under twenty. By contrast, in South Carolina and Kentucky, around 40 percent of all marriages contracted in 1857 and 1856 were by girls under twenty. Indeed, the period "Under Twenty" was the most common time to marry for girls in these states, compared to Massachusetts and Rhode Island, where the most common age frame for contracting marriage (for girls or boys) was between the ages of twenty and twenty-five.

There are a number of explanations for this. First, the phenomenon of a protected childhood was gaining greatest traction in the Northeast, whose residents, for a variety of reasons, were increasingly finding the marriage of youthful people to be an oddity. Combined with the rise of age consciousness (discussed in the next chapter), the marriage of children caused the greatest distress in this region and appears to have been least common there. That said, it had its fair share of practitioners. Youthful marriage remained common in the South, especially among two particular populations: the landed gentry and their slaves. Plantation owners smiled on the marriages of their youthful daughters to suitable mates (sometimes their own relatives). And slaves, who were unable to marry legally and would not be counted in a state's vital statistics, nevertheless wed ceremonially and lived as husband and wife. They often did so at very young ages.

A number of factors combined to make early marriage common in the West as well. The first was demographic: in many areas of the western United States, men far outnumbered women, driving the age of marriage down for girls. This was especially the case when white men confined their marital prospects to white brides or in insular groups that practiced polygamy, like the Church of Jesus Christ of Latter-Day Saints, in both its western locations— Nauvoo, Illinois, and Utah Territory. Second, marriage soon after arrival at puberty had long been the custom among Native Americans, and this continued through the antebellum era. Newly arrived Anglo explorers and speculators took advantage of this by marrying Native girls. Spaniards and Mexicans with claims to whiteness also found it advantageous to marry their daughters off to older Anglo men. Last, historians have found that makeshift life on the frontier, far from what many at the time called "civilization," tended to blur the meanings of age and allow for the marriage of girls who might be seen as too young for marriage in other situations. Travelers on the Overland Trail during the 1840s and 1850s, as well as those who had reached their western destinations, seem to have married at earlier ages, as single men sought wives to make homes and frontier life (and the journey there) gave young girls the experience necessary to become wives at early ages. Although the reasons differed, many antebellum Americans—either in the United States itself or in territories that would be annexed into it by the end of this period—married within the realm of what we would consider to be childhood or adolescence.

MOTIVATIONS AND DESIRES

This chapter focuses on the overarching sociological explanations for early marriage, such as lack of age consciousness and imbalanced sex ratios. Important though they might be, they would probably not have been the reasons that a young person or her prospective spouse would have given for tying the knot.

In explaining why they were marrying each other, most couples, regardless of age, would have cited some combination of love, sexual desire, class- and race-based suitability, and practical considerations like economic self-sufficiency, household competence, or fertility. In the middle of the nineteenth century, the last considerations were much more salient than we like to believe they are now. That is, many couples, especially in the working class, were guided less by notions of romantic love and compatibility than they were by suitability, itself a product of proximity and mutual availability. Of course, premarital sex was also a consideration, particularly if it resulted in pregnancy. Though premarital pregnancy rates were lower in the mid-nineteenth century than earlier or later in that century, many brides continued to marry while already expecting, and some of those were legal minors. Pregnancy could carry a man and woman to the altar sooner than they might otherwise have planned.[3]

But what of motivations that might be particular to minor girls or the men who chose them as brides? Some of these were legal, which I will address in the next chapter. Bear in mind also that in a society less structured around age norms, marrying a minor would be less noteworthy both for the child herself and the man she married. Though there is no way of knowing definitively, most minors and their spouses probably married not *because* of age but rather *regardless* of it. In many places in the antebellum era, age was not meaningful enough as a social category that men sought out especially youthful brides, and those brides were not motivated toward marriage because of their age. Even those who married the young because of demographic shortages of suitable spouses would, most of the time, have been unaware that demography was guiding their choices. And in turn those choices would have further normalized marriage at young ages. The age minimums that legislators were writing into the law were only beginning to have traction among larger numbers of Americans. This was a transitional moment in the history of marriage and of age, where it was still acceptable among wide swaths of people to marry at young ages.[4]

It is possible that people married at younger ages in the past because they also died earlier, but this explanation for the phenomenon is, in the end, unsatisfactory. First, the average age of first marriage has gone up and down over the course of American history—it is not just a slow and steady rise—dipping to one of its all-time lows during the 1950s, by which time life expectancy was many years longer than it had been in the colonial era or the nineteenth century, when average marriage ages were higher. Second, the average age of first marriage, itself related to the number of people who married at particularly young ages, has sometimes varied by region, meaning that it was also a product of such factors as demography, race, culture, and religion. There were, to be sure, also regional differences in life expectancy (especially in the colonial era), but these did not always map seamlessly on to marriage ages and a lengthening of one did not systematically produce a consequential postponement of marriage. Last, I have found little evidence to suggest that people themselves considered their possible youthful demise an incentive to marry early. If they had done so, then surely more men would have married as boys, given that in almost all places at all times, they were far more likely to die before their wives.[5]

Other factors account for the appeal of youthful marriage or, at the very least, the lack of disincentive toward it. One of the primary reasons that most minor spouses were female is that girls, unlike boys, did not need to reach a moment when they could support a spouse and family in order to marry. Indeed, marriage actually relieved some working girls of having to support themselves. Girls were also fully expected to move from a position of dependence in one household to a similar position in another. They did not need to be a certain age for that transition to occur. Although being a daughter was not the same as being a wife, there might actually be little difference in terms of the labor that a working-class girl performed in either her father's or her husband's house, and one of the primary qualifications for becoming a working-class wife was an ability to labor. Middle- and upper-class daughters would arguably have a more marked transition in roles because a middle- or upper-class wife was responsible for the running of a home in the way that a girl's mother, but not she as a daughter, would have been.[6]

From the perspective of a man, the precise age of a girl—especially if she were in the fuzzy region between thirteen and seventeen that we would now call adolescence—might be less important than her attractiveness, capability, and willingness. Americans of the nineteenth century did not identify particular men as child predators or pedophiles, so sexual desire for a younger girl was not stigmatized as it is now. Modern statutory rape laws were not passed before the 1880s. The age of consent to sex outside of marriage was ten in most states. And precisely because a man who married a young girl legitimized his relationship with her through matrimony, socially and legally, both his intentions and their relationship would not achieve the notoriety that it might today.[7]

The girls who married older men may have done so for many of the reasons that contemporary readers might fear: they were tricked, coerced, or were simply naive. Perhaps they did not realize what was in store for them, persuaded as they were by love, infatuation, and promises of devotion. That said, these men were marrying them, not seducing and abandoning them, the great fear of much nineteenth-century literature about young girls, especially in cities. *Charlotte Temple* (1791), the best-selling novel of the early national era, depicts exactly this scenario. Its eponymous heroine, though only fifteen, believes that she is running away to get married; instead, her suitor seduces and abandons her. Had he actually married her, even though her parents would not have approved, she would not have suffered the loss of respectability that is the moral of the story. Charlotte's age, which author Susanna Rowson depicted as adding to her naïveté, certainly did not prevent her from marrying. In the eyes of many around them, the youthfulness of brides simply faded as they aged, their marriages not necessarily better or worse than those who married later in life. Most evidence, then, suggests that minor girls and the men they married did so for precisely the same reasons that many others did, and did not consider their age to be particularly relevant; those around them probably felt similarly.[8]

There were, however, exceptions, one of which gives us as good an idea as we are likely to find of why a man might choose to marry a girl rather than a woman. In 1868, best-selling adventure novelist Captain Mayne Reid published a novel called *The Child Wife*. Reid had been born in Ireland in 1818 but immigrated to the United States in 1840, serving in the Mexican American War, suffering a severe wounding at the Battle of Chapultepec, and resigning his commission soon thereafter and moving to New York. His novels were primarily about men conquering untamed wild settings and their occupants (Theodore Roosevelt was a fan), and although *The Child Wife* is partially about the hero's service in the Mexican War, the Bavarian Revolution, and a number of other conflicts, it is also the story of the wooing and wedding of a child bride. The hero's name in the novel is "Captain Maynard" and at least one edition of the novel comes with a frontispiece endorsement from Reid's own wife, Elizabeth, explaining that "most of the events related in this book were actual incidents in the life of within the experience of the author." Mayne Reid and Elizabeth Hyde were married in 1853, when she was fifteen. Reid was also friends with Edgar Allan Poe, who married his own first cousin, Virginia Clemm, in 1835 when she was thirteen and, according to biographers, may have preferred the company of younger girls to adult women. Although Poe did not leave us with a literary endorsement of child marriage, we are fortunate that Reid did.[9]

When Captain Maynard, who is thirty, meets the girl he will marry, Blanche Vernon, she is thirteen. Reid writes the novel so that Blanche notices

Mayne Reid. The celebrated adventure novelist was thirty-five when he married fifteen-year-old Elizabeth Hyde in 1853. His novel *The Child Wife* (1868) is an extended rumination on why a man might prefer to marry a girl rather than a grown woman. From Elizabeth Reid, *Captain Mayne Reid: His Life and Adventures* (1900).

and becomes attracted to Maynard first. She has agency throughout the courtship—indeed, *she* actually rescues him at one point—though considerable obstacles are thrown in their way (it is an adventure novel, after all). Maynard first sees Blanche at a moment when he had been recovering from unrequited love for another girl, but "he saw a face so wonderfully fair, so strange withal. . . . In less than ten minutes after, *he was in love with a child*." Reid acknowledges that some readers might find this "an improbability" or "unnatural," but it was indeed true for Maynard. When he explains to a traveling companion (the meeting occurs on a ship) that he wants to make the girl his wife, the friend reacts with incredulity: "Wife! A child not fourteen years of age! *Cher capitaine!* you are turning Turk!" He later says that "the girl's only an infant." Maynard responds, "That child has impressed me with a feeling I never had before. Her strange look has done it." Important here is that Reid acknowledges, through having his protagonist do so, that Blanche is indeed a child and that others might think it inappropriate for Maynard to take an interest in her. Indeed, the reference to "turning Turk" indicates that by 1868 there was already clearly an association between youthful marriage and an exoticized Orient. This is not a defense of mistakenly falling for a girl who happened to look older than her years; it is an exploration of knowingly marrying a girl. In this regard, Reid offers a description of the advantages of falling for a thirteen-year-old: "And it is true, though strange, that with them, the man of thirty has more chance of securing their attention than when they are ten years older! Then their young heart, unsuspicious of deception, yields easier to the instincts of Nature's innocency, receiving like soft plastic wax the impress of that it admires. It is only later that experience of the world's wickedness trains it to reticence and suspicion." Reid here explains that a girl is simply more likely to fall in love at an early age than later, in part because she will be more innocent and less jaded; a man has a better shot of winning her if he approaches her when she is a child. Also crucial is that, unlike in *Charlotte Temple*, where the seduction of an innocent girl is a tragedy, this author expects the reader to countenance the seduction because it ends in marriage.[10]

Blanche and Maynard move closer to love throughout the novel, but her cousin, age eighteen and in love with her himself, tries to thwart the relationship. When Maynard finally confesses his love for her and asks, "Blanche Vernon! do you love me?" her father overhears and responds, ominously, "*A strange question to put to a child*!" Blanche is by now fifteen, but her father thinks her far too young for marriage and sends Maynard away. Throughout, Maynard continues to dwell on the fact that Blanche remains a child. In the end, Blanche's father relents when he finds himself on his deathbed and wants someone to take care of his daughter after he has died. Maynard rejoices: "His presentiment was upon the point of being fulfilled; the *child* was to be his *wife!*" Reid also notes that the marriage was to take place not clandestinely, or by abduction, but by consent of the father. The novel ends soon after the marriage, when Captain Maynard and his child wife, Blanche, are happily set-tled in the United States, the wedding having taken place in Blanche's native England.[11]

All of this could easily be dismissed as just so much foolishness, but for the fact that Reid so self-consciously wrote *The Child Wife* as an exploration of marrying a child and that he did so himself in circumstances not unlike the ones he describes in this novel. In her biography of her late husband, Elizabeth Hyde Reid affirmed the broad outlines of their courtship, describing herself at the time of their meeting as "a fair little English girl, a child—scarce thirteen years of age." She explained that she met Reid at her aunt's home, where he had been invited for dinner, and that he immediately took a shine to her and returned to pay her visits repeatedly thereafter. For her part, Elizabeth had little interest in Reid, could scarcely remember who he was, and was otherwise pre-occupied with her dolls. She describes him as "my middle-aged lover" and her-self as still being enough of a child not to fully understand what he was after. Two years passed during which they did not see each other until one day they met again. At that meeting the two were drawn to one another, recognizing each other instantly, and before they could be parted, Reid thrust his address into her hands. She wrote to him the next day and they were soon engaged, though Elizabeth's father was reluctant to give consent. She claimed that a letter Reid wrote to her while they were engaged contained the following lines: "I am getting old, and *blasé,* and fear that your love for me is only a romance, which cannot last when you know me better. Do you think you can love me in my dressing-gown and slippers?" Evidently she could, because they were married soon thereafter. Throughout their marriage Elizabeth was mistaken for Mayne's daughter—to their amusement, she claimed—and sometimes her father for her husband (though he was the same age as Mayne, he looked younger). As she wrote of her husband, "Mayne Reid used to say that he could not have endured having an old wife. . . . Mayne Reid was proud of his 'child-wife,' and liked her to remain the 'child-wife' until the end." Reid died in 1883.[12]

Mayne Reid gives us one way of understanding why a man might specif-ically seek out a young bride: because he found her childishness appealing and because he believed that very youth might make her amenable to him.

Not surprisingly, there is no mention of sex in his or her depictions of their courtship or marriage. Rather, he staged the union as being about romance and affection, with Blanche's youth facilitating both his and her own love. Reid also does not frame Maynard's desire for Blanche as being about the ability to train his bride because of her youthfulness, though he may have considered this, and certainly some men later in the century discussed this practice explicitly. But Reid's novel does give us one view of the distinct advantages to be gained by a man in selecting a younger bride. Even if most Americans were not attuned to the precision of chronological age, they were certainly aware of age as a stage of life, and the youthfulness of a child bride might have been especially attractive to some men. Mayne Reid provides us a view into why a man might have found it appealing to choose a young bride, the selection of which would only become more obvious in later eras as the spread of age consciousness made the disparity in their ages, and Blanche's youth particularly, all the more striking.

THE NORTHEAST

Even though most states in the Northeast and Mid-Atlantic, unlike those in the Midwest, did not have laws that mandated a minimum marriageable age, early marriage appears to have been least common here. As we have seen, by the 1850s, when a few states had begun to collect vital statistics, girls and women married later in New England than they did in the South. By the time the U.S. Census Bureau began to collect comprehensive statistics linking marriage and age, 1880, the Northeast ranked last in terms of minors' marriages. This was partially because northeasterners pioneered the notion that childhood was a stage of life demarcated by precise age boundaries. Marrying below certain ages was seen as unsuitable by citizens of the Northeast before their counterparts in other areas of the country. The Northeast was on the leading edge of a trend that would eventually be embraced by almost all Americans, but it was a trend in its infancy.[13]

Massachusetts began to collect vital statistics in 1842, though in its third published report, in 1844, the compilers would admit that the marriage statistics were "extremely defective," largely because some counties simply did not comply, and even those that did tended to collect incomplete data where ages were often missing. That said, from 1845, when Massachusetts first published its official tally of marriage ages, it offers us the earliest comprehensive calculations for any state during this period (table 2.2).[14]

Table 2.2. Percentage of Marrying Massachusetts Men and
Women below the Age of Twenty by Year, 1844–1861

Year	Boys	Girls
May 1844–April 1845	1.2	15.2
May 1845–April 1846	1.3	17.7
May 1846–April 1847	1.2	21
May 1847–April 1848	1.2	21.4
May–December 1848	1.3	18.2
1849	1.4	17.8
1850	1.8	21.8
1851	1.9	23.2
1852	1.9	23.5
1853	1.9	23.1
1854	1.7	22.7
1855	1.8	22
1856	1.6	22.3
1857	1.7	22.2
1858	1.6	22.1
1859	1.7	21.6
1860*	–	–
1861	1.9	23.5

* Report missing from archives.
Sources: *Fourth* through *Twentieth Annual Reports to the Legislature,
Relating to the Returns of Births, Marriages, and Deaths in Massachusetts*
(*Nineteenth* missing), Massachusetts Archives.

The compilers of these reports are clear that many marriage licenses simply did not record an age—though that remained constant throughout the
period—but the numbers here reveal that between 1 and 2 percent of Massachusetts marriages were contracted annually by men under the age of twenty,
whereas between 15 and 24 percent of Massachusetts brides in any given year
were in their teenage years. In both cases, the greater proportion of these marriages of youthful brides and grooms were concentrated in the eighteenth and
nineteenth year, but a minority of the Bay State's brides and grooms were marrying at younger ages as well. By the 1850s, these reports' compilers had begun

Table 2.3. Number of Massachusetts Grooms and Brides of Certain Ages, 1854–1861

Year	M-13	F-13	M-14	F-14	M-15	F-15	M-16	F-16	M-17	F-17
1854	0	2	0	12	0	35	2	172	6	383
1855*	0	1	0	10	0	40	1	72	7	35
1856	0	1	0	11	0	63	2	176	11	321
1857	0	0	0	11	0	31	3	163	8	348
1858	0	0	0	10	0	30	2	130	11	308
1859	0	4**	0	4	0	47	5	129	8	285
1860†	–	–	–	–	–	–	–	–	–	–
1861	0	0	0	5	0	28	1	137	6	302

* Numbers are organized differently in this year and
seem suspiciously low for ages 16 and 17.
** There was also one bride of 12.
† Report missing at archives.
Sources: *Thirteenth* through *Twentieth Annual Reports to the
Legislature, Relating to the Returns of Births, Marriages, and Deaths in
Massachusetts* (*Nineteenth* missing), Massachusetts Archives.

to note what they thought of as the extremes, the particularly young *and* old who married each year and, by the middle of that decade, to document the youthful numbers systematically (table 2.3). These numbers are also instructive. In a state where parental permission was required for girls below eighteen and boys below twenty-one, significant numbers of people below those ages were marrying, presumably with that parental consent if they were being truthful about their ages when applying for a marriage license.

New York State, which collected and published marriage statistics for only two years in the 1840s, found similar results (table 2.4). Unfortunately New York did not specify the ages of those who married under twenty and after these two years suspended its collection and publication of vital statistics altogether until later in the nineteenth century, so these data are fragmentary, but they make clear that marriage under the age of twenty was just slightly more common here than in Massachusetts.

Anna Cora Ogden provides some insight into why a quarter of New York girls married young. Ogden was born in Bordeaux, France, in 1819 to wealthy American parents. She and her family returned home to New York in 1826. When Anna was thirteen, her older sister, Charlotte, met a New York lawyer

**Table 2.4. Number and Percentage of Total Grooms and Brides
Marrying under Age Twenty in New York State, 1847–1848**

Year	Boys	Percentage	Girls	Percentage
1847	325	3.2	3013	29.5
1848	356	3.1	3050	26.3

Sources: *Report of the Secretary of State, of the Number of Births, Marriages and Deaths,
for the Year 1847*, Senate Report No. 73, April 12, 1848, chart following page 7; *Report
of the Secretary of State, of the Number of Births, Marriages and Deaths, for the Year 1848*,
Senate Report No. 86, April 10, 1849, chart following page 7, New York State Archives.

named James Mowatt while on vacation. He was interested in her; Charlotte
responded that although she was already married, she had a number of
younger sisters, one of whom particularly looked like her. Soon after arriving
back in the city, Mowatt called on the Ogdens and immediately took a shine
to Anna. As she recounted it, he told a friend after their meeting that " 'I feel as
though I should never marry unless I marry that child.' " "From that moment
he conceived the project of educating me to suit his own views—of gaining
my affections, and, the instant I was old enough to be considered marriageable, of taking me to his own home—his child wife." He first proposed when
she was fourteen. He also asked her father, who explained that if they were
both still enthusiastic about the idea when she turned seventeen, he would
consent; for now she was too young.[15]

Not to be stymied, Anna promised Mowatt she would marry him within
the week: "Young as I was, and totally incapable of appreciating the importance of the step I was taking, I did not come to this determination without
much suffering. But once having *resolved*, once having *promised*, nothing
earthly could have shaken my resolution." Working in cahoots with her sister,
she found a clergyman willing to perform the ceremony, and with that difficulty overcome, the couple eloped, and Anna Cora Ogden became Anna Cora
Mowatt on October 6, 1834. As she put it,

> What could a girl of fifteen know of the sacred duties of a wife? With
> what eyes could she contemplate the new and important life into
> which she was entering? She had known nothing but childhood—had
> scarcely commenced her girlhood. What could she comprehend of
> the trials, the cares, the hopes, the responsibilities of womanhood? I
> thought of none of these things. I had always been lighthearted to a

degree that savored of frivolity. I usually made a jest of everything—
yet I did not look upon this matter as a frolic. I only remembered that
I was keeping a promise. I had perfect faith in the tenderness of him to
whom I confided myself. I did not in the least realize the novelty of my
own situation.

The marriage lasted until her husband's death in 1851, by which point she had
published a number of novels and plays and taken to the stage as a well-reviewed
actress. In her 1854 autobiography, Mowatt was clear that she considered her
marriage at fifteen to have been an oddity for which she was ill prepared, happy
though it might have been. Although marriage at fifteen was indeed increasingly seen as bizarre in the industrialized Northeast, especially among the mon-
eyed elite, in many other regions of the country, it was not out of the ordinary.[16]

THE SOUTH

This was true for the South among a number of different racial and socioeconomic groups. While some colonial era planter families had married their
children (as young as eight or nine) to each other in order to solidify family dynasties, this practice had largely been eliminated by the antebellum era.
Some continued to marry in their teenage years, however. Writing a series of
sketches for her grandchildren in 1906, North Carolinian Margaret Devereux,
who grew up in a wealthy slave-owning family and married into another in
1842, explained, "I was so young a bride, only seventeen, when I was taken to
our winter home, and so inexperienced, that I felt no dread whatever of my
new duties as mistress. The household comforts of my childhood's home had
seemed to come so spontaneously that I never thought of *processes*, and naturally felt rather nonplussed when brought into contact with realities." These
realities included the slaves she was expected to manage in her new role as
mistress.[17]

Other elite women shared her experience. Famed southern diarist Mary
Boykin met her prospective husband, the future U.S. senator James Chesnut
Jr., at thirteen and married him at seventeen in 1840. South Carolina governor
James Henry Hammond married Charleston heiress Catherine Fitzsimmons
in 1830 when she was seventeen and he was twenty-four (he would have mar-
ried her when she was sixteen if her parents had consented earlier). Explorer
John Frémont first became engaged to Jessie Benton, daughter of Missouri
senator Thomas Hart Benton, when she was fifteen; the two eloped in 1841

when she was seventeen. Elite white women like these would all have attended school, and it was the expectation of all around them, including their families, that they marry suitable men. Most would have come out formally as debutantes in their teenage years, the very point of which was to secure a husband.[18]

Historian Anya Jabour notes that once they had come out, many elite young women did their level best to postpone marriage because they knew that the period of being a "turned-out young lady" was their last gasp of independence before commencing the duties of wifehood and the dangers of pregnancy and motherhood. Some went so far as to make fun of those who paid them attentions, older gentlemen especially, either bachelors or widowers with young children at home. But in a culture that, Jabour notes, smiled on the marriage of older men and young girls, clearly these men would not have come calling had they thought their attentions unreasonable. Although some young women responded with incredulity—"The idea of an old bachelor of 36 coming to see a girl of sixteen? Preposterous!!!"—others encouraged such attentions and responded in the affirmative when asked for their hand in marriage.[19]

Although it slightly predates the antebellum era, the 1769 marriage of the Reverend John Camm, then a minister and professor at the College of William and Mary (later its seventh president), is instructive. Legend has it that Camm, in his capacity as parish rector, had been prevailed on by an unsuccessful suitor to convince Betsy Hansford, fifteen, to acquiesce to a marriage proposal. When Camm approached Hansford, using the Bible as justification for women's duty to marry, she demurred and pointed him in the direction of a different verse, 2 Samuel 12:7: "And Nathan said to David, *thou art the man.*" Hansford and Camm, then fifty-one, were married that August, though not without comment on their age difference, especially because Camm had been minister presiding over Hansford's baptism. The College of William and Mary also threatened to withdraw his professorship because custom dictated that professors remain unmarried and reside on college grounds. At least one Williamsburg resident thought that all the fuss was overblown. Filling in a correspondent abroad on the local gossip, Martha Goosley explained, "Mr Camms Marriage has made a great Noise here but Pray why may not an old man afflicted with the Gout have the Pleasure of a fine hand to rub his feet and warm his flannells comfortable amusement you will say for a Girl of fifteen but She is to have a Chariot and there is to be no Padlock but upon her mind." A few things are worth noting about this particular marriage. The Reverend Camm, as well as Betsy Hansford's first suitor, both thought her perfectly eligible for marriage at fifteen, as presumably did her parents. Second, though marriage was seen as her destiny, Hansford herself chose her husband, defying the wishes of at least some of those around her. And third, as in the marriage of Arthur and Justina Dobbs mentioned in the previous chapter, the main source of amusement seems to have been with the groom's relative elderliness vis-à-vis his bride, not with her ineligibility to marry based on her age.[20]

Historians have demonstrated for this period that in particular regions, upcountry Georgia, for instance, marriage beginning at fourteen or fifteen was common. In her sample of antebellum North Carolinian planter families' daughters, historian Jane Turner Censer found that 3.9 percent married at fifteen or under, 5.8 percent at sixteen, and 7.1 percent at seventeen. The most common age of first marriage was nineteen, and the average was twenty years, six months. In one family, the Kearneys, the six sisters married at fifteen, sixteen, seventeen, twenty-two, and two at twenty-five. Censer and Jabour are clear that most girls and women married based on their own choices—their parents did not arrange their marriages for them—though location and suitability always constrained marital selections and sometimes induced girls to marry sooner than they might have liked out of fear that another man might not be available later on. During the colonial era it had been much more common for wealthy parents in the South to arrange the marriages of their young children, often to families who lived nearby and were sometimes related. By the antebellum era, most parents had abandoned this practice in favor of the belief that marriage was built on the mutual desire of the bride and groom. Letting girls make their own decisions, albeit with proper guidance, was how marriages were meant to begin. But that this decision might occur at fifteen or sixteen was perfectly appropriate. As one young southerner explained in 1839, "So you see we have the Town full of young girls who will soon be Ladies." Marriage would effect this transformation.[21]

As we saw in the Introduction, Susie Baker, an escaped slave, married at the age of fourteen and made no mention of it when she wrote her autobiography forty years later. That was because marrying in the teenage years was, so far as historians have been able to tell, not unusual for enslaved people in the United States. There are difficulties in assessing slaves' marriage practices, because they could not enter into legally binding contracts, marriage among them. Nevertheless, slaves entered into partnerships that were regarded as marriages by all around them, including their masters, who usually insisted on slaves gaining their permission before doing so. In one instance of permission for an abroad marriage—that is, a marriage between slaves on different plantations—a master sent his slave with a note to another slaveholder: "The bearer 'Billy' has our permission to take your 'Servant Flora' for his wife provided it met with your approbation." As plantation mistress Catherine Edmonston recorded in her diary in 1862,

> A furor of marriage seems to possess the plantation. On Thursday, the 20th, Fanny after bustling aimlessly about the room came out with "Master, Joe, Joe Axe from the ferry wants to see you. He wants to axe you & Miss to let him marry me." So Joe was admitted into the dining room, the preliminaries settled & they left with the permission to fix their own time. This was of the shortest for the next day, Sat the 22d, I was called on for the materials for the wedding supper & then on Sunday came Dempsey with a request for Rachel, on Wednesday Lorenzo Dow to marry Mela, & on Thursday Hercules with a similar request for Chloe! So Cupid gave place to Hymen in a shorter time than usual— primitive customs one will say, but Cuffee strips off the elegancies & refinements of civilization with great ease. White people would have been months in accomplishing what they have been days about!

Here Edmonston demonstrates the way that slave marriages were managed— through asking and granting of permission, then through the master supplying the wedding supper—and also notes, at least from her perspective, how few preliminaries there were to the unions. Of course Edmonston probably did not observe the courtship process that led up to the request for marriage, but she was not incorrect that it was sometimes more abbreviated than for elite white women like herself.[22]

Slaves tended to marry early for a number of reasons. First, they began to work early, often as small children, commencing the hard labor of fieldwork around the age of twelve. The early onset of adulthood in the realm of labor tended to abbreviate their adolescence in other ways as well. On one undated list of slaves purchased as a group from a plantation, for instance, the buyer has them grouped into three columns: men, women, and children. Included on the list of adult women are thirteen-year-old Barbara and fourteen-year-old Rosetta; on the list of men is sixteen-year-old Albert. If youthful slaves were expected to behave like adults in one way—by working—many also sought the perquisites of adulthood, marriage being one of them. They also lived in a world in which far more depended on their physical growth than on reaching precise age markers. Slaves achieved functional adulthood when they were large or strong enough to labor. Although slaveholders often knew the ages (and sometimes birthdates) of their slaves, in case they might need to sell them, slaves themselves sometimes had little sense of their birthdays or ages. Lack of age consciousness was the result. Second, in crowded slave quarters, marriage and the establishment of a family was one of the only ways to gain new accommodations, so there could be distinct spatial benefits to marriage for slaves living in crowded shacks with their natal families. Third, it was always in slave owners' best interests to encourage early marriage, because they presumed (often correctly) that it would lead to childbearing, which would enrich their holdings with more slaves. Although only a minority of slaveholders probably engaged in forced breeding, it was in all slaveholders' interests to encourage marriage at young ages. Rose Williams, interviewed in Texas in the 1930s through the Federal Writers' Project, explained that she had been forced by her master to marry at the age of sixteen. As her mistress had explained it to her: "'Yous am de portly gal and Rufus am de portly man. De massa wants you-uns to bring forth portly chillen." Rose gave birth to two children before being freed; she then left Rufus and never remarried. Some young slaves believed that early marriage to a partner of their choosing would mean they would not be forced into a marriage with a partner not to their liking. That is, the threat of forced breeding or marriage may have encouraged early marriage. Last, many slaves believed (at times correctly) that slaveholders were less likely to sell slaves apart from their conjugal families.[23]

We know from slaveholders' records that most slave women did not bear their first children until their late teens or early twenties; two studies have found average ages of 19.7 and 20.6. It was not uncommon for slave women to begin having (or being forced to have) sex, and sometimes bearing children, before marriage, however. All of this means that the average age of marriage for slave women was probably in the later teens or early twenties, but as with wealthy white women in the South, marriage in the younger teenage years was common enough not to be seen as abnormal. Determining precise marriage ages in plantation records is challenging, however, because masters were far less likely to record precise dates of marriages than they did births. This was because birthdays were necessary to calculating ages, which could be useful in the event of a sale. Marriage dates were monetarily worthless.[24]

There were exceptions to this rule, however. The Dromgoole family of Virginia kept a special book entitled "Negroe Ages," in which they recorded the births, deaths, and a few of the marriages of their slaves. Of the five marriages recorded, it is possible to determine the ages of only a few of the new spouses. When John and Ohio married in March 1860, Ohio was twenty years old and John may have been twenty-four. By 1865, Ohio gave birth to three children, the first one just four months after the wedding. When Frank and Mariah were married in 1846, Mariah was fourteen. She bore seven children by 1863, when she would have been thirty-one. On the Devereux family's North Carolina plantations (the family into which Margaret Devereux, discussed above, married), plantation records do not explicitly record slaves' ages at the time of their marriages but do list family groupings with birth dates of individuals. Births of first children came at a variety of ages for mothers, but ages eighteen and nineteen were not uncommon, indicating that slave girls probably married at least a year earlier. A similar pattern emerges on the Louisiana sugar plantation owned by the Corbin family through the 1860s. John Blount Miller kept a meticulous record of the Cornhill Plantation in Sumter, South Carolina, from 1827 through 1860, documenting the births and marriages of his slaves. For instance, Jim, nineteen, married Ellen, whose age is unrecorded, in May 1838. They had seven children before Ellen died in 1853; one of those children, Maria, married a slave from another plantation, "Mr. Pugh's boy," when she was seventeen. Jackson and Emma wed on Christmas Day, 1842, when Jackson was seventeen and Emma was nineteen; they had four children. Nat and Zilpha wed when they were both eighteen (or twenty-two; the records are contradictory); between 1845 and 1868, they had fifteen children, thirteen of whom survived infancy.[25]

Clearly, not all slaves married when they were in their teenage years. If they worked on small plantations, this would have been particularly difficult because the choice of marital partners was circumscribed by the availability of eligible spouses. Many slaveholders preferred to have their slaves marry within the plantation. On a list of "Negroes rules for government," John Blount Miller of Cornhill Plantation explained: "*Marriages.* Not to marry from House if to be avoided." Francis Wilkinson Pickens of Edgefield, South Carolina, had a similar rule in his plantation book: "No negro man is to have wife off of the plantation, + no strange negro is to have a wife on the plantation." This was because masters could better control slaves if they owned both of them; those who owned men also preferred not to have them impregnate the property of a different master, increasing another's fortune instead of his own. This meant that some slaves lacked the opportunity to marry early. But others, either because of pressure from masters or because of love and sexual attraction, married at young ages. Such early marriages were partially a consequence of living in a society where ages and birthdays were often of little consequence to enslaved people and where slaves became functional adults quite early.[26]

THE NATIVE AMERICAN WEST

By the dawn of the nineteenth century, a once vibrant population of Native Americans had been reduced to approximately 600,000 people. Contact along the eastern seaboard had resulted in death by warfare and disease. European, now American, settlers had also forced Native peoples farther west, a process that continued through the antebellum era, culminating in the forced removal of southeastern tribes to Indian Territory and eventually relocation to reservations. Throughout these years, Native peoples continued to marry according to the Indian custom, and states with significant Native populations sometimes wrote statutory law allowing for Natives to marry by those traditions, those marriages accorded the same legal status as any other union.[27]

Many Native American tribes sanctioned marriage once girls reached puberty. Although talking about "Native Americans" as one group obscures the differences between what was an enormous number of different tribes with a variety of cultural traditions, many historians and anthropologists have demonstrated that what most disturbed European observers of the Indians they encountered were their sexual practices, many of which were similar in regard to marriage. Premarital sex was sanctioned and did not necessarily lead to marriage. Divorce was also possible when a couple chose to end a relationship. Although arranged marriage by tribal elders and parents was common in some tribes, in many tribes young people took up with each other in marriage when they wanted to without benefit of a formal ceremony. Records documenting age of bride and groom do not exist for Indian tribes during this era, so we cannot know what the average age of contracting parties was. Some historians have found an average age of marriage for Indians in California missions (where marriages *were* documented) between eighteen and twenty, but others have demonstrated that sexual relations and also marriage could commence any time after the onset of puberty, meaning that girls and boys could have been in their teenage years when they married. It is also the case that age and birthdays themselves were less important to Native Americans as markers of identity. Most evidence suggests that when that is the case, marriage tends to occur earlier.[28]

These traditions were sometimes documented by Anglos pushing further westward, Spaniards farther north, and French farther south and west, interacting with Indians they had not previously encountered. Father Gerónimo Boscana, for instance, who was stationed at a number of missions in Alta California and spent fourteen years at the mission at San Juan Capistrano between 1812 and 1826, recounted of the Acagchemem tribe (or Juañenos, named for their proximity to this mission) that marriages could be arranged by the couple themselves with parental permission or were sometimes orchestrated by town elders, at times against the consent of the girl in question. Occasionally "some parents, even, when their children were in infancy, by mutual agreement, would promise them in marriage, and the same was ever adhered to, and when parties were of sufficient age, they were united with the customary ceremonies. During the period of their childhood, they were always together and the house of either was a home to both." Boscana himself presided over such a marriage in 1821 between a girl of "eight or nine months" and a boy of two years. Whereas Boscana was clear that some children "threw off the alliance" if it was not to their liking, others considered such ceremonies to be binding. Key here also is that Boscana did not mention specific ages at which girls were expected to marry, with the exception of babies who were betrothed to each other, simply noting that boys might approach girls when they were ready or that tribe elders might arrange for the marriages of "girls." Once these girls reached puberty they seem to have been eligible for marriage.[29]

Intermarriage with Indians was a longstanding tradition among fur traders and trappers as well as explorers and some settlers in the West. In part this was because there were few white women with whom these men might marry in the North American borderlands where they made their living. But these marriages could also cement important alliances between white traders and settlers, who brought European goods with them, and the Native tribes that knew the land around them. Intermarriage and conversion to Catholicism might also prove a boon to Indian women and girls who could call on the power of the church to regulate their new husbands' sexual and marital behavior. Because of the young age of marriage for Native Americans, many of these alliances involved older men and those we would consider to be girls. Famed interpreter and guide to Meriwether Lewis and William Clark Sacagawea was one such girl. Born into a Lemhi Shoshone tribe in present-day Idaho, Sacagawea was kidnapped with a number of other girls by a group of Hidatsas and taken to their village, located in present-day North Dakota, when she was probably about twelve. Soon thereafter, Québecois trapper Toussaint Charbonneau, who was living in the village, took her for his wife. He had already taken another young Shoshone girl named Otter Woman as a wife and may have purchased both girls or won them through gambling. Sacagawea was pregnant with her first child when Lewis and Clark hired her and her husband to be their guides. The kidnapping and marriage would likely have been traumatizing for Sacagawea and Otter Woman, but their young ages at marriage were not the primary issue for them or their new husband. Marrying early was both accepted and common.[30]

Another legend of western American history, trapper, guide, and Indian agent Kit Carson, had multiple marriages that cemented alliances with three cultures. In 1835, Carson married a Southern Arapaho girl named Waa-nibe in the upper Green River region of what is now western Wyoming. Carson was twenty-five and Waa-nibe seems to have been in her mid- to late teens. It is likely that Carson paid her family a customary bride price. Marrying into a Native family made a white man a member of her tribe and thus gave him safe passage as a trapper in that tribe's family. Within two years they had two children together; Waa-nibe died shortly after the birth of their second. In 1840, while living at Bent's Fort, a stopping point along the Santa Fe Trail and a trading point for buffalo hides with both the Southern Arapaho and the Cheyenne, Carson married his second wife, Making Out Road, a member of the Cheyenne Little Bear band. There was no formal ceremony, but such ceremonies were not always part of entrance into marriage in Making Out Road's tribe. Once again, there were particular advantages for Carson in marrying a Native woman, who also seems to have been quite young. Making Out Road's Little Bear Clan was seen as among the elite of the Cheyenne. Carson also needed someone to look after his children. It is unclear why this arrangement did not suit Making Out Road, but in any event, she left Carson within two years, exiting the marriage in the same informal style that it was entered.[31]

Another eastern white man who settled in the West (in his case, Montana), John Owen, helps us to see the makeshift nature of marriage arrangements between white men and Indian women. He recounted in his diary in 1858 that "Myself Mr. Harris & Mr. Irvine did this day Sign marraige [*sic*] contracts with our Indian Wives[.] I have often thought of the Correctness of it & in absence of any person duly authorized to perform the Marraige [*sic*] Ceremony We did it ourselves in the presence of Witnesses[.] I have been living pleasantly With My old Wife Since the fall of 49 and in case of accident I should feel Much hurt if I had not properly provided for her accoding [*sic*] to law." While Owen and his fellow settlers attempted to formalize their ties with Native American women, it is clear that in Owen's case, at least, he had already been living with Nancy (who was of the Flathead or Shoshone tribe) for nine years when he did so. Marriage, even when one spouse was white, was often not formally regulated in frontier communities and when the Indian women to whom these men were married would not necessarily have expected it. Even when they did attempt to formalize their unions, they had no one there to do so, so they did it themselves.[32]

Owen and his friends were clearly attempting to do right by, and provide for, their Indian wives. While this type of loyalty and indeed reciprocity may have characterized many mixed-race unions, others were clearly more exploitative. One of the consequences of the difference between formal sanctioned marriage and marriage according to Indian custom was that some white men took advantage of Indian women, entering into marriages they did not consider to be legally binding. Some of these men had more than one wife, and others simply abandoned their wives once they were ready to move on, leaving behind their children as well. These men may have thought about their "wives" as something akin to concubines. In the 1840s up and down the valleys of the California coast, for instance, white settlers took multiple Native wives, many of whom were in their early teens. Known as "squaw men" by their detractors, these men often left their wives when a more racially suitable woman became available or when they themselves moved on. They had taken advantage of Indian marital practice (both customary marriage and polygyny) but refused to honor its commitment.[33]

THE SPANISH AND MEXICAN WEST

About Kit Carson's third and final wife, Josefa Jaramillo, there is considerably more evidence, in part because they remained married until his death but also because she was not Indian and they were married formally by a Catholic priest. Carson probably met her at the Taos home of his employer Charles Bent, who lived in an informal union with Josefa's elder sister, María Ignacia. In order for Carson to marry Jaramillo formally, however, he would have to convert to Catholicism, which he did in January 1842. The two were married a year later, on February 6, 1843. She was fourteen and he was thirty-three. Marriage into the Jaramillo clan may have provided Carson with advantages in Taos similar to those he gained through marrying two Native girls, but the family was not particularly influential in the town. The age gap between Carson and Jaramillo was large (he was more than double her age), but it was also not uncommon. The Catholic Church, which controlled marriage in the province of New Mexico until it became a U.S. territory after the conclusion of the Mexican American War in 1848, stipulated eleven and thirteen as the minimum ages of marriage for girls and boys, respectively. Historian Ramón Gutiérrez has found that between 1694 and 1846, one quarter of all girls who legally married in New Mexico did so by the age of fifteen. The lowest mean age of marriage during this period, 15.5, was during the first decade of the nineteenth century, itself a result of demographic changes due to a smallpox epidemic. Similarly, Gloria Miranda has found that demographic patterns affected age of marriage in two regions of Alta California, Santa Barbara and Los Angeles: where men outnumbered women and settlement patterns were unpredictable, girls married at younger ages. This pattern tended to characterize the earlier presidial settlements, where girls married at sixteen or seventeen, rather than the pueblos, where most, but not all, married somewhat later. Taken together, we can see that early marriage for girls (and some boys) was culturally and religiously sanctioned in the colonial Southwest during both the Spanish and Mexican periods. A number of factors explain the prevalence of early marriage among Spaniards and Mexicans. Spanish traditions of familial honor were linked with girls' premarital chastity; girls' marriage soon after menarche meant that they had little chance to besmirch the honor of their families through premarital sex or pregnancy. Frontier life also led young people to assume adult responsibilities at earlier ages, and sex imbalances placed pressure on girls to wed young.[34]

The one change to Spanish law governing marriage came in 1776 when King Charles II issued his Royal Pragmatic on Marriage, in which he declared that all people below the age of twenty-five now required parental permission to marry. This was designed to cut down on cross-class marriages and, obviously, youth marrying against the wishes of their parents. The pragmatic cautioned that this should not be used to pressure children into marrying people against their will, but it clearly did give parents a greater say in the choice of spouse. Historians of this region and period debate the degree to which early marriage necessarily meant that parents were controlling their children's (usually daughters') marital choices. Although it remains difficult to know how frequently parents made such decisions, there is clear evidence that some girls were forced into marriages against their will. In one 1842 case discovered by historian Miroslava Chávez-García, Casilda Sepúlveda, who was about seventeen years old, used the Royal Pragmatic to contest a marriage that she claimed her father and stepmother both forced on her. Appealing the case all the way to the Bishop of Alta and Baja California, Sepúlveda won her case and had the marriage annulled. Although this case ended with annulment, far more often girls would simply have remained married to men their parents had chosen for them, some of whom were not well known to them at the time of their marriages.[35]

The church conducted matrimonial investigations (*diligencias matrimoniales*) for each marriage, just as it did for Arcadia Bandini and Abel Stearns, Josefa Jaramillo and Kit Carson; the primary concern remained whether the couple might already be related. Consanguineous and affinal marriages were officially prohibited, but the authorities sometimes were willing to look the other way in an outlying territory like New Mexico or Alta California, where the choice of marital partners was limited by the low population or where prosperous families wished their children to intermarry and were not closely related. The prospective spouses' ages were always a part of the diligencias, even though some were recorded with approximate numbers, indicating the degree to which ages were not always known, even by the people themselves. When Juan Francisco Gutiérrez, thirty-five, and María Concepción Pino, fifteen, petitioned the church to marry in 1809, for instance, they stated that they were related in the third and fourth degrees of consanguinity in the transverse line; this meant that they descended from a common ancestor and were probably second and third cousins to each other. When Father Alvarez questioned them about this, they explained that they were both lifelong residents of the area (Belen, New Mexico) and were "related to most of the people of their station in the area." One witness also appeared to say that he knew María Concepción and that she had her parents' permission to marry.[36]

A bride's poverty was sometimes a factor in why she wanted to marry at a young age, and certainly in why the couple believed the authorities should grant her permission to do so, even if she was related to the groom or was particularly young. In 1805, José Mariana de la Cruz Quintana, twenty-two, and María Antonia Velarde, fourteen, asked for a dispensation to marry even though they were related in the fourth degree of consanguinity. María Antonia was poor and her father had many children; José attested that he would be able to support her and that she had her parents' permission to wed. When the petition was forwarded to Bishop Olivares y Benito, he approved the dispensation. Similarly, the poverty of the bride's widowed mother was a factor in the 1821 diligencia of Pedro Sandoval, a soldier in the National Company in Santa Fe and twelve-year-old María Altagracia Ortiz.[37]

Although blood or consanguineous relationships seem to have been the most common proposed marriage to require dispensation, affinal or spiritual relationships, where one party had had sexual relations with someone related to the second party, also needed to be confessed in order for marriage to be possible. María Soledad Martín, fourteen, was granted a dispensation to marry Antonio José Valdez even after she confessed that she had borne an illegitimate child by her brother-in-law, who also happened to be Antonio José's first cousin. Both were residents of the plaza Blanca in Abiquiu. Because María Soledad and Antonio José were also third cousins, they were mandated to say a rosary of the fifteen mysteries; in penance for the sin of affinity (the sex with Antonio José's cousin), María Soledad was required to go to confession, take communion, cite an additional rosary of the fifteen mysteries, and obtain certification that she had done as ordered. More important for our purposes is that María Soledad lived in a society that sanctioned her marriage at fourteen even though she had already borne her brother-in-law's child, which was probably conceived when she was thirteen. Indeed, that society had well-established procedures for punishing her for having done so, but in ways that were fully designed to facilitate her marriage to another man. The demographics of colonial societies like those of New Mexico and Alta California—few people, especially unrelated; sometimes fewer men than women; and always a state and religious mandate to reproduce and repopulate—meant that girls often married at young ages. Those girls who married foreign men to whom they were clearly not related also did so at early ages, often without knowing their new husbands particularly well before agreeing to become their wives.[38]

As in the marriage of Don Abel and Doña Arcadia, marriages between Anglo men and Mexican or Spanish women could also be used to cement economic and diplomatic alliances. When the cultures into which these men married already sanctioned the marriage of girls at young ages and when explorers, trappers, and merchants were eager to make alliances with long-established families, marriage to one of their daughters could prove a strategic move as well as the basis for a happy union. For similar reasons, Anglo men also married widows with property. Even though Abel Stearns had been in Alta California for some time, uniting himself with the influential Bandini clan only enhanced the status (and landholdings) of a man who was, after all, a naturalized citizen originally from Massachusetts. The same applied for many other men far less established than Stearns. But these unions did not just benefit the man alone. In this case, not only was Stearns himself wealthy, but his unequivocal whiteness as the descendant of Massachusetts Puritans would have been very attractive in Alta California, where there were fewer white men and where many Spanish Mexicans claimed whiteness when they were actually of mixed-race heritage. Even more significant for a girl who married young was the way that Spanish law governed marital property. Unlike the English common-law doctrine of coverture, whereby all a man's property and that which he acquired during a marriage passed to his heirs at his death (his wife retaining the *use* of only a third of the property), under Spanish law a wife not only owned her own property but jointly owned any property acquired during the marriage.

These laws carried over when territories became U.S. states. This meant that a girl like Arcadia who married in her teens could amass significant property by the time of her husband's death, which almost always preceded her own. Wealthy Californios used the Spanish legal code to facilitate the establishment of a Californio elite, much of it brokered through the marriage of young girls, but many of those girls benefited in the process.[39]

MARRIAGE ON THE OVERLAND TRAIL

At the same time that a diverse array of young people were marrying in colonial New Mexico and Alta California, colonists of a different sort were setting out on the Overland Trail, the long trek between Missouri and either California, Oregon, or Utah Territory during the middle third of the nineteenth century. For a variety of reasons, they too married early, both on the trail and once they had arrived at their destinations. In part it was because children had more independence freed from their home communities—some had lost parents who might have objected to the matches had they been alive—but it was also that men were in need of wives if they were going to establish households of their own. And girls needed husbands, especially if they had lost parents, or if they just wanted to relieve their living parents of the burden of supporting them. The pressures toward couplehood that were falling away in urban places— where men were increasingly able to live on their own in boardinghouses, for instance—were intensified on the frontier. Joint male and female labor was necessary to make a successful farming household. There was also, on the Overland Trail, and in the areas in which they settled, a sex imbalance that made men seek out girls to be their wives. Further, the traditional ways that age was accounted for in stable communities did not exist on the trail or in many of the new frontier settlements, if age was even a particularly important way of marking identity to begin with. In this liminal space away from homes, improvisation and spontaneity may have played a greater role than they did in pioneers' "normal lives."[40]

In ways similar to the marriages of Indian women and white men, many of these couples probably married without registering their unions or acquiring marriage licenses. Especially if they were on the trail or in newly established settlements, these bureaucratic steps would have been difficult, if not impossible, to meet. But they were also unnecessary. Under common law the only thing required for a valid marriage was that a couple declare, in the moment, their acceptance of each other as husband and wife. Whether they actually did so—most probably did not—was largely irrelevant, because if they cohabited thereafter and acted as married people in the eyes of their community, they were as married as any other couple, legally and, perhaps more important, socially. Many, of course, went one step further and had a minister perform the ceremony for them, lending an air of official (and religious) sanction to the union. Although the legality of the marriages is not in doubt, one can see how doing away with licensing and the reading of the banns that was common in some locations would allow for more spontaneous marriages, including those of younger people. Some could also marry without the parental consent that might be necessary in stable communities where such laws were more apt to be enforced.[41]

Mary Ackley, an emigrant to California in 1852, explained of a friend that "she was married to a worthy young man when she was sixteen years of age, and later became the mother of eight children. . . . It was customary in early days for girls to marry at fourteen, fifteen, and sixteen years of age." Bethenia Owens, who emigrated from Missouri to Oregon with her family in 1843 and married one of her father's farmhands, LeGrand Hill, at fourteen, regretted the decision almost immediately. As she explained of the 1854 wedding, perhaps alluding to differences between herself and her husband that made consummating the marriage painful: "I was still small for my age. My husband was five-feet eleven inches in height, and I could stand under his outstretched arm." Her son was born two years later, in 1856, but she soon realized that she was unable to remain married to Hill. She was unhappy, and he could not seem to support his family. She explained of her choice to finally divorce Hill: "And now, at eighteen years of age, I found myself, broken in spirit and health, again in my father's house, from which only four years before, I had gone with such a happy heart, and such bright hopes for the future." By contrast, Rebecca Hildreth Nutting Woodson, who moved from New Hampshire to Massachusetts to Illinois to Iowa and finally to California in 1850 before she married in 1852, recounted, "I have never for one moment regretted my marriage to George and so far as I know or believe, neither did he." She was married to George Woodson at sixteen by a Presbyterian minister and without a license ("at that time it was not necessary to have a marriage license"). She had been living with her father and stepmother near Sacramento, where her father and a number of others (including her husband) ran a mill and sold vegetables from a garden they cultivated. As she remembered it, "Father moved away the next morning after I was married, leaving me a girl of a little more than 16 years to cook and do all the work for 20 men, sometimes more." She had her first child the next year.[42]

Charlotte Matheny married her husband, John Kirkwood, in 1852 when she was fourteen. They did so in a double ceremony with her brother Jasper, eighteen, and his new bride, Mary Ring, who was sixteen. As she recounted of the marriage in Oregon Country, "The night before Xmas, John Kirkwood . . . the path finder, stayed at our house over night. I had met him before and when he heard the discussion about my brother Jasper's wedding, he suggested that he and I also get married. I was nearly fifteen years old and I thought it was high time that I got married so I consented." They celebrated that night with a pie baked from dried tomatoes made by Charlotte and Jasper's mother. Another new arrival in Oregon Country, Lucy Henderson Deady, recounted of her youth, "I was fifteen . . . and in those days the young men wonder[ed] why a girl was not married if she was still single when she was sixteen." She married soon thereafter. Historian Lillian Schlissel's study of women's diaries of the westward journey revealed that those who traveled in the early wave of settlement, the 1840s, were more likely to be poor and to marry early; those who came later, when the trail was better established, were better off and came with more possessions. They also married later. Schlissel links their class status with cautiousness, both in making their journeys and in delaying their marriages. But it could be more specifically that the middle class was more likely at this point to demarcate childhood from adulthood in a way that would make early marriage inappropriate. This was not yet so for those with fewer financial advantages; for them early marriage did not foreclose any opportunity that might be awaiting a middle-class girl who postponed marriage. Working people and farmers would marry eventually, regardless; doing it sooner simply allowed them to establish a household more quickly.[43]

The story of Amanda Mulvina Fisk Stout combines a number of these elements. Amanda was born in 1832 in Chautauqua, New York. Her parents were early converts to the Church of Jesus Christ of Latter-Day Saints, and her father died two years after Amanda's birth, "stricken with cholera in the camp in Missouri," where he had been a part of the Zion's Camp expedition. Three years later Amanda and her widowed mother were also heading west with other Saints when Maria Fisk also died. Amanda was now an orphan. As her granddaughter explained, "Amanda was left alone, but she went from place to place, with the Saints, until she was fourteen years old." She finally ended up as a servant to a man named Allen Stout, who had lost his wife on the trail and was left with three children. He and Amanda married in 1848 when she was sixteen, at Winter Quarters, a resting place along the Overland Trail in present-day Nebraska. Amanda would have two children of her own before they would finally make it to Salt Lake in 1851. The tragedies of the trail, for both Amanda and her new husband, combined to make her youthful marriage appealing to both of them. She was in need of someone to support her, and he was in need of someone to care for his children, and himself.[44]

NAUVOO AND THE GREAT SALT LAKE

Many Mormon marriages also occurred at young ages for reasons similar to those of other early white settlers in the West. Mary Minerva Dart wrote that during her journey westward her mother and two siblings died of cholera in 1850 within a week of each other: "We buried them on the plaines wraped in a quilt with out any coffins we buried them all before we reached Fort Larime." After reaching Salt Lake she accompanied her father to Parowan in 1851 to begin a settlement there, where "my oldest sister Phebe M was Maried to R H Gallispie and I became acquainted with Zadok K. Judd and with the consent of my Father we were married November 14 1852 and we had Lusinda A born October 18 1853." She was fourteen at her marriage and fifteen at the birth of her first child. She had fourteen children altogether as she and her husband moved about Utah working to settle the territory and convert Native Americans to their faith. Similarly, Lucy White was born in Nauvoo in 1842 and crossed the Plains to Utah in 1850, after the Mormons were driven out of their Illinois home. She was baptized into the church at the age of ten in 1852, and she and her family lived in Cedar City, Utah, which is where she met her husband, William Flake. She married him at the age of sixteen in December 1858. As she explained it, "Apostle Lyman gave us very good council told us how to treat each other called us children he was 19 in July myself 16 in Aug he said we was not set in our way like we would be if we were older he used most all the evening talking and counciling it was very plesant indeed." This is a rare instance in which someone remarks on the age of the bride or groom at the time of marriage. Lucy Hannah White Flake wrote this account of her life in 1894, more than thirty years after the wedding, but her pausing on her age and that of her husband seems as if it is more than just her own later awe at her youthfulness (if she felt that at all). She claims that the man who married the couple remarked on it at the time. Bear in mind, however, that he did not think their youth an impediment to a happy marriage but rather an advantage, for neither was set in his or her ways and they would be able to adapt to married life, and each other, together.[45]

Although many Mormon marriages began early for the same reasons that other frontier marriages did, some girls became brides at young ages because of polygamy. Mormon Prophet Joseph Smith began speaking of plural marriage as early as 1831, and it was revealed in 1843, after his death, that he had both advocated and practiced plural marriage. Historians debate the number of wives that Smith had during his lifetime (in part because some may have been "sealed" to him posthumously). Historian Todd Compton has been able to document thirty-three actual marriages, but other historians have counted as many as forty-eight. Polygamy in its early years at Nauvoo, or later in Utah, was not a matter exclusively of marrying young girls and women. Although Smith married girls as young as fourteen, he was also married to women in their forties and fifties. Historian George D. Smith has demonstrated, similarly, that the next prophet, Brigham Young, who had 55 wives, did marry six girls below the age of eighteen, but the remaining 49 wives were above eighteen. Some were in their sixties. Smith demonstrates that of the 717 wives of 196 Nauvoo men, 65 were eighteen, 77 were seventeen, 76 were sixteen, 29 were fifteen, 21 were fourteen, 3 were thirteen, and 1 was twelve. There is certainly a pattern here of marrying young girls, yet there were also large numbers of women who were well out of childhood, some quite advanced in years.[46]

The avowed point of plural marriage, the religious commandment dictated by God, was to increase the size of families and the number of children, thus increasing the number of Saints on earth and leading to the "fullness of salvation" (posthumous sealing accomplished the same goal for those who had died). For this reason, younger women would be preferred, though they need not be very young. Historians have argued about the role of the youth of brides in early polygamy. It is clear that Joseph Smith, for instance, married the daughters of families with whom he had become acquainted in his journeys between upstate New York, Ohio, Missouri, and Illinois. Historian D. Michael Quinn argues that this was also a way for Smith to link himself with particular families; by marrying their daughters, he gained the families as allies. As Smith's power grew, moreover, some families may have been eager to unite with him and thus encouraged their daughters to marry him.[47]

Polygamy flourished in Utah after 1852, when the church first went public with the practice, until the 1890s, by which point it had become so controversial that the federal government had sent marshals to Utah to jail polygamists and made renouncing polygamy a condition for statehood. During the mid-1850s some church leaders, particularly Brigham Young and church historian (and later president) Wilford Woodruff, believed that Saints were focusing more on converting Gentiles (non-Mormons) than they were on cultivating their own faith and exhorted church members to rededicate themselves to the founding ideals of the church. The Mormon Reformation of 1855–57 produced, among other things, a 65 percent spike in polygamous marriages, many to young girls. As historian Thomas Alexander explains, "The pressure to conform prompted unprecedented numbers of men and women to apply to Brigham Young for permission to enter plural marriages as evidence of their obedience and righteousness." The numbers were so high that Young had to turn many away. As a sign of dedication and faithfulness Wilford Woodruff himself offered Young his fourteen year-old daughter, Phebe Amelia, in marriage. Young declined. As a result of all the extra marrying the divorce rate also climbed following the Reformation, and Woodruff jokingly wrote to a fellow leader, "All are trying to pay their tithing, and nearly all are trying to get wives, until there is hardly a girl 14 years old in Utah, but what is married, or just going to be." Joking aside, one can see how the combination of demographics and pressures toward plural marriage as a religious obligation would lead to the marriage of young girls in the territory.[48]

Lucy Flake, who was sixteen when she married her husband in 1858 at the tail end of the Reformation, accepted her husband's second wife, eighteen-year-old Prudence Kartchner, ten years later. As she explained: "Sister E R Snow asked me was I willing[.] said yes[.] she asked do you think you can live in that principle and I said am quite willing to try[.] my Mother and sister live in it and I think I can do as much as them and besides I wanted my Husband to go into that principal before I was old because I think it right." She was only twenty-six at the time. One particularly introspective informant, Martha Cox, helps us to understand the motivations of a young girl who chose to enter a plural marriage. Cox was born in March 1852 in Mill Creek Ward in Salt Lake County. Her parents had become converts almost a decade earlier in Nauvoo and fled to Utah in 1849, making "the long trek in wooden wagons across the plains to the Rocky Mountains." In recounting her story, Cox placed less emphasis on the particular man she married and more on the choice to marry a man who already had two wives. The decision did not please her family, but she explained, "I knew the principal of plural marriage to be correct, to be the highest holiest order of marriage. I knew to[o] that I might fail to live the holy life required and lose the blessings offered." Her family was particularly upset that she had chosen to marry "into poverty." As she looked about her little town she saw "but a very few men—not one in fifty of the whole city, who had entered it [plural marriage] at all." She recounted the reaction of a friend to her decision: "It is all very well for those girls who cannot very well get good young men for husbands to take married men, but she (me) had not need to lower herself for there were young men she could have gotten." By her telling Cox was attracted to plural marriage because it fulfilled a religious obligation, not because she was being pressured by her family or her eventual husband.[49]

Martha entered a plural marriage with Isaiah Cox when she was seventeen. She did not claim that plural marriage was easy, but she found great strength in her co-wives: "To me it is a joy to know that we laid the foundation of a life to come while we lived in that plural marriage that we three who loved each other more than sisters children of one mother love, will go hand in hand together down through all eternity. That knowledge is worth more to me than gold and more than compensates for all the sorrow I have ever known." Cox and her sister wives cared for their children together; the first wife, Henrietta, who lost a number of her own children as infants, nursed the babies of her husband's two later wives. When Martha asked Henrietta how she had suffered through such hardships, she explained, "Whenever my heart comes between me and my Father's work it will have to break. And if you have not learned that lesson the sooner you learn it the better." Martha's reaction to this was to call her a "Glorious woman! No better ever lived. Israel never produced a better Latter Day Saint." Martha Cox was an unusual woman; she spent almost fifty years as a schoolteacher and wrote an exceptionally detailed history of her life in order to document the Mormon experience. Her life and choices should not necessarily be taken as representative, and her perspective on those choices may well be skewed by the fact that she wrote this account almost sixty years after her marriage. But they do help us to understand that while demographic and religious pressures may well have forced many young girls into polygamous (as well as monogamous) marriages sooner than they might have wanted, some girls chose plural marriage of their own volition, even against the wishes of their communities, precisely because they, too, believe it to be a religious calling.[50]

Not everyone was so convinced. When Mary Elizabeth Cox, the daughter of Martha's husband and his second wife, was told that Bishop Milton Lafayette Lee was interested in taking her for a second wife, she had a "very pronounced dislike for the man" and said "with a good deal of emphasis that it wouldn't take her long to say 'no.'" Her mother instructed her to pray on the decision, and when her praying brought no immediate answer, "she started fasting and praying often, but still no peace of mind had come to her." Bishop Lee visited Saint George, where Mary lived, and brought his wife to introduce to her: "The sight of them made her joyless, and she felt as if she would collapse." She avoided talking with him for most of his visit. In the meantime a local young man who was interested in her also proposed marriage, but at her mother's behest, she told him that she would need to wait before deciding. Mary recounted her story to someone who recorded it, so the descriptions of her feelings and actions are all in the third person, but they seem to come from her. Mary "felt like she was in a fire without any way of getting out." She prayed and fasted for three more months, growing thinner and paler, but at the end of the period, "her instinctive dislike for Brother Lee had gone from her heart, and in its place was a deep respect and a profound admiration for him." The "change had taken place without any persuasion of any kind from anyone, not even her parents." Mary married Lee in the 1880s, a period when polygamous families were persecuted by U.S. marshals and when some members of the church reacted to this persecution with more avowed adherence to the doctrine of plural marriage. Immediately following Mary's marriage in the sealing room at the Saint George Temple, Wilford Woodruff, now an apostle, "met her and put his hands on her shoulders and spoke words of encouragement and advice to her which gave her renewed strength and assurance." Even if we acknowledge that Mary did eventually make the decision herself to become Bishop Lee's plural wife at the age of seventeen, it is difficult to ignore the prior "instinctive dislike" for her eventual husband or not to see the three months of fasting at the behest of parents who might have wished to link their family with Lee, as being a crucial factor. Although Mary identified the decision as her own, the attentions of a senior church member and the encouragement of her parents and others clearly made the decision fraught for a girl who had not yet reached her eighteenth birthday. These sorts of cultural, familial, and demographic pressures almost always inhere in the history of early marriage, even if the participants themselves were not aware of their influence. Mary Cox reminds us that for every young person who chose marriage with open eyes, there was another who might have had little choice. Determining with any precision how many of each there were is simply an impossibility.[51]

By 1860, many acknowledged Abel Stearns as the most important ranchero in Southern California. Doña Arcadia was by his side as he amassed more and more wealth. In 1847, legend has it that she and her sisters, Ysidora and Josefa, stitched an American flag out of their own clothing and flew it at their father's ranch in San Diego, the first time an American flag would fly in Alta California. Although the story itself may be apocryphal, in this and in so many other things, the Bandinis had embraced the future, which lay not with Spain or Mexico but with the United States. Arcadia's marriage to Abel Stearns (her sister Ysidora also married an American) also exemplified this.[52]

When Arcadia's father died in 1859, he left some of his fortune to Arcadia and Abel. The couple never had children, and when Abel died in 1871, Arcadia inherited everything. She remarried in 1875, this time to Colonel Robert S. Baker of Rhode Island, who had interests in the sheep trade in Southern California. They tore down the Palacio at Main and Arcadia Streets and built the Baker block, reputed at the time to be the largest and most expensive building south of San Francisco, where they maintained a luxurious suite. Their fortune grew, and the Bakers appear in newspapers through the late nineteenth century defending their various interests in lawsuits; they also founded the town of Santa Monica. Robert Baker died in 1894, and Arcadia inherited his fortune as well. When María Arcadia Bandini Stearns de Baker died in 1912 at the age of eighty-five she was the richest woman in Southern California. Her fortune was estimated at between five and twenty million dollars, and fifteen of her heirs would fight over it for a year following her death.[53]

Arcadia Bandini de Baker was anomalous in her wealth, but given where and when she lived, in the circumstances of her first marriage she was not. Because of the racial and gendered demographics in colonial frontiers of the middle nineteenth century, the marriage of young girls with older men was common. Although there were clearly cases of exploitation brokered through such marriages, especially between some white men and some Indian women, in many cases the benefits were reciprocal. Especially because their own societies did not worry about the sexual exploitation of teenage girls and marriage was not allowed to occur before a girl had reached menarche, we must recognize the marriage of some young girls not as exploitation (economic or sexual) but rather as a consequence of the demography and cultural values of a wide variety of antebellum communities.

THREE

Wholly Unfit for the Marriage Condition

Parton v. Hervey *and Struggles over Age of Consent Laws*

On Saint Valentine's Day, 1854, Sarah E. Hervey and Thomas J. Parton were married in the town of Lynn, Massachusetts, about ten miles north of Boston. Sarah was thirteen and Thomas was nineteen. Because Massachusetts had passed a law in 1834 mandating that any girl below the age of eighteen and any boy below the age of twenty-one required the consent of their parents before marrying, Thomas sent his brother-in-law, George Moseley, to obtain the marriage license for them. He lied about their ages, claiming that Sarah was eighteen and that Thomas was twenty and had his father's consent. Once they had the license, they found a justice of the peace who performed the ceremony. On learning of the marriage, Sarah's widowed mother, Susan, enlisted the help of the Lynn city marshal and went to Thomas's house to retrieve her daughter, bringing her back home and refusing to allow Thomas to see her. Not to be outdone, Thomas got himself a lawyer and filed for a writ of habeas corpus, demanding the return of his wife, whom he claimed legally belonged with him now that they were married. He won.[1]

That suit and the ensuing legal wrangling between Thomas Parton and Susan Hervey set a precedent that most judges have followed ever since: even when children break the law in order to wed, they remain legally married. The case, known as *Parton v. Hervey*, is the most important legal precedent in the law governing children and their right to marry. The story of Sarah and Thomas's marriage and the motivations of the various players—Sarah, Thomas, Susan, and the judges who decided the case—are the focus of this chapter. Examining the legality of this marriage helps us to understand how judges interpreted the law, which was designed to prevent child marriage, in a way that actually protected those marriages; why many citizens agreed with such rulings; why legislators refused to update the law; and how this interpretation of the law would have far-reaching consequences long after Sarah and Thomas Parton married.

Susan Hervey was, of course, not the only parent to object to what she perceived as the illegal and premature marriage of her child; others had done so before her and would continue to do so well into the twentieth century. Juxtaposing the subjects of the first two chapters—laws that regulated the ability of minors to marry, on the one hand, and evidence that many children nevertheless did marry, on the other—allows us to understand how the law responded to challenges and to evaluate the motivations of those who did the challenging. The laws remained ineffective at preventing youthful marriage because judges and lawmakers were in a catch-22: although they wished to prevent youthful marriage, they were loath to write (or interpret) the law in such a way that it would dissolve any marriage already solemnized, thereby creating single, nonvirginal, and possibly pregnant girls. The maintenance of public morality through the preservation of marriages, even bad ones, was the heart of the issue.

This and other suits also reveal surprising parental motivations. Many laws were written so as to make age itself the primary criterion for barring early marriage, and the wider spread of age consciousness by the 1850s certainly accounts for a rise in Americans' perception that youthful marriage was inappropriate. But this belief developed unevenly, gaining greater traction in the Northeast and primarily among the middle and upper classes. *Parton v. Hervey* reveals that an equally pressing motivation for objecting to the marriage of a child was actually the loss of that child's labor in her parents' home. For many Americans the fact of a girl's youthfulness was often a secondary reason for objecting to her marriage. Evolving and contested conceptions of childhood were central to these legal challenges. Sarah and Thomas Parton provide a window into all these issues, demonstrating that even in a city like Boston, where age consciousness had made the greatest inroads, many parents continued to think of their minor children as dependents who were obligated to serve them and not as youthful people in need of protection.

WHOLLY UNFIT FOR THE MARRIAGE CONDITION

It is difficult to ascertain much about Sarah and Thomas's lives before the marriage that thrust them into the spotlight. Sarah was the only daughter, and perhaps only child, of Susan Hervey. Her father, Eben Hervey, seems to have died some time before the marriage, though it is unclear when. Susan Hervey's extensive involvement with the courts in the wake of her daughter's marriage is anomalous; typically, fathers brought these sorts of suits. But in Sarah's case, Susan had become the head of household when she was widowed. Sarah and her mother do not appear in Lynn censuses for 1850 or earlier. Susan claimed that Sarah had turned thirteen in December 1853, meaning that she was born in 1840. I can find no record for her birth, though her marriage record claims that she was born in Lynn. (A different record indicates she may have been born farther north in Maine.) Thomas's family, by contrast, was well established in Lynn; census, newspaper, and vital records testify to a large number of Partons in the area. Thomas's roots in the community and his extensive kin network may have made him more attractive to a girl like Sarah with fewer connections in Lynn.[2]

Home to the United States' shoe manufacturing industry, Lynn was incorporated as a city in 1850, when census-takers counted just over fourteen thousand inhabitants. We cannot know how Sarah and Thomas met—perhaps through friends or on the bustling streets of Lynn—but we do know that they married on February 14, 1854, using the marriage license that Thomas's brother-in-law had deceitfully obtained. Deprived of his bride by her mother, within a couple of weeks Thomas had begun legal proceedings, filing for a writ of habeas corpus, his lawyer claiming that Sarah was "unjustly deprived of her liberty and unlawfully detained from the custody of [Parton], her proper guardian." In response to Parton's suit, Susan Hervey explained in an affidavit that she believed Sarah to be "a mere child mentally and physically, not yet having arrived at maturity or womanhood, being wholly unfit for the marriage condition." She also averred that because Thomas was himself under the age of twenty-one, he was also a minor and, even more damning, that he was "a young man of bad character and dissolute habits." She claimed that he had at least once been convicted of being "a common drunkard," and that his sentence (jail time or the work house) was deferred only on the condition that he leave the city of Lynn, which he clearly had not done. Last, the affidavit explained that Sarah had married without her mother's consent, "in a hurried + clandestine manner," and that she was "basely inveigled from her home and induced to

marry the said Thomas Parton." For all these reasons Hervey and her lawyer
claimed that the marriage was null and void; she admitted that Sarah was living
with her but claimed that it was of Sarah's free will.[3]

During the trial, Parton's lawyer alleged that Susan Hervey was an unfit
mother with a history of insanity. By contrast, Hervey claimed that her daughter was "sickly and nervous," and her lawyer produced a witness who claimed
"she was not of good health, her nervous system was affected, her mind quite
disturbed, and she wants as much as one to take care of her; several of the
same family and connections have been insane; her mother was in an insane
hospital once for about eight months." Parton's lawyer called a physician to the
stand who claimed to have examined the girl and testified that he "could discover no symptoms toward insanity, or indicating any unusual want of mental incapacity." After hearing testimony it was up to Justice George Bigelow
of the supreme judicial court to render a decision. Two issues were before
him: whether Sarah Hervey Parton was of sound mind and had consented to
the marriage or instead had been coerced into marrying Thomas Parton; and
whether the law of Massachusetts, stipulating as it did that she required parental consent to marry, nullified the union. Bigelow evaluated the testimony in
order to determine the first issue. He believed that Sarah "freely and willingly
assented thereto, without undue influence or persuasion; that she was not of
weak or impaired intellect, but of competent understanding, and of the ordinary degree of intelligence of persons of her age."[4]

He consulted with his fellow justices on the second issue, a matter of
law. He determined that the laws mandating parental consent were "intended
as directory only upon ministers and magistrates, and to prevent, as far as
possible, by penalties on them, the solemnization of marriages, when the prescribed conditions and formalities have not been fulfilled." That is, he saw
the statute about parental consent as a preventive measure, designed to stop
minors from marrying by punishing those who might illegally issue them
licenses. But he did not believe that the law had bearing on a marriage that
had already been contracted. Because Massachusetts had no law mandating
a minimum age of marriage, he relied on the common-law ages of twelve
and fourteen as its minimums. He also explained that because the legislature
had not passed a statute declaring marriages contracted below the ages of
eighteen and twenty-one to be absolutely void, marriages, even those entered
through fraud, were valid so long as the parties were above the common-law
ages. Because Sarah was thirteen and Thomas was nineteen, they qualified.
He granted Thomas's writ of habeas corpus and ordered Susan Hervey to

release her daughter. In the wake of the decision, newspapers reported that Sarah and Thomas were "well satisfied with the result of the trial" and that the "young man walked out of the court with his youthful wife hanging lovingly on his arm, and both seemed highly delighted that the path of true love had been made smooth for them."[5]

THE GROWTH OF AGE CONSCIOUSNESS

Before discussing the logic of Justice Bigelow's decision and its legal repercussions, it is worth examining how those outside the courtroom understood the marriage, the motivations behind the actions of the other players here—Susan Hervey, Sarah Hervey Parton, Thomas Parton—and the possible motives and desires of other minors who married and parents who tried to prevent or annul their unions. Although most of the newspaper coverage reported the trial in a cursory fashion alongside other legal matters, one longer article in the *Boston Courier* elucidates some of the public attitudes toward the marriage and the subsequent suit by Thomas Parton. Throughout the *Courier's* March 6 article, the newspaper referred to Thomas and Sarah as "bridegroom" and "wife" (their quotation marks). The paper also placed quotation marks around "bride," "Mrs.," and "husband," indicating that the editors did not think Thomas and Sarah worthy of the labels. The article described Sarah as "aged *thirteen* years—an undeveloped girl, scarcely of accomplishments sufficient to entitle her to a seat on the fourth form of a primary school." The reporter then conjured up the scene when the Lynn marshal arrived at the Parton household to claim Sarah for her mother: "The 'wife' pouted a little, ejaculated a few stubborn words—'I won't,' 'I shan't'—then shook her body, shrugged her shoulders, and grimaced." Referring also to Sarah as a "child in pantalets," the newspaper clearly understood the primary issue to be Sarah's age, and occasionally also the youthfulness of her groom, himself still legally a minor as well. The central problem was not, for instance, that Sarah had wed without her mother's consent but rather that Sarah was an age clearly unfit for matrimony. The newspaper was aided in this understanding by the fact that Susan Hervey emphasized her daughter's youthfulness, in age and in temperament, in her affidavit and her testimony at the trial. And she did so, at least in part, because the law was worded so that relying on age gave Hervey her best chance of having the marriage annulled.[6]

To contemporary readers, this makes a good deal of sense, but the notion that a girl's being thirteen was itself enough to make her unfit for marriage—even when many state laws said exactly that—was relatively recent in the United States. As we have seen, young girls and boys routinely married in colonial and antebellum America, and many states continued to abide by the common-law ages of twelve and fourteen as the minimum ages of marriage well into the 1850s, either by statute or by default. Indeed, Massachusetts legislators had earlier debated setting an absolute minimum age of marriage and rejected the proposition. More important to them and many other state legislatures was that children have their parents' consent to marriage. But this can be seen as a matter of parental control more so than child welfare; that is, children needed consent because legally they belonged to their parents, not because they were young.[7]

That a newspaper in Massachusetts would frame the story this way makes sense. Age consciousness, the belief that age is an important characteristic of one's identity, came first to the industrialized Northeast. One of the ways this occurred was through schooling. By educating children together in classes based on their birthdays, schools divided students into differently aged groups, which inculcated the notion that age itself was an important way of evaluating people's abilities. Age-graded schooling then actually produced similar characteristics in same-aged peers. The *Courier* reporter was aware of this when he remarked on Sarah's lack of fitness for marriage: she was "scarcely of accomplishments sufficient to entitle her to a seat on the fourth form of a primary school." Primary schooling was born in Massachusetts, and children were more likely to have access to schooling in urban areas near Boston than anywhere else in the country. If there was one place where people might find it inappropriate for a thirteen-year-old to marry, it was Boston.[8]

Massachusetts was also the first state to collect vital statistics systematically, if unevenly and incompletely, recording from 1842 onward the number of births, marriages, and deaths by county and city. Although the first two reports pay little attention to age in relation to marriage, the 1844 report and those thereafter begin not only to chart the average ages of those who married in Massachusetts but by 1848 also to note the cases at the margins: the particularly youthful and the especially elderly who entered into matrimony. In that report, the authors explained that "we find marriages among person of all ages intervening 13 and 91." They went on to note that the youngest couple was seventeen and fourteen; a number of thirteen-year-old girls were wed; and the greatest age gap seems to have been between a fifty-year-old man and a nineteen-year-old girl. They also noted the comparatively rare cases where the woman was older than the man and the age of the parties who were marrying for the second, third, and fourth time. They explained that the probability of marriage under the age of twenty was nearly fifteen times greater for girls than boys. The point here is less what the numbers demonstrate—we have already seen that youthful boys and girls were marrying in all areas of the country during these years and that it was much more common for girls than boys—than that Massachusetts officials were themselves starting to notice these trends. Age was becoming a meaningful category of identity; people both above and below certain ages were presumed to be unfit for marriage, as were those separated by age gaps perceived to be too large. Of course the collection, publication, and discussion of these vital statistics was not itself neutral; reports like these were one influential vehicle for the spread of age consciousness. They both documented a phenomenon and helped to make it meaningful. First to adopt age-graded schooling, first to rely on birth registration and certification, and first to collect vital statistics, Massachusetts was a pioneer, however unwittingly, in the inculcation of age consciousness. It makes sense, then, that age would be such an important factor both in the argumentation and in the newspaper coverage of *Parton v. Hervey.*[9]

A North Carolina case from 1840 regarding property, guardianship, and inheritance demonstrates the way that age might be understood differently outside of the Northeast. In 1812, a man named William B. Stokes died; Archelaus Carloss was appointed administrator of the estate and guardian to William's only child, Hannah Stokes, responsible for her schooling and for managing the sizable estate left by her father. In January 1824, Hannah married Archelaus's son, Robert Carloss. She was thirteen at the time. By virtue of the marriage and the law of coverture, Robert gained access to his wife's assets. Robert died three years later, and though details are sketchy, he seems to have spent a good part of the fortune that Hannah had inherited. When Hannah remarried in 1830, she and her second husband, George Shutt, filed a bill in a court of equity against Archelaus Carloss, alleging, among other things, that he had facilitated the marriage of his son to his ward so that the son would gain Hannah's fortune. They claimed that Archelaus knew Hannah's age and that the marriage violated an 1820 North Carolina statute that made it a crime to marry a girl below the age of fifteen without her father's consent. The Shutts claimed that Archelaus Carloss was responsible for the losses to Hannah's estate and that Hannah Stokes Carloss Shutt was therefore entitled to compensation for what she had lost through her marriage to Robert Carloss.[10]

Hannah and George Shutt lost their case, the Supreme Court of North Carolina deciding that, no matter Hannah's age, once she married, Archelaus Carloss's guardianship ceased and Hannah's husband's losses were her own. Aside from affirming the legality of the marriage of a minor, what is most interesting about the case is the role that age played. One of the key issues for both sides was whether Archelaus Carloss knew that Hannah Stokes was only thirteen when she married. If he did, then he had helped Hannah and Robert violate the North Carolina law that barred a girl below fifteen from marrying without her father's permission, which was clearly unavailable in this case, Hannah's father being dead. He claimed that he did not; the Shutts claimed he did. To prove his case, Carloss and his lawyer asked a number of witnesses about Hannah's appearance at the time of her marriage to Robert Carloss. For instance: "Was not Hannah Stokes a large and uncommonly well grown girl before her intermarriage with Robert Carloss?" Of the justice of the peace who married them: "What was her appearance as to age & whether she did not look like a well grown woman at the time[?]" He answered: "Her appearance as to age I heard showed that she had size enough for ordinary woman, but in most other appearances looked quite young." Others responded like this: "I think I recollect her weight and it was one hundred & eighteen pounds." "She was very tawl and tolerable well grown of her age." Bear in mind that Archelaus Carloss became Hannah's guardian only two or three years after she was born; he had known her for most of her life. Despite this, and that Carloss made his arguments and asked these questions to win the case, it was still a plausible defense to assert that he did not know her age. The court agreed: "It does not appear that this fact [her age] was known either to the father or the son, and the defendant's positive averment, that he believed her to be over fifteen years of age, is so confirmed by the testimony with respect to her womanly appearance at that time, that the court yields credence to it." The questions and answers all point to a fuzziness about the importance of chronological age. In essence Carloss was asserting that Hannah's appearance as a woman was what he took to be most important and what prevented him from knowing that her marriage was contrary to the 1820 statute.[11]

Carloss also tried to establish that Hannah had spent the time leading up to her marriage living at the home of her mother and stepfather. This was his way of demonstrating both that her mother approved of the marriage (though she denied this in the trial) and that Carloss was not in a position to foist a marriage on her because Hannah was not living with him. We know also that Hannah lived with Robert Carloss for three years, until he died, and that she

bore three children. No one seems to have contested the validity of the marriage during that time (the court claimed, "There is no proof that he treated
his wife ill, or that they lived otherwise than happily"), and indeed, Hannah
filed a suit to do so only after she was married to her second husband, three
years after the death of her first. Taken together, these factors point to a general acceptance of the marriage of a thirteen-year-old, partially because some
people, even those close to her, may not have known her age, and also because
age itself was not a particularly important reason to forbid a marriage in the
mid-nineteenth-century South, even when the law made that a possibility.
The disjuncture between what the law stipulated and what children and their
spouses did stands in contrast to the attitudes expressed by the *Boston Courier*
in 1854 about Sarah Parton, those attitudes a product of the greater spread of
age consciousness in the Northeast fourteen years later.[12]

CHILDREN, PARENTS, AND SERVICE

All that said, it is still difficult to know whether age *was* the primary reason that
Susan Hervey sought to nullify her daughter's marriage. Certainly she made
ample use of the age argument in her response to Thomas's habeas corpus
petition, but this was, in all likelihood, a legal strategy crafted by her lawyer.
The language she employed was unlikely to have been the way she actually
spoke, and the statute was written in such a way that age had to be a key factor
in contesting the marriage. Noteworthy, too, is that Susan Hervey expressed
concern about Thomas's drinking habits and criminal record; these are logical
reasons to oppose a possible son-in-law. Susan Hervey was not alone in her
desire to prevent an older man from marrying her daughter. At least since the
eighteenth century and across the colonies and later states, laws barring minors
from marrying had enabled parents to bring suits to recover damages against
a clerk who had incorrectly issued a marriage license that allowed the union
to take place. Some parents even worked to change the laws themselves. Two
years earlier in Medway, Massachusetts, about twenty-five miles southwest of
Boston, a group of concerned citizens submitted a petition to the Massachusetts State Legislature. Daniel and Candace Nourse and "fifty other citizens of
Medway and their wives" asked the legislature to amend chapter 216 of the Acts
of 1845, which made it a crime to entice any unmarried female away from her
home for the purpose of prostitution. Nourse and his neighbors wanted the
act also to punish the "enveigling [*sic*], enticing and stealing away our Daughters of nonage, carrying them without the limits of our Commonwealth and

there consummating a clandestine marriage against the knowledge or consent of the parents, masters or guardians of the deluded child." The petition elaborated on two events of the past year. On one occasion a thirteen-year-old girl was rescued "from an ignominious flight for a clandestine marriage in another state." In another, the parents of a fourteen-year-old girl learned "an hour to[o] late" that their daughter had been married to her "enticer" "under cover of darkness" in nearby Rhode Island.[13]

The petitioners believed that amending the earlier law would help prevent the enticement of young girls away from their families and would also deter such families (especially fathers) from seeking revenge because the Commonwealth of Massachusetts would itself mete out the punishment. Although the petitioners were outraged about the injustice of these clandestine marriages, the precise reason for the outrage is not altogether clear. The petition contains the following sentence in relation to the Rhode Island marriage: "The insulted father is first presented with this outlandish document which virtually says (under such circumstances as these) I have succeeded in stealing your daughter and now you may help yourself—can it appear strange that men's blood on such occasions boil in their veins with indignation and wrath?" The petitioners seem to be saying that the loss of a daughter means that a father must "help himself," that is, perform himself or pay someone to do the labor that his daughter would otherwise have been doing.[14] The petitioners continued: "In the laws enacted 1850, chap. 303, we find the stealing of our birds our goslins and our lambs punished by law and of the acts of 1845 chapter 216 a partial protection for our daughters." This sentence is more ambiguous. The 1845 act is clearly meant to protect unmarried girls from those who would seduce or entice them into prostitution, but the 1850 act to which they refer extended the crime of larceny to include "the taking, without the consent of the owner and with a felonious intent, of any beast or bird ordinarily kept in a state of confinement." It could be that they were comparing their daughters to poultry and other livestock as a rhetorical strategy to emphasize how unprotected those daughters really were (even chickens being more so). Or it could also be that they were serious about the financial loss they would suffer through their daughters' early marriages. The latter is certainly worth considering.[15]

The petition was read before the Massachusetts Senate on February 27, 1852, and a bill taking up its cause made its way through the house and the senate by early April. The governor approved "An Act in addition to the Act to Punish Abduction" on May 20, 1852. It made the "fraudulent and deceitful" enticing or taking away of "any unmarried female, under the age of sixteen years, from her father's house, or wherever else she may be found, without the consent of the parent, guardian, or master (if she have any) under whose care and custody she is living, for the purpose of effecting a clandestine marriage of such female without such consent" punishable by confinement to hard labor in the state prison for up to a year or a fine of up to a thousand dollars or both fine and imprisonment in the county jail. Although the petition had asked that the law apply to girls below the age of eighteen—which would have been in keeping with the statute on consent to marriage—the legislature had balked and made it applicable only to men who married girls below the age of sixteen. Clearly there was disagreement about how old girls might be before they no longer needed their fathers' (or the law's) protection. This left a two-year gap where one could marry a girl without her father's permission and not risk arrest. A good deal hinged, however, on whether the wooing was "fraudulent and deceitful." This law was in effect when Sarah Hervey and Thomas Parton were married, and Thomas does not seem to have been arrested or charged under it. Indeed, Justice Bigelow of the supreme judicial court found that Sarah had willingly, albeit illegally, married Thomas.[16]

When Susan Hervey lost the habeas corpus suit and Sarah returned to her husband, Hervey remained unsatisfied. Her actions next elucidate the impetus for contesting her daughter's marriage, a motivation she seems to have shared with the petitioners from Medway. She filed a suit against George Moseley, Thomas's brother-in-law, who had secured the marriage license and made the arrangements for the marriage. She alleged that he had "procured her said daughter to be married to a person of bad character and dissolute habits, by means whereof the plaintiff ever since hath been, now is, and ever may be, deprived of the services, society and benefit of her said daughter, to the damage of the plaintiff five thousand dollars." This is approximately $135,000 in today's dollars. Sarah was not, so far as we know, possessed of any special training and might have married in five years without her mother's consent, thus depriving her mother of her labor anyway. It is possible that Susan Hervey was estimating the loss of her daughter's services at approximately $1,000 for each year when her mother might keep her at home—though the average annual earnings for a tradesman were $300 in 1850—or she simply may have been grasping for a high number, hoping to receive anything at all. Either way, Sarah's work in the Hervey home, and perhaps outside of it, was of value to Susan Hervey, especially as a widowed woman. Susan depended on her daughter's labor within her home, and possibly outside of it, to make ends meet. Sarah's marriage to Thomas Parton deprived her mother of those services and helps make clear a further reason that Hervey opposed the marriage. It was not simply that Sarah was young or that Thomas was a drunkard, it was that Sarah's marriage abruptly terminated her service to her mother.[17]

The legal battle between Susan Hervey and George Moseley stretched on for the next three years. In December 1854, a jury awarded Susan Hervey eight hundred dollars as compensation for the loss of her daughter, significantly less than the five thousand dollars she had requested, but still an explicit acknowledgment that Hervey's claim about the loss of her daughter's services was legitimate. Moseley alleged exceptions, contesting the verdict based on evidence that he believed had been wrongly admitted into the record at the trial and instructions that he wanted delivered to the jury that the judge had refused to give. Justice Dewey, who heard the case on appeal for the Supreme Court of Massachusetts, Essex County, sustained Moseley's exceptions and overturned the lower court's verdict in November 1856. Although he did not dispute the notion that a mother was entitled to her daughter's services, his opinion explained that there was no way that Susan Hervey could sustain damages from what the court, in *Parton v. Hervey* (the first case), had found to be a valid marriage. He was disputing Susan Hervey's right to bring the suit in the first place, based on the precedent of the now settled *Parton v. Hervey* and on how the law of marriage worked. Dewey's sustaining of Moseley's exceptions was not the end, however. Immediately thereafter the court ordered a new trial. On the first day of that trial in the summer of 1857, the Supreme Judicial Court of Essex County record book explains: "And now the plaintiff [Susan Hervey], although solemnly called to come into Court and prosecute her suit against the defendant, does not appear, but becomes nonsuit. Thereupon it is considered by the Court, that the defendant recover against the plaintiff costs of suit taxed at eighty nine dollars sixty seven cents." When Susan Hervey realized that she would not win her suit against George Moseley, she failed to come to court. The court thus charged the costs of the entire suit to her. At this point Susan Hervey disappears from the historical record.[18]

Suing for the loss of a child's service or wages was not uncommon in nineteenth-century America. Although the practice was differently regulated over the century (at times falling out of favor), parents regularly sued those who had caused the death of their children and courts awarded damages based on the wages a child might have expected to earn from the time of its death till it reached the age of majority. Parents of dead girls often won lesser awards than parents of dead boys due to this market-based accounting of the value of a child's labor. Parents could also file a civil suit against a man who had seduced and impregnated their daughter. These suits were meant to compensate a parent (usually a father) for the loss of a daughter's services during the time of her pregnancy or for the loss of that daughter's wages if she worked outside the home. It is demonstrably true that parents depended on their children economically and that courts were willing to consider such arguments when children were taken from parents under a variety of circumstances. The point, however, is that these motivations might have trumped the concern that even a loving parent might feel when a child married; the most pressing problem with a child's marriage was a problem for the parent, not the child.[19]

Only a systematic search of all county court records across the country would reveal how frequently parents sued for lost wages or services as a result of their children's marriages, but a number of these cases made their way to state high courts at midcentury. Far more must have been settled in lower courts. Legally children owed service to their parents until they reached the age of majority (twenty-one in most states, though sometimes eighteen for girls, as we saw in chapter 1), but if children below that age married, they became legal adults and were emancipated from their parents. Neither married girls nor boys were obliged to serve their parents any longer. In the case of boys, this meant that they might keep their own wages; in the case of girls, their labor now legally belonged to their husbands (at least until the passage of married women's property acts in the 1850s and 1860s with stipulations regarding wives' wages). Susan Hervey's role in this case, as a woman, was anomalous; normally men brought these suits against other men. The role of children as quasi-possessions controlled by different men during their minority was a well-established legal precedent. The control was necessary because children contributed in important ways to the household economy, that household normally governed by a man. When children married without parental permission, it angered some parents enough to sue: usually the clerk who had issued the license or a third party who had facilitated the marriage in some way. It bears noting also that this kind of suit was precisely what the statutes allowed; they were written to enable a parent to claim pecuniary damages, not to annul the marriage. In these cases, where the validity of the marriage was probably not contestable, it is clear that parents were seeking compensation for the loss of their children's services; this was their primary legal contention with child marriage, not the premature matrimony of minors. In these cases it is helpful to think of a "child" in kin-based, rather than age-based, terms. The father who objected to his child's marriage did so because that child had ruptured the legal relationship between him- or herself and his or her father based on filiation, not because the child was too young for matrimony, per se.

In a case similar to *Hervey v. Moseley*, in 1849 an Iowa father named Rufus Thompson brought a suit against three men who he alleged had assisted Jefferson Goodwin in marrying his daughter, Louisa, who was either twelve or thirteen and therefore below the statutory age of marriage for girls in Iowa, which was fourteen. Thompson claimed that as a result of the marriage, he had "sustained great damage by reason of the loss of her society, service, expenditure of money and time in his endeavors to procure her return, anxiety and trouble of mind, &c." He asked for two hundred dollars in damages. Although a lower court had ruled for Thompson, the Supreme Court of Iowa, hearing the case on appeal, found for the defendants. Because it was clear to the justice that Louisa Thompson had married voluntarily and was at least the common-law age of marriage for girls (twelve), the marriage was valid. If the marriage was valid, then Rufus Thompson could not sue the men who had assisted Louisa and Jefferson in contracting what was now a legal union.[20]

In a pair of Pennsylvania cases from 1844 and 1859, fathers sued justices of the peace for the fifty-pound fine stipulated by a 1729 statute for granting a marriage license to minors without their father's permission. In the 1844 case, Moses Bertron was protesting the marriage of his daughter, Juliann, which had brought him "material injury and damage." In 1859, Strickling English sued R. R. Robinson for performing the marriage of his son, Strickling English Jr., who was nineteen years old and therefore legally a minor. Lower courts had followed the letter of the law and awarded the fines to the fathers. And in both cases the Supreme Court of Pennsylvania reversed those decisions, finding that the fathers had already turned their children out of their homes and ceased materially supporting them. In the first case, the court explained that Moses Bertron had turned "his daughter out on the world, to shift for herself, [and] thereby relinquished his parental rights in relation to her person, and absolved her from filial allegiance." If fathers had ceased acting as fathers, then they were no longer entitled to the fines they might be owed for the loss of their children's services through the emancipation gained through marriage. In this context, the import of these cases is that some parents objected to the marriage of their minor children not only or solely because they believed those children were too young for marriage but because they claimed (sometimes falsely) that the marriage itself caused material damage to them and their households. Although many parents must also have suffered great anguish when their children made what parents saw as unfortunate marital choices—by marrying known drunkards, for instance—these cases remind us that there was more at stake for parents than simply fears about the well-being of their sons and daughters. Especially in a society where age was less meaningful, the youthfulness of a bride or groom might not be the primary reason to object to a child's early marriage. Operative here was a kin-based and not an age-based understanding of the word "child"; it was not that the child was too young but instead that the child belonged to his or her parents.[21]

THE LEGAL BENEFITS OF MARRIAGE

As we saw in the previous chapter, many minor girls and their husbands (sometimes minors themselves) probably married for the same combination of love and practicality that continue to send most couples to the altar. But there were also distinct *legal* benefits to marriage for minors. First and foremost, marriage was one of the only legal ways for a girl to escape her home. Jane Elizabeth Tompkins Milam Hunter, for instance, explained of her 1858 marriage at the age of fifteen, "I was living in San Bernardino when I married Mr. Milam, and married against my parents' wishes. My father was about to go to Salt Lake City. He was a Mormon and belonged to the Mormon Church. I ran away from home, my sister and me both and got married so as not to go to Salt Lake City . . . because I was afraid I would be sealed to some old man." Marriage could also be economically advantageous. In few places in mid-nineteenth-century America was it possible for a girl to find an occupation that would support her. Work in a mill or factory might be available, but it paid poorly. The best-paying option was prostitution, and most people clearly saw marriage, even early marriage, as preferable to that. Marriage also offered an escape from an abusive home. In one of the Pennsylvania cases discussed above, for instance, Juliann Bertron testified that when her father was in "the habit of intoxication," he frequently turned her and her mother out of doors to sleep in the stable. She did admit that he did this only when he drank and that, when sober, he was kind enough, but the drinking was habitual, and she married her husband after an acquaintance of only three or four days. Juliann Bertron married to escape a home life that had become intolerable. Others simply may have tired of serving their parents and believed, probably erroneously, that their lives with new husbands would not be filled with such labors.[22]

Still others may have seen marriage as a route to inheritance. In an 1838 case from Mississippi that echoes the case of Helen Shutt, Frances Nixon Wood used her marriage as a minor to gain control of the estate being held for her by her guardian. Marriage, the Mississippi Supreme Court held, terminated a minor's wardship; her guardian was thus obligated to deliver to Robert N. Wood, Frances's husband, "all the goods, effects, and property, belonging to said ward [Frances], according to law." The doctrine of coverture meant that the property was now controlled by Robert, not Frances. Of course we cannot know if he did a better job in its management than her guardian might have done. From Frances's perspective, however, marriage may have provided access to what she saw as her rightful inheritance. The point is to see how Frances herself, and others like her, might have understood the legal appeal of marriage, even if we can also see the great disadvantages that early marriage held for girls.[23]

THE GENERAL INTERESTS OF SOCIETY

If we can now understand why marriage might have appealed to girls, boys, and the adults they married and why parents might have objected to those marriages, it remains to explore why judges like Justice George Bigelow upheld marriages that seemed to defy state law. There are two primary reasons, and they are related. The first has to do with the interpretation of the law, and the second with the meanings of marriage. Judges like George Bigelow of the Massachusetts Supreme Judicial Court were tasked with interpreting the statutory law (that is, laws passed by state legislatures), the common law (inherited from England and still very much in use throughout the nineteenth century), and past precedent of their own and other state courts (sometimes called case law). In deciding cases, they looked first to the statutes of their state because these were laws passed by their own legislators specifically about the topic at hand. What they found, in the case of minors and marriage, is that state legislatures had not written laws that made marriages utterly void if they were contracted below certain ages or without parental consent, as they did, for instance, with marriages contracted by people who already had living spouses (bigamous marriages). According to the law, a marriage contracted by someone with a living spouse did not legally exist as a marriage, the first marriage making the second an impossibility. Judges argued that if legislators had meant to void minor marriages outright they would have written statutory law that made this explicit, and they had not done so.

Turning to the common law, which guided their decisions when statutory law was not explicit, the judges argued that so long as the contracting parties were above the ages of twelve and fourteen (girls and boys, respectively), had not been tricked or coerced into the marriage, and did not themselves desire to end the marriage (and sometimes even then), the union was valid. Even marriages contracted below the common-law ages of twelve and fourteen but above the age of seven were only voidable and not automatically void. Judges interpreted the statutes that forbade the marriage of people below certain ages, or mandated parental consent for minors, as being "directory," meant to instruct the clerks and justices of the peace and magistrates and indeed minors themselves about who could marry and who should not. In other words, they were preventive measures, designed to curb early marriage and especially marriage without the consent of parents and guardians. They argued that legislatures that meant to void minors' marriages could write statutory law that did just that; until that happened, they would hold the marriages to be valid. As Chief Justice Joseph Williams of the Iowa Supreme Court put it in *Goodwin v. Thompson*, the case cited above, "Statutes will not be construed to have an effect beyond that which is to be gathered from the plain and direct import of the terms used in declaring them. Effect by implication will not be given to them, so as to change a well established principle of common law."[24]

The second reason for upholding these unions had to do with the function of marriage. When judges heard cases about minors and marriage in their courtrooms, the marriages had usually already taken place. As we saw in Chapter 1, in the wake of the Revolution, many states had modified statutory law to limit the ability of children to make contracts, the idea being that they were too young to be properly informed: consent should be informed to be valid. But marriage was more than an ordinary contract; it created distinct kinds of people called husbands and wives. Once previously single people had been transformed into husbands and wives, could they be transformed back into bachelors and maidens? If one of the requirements and expectations of marriage, and thus the making of husbands and wives, was sex, then the answer was almost always a resounding no. Judges had no interest in annulling marriages if this meant turning otherwise married women into single girls who were no longer virgins. This would make for a legal back door into illicit sex because a man could have sex with a girl while married and then petition to have his marriage annulled; marriage itself, and the poor girl, would both be tarnished. Judges were also worried about wives who were pregnant or had already had children; then not only were the lives of the wives themselves at stake but so too were their children, who could be seen as illegitimate if their parents' marriages no longer existed. (Illegitimacy was not only socially ostracizing but also meant that one could not inherit; some states had statutes explicitly stating that children of annulled marriages were legally legitimate because this was such a worry.) In an age where divorce was more available than in previous generations but still hotly contested and often quite limited, preserving marriage was seen as an intrinsic good, for husbands, wives, and their children.[25]

Last, as historian Michael Grossberg has argued, judges preserved minor marriages for the same reasons they preserved marriages contracted without properly executed licenses, marriages performed by nonlicensed officials, and common-law marriages where no ceremony or license had ever been involved: it was a way both to honor the choices of individuals (in keeping with ideals of American liberalism) and to preserve social order through the preservation of what was seen as its cornerstone, marriage. As Justice Bigelow put it in *Parton v. Hervey*, "In regulating the intercourse of the sexes, by giving its highest sanctions to the contract of marriage, and rendering it, as far as possible, inviolable, the law looks, beyond the welfare of the individual and a class, to the general interests of society; and seeks, in the exercise of a wise and sound policy, to chasten and refine the intercourse, and to guard against the manifold evils which would result from illicit cohabitation." In other words, marriage, so long as both parties entered it voluntarily, should be widely available, not strictly limited. And most courts, in part because of Bigelow's trenchant explanation of the issues, followed the lead of *Parton v. Hervey*. While a small minority of judges interpreted state statute to mean that minors' marriages were void because they had broken state law in marrying, *Parton v. Hervey* was used throughout the nineteenth and twentieth centuries as precedent for preserving the marriages of minors once they were contracted. As we shall see in the chapters that follow, in cases involving minors and marriage in the United States, all roads lead back to Sarah Hervey and Thomas Parton. And that case was decided in such a way that the preservation of marriage and fears about illicit sexuality trumped the protection of minors who married.[26]

So what became of Sarah and Thomas Parton, the couple who inadvertently became the precedent for the preservation of underage marriages? Three and a half years after their marriage, on December 9, 1857, Sarah gave birth to a son, named Thomas after his father and grandfather. Within a year and a half, however, Thomas Senior seems to have deserted Sarah, leaving her to raise her son on her own. In April 1865, Sarah returned to the Essex Supreme Judicial Court, this time to ask for a divorce. Through her lawyer she related that in May 1859, Thomas "utterly and willfully deserted her without her consent, and has ever since, without her consent, continued such desertion (being for more than five consecutive years)." She explained that he had not provided any support during that time. Sarah further told the court that even before Thomas's desertion, he had "treated her with extreme cruelty, and on the night of the said day of May, A.D. 1859, without any cause or provocation cruelly struck and beat her in and about her head and face, and threatened to kill her." As a result of this abuse she was compelled to leave him "and to go out to service, and take in work, and to obtain a support for herself and her child." Although she may simply have been recounting what had happened, the actions Sarah ascribed to Thomas—desertion for an extended period, cruelty, lack of support—were what she needed to prove in order to obtain a divorce in Massachusetts. She asked the court to grant her a divorce, custody of her son, and permission to resume use of her maiden name. Thomas Parton did not appear in court, and Sarah Parton was granted all three requests. She was once again Sarah Hervey. The next year Thomas Parton remarried, this time to a woman who shared his own last name, Mary A. Parton; it was her third marriage. At forty-six, she was fourteen years Thomas's senior.[27]

What happened to Sarah Hervey and her son, Thomas, next was a result of her youthful marriage only insofar as the premature end to that marriage had led Sarah to become a single mother at the age of nineteen, precisely the scenario that Justice Bigelow had hoped to avoid. In 1870, a mother and son named Sarah and William Dow, thirty and fourteen years old, appear in the Massachusetts census living with a family and other boarders in a home in Boston's Fourth Ward. It is unclear why they had taken the surname Dow, but later sources make it clear that this Sarah and William are indeed Sarah and Thomas. Fourteen years later, Thomas Parton, who had become a bartender, married in Boston in April 1884 at the age of twenty-six. Following in his father's footsteps, he married a girl, Mary Lanigan, of only sixteen; she gave birth to three girls over the next six years, making Sarah Hervey a grandmother. In 1888, Thomas applied for a liquor license to sell spirits as a wholesale dealer on the first floor and cellar of the building he lived in on Staniford Street in Boston's West End. That same year, however, Thomas Jr.'s troubles began. In September he was sentenced to three months in the house of correction for keeping a liquor nuisance at the Glen Hotel in East Watertown, just west of Cambridge. Two months later police raided his saloon, the Glendome, on Staniford Street: "The most notorious man in the West end is Will Dow, alias Thomas Parton. He is reputed to be the keeper of a number of houses of ill fame, and has a bad character generally."[28]

Two years later, in 1890, the Glen Hotel in Watertown, still owned by Thomas, was gutted by fire. Newspapers reported that Thomas was a fugitive from justice, living in New York to escape the multiple charges of illegal liquor sales against him. Two months before, tragedy had also struck the Parton household. Nellie Parton, aged two months and seven days, died of "diarrhoea and bronchitis" after a two-week illness. Eighteen days later her older sister, Mollie, succumbed to diphtheria at Boston's City Hospital. She was five. Newspapers claimed that Thomas died in New York in 1891, still a fugitive from the law, and his wife, Mary Lanigan Parton, died in 1896, only twenty-eight years old. At the time of her mother's death, Sadie Parton, her grandmother's namesake, was only eight years old. It is unclear what happened to her in the wake of her parents' deaths, though Thomas's properties at 73 and 75 Staniford Street were sold in 1896 "for the Thomas Parton heirs."[29]

And what of the original Sarah Hervey, alias Sadie Dow, precedent-setting child bride? She went into business with her son, running the "notorious" Glen Hotel beginning in the early 1880s when she was in her early forties. Of the opening night, a reporter commented: "Liquor flowed freely, the air was rent with oaths and vile talk, and a free fight was the natural result." Another newspaper recounted that "the hotel was then [under Sadie's ownership] conducted in greater style than ever and Sadie cut a great dash with her spirited grays, which she drove about the suburbs of Boston." It is unclear whether Sarah Hervey was a madam or simply the owner of a roadhouse where liquor violations were commonplace, so much so that her neighbors launched a petition drive to have her hotel condemned as a public nuisance. Her bartenders were regularly called into court, and a man drowned in the hotel pond, perhaps because of intoxication. Sarah Hervey Parton had come a long way from being Lynn's most famous child bride; she had become another person altogether. The last account of her in newspapers comes from 1888, when a man named George Montegriffe was run over by a horse and buggy in Boston. "A woman named Sadie Dow was driving the buggy and, it is said, endeavored to escape, but failed." This sounds like the same Sadie Dow who "cut a great dash with her spirited grays," though one cannot be sure. What became of her after that, or of her namesake, we cannot know.[30]

It is unclear whether Sarah's age was what caused her to make the unfortunate decision to settle on Thomas as her husband. Certainly, social scientists of the twentieth century find that youth at time of marriage is directly correlated with propensity to divorce. Comprehensive statistics for earlier eras are unavailable. The preservation of Sarah's marriage and her subsequent divorce most clearly demonstrate the misplaced faith in marriage evinced by Justice Bigelow and his colleagues across the United States. The very thing that they did not want to happen did so anyway. Sarah was out on her own with a small child, temporarily unable to support herself, and eventually able to do so only through running a house of ill repute. Although the marriages of many minors certainly lasted a lifetime, in this case the judges believed that preserving marriage would ensure the well-being and virtue of Sarah Parton, and neither of those things came to pass. Preserving minor marriages in the name of the social order, even against the objections of parents, came at the cost of protecting children.

FOUR

The Great Life-Long Mistake

Women's Rights Advocates and the Feminist Critique of Early Marriage

As Elizabeth Oakes Smith remembered it, the spring thaw came early to Portland, Maine, in 1823. On March 6 of that year, as rain poured down and the winter's snow melted away, she and newspaper editor Seba Smith married, surrounded by family and friends in the home of her mother and stepfather. She was "clad in white satin, with lace flounces," and wore white flowers in her "long golden brown hair" that reached down below her waist. The preacher from her local church performed the ceremony. As Smith described her husband in the autobiography she would pen almost sixty years later, he was "almost twice my age, wore spectacles, and was very bald. He had contempt for fashionable and conventional usages, and declined to furnish the bridal ring, esteeming it a foolish appendage to a bride." But these were not the real problems. At the time of her marriage, Elizabeth was only sixteen, "a mere baby, no more fit to be a wife than a child of ten years." Smith explained: "I was so foreign to all this: so unfit for the occasion. I, a dreamy, undeveloped child—living my own life, in which worldliness did not form a single ingredient. My poor little head was not furnished with a fibre of the actual." Looking back on an accomplished life as an author and women's rights activist, a life that included a long and unconventional marriage to Seba Smith, Elizabeth Oakes Smith did have regrets, but perhaps none greater than her early marriage. One chapter of her autobiography, called "Maidenhood," begins like this: "This is the most beautiful and the most suggestive period of a woman's life. The girl who has sacrificed this by a premature marriage will carry in her breast, to the end of her life, the sense of a loss—the sense of desecration. . . . To lose this period, to be rushed from the cradle to the alter [sic] is to make the great life-long mistake."[1]

Elizabeth's husband, Seba Smith, was a graduate of Bowdoin College in Brunswick, Maine, and editor of a newspaper called the *Eastern Argus*; he would later invent the fictional Jack Downing, among the most famous literary characters of the age. During their marriage Elizabeth assisted her husband with the management, first, of the *Argus* and, later, of a number of other papers he would run after the Smiths moved to Brooklyn in 1839 and then to Long Island. Elizabeth Oakes Smith began writing pseudonymously in the *Argus* and eventually penned fiction, poetry, and commentary under her own name in a number of New York newspapers. She also published almost twenty volumes of poetry and prose. Although some of Elizabeth's work was necessitated by Seba's inability to provide for their family on his own (they had six children, five of whom survived infancy), he also supported her public life in a way that was exceptional for nineteenth-century husbands. By the 1850s, Elizabeth had become a vocal participant in the nascent women's rights movement, attending conventions and writing and speaking widely on the lyceum circuit on the topics of marriage, divorce, and woman suffrage. Inspired by her experience as a sixteen-year-old bride and mother soon thereafter, one of her primary targets was the early marriage of girls. She became the movement's most eloquent spokeswoman against the practice.[2]

But Elizabeth Oakes Smith was not alone. Early women's rights activists tend to be remembered for their focus on securing the vote for women, but they actually had a much wider set of demands, many of them centered on reforming the institution of marriage. Indeed, some advocated for suffrage precisely so that they could change marriage law, which they saw as the primary arena in which men oppressed women.[3] Early marriage was part of this. Nineteenth-century women's rights activists articulated a nuanced critique of early marriage that focused on how the marriage of girls was detrimental not just to their health but also to that of the nation and its male citizens; they also believed that it was contrary to the laws of man and God. In this chapter I will focus on the first generation of people—notably women—to criticize the practice of early marriage in language that we would now describe as feminist. For many of them, early marriage was inextricable from the circumstances of

Seba Smith (opposite) and Elizabeth Oakes Smith. The couple married in Maine in 1823 when Elizabeth was sixteen and Seba was thirty-one. Seba was a writer and newspaper editor. Elizabeth published widely in poetry and fiction and on the subject of women's rights. She was the foremost speaker in the antebellum women's movement against the practice of youthful marriage for girls. Image of Seba Smith from the Collections of the Maine Historical Society. Image of Elizabeth Oakes Smith in Thomas B. Read, ed., *Female Poets of America* (1849), courtesy of the Library Company of Philadelphia.

women's oppression more generally, both symptom and cause of their greater degradation.

Elizabeth Oakes Smith believed that many of the problems that people saw in marriages all around them, including divorce, were caused by early marriages, when girls did not know their own minds enough to understand the choice they were making, which she called the "great life-long mistake." But more important for Smith, early marriage deprived girls of girlhood itself, the stage of life where they might be educated, have fun, and preserve their innocence before the labor of wife- and motherhood commenced. Like Sarah Parton from the previous chapter, Smith lost her father at a young age, but her mother remarried soon thereafter, and unlike Parton, Smith's middle-class parents believed in education for girls and encouraged her love of reading. Also unlike Parton, Smith's parents employed servants to do the work that Sarah herself performed in her mother's home. Smith believed that her marriage at sixteen, and the birth of her first child the next year, had deprived her of the ability to develop intellectually and physically at her own pace, to become an individual on her own terms before marrying.

But this critique of early marriage must be seen through the lens of class. Although early marriage could be detrimental for working-class girls, it was the daughters of the bourgeois or professional class who might have the most to lose by marrying young, because they had greater access to the protection afforded by childhood and youth as stages of life. Those in the middle class and higher were also most attuned to age consciousness, believing that certain activities were or were not appropriate for people based on their age. Access to education, however foreshortened for girls, both spurred this age consciousness and also serves as evidence of their privileged class status. Women's rights advocates believed that early marriage was problematic because most of them came from families wealthy enough that childhood and youth, stages of life regulated by age, could be protected from adult concerns. Middle-class children did not work in the 1850s Northeast, but working-class children did, meaning that their experiences of childhood might be radically different from one another. Smith and her colleagues who targeted early marriage rarely acknowledged the ways that postponing marriage offered more advantages to girls with greater means, and they had difficulty acknowledging the appeal of early marriage to working-class girls. All that said, their critique was trenchant and astute. The marriage of girls served both as a synecdoche for all that was wrong with the institution of marriage more generally and was a pressing social issue in its own right.

ACTIVISTS TARGET THE CULTURE OF EARLY MARRIAGE

Almost all states, as we have seen, legally allowed for girls to marry before boys and to do so while they were legal minors, but for the most part women's rights advocates did not focus their ire on the laws themselves; instead, they targeted the culture that encouraged girls to believe that their one purpose in life was marriage. They approached the problem in different ways. One was to criticize parents and culture broadly for raising daughters with marriage as their only goal and with no skills other than those for wife- and motherhood, which would make them particularly dependent on their husbands. At the October 1850 Woman's Rights Convention held at Worcester, Massachusetts, Abby Price addressed the delegates by asking them: "Parents, I appeal to you: are you willing to train your daughters with reference only to marriage? Are you willing they should be prey of that sickly sentimentality, that effeminate weakness, which is produced by making that one idea the focus of life?" Earlier in her speech she had exhorted her audience: "If married women have too little stimulus and objects, how much less have young girls, whose very dreams of the future are restricted to getting married! Having no encouragement for great endeavors, excluded from the liberal professions by the law, how many poor victims, who are not obliged 'to labor' but only 'to wait,' are yielded up to be the prey of that frightful disease called ennui." Price believed that the solution to this was occupational training and decent-paying jobs for the nation's daughters as well as its sons. As it stood at the time, "their alternatives are few. The confined factory, the sedentary, blighting life of half-paid seamstresses, perhaps a chance at folding books, or type setting may keep them along until the happy moment arrives, when they have an offer of marriage, and their fears of sustenance end by a union with the more favored sex." Price's point was about more than just marriage—she wanted economic opportunities for women that were commensurate both with their abilities and with the pay of men—but she and other women's rights activists connected the issue to marriage because they recognized that without these opportunities women married because they had to survive, and many did so at young ages. Unlike some of her contemporaries, Price acknowledged that early marriage was a problem not just for wealthier girls but also for working-class girls with far fewer options.[4]

Speaking the next year, also in Worcester, Abby Kelly Foster took a different tack but also focused on the connections between work and marriage. She argued that women lacked equal rights because they were not themselves taking on enough responsibility. Although she did not explicitly address the age of girls' marriages, she advocated that girls be trained and economically independent before they married: "Let mothers take care to impress upon their daughters, that they are not to enter upon the marriage relation until they are qualified to provide for the physical necessities of a family. Let our daughters feel that they must never attempt to enter upon the marriage relation until they shall be qualified to provide for the wants of a household, and then we shall see much, if not all, that difficulty which has been complained of here, removed." Foster believed that daughters who were raised to believe that they were also responsible for the economic well-being of a family would seek out opportunities that had previously been denied them. In so doing they would achieve independence and would also avoid marrying for money or too early. Two years later, speaking at the Woman's Rights Convention in Cleveland, Foster reiterated the point: "A young man is not fit to contract marriage, and is not reckoned worthy, until he is qualified to support a family. It should be the same with woman." In order to do this, however, she could not marry young.[5]

In a letter read into the record at the 1850 Salem, Ohio, convention, Lydia Pierson did not mince words: "The great majority of my own sex are at present incapable of doing service to their country or honor to themselves in public stations." She did not blame women themselves, however; the problem was how they were raised:

> After being taught etiquette, the hypocritical conventionalities of fashion, a little music, a little French phrases—all by rote—they are turned out to use their accomplishments for the purpose for which they have been taught to value them, namely, to win a husband and secure a settlement. They are married at seventeen, soon become mothers, are consigned to oblivion or kept alive by a round of vanity and dissipation. This picture, however humiliating, is a true representation. Such women are fit for nothing but to die, as they have lived.

For Pierson the central problem was education. If boys were given "domestic training" and girls education in the scholastic realm, and if girls were kept in school as long as boys, "we should need no conventions for revolution or reform," that is, women's rights conventions. One central reason that women were not educated longer, however, was that they were married too early. In Pierson's estimation, "early marriage, more than any other cause, prevents the development of the female intellect." Thus, as she explained it: "The greatest bane of woman, and the strongest obstacle to her elevation is the deplorable manner of early marriages.—Very few girls attain their growth, fewer still maturity of constitution and intellect, before they are made wives and mothers." Pierson believed that there were consequences to this beyond simply the detriment of the women themselves, and she used a metaphor from the farm to describe what she meant. "Every man knows that such a course must of necessity deteriorate any breed of domestic animals; and does he suppose himself an exception to the immutable laws of nature?" Pierson believed that women who gave birth when they were too young would lead to the downfall of the next generation. She explained that "woman will never be qualified to fill the positions for which her Creator endowed and designed her, until . . . rejecting early marriage." In Pierson's view this was because early marriage prevented girls' ability to be educated in a manner that would allow them to pursue the positions, plural, for which they might be suited.[6]

Pierson would have been pleased that the Blackwell family made similar arguments throughout the 1850s; indeed, it is possible that Pierson was actually influenced by their writings. Elizabeth and Emily Blackwell were the first and third women, respectively, to graduate from medical school in the United States. Their brother, Henry Brown Blackwell, a social reformer, was married to Lucy Stone, who kept her own name when they wed in 1855 (others who did the same were sometimes called "Lucy Stoners"). Their sister-in-law was Antoinette Brown Blackwell, the first woman minister ordained by an American church. All were committed to women's rights. Elizabeth Blackwell's influence on the rest of her family is especially notable in the debate about marriage, and age of marriage specifically, because it related directly to her own work in medicine. In *The Laws of Life* (1852), a series of lectures on the physical development and education of girls, Blackwell argued that the age when girls finished their education (which she said was sixteen) and the age when they had actually finished growing (between twenty and twenty-five) should be more closely aligned: girls should be allowed to continue their education past the age of sixteen, when they would be more capable students. The years between sixteen and twenty-five would attain "grandeur" for girls if they were spent "in preparation for the duties of adult life." Girls were not currently achieving this sort of grandeur or the "full preparation of a mature nature" because, according to Blackwell, "in America the large majority of marriages are made too early. A young lady is thought to be getting rather old at 20, but at 25 is already an old maid; and yet, as a general rule, before the age of 25, she is not prepared to enter on the marriage relation; it is only from 20 to

25 that the body attains its full vigor." Although these were obviously political arguments for Blackwell—she wanted girls to have more opportunities for education—they were also arguments grounded in her expertise in medicine. She believed that early marriage was physiologically harmful for girls, in part because of the sex they would be expected to have and the children that might result from it.[7]

The Reverend Antoinette Brown Blackwell spoke to similar issues at the tenth National Woman's Rights Convention in 1860. She believed it wrong that a girl's one purpose in life from the time she was fifteen should be marriage. Instead,

> Let her be taught that she ought not to be married in her teens. Let her wait, as a young man does, if he is sensible, until she is twenty-five or thirty. (Applause.) She will then know to choose properly, and probably she will not be deceived in her estimate of character; she will have had a certain life-discipline, which will enable her to control her household matters with wise judgment, so that, while she is looking after her family she may still keep her great life purpose, for which she was educated, and to which she has given her best energies, steadily in view.

Blackwell's argument was designed to demonstrate the benefits of delayed marriage, not just for girls themselves, but also for the families they would be raising.[8]

Her brother-in-law Henry Blackwell's argument against early marriage echoed and expanded on some of these themes. He explained in 1853 that young women "fall in love before they are out of their teens, and from sheer vacuity get married, when, even in a physical point of view, marriage is a monstrosity and a crime. . . . Condemned to hopeless imbecility of body and immaturity of mind, they make nothing but mere wives and mothers, and very poor ones at that." But Blackwell thought that early marriage was detrimental, not just for the women themselves, but for society more generally. He believed that American civilization was degenerating, especially as compared to the English. Although some blame might be laid at the door of alcohol, tea, coffee, tobacco, or the habits of city life, "the greater part of it, is owing to these early marriages, without strength of muscle or of brain. . . . They should be trained for an active, independent life, before and after those years when children are to be reared. They should be taught, that it is a crime to enter marriage bonds before they are properly developed." His plea was on behalf of women but was also designed to appeal to men: "For myself, I could not desire a degenerate family. I would not wish for a race which would not be head and shoulders above what I have seen. Let me say to men—select women worthy to be wives. The world is over-stocked with these mis-begotten children of undeveloped mothers." Blackwell's argument skates dangerously close to a class-based argument about proper wife- and motherhood, and no doubt he was primarily targeting middle-class men in his remarks, yet he was actually making an age-based argument: "unde-veloped" mothers were too young for marriage and produced "mis-begotten" children. If men could marry women instead of girls, they would avoid this problem. Blackwell was a devoted advocate of women's rights and a member of one of the nation's foremost families fighting for that cause, but he recog-nized that he needed to convince others by means not just of the injustice done to women but of the benefits of women's rights for all. He employed quasi-eugenic language that would gain much wider popularity later in the century and appealed to a spirit of patriotism and nationalism to make his case.[9]

THE MEDICAL CRITIQUE OF EARLY MARRIAGE

Many others also employed physiological arguments against early marriage. By the middle of the nineteenth century, a wide array of doctors, reformers, and lecturers had begun a public dialogue about the role of sex and marriage in the lives of Americans. Some were more mainstream than others and some had greater claims to medical legitimacy, but the end result was a vast swath of literature covering everything from courtship to masturbation, prostitution to childbearing. Marriage, and specifically the age of marriage, was often a compo-nent of these tracts, which were widely available throughout the United States. Bear in mind that the writers' sentiments about women's rights varied widely. To begin with, most of the authors were men. Some, however, wrote in the tradition of the women's rights advocates we have already met in the hope that they might contribute to the emancipation of women. Others were more clearly geared toward men; women's rights were not their primary concern. Instead they worried about the degeneration of civilization; they saw early marriage as a sign of this. Taken together, however, they reveal a preoccupation with the proper age of marriage from a physiological standpoint; the majority, especially among those who claimed medical expertise, advised against early marriage.[10]

Dio Lewis, who lectured around the country beginning in the 1850s, believed that open discussion and reading about sex were the best protection for women "against sexual abuses." He was opposed to early marriage. He explained that "premature marriages are bad for both parties, and that their offspring are sure to lack vitality. It is well known to cattle-breeders that if their animals breed too young their progeny are hardly worth raising." In an era before Darwinian understandings of heredity, many believed that the health of the mother descended directly to her children, affecting the march of civilization. Although Lewis acknowledged that throughout human history (in his estimation) men had married younger women and that "children of good temper and fair physical proportions may be born of girls not yet sixteen years of age, but I have not read of a single *remarkable* man who came from so young a mother." Tracts like these almost always relied on shoddy evidence and their authors' interpretations of it were usually contradictory, but in this case Lewis believed that early marriage denoted a lack of civilization. Lewis went on to document what he considered the best civilizations, where citizens married later, and then recorded the thoughts of those he considered experts on the subject, all of whom advised that women should wait to marry, till a minimum of nineteen years. He believed that the natural result of early marriage was a "puny, sickly offspring."[11]

William Alcott, one of the most widely read doctors of the mid-nineteenth century, agreed with Lewis. In *The Moral Philosophy of Courtship and Marriage* (1857), he advocated that women and men not marry till they were physically mature, which in the male came in the twenty-fifth or twenty-sixth year and in the female in the twenty-first or twenty-second. He acknowledged the "strange preference for inequality of age" that was more frequent among men, many of whom "are exceedingly fond—at least to a very great and greatly increasing extent—of being wedded to very young women," but he believed that men and women should marry those who were close in age. This was not because one might outlive the other but because of a "difference in taste, which is inseparable from age, and which forever prevents a full and complete and perfect sympathy." Although Alcott was concerned about the individual couple, in the end he also brought it around to physiological arguments about society as a whole. In *The Physiology of Marriage* (1866), Alcott warned that what he called the "new fangled doctrine of early marriage" led to "premature physical decay of the corporeal fabric," which itself would be repeated in successive generations. The argument was not so much about the best interests of the bride and groom but about what their early marriage would mean for future generations. Echoing others who took recourse in metaphors of animal husbandry, he asked: "Why, what can be more plain, than that a young tree or a young heifer which, instead of bearing fruit or rearing progeny as early as possible, should be restrained from bearing for one year, would be gaining a physical strength and vigor, and would attain to a greater average degree of strength, in fully maturity, than if it propagated itself a year earlier?" For Alcott, then, the problems of early marriage were not so much that young brides might suffer but that their progeny, and hence all of society, would do so.[12]

Some of these doctors worked in the tradition of phrenology, a now-debunked science that purported to explain behaviors and cognitive capacities by locating them in different areas of the brain. In bringing phrenology to the masses—through both lectures and widely available publications—their goals were avowedly prescriptive: they wanted to fix the ills of modern society by recommending proper sexual and marital behaviors.[13] The debate over early marriage was featured in many of their writings. Although some authors who made little claim on medicine or science might advocate early marriage, explaining that a girl "may marry at fourteen, or as soon as she attains her full stature, and experiences the usual monthly change peculiar to the sex," most phrenologists would have agreed with O. S. Fowler that "marriage should be postponed till the growth is completed, the physical organization well nigh consolidated, the judgment fully matured, and both parties have obtained a good *practical* knowledge of Physiology, as well as of the best method of nursing and educating children." Fowler's brother and fellow phrenologist, L. N. Fowler, agreed. He bemoaned that

> it is almost an every day occurrence that persons, particularly females, hurry into married life before they are fully developed, either mentally or physically, before they have either judgment, reason, or experience.
>
> Several young ladies, hardly in their teens, in New York, whose names I might mention, had an idea that it would be a fine and pleasing thing to marry, which they did, although contrary to the wishes of their parents; and, the consequences are disease, illness, dissatisfaction, and premature death.

Fowler finished these thoughts by explaining also that on marriage a woman tends to enter "at once upon the duties of a parent" and because of this she has very few opportunities for "mental culture" once married: "as education is absolutely necessary to train and educate children properly, she should, before marriage, store her mind with useful information." Even as the Fowlers and others of their ilk discouraged early marriage, often their greater concern was the children the young wives would likely bear or the future generations who would suffer if they bore them too young.[14]

THE CRUSADE OF ELIZABETH OAKES SMITH

Not so Elizabeth Oakes Smith, with whom we began. Smith was by far the most articulate opponent of early marriage in the women's rights movement and certainly the one to devote the most energy to arguing against the practice. After attending the 1850 Woman's Rights Convention in Worcester, Smith embarked on a series of ten editorials published in Horace Greeley's *New York Tribune* in 1850 and 1851 called "Woman and Her Needs." She would also publish them in a volume of the same name in late 1851. Into the later 1850s she was a regular on the lecture circuit, beginning in New England and moving west to Saint Louis, Cincinnati, and Chicago. The ideas she discussed in her editorials would surely have informed the talks she was giving across the growing nation, meaning that readers and audiences would have had access to Smith's opinions about early marriage in a variety of forms.[15]

In the editorials Smith laid out the case for women's rights as she saw it. Smith's primary concern was that woman lacked the opportunity to be an individual as man did. She argued for the "recognition of the entire individuality of Woman, her claims as a creation distinct, and one; not as a half—a supremacy—an appendage—a mere luxury for the delectation of man." Although she was not opposed to demonstrating how granting women equal rights would also benefit men, marriage, and children, her primary concern was that women themselves deserved better for their own sake. And a primary way that women suffered was through early marriage.[16]

In her fourth installment in the *Tribune*, Smith argued that girls and boys were raised differently and that this was to the detriment of girls. Boys were trained "to earn an honorable position" and allowed to make mistakes, whereas a girl "is not allowed to grow and blossom under the sweet dews of divine guardianship; to develop into holy and truthful womanhood." Instead, "the one great object, supposed to be the end and aim of womanhood, marriage, is forced upon her at every step of her life." Early marriage robbed girls of the chance to develop into womanhood on their own terms: "She is defrauded of her girlhood by premature marriage, and taught to feel a triumph in what in a true state of society would be a degradation; for surely there is something painfully sad, to say nothing of humiliating, in the sight of these baby wives to men old enough to be guides and fathers to them, and girl mothers, hardly escaped from pantelets." Here she used the same language that she would use some thirty years later when writing her autobiography: not only were girls trained for marriage when they could be training for a career, but they were robbed of their youth through early marriage. In a later installment, Smith acknowledged that men spoke of the beauty of "sweet sixteen" and the "loveliness of girlhood," explaining: "most lovely is it, and sacred should it be held; and therefore the woman should not be defrauded of the period; she should not be allowed to step from the baby-house to the marriage altar. It should be considered not only unwise to do so, but absolutely indelicate." As in her autobiography, Smith was adamant that girls have the chance to develop into womanhood before they could marry. This was, though Smith did not acknowledge it, a class-based argument, for it was generally only those girls of the middle class and higher whose parents could protect their girlhood by keeping them in school. Working-class girls or those raised on farms were working from a young age, either in their own homes or increasingly in the growing industrial economy of urban America. Postponing marriage in order to experience girlhood would have made little sense to them.[17]

Smith challenged the idea that girls matured more rapidly than boys, the logic behind their lower ages of consent to marriage and phrenologists' and doctors' advice on differential ages of marriage. She believed that it was a "popular error that our sex are earlier developed than the other, and there-fore soonest adapted to marriage"; this was male bias, in other words, not sci-ence. Instead she believed that "girls are married and perplexed with the cares of housekeeping, when the pretty ordering of 'wee things' of the playhouse would be in better keeping; they suffer the anxieties and sorrows of mater-nity at an age pitiful to contemplate." She railed against the notion that girls were created for the "one purpose of family relation" and worried that girls who married and became mothers at fifteen did so "at the expense of health, happiness, and all the appropriateness and dignity of life." And yet, "men seem quite proud of these baby-wives, when in truth they should blush at their self-ishness." Smith skirted around the issue of sex itself and the consummation of marriages between girls and men, and yet it lurks just below the surface of her writings. Arguing that "ungenial relations" produced insanity in those not old enough to comprehend marriage, Smith alluded to the shock that intercourse might present for those intellectually and physiologically unprepared for it.[18]

At times Smith seemed less to be arguing against early marriage than to be intent on shaming men out of the practice; her use of the phrase "baby wives" is indicative of this strategy, and it echoes her belief that men achieved dominance in their marriages by choosing youthful brides. At other times, she almost seemed to be indicting the "baby wives" themselves for their mar-riages. As she explained, there is "something appalling when I see a mere girl promising at the altar to love, &c. 'till death.' What does she know of human emotion, of the depths of her own soul or that of another?" Arguing that no one, "even at mature age," could actually know that they would love another forever, given the "arbitrary nature of human emotions," still, when people made this promise, "they should be of years to realize the solemn import of the words, and willing to hazard the test." A girl who was yet "blind, undiscerning, and irresponsible" was not capable of making such a promise. Smith's opposition to divorce and her concern about early marriage led her to acknowledge the truth about marriage that few others discussed openly: no matter the age of a bride or groom, it was always a great risk. This was not just because it was unequal but also because no woman (or man) could actually know how she (or he) would feel, or the spouse would act, in the future. Smith's position on youthful marriage had led her to a greater truth about the uncertainty of all marriages.[19]

Perhaps her most stringent critique of early marriage centered on what she saw as its illegality, and here she was engaging with the issues of a child's legal capability to contract that were also bedeviling judges, who had come to the conclusion (as we saw in the previous chapter) that the marriage contract was sui generis because it both created a legal relationship and changed the status of the contracting parties, creating husbands and wives. For this reason, age (or non-age, in legal terms) could not alone be enough to nullify the marriage contract. In Smith's estimation, contracts should be made between equals, both of whom were capable of understanding the terms of their consent. "For this reason," she wrote, "all contracts with children under age, with wards and idiots, are void in law." As historian Holly Brewer has demonstrated, this need for informed consent was in part a legacy of the Revolution, after which children were generally barred from contracting, from being called as witnesses, and from being held responsible for many crimes, all because they were not presumed to be fully formed enough to exercise sound reason and judgment. Almost all American jurists were agreed on this point: children could not contract. Except marriage.[20]

Picking up on precisely this discrepancy, Smith wrote:

> Now, here is a contract. One party is mature in life—experienced
> not only in the world, but in the nature of his own soul, its needs, its
> capacities, infirmities, and powers. The other party is a child, an infant
> in law, whose pen to a commercial contract would be worthless. . . .
> Yet this girl, this child, is party to a contract involving the well-being

of her whole future life; a contract by which she is consigned to
sickness, care, suffering, coercion, and her individuality completely
suppressed.

Using the actual legal language of the common law and some state statutes—
"infant" and "idiot"—to talk about those who were incapable of contracting,
she highlighted the problem with allowing children to contract marriage: "Can
she, who is an infant, an idiot in a worthless account of dollars and cents, be
capable of entering into a contract involving such tremendous interest? Can
this child, whose nature has been so outraged even before she can even understand its laws, be held responsible for after results?" Smith went on to indict
any man (which would presumably have included her husband) who would
enter such a contract with a legal infant, precisely because he was availing himself of her inexperience in gaining her assent to the marriage in the first place.[21]

Smith was astute here. She recognized that when it came to legal understandings of childhood and consent and contract, there was an established
consensus that children were incapable of binding themselves to a contract.
The main exceptions to this were marriage and military service, to which boys
routinely consented, to which they were sometimes bound by their fathers,
and from which they often found it difficult to extricate themselves using age-
based arguments. Because the marriage contract changed single people into
husbands and wives, judges often thought of it as less a contract than a status or,
at the very least, a special contract. Blackstone, who codified the common law
in his mid-eighteenth-century treatise, acknowledged that "want of age . . . is
sufficient to avoid all other contracts, on account of the imbecility of judgment
in the parties contracting; *a fortiori* therefore it ought to avoid this [marriage],
the most important contract of any." Blackstone believed that it *did* in part
void the marriage contract, because those below the ages of twelve or fourteen
could not contract marriage under the common law (or at least could have
their marriages nullified on reaching those ages). But by the mid-nineteenth
century many felt that those ages were far too young for marriage, especially
given that they were well below the age of majority (the age of legal adulthood,
twenty-one under the common law). This recalibrating of "proper" ages for
marriage was in part a consequence of the greater spread of age consciousness, particularly in the industrializing, urbanizing Northeast. The difficulty,
also not lost on Smith, was that most other contracts could be dissolved if the
parties did not meet their obligations (a conveyance of real estate, for instance,
where one party did not pay in full) or were not made for life (as in a labor

contract or a rental agreement). By contrast, the contract that female children regularly entered, marriage, was binding for life. Though divorce was increasingly available by the middle of the nineteenth century, it remained rare and for many years in many states was available only through legislative decree, not through the courts, which made it difficult and costly to obtain. Smith was pointing to an obvious hypocrisy in the law and demonstrating that the very thing that lawmakers normally used in order to regulate children's capacity to consent—their age—seemed irrelevant in the case of girls.[22]

Smith was partly correct: as we have seen, girls were everywhere permitted to marry before boys and almost always below the age of majority. The only flaw in her argument was that boys were also permitted to marry below the age of majority in all states, particularly if they had their parents' permission. Outside the realm of the law, however, Smith was on solid ground, because in comparative terms, few boys actually did marry as children, whereas many girls did so before they reached legal adulthood. And Smith's arguments were always bigger than simply legal ones: she wanted her readers to understand that this was a societal and a parental responsibility, not simply one accorded to legislators. In order for girls to stop marrying, they had to be presented with options that were more attractive, and their childhood had to be protected from adult concerns. This was not something that the law alone could remedy, though it could certainly be modified if Americans changed their view on its suitability.

The other difficulty with the marriage contract for activists like Smith was that it was universally the same. Many other contracts were individualized; the parties entering them set their own terms. Not so marriage, which had only one set of terms for all who contracted it. As a legal treatise explained of the marriage contract: "But this agreement differs essentially from all others. This contract of the parties is simply to enter into a certain status or relation. The rights and obligations of that status are fixed by society in accordance with principles of natural law, and are beyond and above the parties themselves.... They cannot modify the terms upon which they are to live together, nor superadd to the relation a single condition." And those terms, under the common law, which still governed most of what were called the "domestic relations," were almost completely unfair to women. As Smith put it, "The wife is not the help-meet for the man, but the appendage, the housekeeper, the female, of the establishment; ... her very existence is merged in that of her husband, the children of her blood are not hers; her property is not hers; she is legally dead." Elizabeth Cady Stanton agreed. In an 1860 letter to the editor of the *New York Tribune,* Stanton explained:

The contract of marriage is by no means equal. The law permits the girl to marry at twelve years of age, while it requires several years more of experience on the part of the boy. In entering this compact, the man gives up nothing that he before possessed—he is a man still; while the legal existence of the woman is suspended during marriage, and henceforth she is known but in and through the husband. She is name-less, purseless, childless—though a woman, an heiress, and a mother.

Although women's rights advocates targeted all of these things in their own right—and had achieved some success by the 1850s, especially in regard to married women's right to their own property—for Smith and others like her, early marriage was particularly problematic because the contract itself was so detrimental to women's autonomy. It was one thing for grown women to sub-mit to its terms, quite another for a girl who did not understand what she was getting herself into to agree to be bound by its strictures. That these activists recognized the cruel unfairness of the marriage contract—for all women— only intensified their belief that girls should not be encouraged or permitted to enter it.[23]

Elizabeth Oakes Smith always defended the institution of marriage, even when she criticized how it was regulated or how girls were forced into it at tender ages; indeed, she opposed divorce and often framed her objections to early marriage as being for the good of marriage itself. She claimed that she had not known "a case of discomfort in the marriage relation, in which the contract did not take place during the girlhood of the woman, when she was so young and immature that she could form no estimate of the importance of the step she took." In other words, early marriage was to blame for bad marriages. Not everyone took this tack. Perhaps the nineteenth century's most notorious critic of marriage, Victoria Woodhull, had also married young. Woodhull is remembered today as the first woman to run for president (in 1872), as one of the newspaper editors (her sister, Tennessee Claflin, was the other) who exposed the notorious Beecher-Tilton adultery scandal, and for her champi-oning of free love. Woodhull believed that legal marriage perverted the rela-tionship between a man and a woman. If instead they came together without any legal obligations to each other, they would achieve a better union; they could also leave the relationship when love left them. Woodhull did not focus on the issue of early marriage the way Smith did, but it is difficult to believe that her own early marriage did not influence her stance on the institution.[24]

Woodhull was born Victoria Claflin in 1838 in Homer, Ohio, a full thirty-two years after Smith. As one of ten children (nine of whom survived) to parents who partially depended on Victoria and Tennessee for their own subsistence, she had few of the advantages of Smith. At the age of fourteen she met Canning Woodhull, an itinerant doctor twice her age, who claimed (erroneously) to be the son of a judge and the nephew of the mayor of New York City. In part to escape her home she married him in November 1853, just two months after her fifteenth birthday. She bore her first child at sixteen. Canning Woodhull was an alcoholic given to long bouts of intoxication; he was also unfaithful and largely unable to support his family. As Victoria wrote of her first marriage (she had two others):

> I supposed that to marry was to be transported to a heaven not only of happiness but of purity and perfection. I believed it to be the one good thing there was on the earth, and that a husband must necessarily be an angel, impossible of corruption or contamination. . . .
>
> But alas, how were my beliefs dispelled! Rude contact with facts chased my visions and dreams quickly away, and in their stead I beheld the horrors, the corruption, the evils and hypocrisy of society, and as I stood among them, a young wife as I was, a great wail of agony went out from my soul, re-echoing that which came to me from almost every one with whom I came in contact. I soon learned that what I had believed of marriage and society was the nearest sham, a cloak made by their devotees to hide the realities and to entice the innocent into their snares. I found everything was reeking with rottenness.

Woodhull's solution was to swear off marriage, at least publicly (she actually married for the third time after embracing free love). As she explained it in a famous and oft-quoted 1871 speech, "I have an *inalienable, constitutional* and *natural* right to love whom I may, to love as *long* or as *short* a period as I can; to *change* that love *every day* if I please, and with *that* right neither *you* nor any *law* you can frame have *any* right to interfere." She also regularly compared marriage to "sexual slavery" and legalized prostitution. Although she did not frame her position on marriage directly in terms of her disastrous first union, or that disastrousness as a consequence of her youthfulness at the time, drawing the links between them is no great stretch. The doctrine of free love—the belief that each person's love should not be regulated by the law of marriage—would have allowed her to part from the man she had married at fifteen much sooner than she actually did. Indeed, she would never have been legally bound to him at all.[25]

Woodhull was active at a later moment than Smith and she was much more radical; by the 1870s and 1880s, a whole host of reformers were questioning marriage much more fundamentally than Smith had done. Although Smith's plan for more equal marriages depended not just on wives marrying once they had reached adulthood but also on greater opportunities for education and economic self-sufficiency for women, she still had more faith in marriage than Woodhull. But even Smith had her moments of doubt. Writing in 1851 in the *Tribune*, Smith explained of her previous columns: "I have heretofore urged the importance of denying the marriage rite to those incompetent by the laws to enter into other contracts [children]. I might say, but the sarcasm is even too severe, that a being held as an infant, a chattel, an idiot in law, never reaches her majority, and is therefore morally irresponsible even in this." By this she meant that even grown women, who shared much in common with children under the law, were legally incompetent to make the decision to marry. And in this assertion her sarcasm was not too severe. Discouraging young women from entering marriage too early no doubt would make for many happier wives, especially those among the middle class who were most able to take advantage of girlhood itself. But the laws that governed marriage, even between people of similar age, were so hopelessly skewed against women throughout the nineteenth century that the disempowerment that young girls were subject to in marriage was just a symptom of the larger problem that all married women experienced. Even Elizabeth Oakes Smith, who never divorced and had an exceptionally uncommon marriage for the nineteenth century (or indeed our own), still felt there were great limitations in marriage. Although she enjoyed the support of her husband in her publishing and speaking on women's rights and the couple gave their six sons the surname "Oaksmith" as a merger of both their names, Smith would write resignedly near the end of her life: "At best, even now a wife and mother can rarely do as she may wish, but only as she can—and to most of us this is enough."[26]

FIVE

My Little Girl Wife

The Transformation of Childhood and Marriage
in the Late Nineteenth Century

In November 1894, newspapers across the country announced the news that Civil War general Cassius Marcellus Clay, former minister to Russia and cousin of Senator Henry Clay, had married for the second time. The major focus of the stories was that he was eighty-four years old and his new bride, Dora Richardson, was fifteen. The two had met after Dora, an orphan, moved in with relatives who lived as tenants on Clay's Kentucky estate, White Hall. Clay's first marriage had ended in divorce, and his ex-wife and children all protested the marriage. But both General and Mrs. Clay defended their union, at times by force, and this, too, made headlines. When a posse of local men arrived at White Hall to claim the youthful bride, Clay fired on them with a cannon as Dora watched from an upstairs window, shouting to the crowd that she chose to stay at White Hall and look after the general. About three years after the marriage, Clay explained to a reporter,

> It was a long time before I could get her to comprehend that she was
> mistress of my big house and of the landscape about her. . . . She was
> a child and I treated her as such, and have faithfully endeavored to
> develop her mind and make a model woman of her, and believe I shall
> elevate her thoughts and aspirations. At first she sat in a high chair that

raised her feet off the floor, but she has grown beyond that and is now a budding beauty, with a perfect oval face and golden hair.

He also recounted that he had recently purchased a guitar, "for my little girl wife, who is becoming quite accomplished in music." Dora herself claimed that he had bought for her "oceans of candy, and bananas, and many other nice things."[1]

The marriage of Clay and Richardson was anomalous, both in their extreme age difference and because he was a figure of renown. That said, by the 1870s and 1880s stories about child brides began to appear regularly in newspapers across the nation, many of them documenting cases of marriage far outside the region that the paper covered. They appeared in even greater numbers during the early twentieth century. And like the reporters who covered Cassius Clay's marriage, many of these stories emphasized the childishness of the girl (and it was almost always a girl) who married. Most of these brides were not depicted as being unusually mature or large for their age: instead they were described as children. Through their descriptions, and by their very publication, the stories implicitly (and sometimes explicitly) called attention to the inappropriateness of the marriage of children.

At the same time that these stories were being published, a marriage reform movement developed in the United States. Child marriage was not the reformers' main focus—preventing divorce was—but one consequence of the focus on divorce was a reevaluation of the law that governed marriage. The logic went like this: The rise in divorce (and the numbers were rising, though incrementally) could be stemmed by barring the wrong people from marrying each other. If the right people married, they would stay married. All of this could be accomplished through passing new laws that barred certain people from marrying: the diseased, those who were already related, and those who were too young. In addition, unsuitable matches might be prevented if couples were made to wait longer between obtaining a license and becoming legally wed; mandatory waiting periods accomplished this goal. And all of this could be better regulated through increased reliance on marriage licenses and through the abolition of common-law marriage. Historian Michael Grossberg has memorably called all of these efforts "guarding the altar."[2]

These two trends, child brides in newspapers and antidivorce reformers, indicate that childhood and marriage had changed by the late nineteenth century and that those changes were spreading beyond a small group of reformers in the urban Northeast. In this chapter I focus on a number of

Cassius Marcellus Clay and Dora Richardson Clay (opposite). At the time of their marriage, Cassius Clay was a renowned Civil War general, longtime believer in slave emancipation, and former minister to Russia. Dora was an orphan living with relatives, tenants on Clay's Kentucky estate, White Hall. He was eighty-four and she was fifteen. Their marriage caused a scandal in Kentucky that rippled across the country. Both images courtesy of the Filson Historical Society, Louisville, Ky.

interrelated phenomena—publicity around child brides, purity campaigns to raise the age of consent to sex, and antidivorce reformers' campaigns to raise the age of marriage—all of which demonstrate the ways that larger numbers of Americans were grappling with the meanings of childhood, sex, and marriage. Although many of these reformers did not yet frame their concerns around protecting children themselves—their anxieties were instead about eradicating illicit sex, preventing prostitution, and protecting the good name of marriage—they nevertheless gained traction because of the growing belief that children were fundamentally different from adults and that marriage was an adult institution that needed protecting from those who might not take it seriously, children among them. Their work would have real consequences for limiting the rights of children to marry: by the later 1800s and the first decades of the twentieth century, lawmakers had raised the marriageable age in more than half the states. Through changing the laws and publicizing their efforts they had also given parents the tools to help prevent early marriage and control their children.[3]

CHILD MARRIAGE MAKES THE NEWS

Child brides began to appear in newspapers across the country during the 1870s and 1880s. Although newspapers had certainly reported on the weddings of youthful brides (and some grooms) in the antebellum era, the fact of their youth was rarely the focus of the story. It now was. Some of these stories ran in papers far removed from the regions that they covered, indicating that the stories were meant as novelty items, not necessarily to inform a readership about people whom they might actually know in their communities. Although this focus on everyday people was a longstanding tradition of the penny press, the fact that children were now seen as unfit for matrimony was new and noteworthy. In July 1872, a *San Francisco Bulletin* reporter wrote from Visalia, California, that he had happened upon a child bride of twelve, married three years earlier to a man of fifty. "Mrs. Lou Peyson, the little matron, is very small even for her age, wears short dresses, and conducts herself in most matters precisely as the child she is." In emphasizing the brides' childishness, many accounts discussed the fact that they were still in short dresses, not being old enough yet to have graduated to the longer frocks that fully grown women wore. The next year in upstate New York, a reporter for the *Albany Argus* elaborated on a child bride who had been forced into marriage by her father (for reasons unclear) when just eleven years old. The reporter explained that "in manner and general appearance she was simply a child." In 1897, the *St. Louis Republic* reported that Clementine Pope, aged fourteen, "is a beautiful child, possessing a striking figure in her short dresses." She was married in April to sixteen-year-old H. H. Brown. Marie Cecelia Kartese, married at thirteen to Michael Jones, twenty-two, in New York City in 1905, was described as "a small frail little creature." "Up until yesterday Miss Kartese had worn short dresses, all white." The *Wilkes-Barre Times* reported in 1908 in a case of one child bride citing another's seduction of her own husband in divorce proceedings that "both the child wives looked like school children, their dresses scarcely reaching their shoe tops. The two had been playmates before marriage." Last, when H. S. Hunt, thirty-five, and his eleven-year-old bride left Texas for Kansas on their honeymoon trip in 1908, Mrs. Hunt traveled on a half-fare ticket because of her age.[4]

These newspaper articles sometimes discussed the pastimes of child brides as a way to denote their youth. For instance, in 1908, fifteen-year-old Lucy DiAngelis, though a married woman, still enjoyed playing with children, and on one occasion was pretending to be a highwayman when she accidentally shot and killed six-year-old Elizabeth Dumbrosio. Helen Stobba, fourteen, due to marry her twenty-six-year-old fiancé the next week, confessed that she did not intend to give up playing with her two favorite dolls after her wedding: "I admit I like to play with dolls, and my getting married won't make me care less for them," she said. In one of the more disturbing stories, the *Philadelphia Inquirer* reported that Captain John W. Morse, forty-five, was wed to fifteen-year-old Nora Theresa Shaughnessy in June 1904. The reporter explained that the wedding "is the culmination of a romance dating back five years ago, when the captain saw little Nora, who was only ten years of age, playing in Penn Treaty Park, which is in front of her home. He had amused himself then by tossing pennies to the child and her little playmates." Nora would become stepmother to Morse's three children from a previous marriage, the youngest of whom was five years her senior. One of Nora's bridesmaids whispered to the reporter that "the white silk gown of the bride concealed a copper penny hung about her neck by a ribbon, and that it was one of the same identical pennies tossed to her by her husband five years ago."[5]

In all of these instances the girls are portrayed as being just that: girls, not prematurely developed young women who happened to be chronologically younger than they appeared or acted. Although this emphasis on their girlishness was clearly one of the ways that newspapers could sell the story, it bears noting that what would sound to our ears like clear cases of pedophilia—Captain Morse grooming little Nora Shaughnessy from her tenth birthday into his fifteen-year-old bride—are celebrated openly in church weddings and reported in major newspapers. These were men marrying children but with little of the shame and embarrassment we might associate with doing so today. Although the reporters and newspapers, by publishing the stories, clearly thought that there was something weird and titillating about the unions, there were ample numbers of American men who thought the marriages perfectly appropriate and families and communities around them that, to varying degrees, accepted and supported these decisions. There were competing understandings of childhood in play: one that understood girls below a certain age as inappropriate for marriage and another that did not. The two discourses met—and clashed—in these accounts.[6]

THE PURITY CAMPAIGNS: AGE OF CONSENT (TO SEX) LAWS

Reflecting this new understanding of childhood as distinctly different from adulthood, updated laws that criminalized nonmarital sex between a minor girl and an older man—what we now call statutory rape laws, because through statute they declare to be rape what is otherwise consensual sex—are a product of this era. Following a trumped-up 1885 press exposé of what reporters claimed was a sex trafficking ring involving young girls in England, Americans examined their laws and many were shocked to discover that in the United States the age of consent to sex was either ten or twelve (or, in the case of Delaware, seven). Reformers set about changing state laws one by one. These "purity campaigns," led largely by activists affiliated with the Women's Christian Temperance Union, who were already committed to reforming men's behavior and eradicating the double standard, were remarkably effective, transforming almost all state laws between 1885 and 1920. Thereafter it was a crime for a man to have sex with a girl below the age of sixteen or eighteen (or fourteen in Georgia), whether or not she consented. Her youthfulness meant that she was legally incapable of consenting.[7]

For all that the issues might appear similar, the campaigns to raise the age of consent to sex were fundamentally different from, and usually unrelated to, efforts to raise the marriageable age. Because they are so often confused, however, it is important to explore the logic of the purity campaigns. Doing so also illuminates the fundamentally different way in which Gilded Age reformers understood sex in and outside marriage, even in cases when the bride was legally a child. It demonstrates further that new understandings of childhood as being incompatible with marriage were usually *not* framed, at least publicly, around discomfort around married girls' sexuality.

While the purity campaigns are often seen as evidence of the beginnings of the legal codification of childhood, and to a degree this is true, it bears remembering that some reformers were primarily worried about prostitution and the reason they sought to protect *girls* was because they were not yet married. *Women* were thought to be able to know their own minds enough to say no to sex outside of marriage, but reformers also presumed they would already be married. For many, the concern was that if girls were "ruined" through premarital sex, they never would marry and would likely descend into prostitution. This was not necessarily a worry about the physiological harmfulness of youthful sex; instead, it was about keeping sex where it belonged, within marriage. It was also about reforming men.

Indicative of this is that statutory rape laws, either implicitly or explicitly, exempted marital sex. New York State's 1895 law begins, "A person who perpetrates an act of sexual intercourse with a female, not his wife, under the age of eighteen years . . . ." It was perfectly plausible to New York's legislators that a man might have a wife under the age of eighteen and that he would have sex with her. Although many states continued to have marriageable ages below the ages designated by statutory rape laws—sixteen and eighteen—the crusaders who had worked for these laws did not think about sex within marriage in the same way they did sex outside of it.[8] Indeed, they often contrasted the ability of a girl to consent "to her own ruin" with what they believed (erroneously) was her *inability* to marry at a young age. As reformer Helen Gardener asked rhetorically in an 1895 forum on the age of consent (to sex): "What good can it do any human being to have the age of consent below that at which honorable marriage or the right to sell property comes to a girl?" Although some purity reformers connected the two ages of consent (to sex and to marriage) and argued that both ages should be raised, most saw sex within marriage as safe precisely because it was marital, and it must be said that many did not have a strong understanding of marriage law, presuming that parental consent laws meant that young girls did not marry all that often.[9]

The most radical—or conservative, depending on how you see it—of the purity reformers believed that age of consent laws, of any variety, should be abolished altogether as unbefitting a civilized or Christian nation; this was because the laws tacitly implied that there was some age at which it *was* acceptable for an unmarried woman (or man) to have sex. There is a reason, after all, that these were called "purity" campaigns. Some of the most vocal proponents of the laws compromised on the ages of sixteen or eighteen only because they hoped that girls would already be married by those ages. In calling for an abolition of age-of-consent laws, the president of the Wisconsin chapter of the Women's Christian Temperance Union, Vie Campbell, explained, "We might, with greater propriety, have an age at which murder, arson, or any of the high crimes and misdemeanors could be committed, than to have an age recognized by law for this great crime." Campbell was being facetious, but her point was that in fixing on particular ages, statutory rape laws implied that premarital sex above those ages was perfectly acceptable. She thought not, and in this context her point is important because it shows the degree to which the purity campaigns, for some of their reformers, were distinctly *not* about age; they were about sex outside of marriage, no matter the age of the participants, and about preventing prostitution, which they believed followed from "ruin."[10]

Many purity reformers believed that sex in marriage was categorically different from sex outside of it, generally without much regard for the age of the wife. As Carrie Clyde Holly, a suffrage activist and one of the first women elected to the Colorado House of Representatives, explained on the floor of the Colorado house in sponsoring an age-of-consent law, "The consent for marriage is not at all like the consent mentioned in this bill. Marriage protects, and does not destroy. A man seeking her [a girl or woman] in marriage needs no law to induce him to protect her, even from himself. Marriage, if not a sacrament, is not a crime. It is the cement of society." It was as if these reformers (and Americans generally) believed that a youthful wife was no longer a child; marriage protected her and, in transforming her into a wife, made her an adult. Legally this was true, and many purity reformers seemed to abide by this belief, so profound was their investment in the powers of marriage.[11]

All of this helps us to see why many would not have put men like Captain Morse, who married fifteen-year-old Nora Shaughnessy, in the same category as those who might seduce and abandon a girl of the same age, precisely because they were making an honest woman of her and committing to her for life. Even if contemporary readers might cringe at the description of their nuptials, there was not yet a coherent idea of a pedophile in circulation, such that actions like those of Morse would be seen as characterizing a particular personality that should be avoided, condemned, or imprisoned. Even those older men who seduced girls and then abandoned them were not generally described as perverted; rather, they were doing what all men might be presumed to want to do if they could get away with it. They were bad, not sick. Statutory rape laws were designed to curb a double standard seen as prevalent enough that it was a problem for all men, not a small subset who seemed to prefer sex with "underage" girls. So although there was a good deal of activity in the late nineteenth and early twentieth centuries to protect girls from precocious sex, the drive to raise the marriage age did not come from the same campaign, because marital sex, even at young ages, was usually presumed to share a sanctity and a safety with marriage more generally.[12]

THE MARRIAGE AND DIVORCE REFORM MOVEMENT

Whereas the campaign to raise the age of consent to sex was unrelated to worries about youthful marriage—precisely because of reformers' faith in the magic of marriage—other reformers concentrating on preventing divorce were absolutely concerned with youthful brides and grooms. Divorce had been available under limited circumstances from the colonial period, particularly in the North, but following the American Revolution most states had liberalized their divorce laws to expand the grounds on which a person could sue for divorce from the original ground, infidelity, to include desertion and cruelty. Some went so far as to include an omnibus clause, which allowed judges to award divorces for reasons that might not fit within the traditional grounds, thus expanding the availability of divorce. Although it is undeniable that making divorce more accessible did lead to the end of more marriages, it is more important to understand that the only reason that states changed their divorce laws in the first place was because Americans were changing their understanding of marriage. Even though states retained the need to prove fault (no-fault divorce was a century away), more and more Americans were coming to believe that unhappy husbands and wives, particularly those who were ill treated, should be able to end their marriages.[13]

The increased availability of divorce may have been a godsend for the couples that took advantage of it, but those who believed in lifelong marriage met the rising numbers with fear and trepidation. In one way, the antidivorce reformers were a throwback; most were religiously inclined (many were ministers), and their fear about the rise in divorce was that people did not fully appreciate the religious obligation that they believed inhered in marriage. What they bemoaned was that by the end of the nineteenth century, marriage had been transformed into a relationship not of religious duty but instead of love. This understanding of marriage led some couples, almost inevitably, to want to exit their marriages when they no longer loved each other. To document the problem, Congress for the first time passed a resolution charging the head of the U.S. Department of Labor with collecting and tabulating a nationwide report on the incidence of marriage and divorce across the country (or at least where states collected the data). Carroll Wright released *A Report on Marriage and Divorce in the United States* in 1889 and included a detailed description of the marriage and divorce laws in each state. A second volume followed in 1909. Both reports demonstrated what had prompted their release: divorce was on the rise. To combat the rising divorce rate, many urged restricting the grounds for divorce, or doing as South Carolina did, and barring the practice altogether. But most were more reasonable, arguing that divorce needed to be available for those in dire need. Some believed that the better strategy was to make it harder to marry in the first place; this would prevent people from marrying who were more likely to divorce.[14]

This is where age restrictions come in. In an 1884 piece in the *North American Review*, commentator Noah Davis argued that "restrictions ought also to be imposed upon the marriage of infants. The common-law rule of twelve years for females and fourteen for males is not a fit or decent one for this country. The age should be at least fifteen and eighteen years." Davis spent most of the article railing against "the great antagonizing evil" of divorce; though his main concern here was not so much about protecting children as it was protecting marriage, he clearly subscribed to ascendant understandings of childhood that made it incompatible with marriage. So, too, did William C. Robinson, a Yale law professor. In an 1881 article called "The Diagnostics of Divorce," he explained that the "most prolific source of the disease [divorce] proves to be the unfitness of young married people for the discharge of their marital obligations." He believed that it was "absurd that an infant, who cannot bind himself to pay a borrowed dollar, is permitted to enter the most sacred of relations. . . . No person should be marriageable under the age of 21, and a marriage celebrated between persons, either of whom is under age, should be *ipso facto* void." Again, even as Robinson relied on middle-class notions of protected childhood that were common by the later nineteenth century, he framed the problem not as being about suffering children (or suffering women, as Elizabeth Oakes Smith did) but about where that sort of suffering might lead: divorce.[15]

Even though age of marriage was never the primary target of the marriage reform movement, because they cared most about divorce, increasing the marriage age was an instrumental way of preventing divorces. So, too, were instituting waiting periods between application for license and marriage, as well as publication of banns to alert parents that their children might be planning to marry. One of the problems, however, in proposing changes to both marriage and divorce law was the great variety of laws from state to state. A couple unable to marry in one state (because of age or parental consent, for instance) could easily cross state lines and marry elsewhere. Or a couple who lived in a state with strict divorce law could go to a state known to be a divorce mill (Indiana was one), where rules were laxer. Critics referred to these practices as migratory marriage and divorce. As one put it in 1882, "A citizen of the United States journeying with his wife from Maine to Louisiana, passes, in succession, within thirty hours, under a dozen different systems of law regulating the relation that UNITES them, systems differing as to the nature of marriage, the manner of contracting it, the consequences of divorce, the effect in one State of a divorce decreed in another, and in very many other respects." This individual state control of marriage meant that the problem had no easy solution.[16]

Two seemed feasible. From the mid-1880s, nearly every year through the early 1930s, at least one member of Congress proposed an amendment to the Constitution that would allow the federal government to regulate marriage. This proposal had its fair share of critics, which I discuss in Chapter 7, but it also had many supporters. With such an amended Constitution, Congress could pass laws to make both marriage and divorce uniform across the United States, making it more difficult for a couple to evade the laws of their home state because those laws would, of course, be the same everywhere. The other solution, and it amounted to the same thing by a different route, was to make state laws uniform by having individual states adopt a common standard. The National Conference of Commissioners on Uniform State Laws, as early as 1895 weighed in, recommending a number of uniform laws on marriage and divorce, including that all states institute the ages of eighteen and fifteen for boys and girls, respectively, as the minimum marriageable ages. Speaking at the World's Congress of Jurisprudence and Law Reform in 1893, Edmund Bennett argued that allowing young people to marry "before the characters of the parties are formed," "not only leads to many unhappy marriages, but sooner or later naturally lands the parties in the divorce court." He advocated raising the marriageable ages to eighteen and twenty-one, explaining that "uniformity here and in the other essentials of marriage is not only desirable but imperative." The National Divorce Reform League followed these developments, reporting affirmatively that the National Commission had recommended fifteen and eighteen as the minimum marriageable ages for girls and boys, respectively, in 1896.[17]

RAISING THE MARRIAGEABLE AGE

It is no wonder that this much conversation about raising the marriageable age would lead to changes in the law, though this occurred slowly over the second half of the nineteenth century and increased in the 1890s and early twentieth century. Including both states and territories that would later become states, three states changed their law in the 1860s (Kansas, New Jersey, and Texas), seven in the 1870s (California, Georgia, Indiana, Missouri, New Mexico, North Carolina, and the Kingdom of Hawai'i), five in the 1880s (Arizona, Idaho, New Hampshire, New York, and Ohio), and eight in the 1890s (Michigan, North Dakota, Rhode Island, South Dakota, Tennessee, Utah, West Virginia, and Washington, D.C.). Thus, over forty years, twenty-two states and Washington, D.C., changed their laws: almost six changes per decade on average, with a clear increase toward the century's end. These modifications included raising the minimum marriageable age (from twelve to thirteen for girls in New Hampshire in 1887, for instance); instituting minimum ages where they had not previously existed (fourteen and seventeen for girls and boys in Georgia in 1873, for instance); or changing the ages below which a child might need parental consent (below eighteen for girls in Michigan in 1895). Almost all of these states or territories raised the qualifications in some way, and those that lowered them did so in the earliest decades, sometimes then revising them upward again. The trend, however, was clearly toward making it harder for boys and girls to marry young, recognizing that marriage was incompatible with childhood and that children became spouses who were more likely to divorce. Many of these laws were also passed in states where previously there had been no minimum ages and the new laws were, in essence, catching up to the rest of the country.[18]

Discussions of the law in the press help to make this clear. When California lawmakers were drafting a new civil code in 1871 and 1872 that included a recommendation to institute minimum marriageable ages, the editors of California newspapers weighed in on the proposed changes. Their commentary gives us a good sense of the combined concerns for childhood and the stability of marriage that were sweeping the nation by the 1870s. The editors of the *Sacramento Daily Union* believed that the current laws, which permitted children at the common-law ages to marry with parental permission, were "so shocking to common sense and popular judgment, and so dangerous to the well-being of the parties themselves, that some better limit ought to be established. Either raise the age of consent to fifteen and eighteen, or make the marriage absolutely void if consummated without the consent of parents or guardians or a Probate Court." The *Daily Alta California* had stronger language. Objecting both to the wording of the new code and to the legal precedents that preserved minors' marriages (as in *Parton v. Hervey*), the editors wrote: "We find nothing in the Code preventing children of the most immature years from marrying—nothing to prevent a boy of twelve and a girl of ten from becoming adults by marriage, with full power to sell their real estate and make such contracts as others can make." Here they were also noting the power that marriage had to turn children legally into adults, which they clearly believed was absurd. They explained cynically that "they are men and women in the eyes of the law, except that the little man would not be able to vote or hold office." They also commented on the provisions for the annulment of marriage, which was sometimes available to those who married below the legal marriageable age (proposed at fifteen and eighteen in the code): "If you are a girl under fifteen, or a boy under eighteen, and your bliss is not as extatic [*sic*] as you anticipated, the courts will annul the marriage for you and set you free." This editorial combined a new understanding of the inappropriateness of marriage for young people with the rising fear that their marriages would lead inexorably to divorce (or its legal cousin, annulment). It also highlighted, albeit cynically, the changed expectations for marriage: spouses now were expecting ecstasy.[19]

If change before 1900 was gradual, after the turn of the century more states (and future states) embraced the trend of raising both the established minimum marriageable ages and the ages below which children required parental consent. This trend is the clearest example of legislatures that were rethinking the proper age of marriage in light of changes to understandings of childhood and fears about the rising divorce rate. In the first decade of the twentieth century, eight states and the District of Columbia passed legislation modifying the marriage age in some way, and in the second decade, seven states also did so (two of them, Arizona and Kansas, did so in both decades). All the laws made it more difficult for children to marry at younger ages or limited their ability to do so without their parents' consent. Many were passed without much fanfare, some clearly mimicking nearby states and others being passed at the urging of local women's groups and legislative reformers.[20]

Perhaps no state was more active in amending its marriage laws than New York, not just as they related to age but in ways that indicate how legislators were trying to gain control over the process of becoming married in the Empire State. Between 1850 and 1900, the state legislature amended its

marriage law twelve times and in the twenty years following 1900 changed it at
least eighteen more times. Many of these revisions were minor and concerned
the registration of marriages, those who were qualified to perform a marriage,
and marriage license fees. But it is also clear that New York was continually
faced with new challenges when it came to the issue of early marriage. Following the repeal of its minimum marriageable ages in 1830 (discussed in Chapter
1), the only statutes that New York maintained relating to age of marriage were
two midcentury laws: one that made it a crime to take a girl below the age of
fourteen and marry her without parental permission, and one that allowed a
parent to bring a suit to have the marriage of a daughter nullified if she married
below the same age. In 1887, New York amended the latter law to make the
age sixteen instead of fourteen and to set minimum marriageable ages: sixteen
for girls and eighteen for boys. As the *New York Herald* explained, the nam-
ing of those ages did not actually prevent children below them from marrying
because the law did not declare their marriages void, merely voidable. The law
did, however, "make it a misdemeanor for any minister or magistrate to solemnize a marriage when either of the parties is known to him to be under the age
of legal consent," thus putting the onus on the official to verify the parties' ages
or risk prosecution. In 1896, however, the legislature repealed the minimum
marriageable ages and passed a new comprehensive law on marriage. This law
stipulated that any marriage contracted below the age of eighteen (for girls or
boys) could be annulled under certain conditions, but it set no minimum ages
or ages below which consent was required. New York's minimum ages would
thus have been twelve and fourteen.[21]

In the first decade of the new century, New York instituted eighteen and
twenty-one as the ages below which a girl and boy needed parental consent
(in 1907). The state also declared that children of a marriage annulled for
lack of age were to be legitimate (1903), and then it loosened the parental
consent law to enable children of divorce or children with only one parent
living (or living in state) to obtain permission from only one parent (1912).
Four years later it declared that annulments were open not just to children
below the age of eighteen (which the 1896 statute had declared) but to any
child who was below the age where parental consent was required. This
would extend the possibility of annulment to twenty-one for boys, though
only so long as they did not have the permission of one or both parents.
Many of these changes were supported not just by marriage reformers and
lawmakers who passed them but also by ministers who were increasingly
concerned about the ways couples seeking to circumvent the laws might take

advantage of their position as officiant. All of these changes demonstrate two things: first, that New York was gradually regulating the ability of its children to marry, and second, that some of those children were marrying anyway, hence the need for more loopholes in consent laws and the greater accessibility to annulment when those youthful marriages turned sour. New York was an extreme case in the number of times it modified its marriage law and in being a state without a minimum marriageable age for large stretches of time, indeed for passing and then repealing such ages more than once. But precisely because New York was home to a large contingent of marriage reformers and, because of its location in the industrialized Northeast, an early subscriber to the belief that marriage was inappropriate for children because of their age, it makes sense that New York would have such a conflicted relationship with its marriage laws.[22]

THE USES OF PARENTAL CONSENT

State legislators placed great emphasis on parental consent in writing these laws. Although only some states had minimum marriageable ages below which no one was supposed to marry, almost all had ages below which a girl or boy needed her or his parents' consent to do so (table 5.1). The New England colonies had first written their laws this way, but increasing numbers of states were falling into this line of thinking. It is possible to read this adoption of parental permission by more states as a reflection of the changes wrought by urbanization, industrialization, and mobility. Insisting that children gain their parents' consent was one way of preserving patriarchal authority in the face of a society that presented youthful people with many more options outside their natal homes and many more ways to defy their parents. These laws put the onus on parents to decide whether their children were ready for marriage and, just as important, whether the parents were ready to be without their children's labor. Because marriage legally turned children into (differently gendered versions of) adults, these laws somewhat paradoxically said that people below certain ages were too young to make the decision to marry on their own, but if their parents consented, then marriage could transform them into adults who now were capable of making such decisions. They were now legal adults, but only because *real* adults had said that they could be. It is not that this was an inherently flawed strategy; it is more that it demonstrates an instance where the law, in attempting to meet a variety of circumstances, produced contradictions around childhood and marriage.

Table 5.1. Changes in Marriageable Age and Age of Consent, 1865–1920

State (Year Became State)	Marriage Ages in 1865 or When First Passed (Year)—Girls/Boys Marriageable Minimums; *Age below which Consent Required*	Marriage Ages in 1920—Girls/Boys Marriageable Minimums; *Age below which Consent Required*	Change
Massachusetts (1788)	*18/21*	*18/21**	Same
New Hampshire (1788)	12/14	13/14; *16/18*	Raised
Connecticut (1788)	*21/21*	*21/21*	Same
Rhode Island (1790)	–	*21/21*	Raised
Vermont (1791)	*18/21*	*18/21*	Same
Maine (1820)	*18/21*	*18/21*	Same
Delaware (1787)	*18/21*	*18/21*	Same
New Jersey (1787)	*21/21**	*18/21**	Lowered
Pennsylvania (1787)	*21/21*	*21/21*	Same
New York (1788)	–*	*18/21*	Raised
Virginia (1788)	*21/21**	12/14; *21/21**	Same
Maryland (1788)	*16/21*	*18/21*	Raised
Georgia (1788)	–	14/17; *18/–*	Raised
South Carolina (1788)	–*	14/18; *18/18**	Raised
North Carolina (1789)	14/16*	14/16; *18/18**	Raised
Kentucky (1792)	12/14; *21/21**	12/14; *18/21**	Lowered
Tennessee (1796)	–	*18/18*	Raised
Louisiana (1812)	12/14; *21/21*	12/14; *21/21*	Same
Mississippi (1817)	*18/21**	*18/21**	Same
Alabama (1819)	14/17; *18/21**	14/17; *18/21**	Same
Missouri (1821)	*18/21*	15/15; *18/21*	Raised
Arkansas (1836)	14/17; *18/21*	14/17; *18/21*	Same
Florida (1845)	*21/21**	*21/21**	Same

Texas (1845)	12/14; *18/21*	14/16; *18/21*	Raised
West Virginia (1863)	12/14; *21/21**	16/18; *21/21*	Raised
Ohio (1803)	14/18; *18/21*	16/18; *18/21*	Raised
Indiana (1816)	14/17; *18/21**	16/18; *18/21*	Raised
Illinois (1818)	14/17; *18/21*	16/18; *18/21*	Raised
Michigan (1837)	16/18	16/18; *18/–*	Raised
Iowa (1846)	14/16; *18/21*	14/16; *18/21*	Same
Wisconsin (1848)	15/18; *18/21*	15/18; *18/21*	Same
Minnesota (1858)	15/18; *18/21*	15/18; *18/21*	Same
Kansas (1861)	12/15; *18/21*	16/18; *18/21*	Raised
Nebraska (1867)	16/18; *18/21* (1866)	16/18; *18/21*	Same
North Dakota (1889)	15/18 (1877)	15/18; *18/21*	Raised
South Dakota (1889)	15/18 (1877)	15/18; *18/21*	Raised
California (1850)	*18/21*	15/18; *18/21*	Raised
Oregon (1859)	15/18; *18/21*	15/18; *18/21*	Same
Nevada (1864)	16/18; *18/21*	16/18; *18/21*	Same
Colorado (1876)	*18/21* (1864)	*18/21*	Same
Montana (1889)	–	16/18; *18/21*	Raised
Washington (1889)	*18/21* (1854)	15/–; *18/21*	Raised
Idaho (1890)	16/18; *20/21* (1864)	*18/18; 18/18*	Lowered
Wyoming (1890)	16/18; *21/21* (1869)	16/18; *21/21*	Same
Utah (1896)	–	14/16; *18/21*	Raised
Alaska (1959)	18/21 (1900)	18/21	Same
Hawai'i (1959)	12/14; *18/20* (1842)	15/18; *18/20*	Raised
Oklahoma (1907)	15/18 (1890)	15/18; *18/21*	Raised
New Mexico (1912)	–/21 (1863)	15/18; *18/21*	Raised
Arizona (1912)	*16/18* (1865)	14/18; *18/21*	Raised
Washington, D.C. (1790)	12/12; *18/21* (1857)	14/16; *18/21*	Raised

* Crime or punishment for marrying a girl below certain age.
Sources: statutes and codes in chapter 5, notes 18, 20, 21, 22.

There is no way to know what a majority of parents thought about their children marrying. Some probably encouraged it, particularly for daughters who might be marrying a man who could provide for them. Some consented if they lived in areas where early marriage was the norm; the parents themselves might well have married young. Others were clearly opposed, perhaps because marriage would deprive them of a daughter's or son's service, because they feared that their child was being married for the money, or because, like many, they had come to believe that marriage in the teenage years was inappropriate. These last cases are prime examples of the new doctrine of marriage—that it should be based on the free and loving choice of both parties—running head-long into evolved notions of childhood as a stage of life deserving of protection and defined in part through children's *inability* to make choices. Parents were objecting to their children's marital choices at least in part because children themselves were making them.

Because of this emphasis on parental consent, clerks whose job it was to issue marriage licenses were a key site where parents could call on the state to help them regulate their children; local government acted as a wedge to maintain parental authority. Some county clerks and registers of deeds kept the paperwork that allowed them to issue marriage licenses to minors as well as the letters that denied that consent. Although it is impossible to gauge which was more common because we do not know the method by which these county officials saved what they did and what made its way to the archives, a sampling of North Carolina denials of consent allows us to see the way that parents, usually fathers, spoke of their children's plans to marry. We can see the willfulness of children in pursuit of their goal and parental resistance to that goal. The frequent insistence on chronological age, while necessary under the statute, is also indicative of a moment when numerical age was used as a means to argue that children should not be allowed to be self-determining, that they still belonged under the authority of their parents.[23]

On January 16, 1913, Joseph Campbell of Maiden, North Carolina, wrote a letter to the register of deeds for Lincoln County: "This is to notify you that you are not to issue license for my daughter Susie Campbell to marry any one, she being under lawful age." The register of deeds, W. H. Sigmon, responded the next day to ask that Campbell write immediately with Susie's exact age. He explained that he was legally obligated to issue a marriage license to any two people who both claimed under oath to be eighteen years of age and that some were under the mistaken impression "that 21 is the lawful age." Campbell replied that Susie was "not quite 16 years of age." He continued: "Any certificate purporting to be from me will not be genuine." The certificate to which he referred would have been his written permission allowing Susie to marry. Although North Carolina statute did not forbid a girl of Susie's age from marrying (fourteen was the marriageable age for girls, sixteen for boys), state law did mandate parental consent for those below the age of eighteen and made obtaining a marriage license for those below eighteen "under false pretenses" a misdemeanor.[24]

Almost all the rest of the correspondence is one-sided, but many of the same themes are present: parents calling on the state to regulate their children and prevent them from marrying too early. In 1902, J. C. Capel wrote to his county register of deeds: "I am informed that my daughter (Edna) and Andy Bowers are expecting to run away and get married. This is to notify you that Edna is only 17 years old and that I am opposed to the marriage." In 1906, the register of deeds for Stanly County in Albemarle, North Carolina, wrote to his colleague in Montgomery County to let him know that Frank Blalock, a Montgomery resident, feared that his seventeen-year-old son, Littleton, was about to elope with "one Miss Hinson." Blalock had requested that neither register issue the license. On April 3, 1912, Livvie Burns wrote to the register of deeds of Halifax County to ask that he refuse to issue a marriage license to James Gibbs, who intended to marry her daughter, Lizzie, who was fourteen. These were fairly straightforward requests made by parents who suspected that their children might be contemplating marriage with specific people and who opposed those unions because of either the prospective spouse or their child's age, or both. They could call on county officials to help them stop the unions because their children were young enough that they required parental consent. But that they wrote to the registers of deeds at all indicates that they feared their children were on the verge of defying parental wishes. Doing so through marriage would effectively terminate the rights that parents had in their children, and it was at least partially for this reason that parents sought to bar the children from marrying.[25]

Other requests were more curious. In December 1914, a parent named A. M. Lutz wrote to the register of deeds of Lincoln County: "I hereby forbid you to issue marriage license to my son Fred A. Lutz to mary [*sic*] any one without my consent in writing, as he is only 16 years old." Lutz did not specify a prospective bride, but was quite clear that Fred did not have permission to marry, no matter who she was. Two years earlier, in July 1912, a parent named C. A. Spencer similarly forbade the marriage of daughter Pearl Spencer, "she being only 14 years of age," "to any one." Exceptional among notices of this kind is a 1917 missive that seems to have been mass-produced. Printed on cheap newsprint, it is headed "WARNING" and explains: "I hereby forbid any one to issue marriage license, convey or assist in anyway, for the marriage of my daughter, Candas, who is only 15 years of age. S. R. Beam, Bessemer City, North Carolina." Beam sent the notice to the register of deeds for Lincoln County, though he lived in Gaston County; he may have had the notices produced in bulk and sent to many counties in order to prevent his daughter from marrying anywhere in the state. It is unclear, however, whom any of these parents thought their children might be attempting to wed. Perhaps they did not say because they felt it necessary only to name their own children, but some of the letters are quite clear that sons and daughters be forbidden from marrying "any one," suggesting either that the children had a number of options or that the parents simply suspected that marriage might be one way to escape their own households, an escape they hoped to prevent.[26]

Some parents did not fully understand the state statute and attempted to bar their children from marrying even when they were legally entitled to do so. In March 1913, Mrs. L. B. Conrad wrote to the register of deeds of Lincoln County to forbid her son Russell from marrying Linda Ward. She noted that he was nineteen years old, which in North Carolina entitled him to marry without parental permission. Others used the phrase "not of age" or "under the lawful age," as Joseph Campbell had, though they did not specify what they believed that age to be. Combining both of these trends—prohibition of a child legally entitled to marry and a blanket denial without regard to that child's actual prospective spouse—in January 1913, a parent named P. V. Cobb wrote to the register. "If any body comes for Grover Cobb license. Do not let them have them, he is not but (18) eighteen years old. I don't much think he will come but if he does be sure and don't let him have any." Because Grover seems to have been eighteen, his parent, probably his father, was incorrect in his belief that he could forbid his son from marrying, but noteworthy here is that he is not even sure Grover wanted to marry; this was just a preventative measure in case Grover should decide he might want to avail himself of the option. Even the remote possibility of marriage was worth attempting to prevent for this North Carolina parent.[27]

Another parent, F. L. Little, in an almost illegible note, gave consent for his or her child to marry because "they are going to Run of[f] to S. C. anyway to marry if they don't mar[r]y here." This letter is not dated, but if it comes from the same period as the other letters filed along with it, it was a moment

WARNING

I hereby forbid any one to issue marriage license, convey or assist in anyway, for the marriage of my daugnter, Candas, who is only 15 years of age.
June 23, 1917.   S. R. BEAM,
                              Bessemer City, N. C.

Notice forbidding the marriage of Candas Beam. Candas's father, S. R. Beam, had this notice printed on newsprint and may have sent it to county clerks across North Carolina in an effort to prevent his daughter Candas from marrying. Beam was using updated marriage law and local government to prevent his daughter from leaving his home via marriage. Image courtesy of the State Archives of North Carolina.

in which South Carolina had just instituted an age of consent to marriage. In 1911, the state updated its statute mandating consent for those below age eighteen and prohibiting the issuance of a license to boys below eighteen and girls below fourteen. Even if this letter was sent after 1912, it is plausible that Little's child simply did not know that the law had changed, assuming that there was still no age of consent to marry in South Carolina. Either way, Little was resigned: a parent giving consent but only because he knew he had no chance of stopping his child, that child being willful enough to run to another state if s/he did not have parental permission.[28]

Filed in among these letters forbidding officials to issue licenses are also many letters of consent, both for children who legally did not require it and for those who did, some as young as fourteen.[29] There are also scribbled memos where a register has simply noted two names and ages with the words "Forbidden" or "Consent." Presumably these were moments when parents visited in person to make their wishes known and the register kept a record so that he would remember when the applicants came to his office. Also included are boilerplate refusals of consent on official stationery, signed with an *X*. These seem to have been written by a register of deeds and then signed by a parent who was concerned enough to come to his office but unable to write a letter to convey his or her wishes. They demonstrate that even illiterate parents in rural North Carolina had been touched by age consciousness. Taken as a whole, they attest to a high degree of interaction between local residents and their county officials regarding their children but also, more important for our purposes, to a concerted effort to control those children and, in many cases, to deny them the right to marry as they seemed to have wished. Although few parents said precisely why they forbade the marriages, most made mention of their children's ages and asserted their rights as guardians of minors to make those decisions for them. This heightened oversight makes most sense when read in the context of a society that was increasingly understanding childhood as a separate and protected stage of life, cordoned off from adulthood, and fundamentally incompatible with the rights and duties of marriage. In partial acknowledgment of this, C. C. Rowe wrote to his local register in 1914: "Please do not issue any marriage license to any one for Rose Bud Lowe my daughter. She is only a child and don't know what she is doing. There is to[o] many children getting married now so turn any one down that ask for papers for her."[30]

Dora and Cassius Clay, whom we met at the beginning of this chapter, divorced within a few years of marrying, Dora retaining a farm that Cassius had given her as they separated amicably. Dora remarried about four years after her first marriage, and newspapers around the country covered that story, too. Cassius Clay died seven years after marrying Dora, in 1903. It was because of high-profile marital endings and new beginnings like theirs that reformers pushed for laws that would protect both childhood and the institution of marriage. Dora and Cassius, especially after their divorce, served as a symbol (albeit in extreme form) of all that was going wrong with the institution of marriage: inappropriately matched couples who seemed to marry on a whim and did not take the obligations of marriage seriously, thus winding up divorced. One way to prevent marriages like this one was to limit the ability of minors to contract marriages at all. In a moment when children were increasingly understood as unfit for most of the rights and responsibilities of adulthood, this made a good deal of sense to increasing numbers of Americans. Marriage had largely been redefined as a union entered for love and companionship. Because childhood had also been redefined, however, Americans increasingly saw children as incapable of making the choice to contract marriage.[31]

As we shall see in the next chapter, however, and like the willful children of North Carolina whose parents sought to bar them from marrying, many of these new laws met with substantial resistance by young people. Throughout the late nineteenth and early twentieth centuries they continued to marry illegally; one of the effects of this was to contest the very status of "children" that legislators were working so hard to offer them.

SIX

I Did and I Don't Regret It

Child Marriage and the Contestation of Childhood, 1880–1925

On July 7, 1908, Imogene Glenn and Grover Hollopeter were married in Olympia, Washington. She was fourteen, he nineteen; they had known each other for about four years and had been "going together" since Easter Sunday of that year. Because Washington mandated parental consent below twenty-one for boys and eighteen for girls in order to issue a marriage license, Grover and his sister Edith Gilbert obtained the signed consent from his parents, while Imogene forged her own mother's signature. Following a ceremony by a fully licensed minister, the Hollopeters left for a trip through Reston, Tacoma, and North Yakima, Washington. By this point, Imogene's parents had discovered what their daughter had done, and as the newlyweds made their way back home via Tacoma, police intercepted them and took the couple into custody. Imogene's parents (whom she later accused of abuse) took their daughter home and refused to let her see her new husband. As Imogene explained to the *Morning Olympian*, "Grover and I love each other and that's all there is to it. We have been planning our marriage for some months and we decided that we should be married last Tuesday. It's no worse for me to get married at 14 than it is for girls to get married at that age in the olden times. They made good wives and good mothers then and I don't see that piling up years upon a girl makes her love a man any better when she's older."[1]

Following in the now well-worn path of Thomas Parton, whom we met in Chapter 3, Grover petitioned for a writ of habeas corpus, claiming that the Glenns were holding Imogene illegally. The Glenns responded with a suit to have the marriage annulled outright. The trial in Thurston County Superior Court primarily investigated whether Grover and Imogene were capable, because of their age, of being married in the first place; whether they had parental permission; and whether Grover had coerced Imogene into the marriage. Imogene claimed that she had not been coerced and admitted that she had signed on behalf of her mother, though with her mother's permission and in her presence; this claim seems dubious (and indeed Mrs. Glenn denied it). The issue of the couple's fitness for marriage was of special interest to her counsel. Lawyers for both sides dwelt at length on their chronological ages. Asked if he knew when he was born, Grover answered, "No sir, I don't know exactly," but then explained that he knew that he was nineteen because his parents had told him so and because it was written in the family Bible (which was later entered into evidence). Grover's mother, Clara Hollopeter, also averred that she was positive that Grover had turned nineteen on July 4 but could not say in which year he was born. His father, when asked if he thought it wise for "a boy of 18 and a girl of 14 to go out into the world," responded, "If they saw fit, yes." Grover was also asked how long he had been out of school (two or three years, he believed), what he did for a living (worked in the oyster beds), how much he made (about four or five dollars a day), and whether he was under his father's control (he was not).[2]

Nat Glenn, Imogene's father, claimed that his daughter was fourteen and that he thought she had been born on February 14 or 15. In a petition to the court the Glenns' lawyer explained that Imogene was a "minor child" and that her parents had a duty to "protect and control her." The lawyer further argued that because Grover himself was still a minor, he was "not capable to maintain an action at law to recover the person of the said Imogene or any other." Claiming that Grover had no house or means of supporting himself, the Glenns' lawyer said that Grover certainly could not support their daughter. Not to be outdone, Grover responded through his lawyer that "he is physically a full grown man, that he is able to earn a livelihood for himself and sufficient to support his wife; that he already has some property and has made plans for a home for his said wife."[3]

The questions, answers, and various petitions, even though they were asked or written in a language designed to accord with the statutory law, reveal conflicting understandings of age, as well as confusion about its meaning and import. First, although everyone concerned knew that Imogene and Grover were quite specifically fourteen and nineteen, they also demonstrated varying levels of confusion about when exactly they were born or how they knew their precise ages, even in court, when they had presumably known that they would be asked these questions. The Glenns and the Hollopeters were aware of calendar age, but it does not seem to have been central to their understanding of their children. Second, calendar age competed with physical ability and financial stability in determining what counted as adulthood. The legal statutes on which the Glenns relied stipulated particular ages below which a person was a minor and thus incapable of marriage without consent. But Grover and Imogene based their arguments on Grover's job, his income, and Imogene's love for her husband, none of which they seemed to believe were contingent on chronological age. They had a functional understanding of their capability for marriage rather than a bureaucratic and legal one. It was not that they were unaware of their ages or that those ages denied them certain privileges, marriage among them, it was that they disagreed with the law. They did not believe that age *mattered* in the way that the Glenns or the state of Washington did.

Imogene's parents were successful in their suit, but Grover Hollopeter appealed the ruling to the Washington Supreme Court. The court ruled in his favor, stating that in the absence of a statute declaring a marriage without a properly executed license to be absolutely void, the marriage must be held valid. Parties who had forged the documents or an official who had wrongfully performed the marriage could be prosecuted, but the couple remained married. The justices declared that the bride was "within the common law age of consent," twelve, and thus capable of consenting to the marriage. Both court and newspaper accounts were clear that the Hollopeters had consummated their marriage, but the court stipulated that Washington's statutory rape law, which criminalized sex with a girl under eighteen, could not apply to the couple. Of the groom the court declared that "the ordinary legal consequences follow his marriage, and he is entitled to the society and services of his wife." The court also explicitly held that marriage emancipated the Hollopeters from their parents, in essence making them adults before they reached the legal age of majority. The Hollopeters had used marriage to emancipate themselves and to become legal adults.[4]

The logic in *In re Hollopeter* was almost exactly the same as that laid out in *Parton v. Hervey*, decided in Massachusetts more than half a century earlier, and even though the justices did not cite that case, Grover's counsel certainly did. Although the legal justification for upholding the marriage of a minor had not changed in those fifty years, much else had, and in ways that might have made marriage look particularly appealing to minors. We cannot know precisely why Imogene Glenn and Grover Hollopeter married—aside from the usual combination of romance and pragmatism that still sends millions of couples to the altar—but a number of factors might have made marriage appealing to minors in the late nineteenth and early twentieth centuries. As in earlier eras, marriage legitimized children who, born out of wedlock, would otherwise live under the stain of illegitimacy. It also retroactively legitimized premarital sex, "righting the ruin" of a girl's loss of virginity. As more and more girls, particularly in the working class, had sex before marriage, this was crucial, both for them and for their parents. Following the passage of statutory rape laws in the 1880s and 1890s, marriage also legalized sex that was criminalized outside of it. Last, marriage legally emancipated children, giving them access to their wages and the ability to live apart from parents and make their own decisions. Whereas the first two explanations concerning the legitimacy of children and sex were true for people of all ages, the final two were particular to those defined through chronologic age as children. The marriage of minors, which increased gradually during this period, must be seen as a move toward adulthood enacted in a society that, as we saw in the previous chapter, was becoming increasingly rigid in its classification of the divisions between children and adults and relying on chronologic age to do so.

One possible reason for the strong resistance at this moment was the newly developed category of adolescence, a term made popular by psychologists and social workers, but also given cultural weight by the increasing prevalence of high schools, which segregated children in their teenage years, removing many from the workforce and making it appear as if adolescents really did share many characteristics. The publication of G. Stanley Hall's *Adolescence* in 1904 was the intellectual bulwark of this movement, but adolescents were being treated differently in a variety of ways: child labor laws, juvenile courts with different sentencing guidelines, campaigns for mandatory schooling, and municipal curfew laws. All, to varying degrees, fixated on precise age categorizations to do their work and all came into their own during this period, roughly from 1880 to the 1920s.[5]

Psychologists and social workers may have distinguished adolescence both from childhood *and* from adulthood, but within the realm of marriage law those in their teenage years were usually lumped in with children, not with adults. When state legislatures raised the statutory age of marriage during this period, the result was to treat teens like children. And yet, by the 1900s and 1910s, experts believed that adolescence was also a period of transition away from childhood in many ways, one of them sexual. In the realm of marriage law this "in between" category did not exist; one legal scholar has likened adulthood in the realm of the law to being akin to an "on/off switch." In the debates about youthful marriage we see parents and lawmakers insisting that adolescents should be regulated in ways similar to children; adolescents them-selves resisted, asserting that they were really more akin to the adults they were becoming.[6]

The marriage of children was most common and least contested in more rural areas, particularly in the South and Southwest. These areas had a longer tradition of early marriage, but they were also areas with a less entrenched community of social reformers intent on monitoring and protecting children. Both factors point to a larger truth: by the turn of the century, rural areas of the United States were less influenced by the notion that childhood was a separate and protected stage of life. This trend would continue well into the twentieth century. When children married in these areas they did so with much less con-troversy and, perhaps, with less sense of what they might gain from marriage. They married because culturally it was what many people did, often at young ages. In order to "contest childhood," then, an ideal of childhood itself, com-plete with rules and norms and expectations, had to be in place. This was most true for urban areas in the Northeast, Midwest, and Northwest. In those areas marriage allowed young people to contest that ideal, and there was a greater outcry when they did so. At a time in U.S. history when reformers were fash-ioning and policing the norms of childhood, we must see these contestations not just as the work of individual children intent on their freedom but also as the symptoms of discontent over these new norms.[7]

THE INCREASE IN YOUTHFUL MARRIAGE

Though it is clear that child marriage was increasing incrementally from the late nineteenth through the early twentieth century, ascertaining whether this was a rise from the mid-nineteenth century is difficult, because census publi-cations before 1880 did not link the age of the populace with marital status.[8] Earlier chapters, though they include vital statistics reports for select states for earlier periods, leave us with an incomplete picture, and they tend to focus on areas like the Northeast, where the numbers of minors marrying would have been lowest. Indeed, the age consciousness that partially prompted the

Table 6.1. Percentage of Married Girls Age Fifteen to Nineteen, 1880–1930

1880	1890	1900	1910	1920	1930
11.71	9.49	10.96	11.31	12.54	12.63

Source: Carter et al., *Historical Statistics of the United States*, vol. 1, 77–78.

collection of the statistics was also mitigating the marriage of young people. Even when census reports do categorize the number of married people at various ages, they often use age brackets that make determining precise numbers challenging. For instance, late-nineteenth-century censuses categorized the number of married girls and boys below the age of fourteen and then lumped together all those between the ages of fifteen and nineteen. This lumping permits no differentiation between a fifteen-year-old wife and one who was nineteen, even though legally and culturally these were very different phenomena in many states. Still, records show that in 1880, 11.7 percent of girls aged fifteen to nineteen were married; in 1890, this number dropped to 9.5 percent; and in 1900, it rose again to 11 percent (table 6.1). Using these same imprecise brackets for later years, 11.3 percent, 12.5 percent, and 12.6 percent of girls aged fifteen to nineteen were also wives in 1910, 1920, and 1930, respectively.

Starting in 1910, the Census Bureau published a much more precise age breakdown, and although the increase is less dramatic, it is still apparent. From 1910 through 1930, between 5 and 10 percent of fifteen-, sixteen-, and seventeen-year-old girls were wives (table 6.2). For instance, 3.7 percent of sixteen-year-old girls were wives in 1910; in 1920, 4.2 percent; and in 1930, 4.3 percent. Not surprisingly, the percentages for seventeen-year-old wives were higher, and those for eighteen-year-olds were much higher. Bear in mind that these numbers come from the U.S. Census Bureau, not from State Vital Statistics Bureaus. This means that they reflect not the percentage of girls who *got married* at those ages but rather the percentage of girls who *were wives* at the time that a census agent came to their door; many of them (particularly among the eighteen-year-olds) could well have married earlier.

The increases are, of course, incremental, but all told they amount to hundreds of thousands of underage wives. In 1920, for instance, there were 344,869 teenage wives in the United States, out of a total of 3,382,430 girls aged fifteen to eighteen, or about 10 percent of the total. Increasing at a far greater rate was the newspaper coverage of child marriage and reformers' attention to the phenomenon, both born of growing fear about its prevalence.[9]

Table 6.2. Percentage of Married Girls Age Fifteen to Eighteen, 1910–1930

Age	1910	1920	1930
15	1.2	1.4	1.3
16	3.7	4.2	4.3
17	8.7	9.8	9.9
18	17	19.2	19.2

Source: U.S. Census Bureau, *Fifteenth Census of the United States: Population*, vol. 2, 845–46.

Reformers and jurists believed that child marriage was common and becoming more so. That belief came in part from their heightened sensitivity to childhood as a stage of life. But it also could have stemmed from an actual rise in children marrying during this era of increased regulation of young people. In 1909, while deciding on an annulment case of a seventeen-year-old wife, New York county justice Samuel Greenbaum noted the "apparently increasing number of suits for the annulment of marriages contracted under the legal age of consent." His colleague on the New York bench, Justice Walter Smith, echoed him in 1924: "Actions for annulment of marriage on the ground of non-age of parties account for a large proportion of the matrimonial problems presented to the court." These justices were adjudicating over annulment proceedings of children who themselves wished to be freed of their marriages as well as parents who sued for this action. That these particular youthful marriages were unhappy does not detract from the judges' belief that the phenomenon itself was both prevalent and growing.[10]

MARRIAGE AS AN END TO CHILDHOOD

What is at first noteworthy about the Hollopeters' victory—that the court affirmed the marriage despite state law designed to make it impossible—was actually quite common.[11] Indeed, when judges annulled marriages, it was almost always at the behest of the underaged party who later disaffirmed the marriage by living apart from her or his spouse; the party who *had* married as an adult was usually denied the right to sue for annulment.[12] This was especially the case if only one party to the marriage sought an annulment and the second, and also underage party, did not.[13] Most judges also dismissed the claims of parents who sought to annul their children's marriages; certain jurisdictions excepted, only a husband or wife could bring a suit of annulment. If those parties did not contest their marriage and continued to cohabit past the statutory age of consent, they remained married.[14] Indeed, women who married as girls, remained married past the statutory age of consent, and then retroactively attempted to use their previous underage status to nullify their marriages were usually denied.[15]

Some children married by unorthodox methods or took advantage of common-law marriage in order to be with each other or with their older spouses. Doing so indicates that they were aware of the law and used it to their own ends to be together and to negate the need for the parental consent required in many states. In the mid-1880s, for instance, John Beevers and Lou Jacobs, twenty-one and fourteen, respectively, eloped from Hollister, California, to Monterey to be married on the high seas. Maritime law, they believed, would help them escape "the difficulties to marriage presented by the girl's tender years"; fifteen was the marriageable age for girls in California. Because the seas were "too boisterous," they were unable to obtain a boat to take them out, so they simply returned home, telling their friends and families that they succeeded in their plan. They lived together as husband and wife for four years, during which time they had a child. Although the marriage did not work out, Lou Jacobs Beevers and her erstwhile husband had evaded the law to be together and emancipate her from her parents, who seem to have opposed the union. In a similar move, Hiram Bittick and sixteen-year-old Bertha Bice performed their own marriage ceremony in front of witnesses when Bertha's mother refused her consent, which prevented them from obtaining a license to wed in Missouri. The court affirmed that this cagey maneuver had, in fact, created a common-law marriage and that Bittick could not be convicted of the crime of taking a girl under eighteen for the purposes of concubinage.[16]

In 1890 in Newberry, Indiana, Owen Palmer, age thirty, and Pearl Wolfe, fifteen, were married. The bride's mother promptly had Palmer arrested for kidnapping. The court acquitted him of the charges, but while he was detained in jail, Pearl's mother reclaimed her. On his release Palmer, like Grover Hollopeter, petitioned for a writ of habeas corpus, alleging that Pearl's mother and brothers were unduly restraining her. He was successful, and Pearl, turning her back on her family, left the city with her groom. In 1892 in Georgia, the state convicted a man named Cochran for kidnapping a girl and marrying her. On appeal, the Supreme Court noted that Cochran had "obtained the voluntary consent of the lady to run away and marry him" and that "since the law makes a child capable of giving her consent to a marriage, this consent must count for something, unless it is procured by improper means." Because the Court found that Cochran had not used fraud or force with his new bride or her parents, the conviction was reversed and the couple remained married.[17]

Sometimes the child's labor and services were at issue between parents and a new spouse. In Richmond County, Georgia, fourteen-year-old Josephine Gibbs married Thomas Brown in October 1881. Josephine's mother, Anna Gibbs, had brought a suit of habeas corpus before the Richmond Superior Court to have her daughter returned to her. At that court and in the Supreme Court of Georgia, she was denied because Josephine had been above the age of twelve at her marriage. In this case and others like it, judges tended to note that a child, during its minority, owed its service to its parents, but that following marriage, a female child was both emancipated and owed service to her husband. In a North Carolina case from 1921, in which a father alleged that his sixteen-year-old daughter had been abducted and taken to South Carolina for the purposes of marrying an older man, the father sued her supposed abductors—two friends of the groom—for emotional damages and for the loss of his daughter's services, which resulted from her marriage. The father did not sue the new husband precisely because the law held that the daughter's services now to belonged to him and because he had not been the one to deliver her to South Carolina. The marriage itself remained intact (annulling the marriage had never been the father's suit), but the court ruled for the father. However, in a scathing dissent Justice William Allen made it clear that he believed the daughter had chosen to go with the men in order to marry her now husband, thus willingly depriving her father of her services.[18]

In the opinion for the majority Chief Justice Walter Clark explained, "It is not unusual among working people and those in moderate circumstances to rely to a large extent upon the services and wages of the older children, and often, in granting their consent to the marriage of a minor, if a daughter, it is upon an agreement that the husband shall work with the parents on some agreed terms. This is by no means unusual." Twice noting the regularity of the practice of girls' early marriage, Clark was cognizant of the key issue behind this suit: not that Frank Little's daughter had married below the age of consent but that in so doing Little had been deprived of her services, which she now owed to her husband. The suits that made their way to high courts in the southern states during this period focused less on the issue of children's marriages for their own sake—what we might call child protection—and more on issues like the loss of service, questions of inheritance or bigamy, or suits for damage against the official who married a child. Older notions of children as quasi-property of their parents that were becoming outdated in the North during this period still survived in the South.[19]

An 1881 Mississippi case, *Holland v. Beard*, is representative: Richard Holland sued a clerk for damages when the clerk issued a license to his young daughter, allowing her to marry and thus depriving Holland of her services. Holland lost, the court finding that the marriage was legal and that it was not possible to award damages resulting from a legal act. Cases like these certainly pertained to child marriage, but the main issue was not the ability of the young girl to marry; it was the effect of that marriage on others, in this case, her father. In other cases inheritance was at issue, itself resting on the validity or invalidity of an early marriage. Unlike cases in northern states where the focus was more often on the actual marriages from which parents sought to extricate their daughters and sons, early marriage remained accepted in many southern states. It was contested, or became a legal strategy, more when other parties were affected by those marriages either through loss of services or inheritance or the possible invalidity of subsequent marriages. The chronological boundaries of childhood continued to carry less cultural currency in the South.[20]

There were, of course, exceptions to this general rule, southern parents who, like their northern counterparts, contested their children's marriages based on their belief that a young age made them unsuited for matrimony. In January 1924, Rose Armour and Mike Nolte of San Antonio, Texas, began seeing each other. As Rose's mother, Annie Armour, explained it: "She went out with him just once or twice a week, and later, more. I asked him to stay away from the house. I said, 'The child is only fifteen and you are a much older man.' I asked him politely and nice to stay away from the house and let her alone." Armour explained further that she believed that the romance would blow over because Mike, who seems to have been in his early twenties, claimed that he was leaving for Europe with his father. Instead, on June 12, 1924, Rose and Mike were married where no one knew them, in Boerne, Texas, about thirty miles from their homes in San Antonio. They married without her parents' consent; Mike swore out an affidavit to a county clerk, claiming that he was twenty-one and that Rose was eighteen. Although Rose's parents objected to the marriage, her mother duly announced it in the paper and seems to have decided to accept it. That September, however, as the "next friends" of Rose, her parents filed a suit to annul the marriage, claiming that "by false representation she [Rose] was decoyed from her father's house and that upon the entreaties and importunities and representations so made to her by the defendant that her parents would consent she finally, to avoid further importunities, gave her consent to the marriage." They also alleged that Mike had tricked Rose into marrying him in a variety of ways and that he had beaten and abused her after the marriage, allegations that Rose vehemently denied. When Rose was called to the witness stand, the transcript indicates that she explained, albeit in a formulaic summary: "When I got married I did that of my own free will, nobody persuaded me outside of Mr. Nolte, and I knew what I was doing. I went voluntarily to Boerne to get married, knew where I was going when I started, and I went up there and was married there." She also testified, "I love my husband and want to live with him, or I wouldn't have gone back with him [after a visit to her sister's]. It is my purpose and desire to remain with him. I have absolutely never felt at any time that I was being held captive by my husband, and wanted to get away. My actions have been voluntary." The Court of Civil Appeals for the Fourth District explained that the time for Rose's parents to intervene in her life had ended at her marriage: "The mother should have exercised restraint over her daughter when she was under the family rooftree and when it was her duty to have exercised such restraint, but it is ill[-]timed after the daughter has willingly entered into the marriage state and desires to remain in that state for the mother to seek to destroy the marriage." The court thus denied the annulment petition, and Rose and Mike remained Mr. and Mrs. E. M. Nolte.[21]

Typical of claims in northern courts was the case of Alex and Sadie Scott. In 1899 in Saint Paul, Minnesota, thirty-two-year-old Alex Scott married thirteen-year-old Sadie Lowell without her parents' knowledge or permission but in a proper ceremony executed by a minister. Her parents forcibly took her from her new husband's home and held her in their own; Scott petitioned for a writ of habeas corpus to have her released. The lower court refused him, and he appealed to the Minnesota Supreme Court, which recognized the primacy of the common law and held that the marriage was valid, notwithstanding the state statute on age of consent and parental permission. The Supreme Court explained: "Marriage emancipates a minor child from parental control. Accordingly it is held that, where a girl of only 13 years and 11 months old marries, her father has no legal right to restrain her from living with her husband, if she elects." Asked by the lower court what she preferred, Sadie had said, "Well, I would like to go with him," referring to her husband. Here the parents' prime complaint seems to have been the marriage itself, which Sadie and Alex had used in order to be together.[22]

The year after the Hollopeter case and also in Washington State—perhaps inspired by the success of Imogene and Grover, suggesting forethought about how best to employ the law—seventeen-year-old Robert Cravens and fifteen-year-old Florence Simpson ran away from home and eloped to Victoria, British Columbia. On their return to Seattle, Florence's parents seized their daughter and charged Robert with abduction. Robert, like Grover Hollopeter, petitioned the court for the return of his bride, alleging that she was being held illegally. One judge dismissed the charges against Robert while another, Judge Mitchell Gilliam of the King County Superior Court, found for Robert in his plea, explaining, "If Cravens committed perjury at Victoria by swearing that he and his bride were of legal age, that is a matter for the British Columbia court. The fact before this court is that he is legally married to Florence Simpson and that the act of marriage makes him of legal age. This court cannot take his wife away from him and the only dispisition [*sic*] I can make of the case is to grant the petition and award the husband his bride." A local newspaper reported that while the parents of both bride and groom were attempting to use the newlyweds' crimes as leverage against them to annul the marriage, "the young husband has rented a room from his brother in the Fairbanks apartments, where the young couple will make their home. From his brother he receives employment at $2.50 per day with which to provide for his 'family.'"[23]

Two New York City cases, though atypical in that they featured underage grooms and not brides, nevertheless illustrate the ways that young people used marriage to be with their lovers despite their parents' wishes. In 1918, Albert Marone, who was below the age of consent, was married to a twenty-year-old woman in New Jersey. Although they lived in New York, they had gone to New Jersey to marry precisely because it would be easier there. As his guardian ad litem, Albert's mother, Angelina Marone, sued to have the marriage annulled. The court ruled against her: "In this case both the plaintiff [Albert] and the defendant [Catherine Marone, his wife] object to the annulment of the marriage. Each has testified that not only since the action was commenced, but up to the time of the trial thereof, they have continuously cohabited as husband and wife." Because county marital records in New York State are sealed to all but the parties involved for one hundred years, we have no access to the testimony of the Marones. We cannot know why marriage was so important to them or why Angelina Marone so opposed it; all we know is that they were successful.[24]

But in a 1916 case that made its way to the New York Supreme Court, *Herrman v. Herrman*, we have a better sense of the parties' motivations. It is clear that Philip Herrman's parents found out about his courtship with Dorothy Gates, a chorus girl, before they married. Philip's father, James Herrman, visited Gates at her home and urged her to cease her relations with his son. She was eighteen, and Philip was seventeen and still in school. It seems likely that Philip's parents believed that Dorothy was unsuitable company for their son precisely because she was a chorus girl. James repeatedly emphasized that Philip was "a schoolboy" and under the age of eighteen: "I notified her that he was in school and was home on the Christmas holidays, and I forbade her to have anything to do with him whatsoever, that he was only just past 17." The testimony of Philip and Dorothy diverges on whether they had sex before marriage, although both agreed that they had intercourse several times afterward. Both agreed also that Dorothy told both Philip and his father that she was pregnant and that this may have precipitated the marriage, but the testimony is inconclusive on this point and she never gave birth to a child. What we do know is that both Philip and Dorothy filed defense briefs opposing the annulment. Because they had had intercourse following the marriage and following Philip's eighteenth birthday, the judge ruled in their favor, ending the Herrmans' effort to annul the union. And whether Dorothy had used marriage in hopes of bettering her station in life—clearly the implication of Philip's parents—Dorothy and Philip had also used marriage to defy his parents and be together.[25]

An Alabama case from 1924 illustrates how some children used the emancipatory powers of marriage to free themselves not just from parents but from the state. Lizzie Johnson, a twenty-year-old ward of the court, got married while on parole from the State Training School for Girls at Mount Pinson, where she had been committed till the age of twenty-one. The Jefferson County Circuit Court ruled that Johnson's marriage had immediately emancipated her and that she was no longer a ward of the state. The state of Alabama lost the case on appeal; that court declared that marriage "had the effect to immediately remove her disabilities of minority." Although it is unclear whether Lizzie Johnson (now DeMarco) married so that she could be emancipated, that was the effect.[26]

Marriage likewise provided a way for couples to have sex in states that criminalized it between men and minor girls, even in cases where parents appear to have supported the relationship. That is, illegally entering into state-sanctioned marriage had the effect of preventing the state from interfering in the relationship between a minor girl and her new husband. In June 1918 in Detroit, Francisco Pizzura and Anna Pizza became acquainted; he was twenty-eight, and she was not yet fifteen. They eloped and began to live together, soon moving in with Anna's parents, who approved of the union.

After joining the military, Francisco returned to Detroit on furlough, and on the night of November 28, 1918, Anna and Francisco had sex. It is unclear whether this was the first occasion or who brought charges against him for statutory rape, for which he was initially convicted. Appealing the case, Francisco explained that he, Anna, and Mr. and Mrs. Pizza all understood the couple to be married and that even though the marriage may not have been solemnized, he had obtained a marriage license, and they had lived together as common-law husband and wife since soon after meeting. He, like all of the parties concerned, seemed to believe that marriage had legitimated the sex between himself and Anna. The court affirmed this belief: "When the defendant began and continued his relations with Miss Pizza he was of consenting marriageable age and as to him the marriage was valid. Their relations were voidable only at the option of Miss Pizza. She has not desired to repudiate the marriage contract, but, on the contrary, she desires, so far as the record shows, to hold the defendant to it."[27]

As we saw in the previous chapter, stories of youthful marriages are plentiful in newspapers from the time. In demonstrating their oddity to newspaper readers, many also showed the lengths that children were willing to go to marry, often in opposition to their parents. Marriage liberated them from that very opposition. In 1902, for instance, thirteen-year-old Ella Green and her fiancé, Frank Maines, sixteen, waded into the Ohio River to escape her angry, gun-wielding father; there they jumped into a johnboat and made their way across the river to Lawrenceburg, Kentucky, where they were married. The reporter explained that they "left Lawrenceburg and decline to return until [the] angry parent's temper has cooled." In 1906, Frank Diggs and Lucy Patton, fifteen and thirteen, fled Postum, Missouri, for Tulsa in what was then Indian Territory. There they were married. As Diggs put it, "Knowing it would be folly to ask for our parents' consent to be married at home, we decided to elope last week, to run away to the new state, which we heard was a young folk's country, and get married, and here we are." Not only were Diggs and Patton aware of the barriers to their marriage posed by the need for parental permission, Diggs's use of the phrase "young folk's country" also indicates that he recognized his position as a young person; he wanted to be around those who were similarly aged but did not want to be regulated because of that age. Also in 1906, Boston's Gracie Jenkins, fifteen, explained the reasons for marrying sixteen-year-old John Jenkins: "There's nothing to make so much fuss over. . . . John loved me and I loved John so when he found that he could make $1 a week here in a grocery store he asked me to come with him. I did and I don't regret it." Last, in 1907, the *Daily Oregonian* reported on a young Portland couple who married despite her parents' concerns. Anna Donkers was fifteen at the time of her wedding. When the sheriff asked the husband why he and his bride had married in secret, "young Hogan replied that Anna came to him in tears in the morning, saying her mother had threatened to kill her if she persisted in keeping company with him. She left home, he said, and announced that he must marry her then or never, and he married her, feeling that if he hesitated he would lose his prize." One cannot know whether sex was at the heart of Anna Donkers's parents' objections to her match with William Hogan or indeed whether sex was the reason the young couple sought to be together. But Hogan explained that the couple, the bride particularly, saw marriage as a means of safeguarding the relationship from her parents; she knew that marriage would protect her and her husband.[28]

COERCION, EXPLOITATION, AND FORCE

There is a good deal of variation in these cases, notably between those couples who were close in age and those where the bride was considerably younger, sometimes fully half the age, of the husband. In some there is evidence of coercion, exploitation, or force. Although children could use the law of marriage to their own ends, unscrupulous parents and scheming men could also use the law to unload a daughter or gain a laboring wife and youthful sexual companion. Theoretically a marriage was voidable if entered through force or coercion, but in practice many girls were either pressured into marriage with men not of their choosing or forced outright into unions. Though these cases seem to be in the minority, there is no way to know which variety of marriage—by free choice or by coercion—predominated.

It is worth pausing to examine a number of cases where child wives were exploited, because the same legal device that could emancipate a girl from her parents also bound her to her husband; the outcomes were two sides of the same coin. In some cases parents pressured or forced their daughters into marriage for pecuniary gain. In Philadelphia in 1884, for instance, the father of thirteen-year-old Katie Ferraro forced her to marry twenty-two-year-old Angelo Gileberto. After being married by a magistrate, her new husband insisted they also be married in the Catholic Church. As Katie was being fitted for her wedding gown, the seamstress advised her to go to the Philadelphia Society for the Prevention of Cruelty to Children if she did not want to be married. The newspaper that reported the story alluded to significant class differences between the father, a ragpicker, and the groom, a tailor, claiming also that Katie was "decidedly pretty." In this case it seems as though Gileberto had made some sort of deal with Katie's father, even if it was just in taking her off her father's hands. In 1891, a California mother named Mrs. Cram was turned away from her county clerk's office when the clerk realized that her daughter was only fourteen and thus ineligible for marriage. " 'Why,' said the irate lady, 'I married off my other daughter in May, and she was only 13 years of age. I got the license in this office, too.' " Although it is unclear whether Mrs. Cram was benefiting financially from marrying off her teenage daughters, clearly she was very much involved in effecting the unions. In 1897, also in Los Angeles, the *Herald* reported that a man the article referred to variously as a "Chinese" or "Mongolian" had paid an impoverished woman named Mrs. Atwater approximately $150 so that he might marry her daughter, Rachel Beaver, who was fourteen. Because Rachel was too young for matrimony in California, they were married at sea, where maritime law prevailed. In an early twentieth-century case, a woman from Missouri's Ozark mountains sold her nine-year-old daughter into marriage with a sixty-year-old Iowan named John Leeper. As the newspaper reported, "Her mother told her, she said, that she was Leeper's slave and must obey him in all things so long as she lived." Two years later she was able to escape and file for divorce. In these cases parents orchestrated marriages for what seems to be financial gain, marrying their daughters to men who were intent on having them labor or perhaps were just attracted to them.[29]

Marriage as economic opportunity could sometimes be more systematic as well. Throughout the late nineteenth and early twentieth centuries, white men moved to Indian Territory in hopes of marrying Native American girls and women who were eligible either for cash payments or lands through the allotment process. Even if these so-called squaw men were ineligible for funds or lands, their wives could claim it and the men would benefit by virtue of marriage. Newspapers throughout the country both described the practice and served as advertisements for more men to take advantage of it. The *St. Louis Republic*, in an 1894 article titled "Money Value of a Squaw: Why Even an Ugly One Is Matrimonially Desirable," explained that an Indian "squaw," pretty or ugly, young or old, was "literally worth to a keen white husband her weight in gold." This article recounted the story of a man who had married a sixteen-year-old Choctaw-Cherokee girl and "boasted proudly that he was able to collect for his wife for both her tribes." In a 1901 article in the South Carolina *State*, the reporter warned and advertised in equal measure. Under the headline "Indian Girls of Beauty and Fascination," he explained that the great beauty and civilization of Native girls in Oklahoma was a result of prior inter-marriage and education: "They are to all intents and purposes on the same plane with white women of education and refinement, except that the strain of wild, strong Indian blood in their vains [sic] gives them a tinge of richer color, a brighter eye, a more lissome grace than their white sisters possess." They were like white women, only better! After explaining the various ways that the Cherokee and Chickasaw nations had attempted to prevent intermar-riage, the reporter closed by emphasizing to the paper's white, southern read-ers the wealth and beauty of a number of eligible Native girls. Subtitles for a *Cleveland Gazette* story from 1899 summarized it perfectly: "There Are Many Charming Girls in Indian Territory: They Don't Wear Blankets, nor Live in Teepees, but Are Well Dressed and Dwell in Houses with Modern Conveni-ences." Historian Rose Stremlau notes that the reporters in these stories often reassured readers that they could have it both ways: the girls could pass for white when necessary but were also entitled to a fortune by virtue of tribal membership. Of course, not all of the young women who married white men during this era were legal minors, and although we cannot know the degree to which these girls and women may have been enthusiastic about the unions, certainly eastern and southern men were leveraging their whiteness in order to marry in financially advantageous ways.[30]

Some girls in this era told tales of being forced to marry men against their will through threat of violence. Seventeen-year-old Mary Jackson explained that James Jackson pulled a revolver and forced her to marry him in San Francisco in 1909. Nellie Williams, fourteen, was given an annulment in 1904 after explaining that her husband, Henry Brose, had coerced her into marriage by threatening to kill himself if she did not consent. When she protested, he then threatened to kill her, too. In 1908, a girl named Linda Brown claimed that a Hawaiian named Liiwalana had hypnotized her, held her captive in a room on Third Street in San Francisco, and forced her to marry him. Within a week of the marriage, he deserted her, and she had not seen him for two years. In these cases of forced marriage, the reason is not clear. Perhaps youth made girls susceptible to such measures, but adult women could have been forced—by gunpoint, threats, and hypnosis—into marriage as well.[31]

Tales of forced marriage were also commonly associated with immigrants, even though child marriage was less common among immigrants than among native-born Americans (an issue I return to in the next chapter). The annual reports of the Brooklyn Society for the Prevention of Cruelty to Children make little mention of child or forced marriage as a common problem, but the society included a picture of eleven-year-old Francesca Carboni in its 1891 report (below). According to the society, girls like Francesca were brought from Italy and married against their will. Francesca was forced to marry a twenty-seven-year-old man who beat and kicked her before she was able to escape from him. Child marriage was not a focus of the New York Society for the Prevention of Cruelty to Children across the river, in Manhattan. The society did note, however, in its 1890 annual report, that "'marriage for convenience,' it would appear, is not confined exclusively to the wealthy; for such marriages are not infrequently contracted by the poorest of Italians." Explaining that it was "not altogether an uncommon event in little Italy" for a thirty-four-year-old man to marry a fourteen-year-old girl, the report described the mercenary ways in which mothers might try to get rid of their daughters and potential husbands might take on young wives. The society highlighted the cases of three Italian American girls, Filomena C., Annie E., and Kate T., who had either been abducted or coerced to leave home through promises of marriage. But none of the men who had taken them actually married them, save one who seems to have performed the marriage ceremony himself; in these three cases, marriage was a tool to lure the girls from their homes, rather than the endgame the society claimed to be describing. Last, in 1913, the *San Francisco Call* reported that Donaldina Cameron of the Presbyterian Mission Home had rescued thirteen-year-old Lym San Toy from her husband, explaining that San Toy had been given in marriage by the Lym Family Society (a tong, or fraternal organization) to a member of the Wong Friendly and Benevolent Association (another tong) for $1,100. The *Call* speculated that war might erupt between these powerful tongs in Chinatowns across the nation if the girl were not returned to her husband; Cameron was doing all she could to prevent that from happening. Although these cases indicated that young girls from other countries were sometimes forced into marriage, they also demonstrate that immigrants were often scapegoated as being responsible for the high numbers of child brides in the United States.[32]

Cases of sensationalized violence against child brides also make repeated appearances in newspapers during this period. It would be impossible to know whether younger brides were any more likely than adult women to suffer at the hands of their husbands, though the age of some brides clearly made them ripe for newspaper coverage. In 1906, in Manzu, Oklahoma, a forty-year-old man named William Goodnight killed his sixteen-year-old bride and then turned the gun on himself; the newspaper reported that he was "insanely jealous

of her." The next year a Kentucky man named Ed Turner fatally stabbed his young wife, Lillie, because he believed that she had been unfaithful to him. In 1911, sixteen-year-old Chun Ah Lee of Jackson Street in San Francisco was found with her throat cut; police suspected her husband, Leong Soon, of killing his wife in a fit of jealousy. Although husbands killed wives of similar ages with some frequency in the United States, it is also likely that some men sought out younger wives precisely because they believed that they would be more docile and acquiescent. When that proved untrue in some cases, these men reacted with violence.[33]

The twinned issues of sex and reproduction were important in the meanings and struggle over child marriage at the turn of the century. As historian Stephen Robertson has demonstrated for New York City, parents often conspired with judges to use marriage to "right the ruin" of their daughters' premarital pregnancies or simply their loss of virginity. At times these girls were married off to men who had raped them, both statutorily and forcibly. Often courts were sympathetic, recognizing that the stain of illegitimacy on a child was a terrible burden and that a "ruined" girl's future could be saved only through marriage. In a trend that would continue through the early twenty-first century, marriage became a back door out of civil seduction suits (where a girl's parents sued the man for obtaining sex through promise of marriage), as well as statutory rape charges (and in some of these early cases, charges of forcible rape). Robertson finds that 30 percent of the statutory rape cases he surveyed between 1896 and 1926 included "an effort to resolve a case by means of a marriage or by a financial payment in lieu of marriage." In an 1897 case from California, for instance, Richard Earlston, a famous balloonist, had charges of statutory rape against him dismissed when the parents of his fifteen-year-old victim, Beulah Minot, agreed to let him marry their daughter instead of being charged. In this case, it should be noted, Beulah seemed quite amenable to the marriage and declared her unwillingness to testify against Earlston, but in other cases parents clearly pressured girls into marriage to retroactively legitimize sex and pregnancy.[34]

Francesca Carboni, rescued child bride, 1891. This picture appeared in the *Eleventh Annual Report* of the Brooklyn Society for the Prevention of Cruelty to Children. According to the original caption, Carboni was eleven years old and had been brought from Italy and forced to marry a twenty-seven-year-old man. After he beat her and left her tied to a bed, she managed to escape his home on Long Island and was found by a police officer in Prospect Park, Brooklyn. She is pictured here with an agent from the Brooklyn society. Image courtesy of the Brooklyn Collection, Brooklyn Public Library.

Beulah Minot's case forces us to look at the marriage of a minor from at least two perspectives: that of the state and her parents, who presumably did not want her to have sex at fifteen, and that of Beulah and Richard Earlston, who were using marriage to be together legally. Though we cannot know with any certainty, the Earlstons' joint perspective may be further divisible: Beulah loved Richard and wanted to be married to him; Richard did not want to go to jail and was using marriage to Beulah to evade it. In a similar San Francisco case from 1915, Mabel Kressig's mother lied about her age (saying that Mabel was fifteen instead of fourteen) so that she could marry the man (John Souleotes, a guest at her parents' hotel) with whom she had been having sex for a month. When the state charged Souleotes with statutory rape, he was eventually able to use the fact of that marriage to have his new bride's testimony excluded as evidence and win his freedom. Although there clearly were many cases where adults (both parents and husbands) used the law of marriage to exploit daughters and wives, there is also ample evidence that child brides and sometimes boy husbands were using the law to evade oversight by those very parents. The law of marriage allowed them to do so. Not incidentally, it also protected the relationships with their new spouses. In newspaper coverage or court decisions, it is also often noted that the parties involved, though legally children until their marriages, were either mature for their age or, in the cases of Robert Cravens, John Jenkins, and Grover Hollopeter, were already supporting themselves. In working for wages, these children evaded the newly emerging mandates of childhood that saw school as the proper place for juveniles. It was not in marriage alone that they defied the ideals of childhood.[35]

Even as marriage could transform these children into legal adults, it could not necessarily make them adults in other realms. Biologically they might still be developing, and this might mean that others would still interact with them socially as children. They might not be hired as, or paid at rates suitable for, adults. This, in turn, would mean that they might not be able to support themselves as many adults could and might still be financially dependent on parents in ways that significantly undercut their claims to legal adulthood. It is impossible from the records we have to fully explore these possibilities, but it is worth emphasizing that the story I have told in this chapter is a legal one, and that marriage might not financially, socially, or culturally transform these children into adults in the eyes of those around them.

That said, it also bears noting that these children used the law, as administered by the state, not only to legitimize their sexual activity but more radically to contest their very status as children. Most historians have rightly seen an expansion of the state during this era as one of the prime ways that children were increasingly controlled, indeed a means to cement childhood itself. Influenced by Progressive Era reformers, state legislators passed laws to protect and segregate children in schools, courts, correctional facilities, and (outside of) workplaces. Precisely because adults create and wield it, the law was largely a tool for the policing of childhood and adolescence, not its contestation. But although legislators create the law, judges administer it, and many judges were loath to break up contracted and consummated marriages, thus interpreting statutes narrowly and leaning on the common law to guide their decisions. A longstanding belief in the sanctity of marriage and its importance as a social institution trumped more recent conceptions about childhood as a protected status in these judges' rulings. Although most children, and adults for that matter, would not have understood the difference between common and statutory law, many children were able to take advantage of that difference in order to gain rights through marriage that would have been denied them by virtue of their chronological age. The import is twofold. First, the law was not always as overarching or effective as reformers might have hoped. In this case, bureaucrats at the local level were clearly not equipped to implement the law in ways that legislators had intended; they regularly allowed minors to marry when the law said they should not have. And because they were ruling on marriages that already existed, judges largely followed the letter but not the spirit of statutory law, gutting it of the constraints legislators had intended. Second, not only was the law sometimes ineffective, but children could actually use it to counter the very goals of those who passed it. In terms of marriage, and contrary to most other Progressive Era reforms, the law was often on the side of children, not of adults. These marriages indicate that even as childhood as a life stage had made serious inroads into cultural consciousness, it was not without its detractors, chief among them those named by the category.[36]

The year after Grover and Imogene were married, Washington State passed a new law stipulating that it was against the law to issue a marriage license to any girl under the age of fifteen; Grover's fifteen-year-old sister Lottie was married the same year. Two years after Grover and Imogene's marriage, Imogene gave birth to a daughter named Lois. Two years after that, however, Grover sued Imogene for divorce on the grounds of abandonment and desertion, alleging that she spent nights out late, came home under the influence of drink, and was verbally abusive toward him and Lois. He won his divorce and custody of their two-year-old daughter in November 1912. This was itself rather unusual, but Imogene appears not to have contested Grover's application for custody, asking only for visitation rights. At the time of the divorce, Imogene expressed regrets for having "listened to his tales of wedded bliss that never materialized." Marriage may have allowed Grover and Imogene to be together, transforming them into legal adults, but it had not transformed them into different people or made their relationship any more "blissful" than it was already, as Imogene had perhaps envisioned. Grover remarried a year later, and this marriage lasted until his death by accidental drowning in 1947. Imogene seems also to have remarried (in 1915) and thereafter disappears from the historical record. Although we could certainly tell the same story about any number of other couples with greater access to divorce in the early twentieth century— and although many youthful marriages lasted until the death of a spouse—it seems fair to say that Grover and Imogene's youthfulness at the moment of matrimony also contributed to the brevity of their union. Certainly Imogene thought so.[37]

The significance of the Hollopeters' marriage lies in the way that they were able to use the law to be together, outsmarting both their parents and a legal order that was, by and large, designed to keep them from having sex and living together. Marriage, as a legal device, allowed for this; it emancipated them and protected the sex that would otherwise have been punished under statutory rape laws. Of course it was also, and many believed increasingly, a way for older men to exploit younger girls, the fear of the reformers discussed in the next chapter.

SEVEN

Marriage Reform Is Still an Unplowed Field

Reformers Target Child Marriage during the 1920s

Edward West Browning, New York City multimillionaire and real estate magnate, met Frances Belle Heenan, a student at the New York Textile High School, in March 1926. He was fifty-one and she was fifteen. The meeting took place at a high school sorority dance at New York's Hotel McAlpin; Browning sponsored the sorority, and Heenan was pledged to it. He fell for her immediately, and by the next month rumors were circulating that they might marry. The *New York Times,* among many papers, was already covering the story of this outlandish couple, known as "Peaches" and "Daddy" for the nicknames they called each other. Though Heenan's mother publicly denied the rumors through early April, claiming that Frances was too young and just a "little girl," they were married on April 10 in Westchester County, New York, away from the press. Nevertheless, the wedding made the front page of the *Times.* Heenan's divorced parents were present and had consented to the marriage. Fearing precisely this outcome, Vincent Pisarra, superintendent of the New York Society for the Prevention of Cruelty to Children, lodged a suit in New York Children's Court to have Frances's mother deemed an improper guardian, guilty of neglect. The society sought to appoint a guardian who could stop the marriage. Justice Franklin Chase Hoyt was unable to grant the petition; under New York State law a girl could marry with parental permission as long as she was above the common-law age of twelve. If Catherine Heenan gave that permission, she was simply abiding by the law, as were Peaches and Daddy in taking advantage of it.[1]

Peaches and Daddy were sensations in the Roaring Twenties. The tabloids covered their whirlwind courtship and marriage exhaustively, including with their stories some of the first doctored photographs, called "composographs," featuring Peaches and Daddy together in compromising or outlandish situations. The coverage included tales of lavish shopping sprees, an unknown assailant throwing acid in Peaches's face (she survived, largely unscathed), and the bizarre acquisition of an African honking gander as a family pet. When Peaches died many years later, the *Times* eulogized her as a "Symbol of the Twenties." As couples went, even couples with more than a thirty-year age gap between them, Peaches and Daddy were spectacularly unrepresentative. The difference in social class between them made them anomalous, and West's wealth and personal history (he had previously undergone a public divorce and adoption scandal) made him an object of public fascination long before he met Heenan. Nevertheless, the couple warrants consideration for two reasons. First, they were famous enough that their relationship redefined the terms by which many Americans (and indeed international observers) understood child marriage. Their very famous relationship was depicted in a way that cast relationships between older men and younger girls, even if joined in legal marriage, as possibly pedophilic. Second, elements of their story serve as a prism for understanding the changed landscape of youth, sexuality, and reform movements in the 1920s.

Reformers during the 1920s were intent on eradicating what a new generation of activists saw as an epidemic of child marriage. These reformers were reacting in part to a youth culture that was public, cohesive, and sexually assertive for the first time in American history. Along with smoking, drinking, and dancing, standards of sexual morality—including necking, petting, and sometimes premarital intercourse—underwent a revolution in the 1920s. Young people, including those in the middle class, increasingly accepted some form of sexual expression within relationships. And among working-class youth, treating—the practice of a girl exchanging sexual favors for a date—was well established and not a matter of shame or regret for those youth. To the horror of social workers and reformers, many working-class girls were well aware of their sexuality and were unafraid to act on it. Although most reforms of the Progressive Era (and its aftermath in the 1920s) around youth and sexuality targeted sex outside of marriage,

Frances and Edward Browning. "Peaches" and "Daddy" were among the most widely publicized tabloid sensations of the 1920s. Here they are pictured strolling along the beach in Atlantic City, New Jersey, on June 1, 1926, soon after their wedding, when she was fifteen and he was fifty-one. The bandage on her face covers damage from acid that was thrown at her. Image © Bettman/Corbis.

some reformers began to see youthful marriage as exploitative in a new way. In essence, they had begun to question just how protective marriage necessarily was for girls who entered it. Especially now that divorce was readily available, marriage could easily provide a back door to sexual activity that men could not procure outside its bounds. Combined with new fears about child predation by older men, marriage, once seen as a safe haven, could now be a site of exploitation.[2]

A focus on child marriage must also be understood in the context of changes to marriage. Over the nineteenth century, most American had come to believe that marriage should be a union grounded in love and companionship, but a further wrinkle developed in the 1920s. Marriage experts increasingly emphasized the key role that sexual fulfillment played in marital happiness, especially for wives. In a society where healthy marital sex was discussed much more openly, the sex lives of "underage" wives were bound to cause more consternation, especially if they were married to much older men. Such marriages flew in the face of the increasing emphasis on marital compatibility and complementarity.[3]

If child marriage reformers of the nineteenth century could roughly be divided between those who tried to end child marriage because it was bad for women (motivations we could call feminist) and those who were bent on protecting the institution of marriage by preventing divorce (and who often had religious motivations), the 1920s generation framed its crusade in the language of child protection: youthful marriage was bad for children. These reformers had come of age professionally in the Progressive Era, were often trained as social workers, and used the tools of social science in their aim to help children and families by postponing the age of first marriage. That said, no matter their stated motives, much of their correspondence reveals that they were almost as invested in protecting the institution of marriage from those who gave it a bad name as were some of their forebears in the Divorce Reform League. Their focus on immigrant child marriage (even after discovering that immigrants made up a minority of underage spouses) and their occasional dabbling with eugenics, demonstrate how even their best child-protectionist ambitions were tinged with fears about societal woes and class and ethnic prejudice. Taken together, the work of reformers bent on eradicating child marriage and saving its victims gives us another view into worries about sex and youth in the 1920s, one that reveals that as discussion of sexuality itself increased, faith in the institution of marriage to contain sex and protect girls was increasingly eroded.

PEACHES AND DADDY

Vincent Pisarra of the New York Society for the Prevention of Cruelty to Children sought to bar Frances Heenan from marrying Edward Browning because he believed marriage of a fifteen-year-old girl to be wrong, especially one to a fifty-one-year-old man. Intervention in the lives of working-class families like the Heenans, though framed around protecting children, had been standard fare for social service agencies in the Progressive Era and into the 1920s. The society focused on child abuse, yet many Progressives also targeted working-class families for what they perceived as neglect, which was sometimes just a class-based difference in childrearing. In this particular scenario, it is difficult to believe that Peaches's mother or Edward Browning really were exploiting Peaches, as the society asserted. Peaches met Daddy independently of her mother and seems to have cultivated the relationship when her mother was not around. In addition to the impending marriage, one of Pisarra's indictments of Catherine Heenan's parenting was that she had allowed Peaches to appear as a chorus girl in the show "Vanities" at the Earl Carroll Theatre. Though she did not last long there—the stage manager said she did not measure up to "Vanities" standards—that she was even qualified was a testament to her precocity and her ability to project a certain sexuality. In a roundabout way those were the things that Pisarra was using to indict her mother: if Peaches was precocious and sexual, it was because of her mother's influence or neglect, or both.[4]

But what Pisarra seemed unable to comprehend was that Peaches herself may have been calling the shots. Edward Browning was already well known as a strange and wealthy man; he had gone through a public divorce and adoption scandal. Peaches could have known about all of this when she met him or would have found out soon thereafter; the earlier cases were widely publicized. As later testimony makes clear, though Daddy Browning may have been strange, he does not appear to have been cruel to Peaches, and if nothing else, he lavished her with expensive gifts. In short, Frances Heenan may well have been quite aware of how she could use her youth and sexuality to attract Edward Browning. Peaches was just one manifestation—albeit an enormously publicized one—of new mores in youthful sexuality that historians have demonstrated emerged during the 1920s. While few young people lived up to the flapper image that is the symbol of the decade, in reality much did change for young people. Reformers, like those at the society, could not conceive of Peaches as anything other than exploited, whereas in reality she may have been manipulating the situation to the best of her abilities. This was no less true for other working-class girls who married men with far less capital than Browning. That Peaches and Daddy achieved such notoriety had everything to do with Daddy's wealth, but the effect was to turn a spotlight on working-class girls' assertive sexuality, demonstrating publicly the transition that was occurring during the 1920s. It also showed that Americans continued to understand that transition in different ways: some saw girls making their own choices; others cast this as exploitation.[5]

The case of Peaches and Daddy, more than just a bizarre footnote to the 1920s, led to new understandings of youthful marriage, particularly when a bride's husband was considerably older than she was. Although we have already seen plentiful evidence of older men marrying girls through the nineteenth and early twentieth centuries, generally speaking those men were not themselves seen as strange for having done so. If the age gap was too large (think of Cassius Clay and Dora Richardson), sometimes the men were portrayed as being foolish for marrying younger women, but not abnormal in a sexual way. Certainly women's rights advocates portrayed men marrying girls as exploitative, indicative of the men's need to be powerful and controlling, but not as if they had any particularized sexual predilection. This is the key difference that emerged by the 1920s; while people may not have used the word pedophile to describe Edward Browning, they were applying that logic to the case. The growth of psychiatry and the development of particular categories of psychiatric disorders, including pedophilia, first coined in 1886 by Richard von Krafft-Ebing, gained wider dissemination beginning in the early twentieth century. Like all kinds of sexual categories, people may well have been doing and feeling various sexual things before then, but they didn't become pedophiles (or masochists or homosexuals or heterosexuals) until they were recognized and named as such. It is not, then, that men in earlier eras might not have used the institution of marriage in order to satisfy desires we would now categorize as pedophilic; they probably did. But those around them did not see the marriages this way. By the 1920s, they were beginning to do so.[6]

The marriage of Peaches and Daddy was a key case in solidifying that understanding, in part because it was so widely publicized, but also because of Browning's history. First, Edward Browning was divorced. His first wife, whom he had married in 1915, had had an affair with her married dentist and then fled to France when Browning had initiated divorce proceedings. He had eventually obtained the divorce in France. Although the demise of Browning's first marriage was clearly not of his own doing—she was legally at fault—that it had ended at all called attention to the possible impermanence of matrimony. That Adele Browning, the first wife, was also younger than Browning was certainly noted when they wed, but this was hardly unusual; many older men married younger women (they still do). At the time of the divorce, however, Adele was rumored by reporters to have said, "He is interested in other women very much younger than I." Whether she actually said this—and there is little way to confirm it—is largely irrelevant. More important is that the rumor had traction; it now *meant something* that a man might be interested in women very much younger than himself, and it meant something about his sexuality in particular.[7]

The second issue in Browning's history has to do with his children. Edward and Adele were unable to have biological children of their own, so they adopted two toddler girls in 1918 and 1920. Though none of this was particularly unusual, Browning's attempt to adopt a third child after his divorce from Adele was. In the summer of 1925, Browning claimed that he was interested in finding a playmate for the one child (Dorothy Sunshine) he had retained after the divorce, and so he placed an advertisement in various New York newspapers: "Pretty refined girl, about 14 years old, wanted by aristocratic family of large wealth and highest standing." Responses poured in. When the tabloids discovered that Browning was behind the ad, they reported his identity to the world, dubbing him Cinderella Man. One applicant, Mary Louise Spas, claimed to be sixteen, just slightly older than the age Browning had mentioned in the ad. Browning was so taken with her that he picked her immediately and arranged the adoption with her parents; the tabloids reported all of this. As it turned out, however, Browning paid Spas's parents a nominal sum to ease their suffering. When word got out, the authorities commenced an investigation: paying for a child was illegal in New York State. At the same time, the tabloids discovered that Mary Louise was twenty-one, not sixteen. Browning was able to have the adoption annulled, but the damage was already done. Showing pictures of her sitting cozily on Browning's lap and relating stories of him "paddling" her, Mary Louise explained to the tabloids: "I know he is not fit to associate with young girls."[8]

It remains unclear what Browning's motivations were in attempting to adopt Mary Louise Spas or whether he had a predilection for young girls. Either way, he was certainly portrayed that way. That marriage—in this case, to Peaches—might be one means of satisfying his desires was part of the subtext to the scandal. Indeed, he may well have married Peaches precisely because he could not adopt her. Marriage was a legal way to gain access to what he most desired, but in making this choice, Browning called into question both the legitimacy of marriage itself and the safety it was presumed to provide for the women who entered it. Browning appeared to be perverting the legal institution of marriage to gain what he could not have outside its bounds.

Reporters publicized other marriages through this narrative. Charlie Chaplin, for instance, married his first wife, Mildred Harris, in 1918 when she was seventeen, believing that she was pregnant (she wasn't). He married his second wife, sixteen-year-old actress Lita Grey (who really was pregnant), in 1924, when he was thirty-five. They wed discreetly in Mexico, in part because of the age difference and because he could have been charged with statutory rape in California, where they lived. The couple divorced within a few years, and Chaplin married and divorced a third time before marrying his fourth and final wife, Oona O'Neill, barely eighteen to his fifty-four in 1943. The age gap (and his having just been named in a paternity suit by an ex-girlfriend) caused a scandal. Chaplin does seem to have had a pattern of dating and marrying women and girls much younger than he, though his marriage to O'Neill lasted until his death in 1977. Although the outrage was obviously fueled in part by the development of a greater understanding that some men were especially attracted to women far younger than they—pedophilia, or something like it—Chaplin's previous three divorces did not help matters. If marriage was not necessarily permanent, and Chaplin's history certainly demonstrated this, then the institution could easily be seen as a back door to sexual exploitation. In an earlier age when marriage was understood to be permanent, and crucially, when girls' and women's marital sexuality was rarely considered, such an understanding of youthful marriage would not have been relevant. It was the combination of marriage's relatively new impermanence and fears about a newly sexualized adolescent girl that made youthful marriage—even among those who were not so famous—fodder for reformers during the 1920s.[9]

MARY ELLEN RICHMOND AND THE CRUSADE
AGAINST CHILD MARRIAGE

The twentieth-century campaign to ban child marriage in the United States had begun at least by 1918, when the American Association for Organizing Charity, a nationwide network of social welfare agencies (what would later become the Family Service Association of America), commenced a survey of family welfare organizations in various states to determine their marriage laws. The next year they established a standing committee on marriage laws, which met regularly to ascertain problems and to advise local activists how best to change state laws and assist their local license issuer in preventing child marriage. The movement had grown significantly by the mid-1920s. Until her death in 1928, Mary Ellen Richmond of the Russell Sage Foundation was at the center of the campaigns. Richmond was a leading figure in the development of social work, particularly the method of casework, and was also active in Progressive Era campaigns against child labor and for compulsory schooling. She would publish a number of books on the subject, including the coauthored *Child Marriages*, in 1925, the bible of the movement. Writing to a friend and fellow reformer in that year, Richmond noted that in contrast to the work already accomplished in the realm of child labor, "marriage reform . . . is still an unplowed field." She saw much work to be done. The campaign's stated goals were twofold: to help children and families via the practice of social work, thus preventing child marriage; and to amend the laws and better enforce the existing laws to make it impossible for children to marry. Reformers wanted not only to raise the marriageable age and the age under which children required consent but also to implement new laws to require documentary proof of age at a license bureau and mandate waiting periods between application and issuance of license. Continuing work begun by divorce reformers in the late nineteenth century, some also advocated a constitutional amendment allowing the federal government to regulate marriage, along with legislation to standardize marriage law across the states so that couples denied a license in one state could not simply cross state lines and marry elsewhere.[10]

Joining Richmond, the American Association for Organizing Charity, and the Russell Sage Foundation was a loose confederation of women's clubs, leagues of women voters, and other concerned citizens across the nation. Marriage laws are determined at the state level, of course, and some states (particularly those of the Northeast and Midwest) had many more active reformers than others; they achieved the greatest successes in those regions. These reformers usually couched their arguments in the language of child protection, and given their training as social workers and their background and experience in the campaigns for schooling and against child labor, it is clear that the welfare of children was their primary goal. In contrast to the purity campaigns of the later nineteenth century, Richmond and her colleagues were less interested in eradicating prostitution as a moral stain on the land and more focused on helping individual children. And unlike the earlier divorce reformers, for instance, these activists were not ministers intent on bringing Americans back to Christian understandings of marriage. That said, throughout the campaigns

Mary Ellen Richmond with her cat. Richmond was the leading crusader against youthful marriage in the 1920s and coauthor of *Child Marriages* (1925). An innovator in scientific methods in the field of social work, Richmond worked at the Russell Sage Foundation in New York City at the time of her work against child marriage. Her concern for children and families was always of the utmost importance, yet by the 1920s, Richmond, who herself never wed, still clung to increasingly outdated understandings of youth, marriage, and sexuality. Image courtesy of the Rockefeller Archives Center.

one also finds a remarkable preoccupation with the institution of marriage. These activists, though very different from the purity and divorce reformers of the previous century, were also very much following in their footsteps. While framing their campaign in the language of child protection, they still strongly believed that matrimony was the building block of a civilized society and that allowing children to marry sullied its reputation. They worked to protect marriage by barring children from entering it.[11]

In her keynote address at the annual meeting of the New York League of Women Voters in 1925, Mary Ellen Richmond called on New York State to raise its marriageable age to sixteen (from the common-law ages of twelve and fourteen) and to institute a five-day waiting period between the application for and issuance of a marriage license. She told the story of a fifteen-year-old New York girl who had met a junior from a local college the previous year; three days after meeting they procured a marriage license by swearing that she was eighteen years old (below that age, a girl needed her parents' permission to marry in New York State) and were united in marriage that day. As Richmond explained, "The bridegroom then took his bride to a hotel where they spent two days and two nights, at the end of which time he abandoned her and never lived with her again." The bride later gave birth to a child. In this case, a judge was willing to annul the girl's marriage (permissible under New York law), but the problem remained: a single nonvirginal girl, now a mother, because her husband had abandoned her after using marriage to have sex with her. In Richmond's view, better laws could have prevented the whole scenario from occurring.[12]

Sex between a man and a girl was protected within marriage, meaning that the college junior could legally exploit his fifteen-year-old bride with no reprisal. Similar cases made their way to courts in ever larger numbers in the early twentieth century, and reformers paid attention. In one 1909 case also in Manhattan, a girl named Anna Kruger explained that she had married her husband in April 1908 at the age of seventeen and lived with him for a short time before he abandoned her. She was petitioning for an annulment; her husband did not show up in court. At trial it became clear that Mr. Kruger also went under another name, Krugerman. The implication by Anna Kruger's attorney was that only a criminal would have aliases and that his treatment of his wife was just part of his larger criminal identity. Clearly, Kruger had married her and then abandoned her, taking advantage of marriage in order to have sex with her. In a similar 1914 case from Washington State, an eighteen-year-old University of Washington student married a seventeen-year-old girl after a courtship of less than a month, lived with and had sex with her for at least a month, and then petitioned for an annulment on the grounds that *he* was below the state's statutory age of marriage (twenty-one for boys without parental permission). He won his case in lower court, but on appeal to the state supreme court, the girl's attorneys argued that granting the annulment would mean that

> any male who happens to be under twenty-one years of age when he marries, irregardless [*sic*] of how large his physique, or bright his intellect, can perpetrate a fraud upon an innocent and virtuous girl, through the ceremony of matrimony, and stay with her until he has satisfied his passionate nature, ruin her life, then leave her, come into court, and plead his non-age, and on proving that simple fact, secure a decree annulling his marriage, thereby protecting himself from a criminal prosecution, committing a rape upon a girl under the protection of the State of Washington.

She won her case, preserving the marriage. The difficulty was that marriage both legalized sex between a minor girl and her husband and served as the bargaining chip a man could use in order to obtain sex from a girl unwilling to consent without marriage. It was true, of course, that the numbers of youthful marriages *were* increasing, albeit incrementally, but because the divorce rate was also growing, increasingly marriage looked like a back door to sexual activity that men could not obtain outside of it.[13]

Reformers had also come to believe that marriages contracted because of prior sex or pregnancy were often miserable or abusive and more likely to end in divorce. A case like the following was typical of an earlier understanding of the powers of marriage: the 1891 report of the New York Society for the Prevention of Cruelty to Children detailed the story of a Massachusetts girl named Frances who left her home with a young man (also a minor) and went to New York City. They lived together, representing themselves as married, though they were not legally so. At the behest of Frances's family, the police investigated, and eventually the society became involved. But there was no easy solution: a jury was unlikely to convict the boy, and Frances was yet too young for marriage in New York State (at this time, the state had minimum marriageable ages). "The police justice considered marriage the only proper solution, and when he learned that the age of consent for females was fourteen years in New Jersey, he directed them to go there and marry, paroling the defendant for that purpose." As the report explained, after the marriage, "they went forth man and wife, for better or worse." Although the organization clearly did not view what happened as a good thing—hence its inclusion in the report—marriage was still seen as the only viable *solution* to the original problem, which was sex outside of marriage; indeed, a judge actually recommended that the couple evade state law in order to procure the union. This stemmed from a belief—shared by many Americans, not just those in the judiciary or reform circles—that marriage was the only way to "fix" the problem of premarital sex (and certainly resultant pregnancies).[14]

By the 1920s, however, reformers were beginning to consider whether this was really the best course of action. As one reformer put it in 1920, "Experience abundantly demonstrates that such marriages usually turn out most unhappily." Although reformers (and many parents) had earlier believed that marriage "righted a girl's ruin," this had been grounded in a faith in the institution of marriage itself, a faith that was being tested both by the children who entered it and the thousands of couples who left it. Marriage following sex or pregnancy had long been a tradition supported by many, even if the girl had been raped by the man now proposed as her husband. In 1926, Russell Sage social worker Joanna Colcord (and Richmond protégée) minced no words in her evaluation of this custom: "To hear marriage being proffered to a man who has raped a young girl, as an alternative to a prison sentence, makes one feel as if this world we live in were as topsy-turvey as a madman's dream." Even in less extreme examples, where the parties had simply had sex while single, it was unclear whether marriage was necessarily the solution. If marriage were not a lifelong commitment entered into by ideal husbands and wives, then one or the other parties to it might end up suffering. As reformer Jane Deeter Rippin put it in 1918 of girls who married after it was found that they had had sex, "Some [reformers] believe that marriage will settle any situation and that after marriage the child is a woman and a different factor to be dealt with. Personally I do not agree with this opinion." Rippin and others like her were questioning just what marriage was capable of doing for the parties who entered it, just how transformative it really was. Where before reformers had believed that, in Rippin's words, "after marriage the child is a woman," now they were unsure. The child had done something "womanly" that necessitated marriage (sex), but marriage was not necessarily transforming her into an adult wife. The difficulty for reformers was that young people were behaving in ways that were out of keeping with their chronological age, whose growing importance was making these age-inappropriate behaviors that much more glaring.[15]

With her colleague Fred Hall, Mary Ellen Richmond published *Child Marriages* in 1925, a call to arms for social workers, legislators, and reformers. The book reviews both the state of youthful marriage in the United States and the laws that permit it. It is, of course, meant to prod its readers toward fixing those laws and working to prevent child marriage in a variety of ways. For our purposes, however, what is worth focusing on is the language the authors use to describe the problem. Noting the "physical and mental immaturity of these [married] children," Richmond and Hall recounted a variety of reasons that children should not be able to wed. Among them were connections to "immorality," both the sex that girls between eleven and sixteen had with their husbands and their links to exploitation, prostitution, and disorderly houses. They emphasized the abbreviated length of many of these marriages—"we were not prepared for the temporary character of this group of marriages"— some lasting as little as a few days. This was clearly enough time for sex. One study found that being under legal age was the third leading cause of annulments in the United States in 1927 and 1928. The authors also noted with horror the growing number of states that made exceptions to their marriage laws when a prospective bride was pregnant, in effect countenancing the sex she and her partner had while unmarried in an effort to legitimize the child or avoid prosecution for statutory rape.[16]

A key difference between Richmond, Hall, and others' understandings of child marriage and reformers' focus on young people and sex more generally was that they were more likely to see child brides as being exploited. This stands in contrast to their view of unmarried, working-class girls who had sex as promiscuous, sometimes little better than prostitutes. Youthful brides were usually, but not always, understood to be victims. The irony here is that young wives were doing what they were supposed to be doing, albeit prematurely, and yet reformers and social workers seemed unable to recognize the girls' agency, usually blaming older men or parents for the marriages. By contrast, sexually active unmarried girls' agency was precisely the problem; they were willful, and though their parents, too, might be to blame, large numbers of these girls were incarcerated for their "crimes." Both reactions illustrate reformers' perceptions of changing norms of sexuality: they attempted to control it, but in different ways. The campaigns to ban child marriage must thus be seen as a variation on the regulation of sexuality that other historians have studied.[17] Reformers increasingly viewed marriage as a back door into illicit sexuality—which it clearly sometimes was, both a bargaining chip in sexual bartering and a legal device to protect an older man. But reformers almost always construed the situation this way, unwilling to consider how girls might have seen real advantages in the institution. In one way they had made real progress because they could question the powers of marriage itself. In another, however, their class and generational positions blinded them to how young people themselves might have understood marriage.

RAISING THE AGE OF CONSENT

The legal goals of the child marriage reform movement were myriad and included instituting waiting periods between application and issuance of license; requiring documentary proof of age when applying for a marriage license; and improving training for the clerks who issued marriage licenses. Reformers were also intent on eradicating the financial incentives (at both state and county levels) that encouraged the issuing of licenses and, the other side of the same coin, increasing the penalties on clerks who knowingly issued licenses to the underage and the ministers and justices of the peace who married them. As one minister explained of why he married a fourteen-year-old girl without her parents' permission for a two-dollar fee: "When they come to you, I marry them, and that is all there is to it. The law only requires me to ask certain questions as to name, age, birthplace, and names of parents. I am free to take their answers, be they right or wrong. I am not legally responsible for anything further, and I don't hold myself morally obliged to look further into these matters." This minister seems to have been particularly mercenary, yet there is plentiful evidence—in the form of hundreds of thousands of youthful brides—that others also turned a blind eye or were simply unaware of a child's age. In a 1909 New Mexico case, the state prosecuted a minister named Thomas Harwood for illegally marrying Amalia Perea, thirteen years old, to Manuel Chaves, even though fifteen was the statutory minimum age for girls in the territory. Though Harwood had been told that the priest who had baptized her alleged that she was only thirteen, he performed the marriage anyway. After all, the couple had a legally executed license, and Amalia's parents both supported and witnessed the marriage. Reformers were facing an uphill battle; they wanted ministers and county clerks to care about their jobs enough to prevent youthful marriage, even when financially it benefited them more to issue the licenses and perform the ceremonies regardless of the age of the bride and groom. If they could not induce them to care, then they backed reforms that would punish them, even though such statutes had often been on the books for as much as a century. Mandating that clerks both ask for and keep copies of documentary proof of age thus became an effective weapon in the fight against child marriage; as birth certificates became more widespread in northern cities, themselves a result of increased state bureaucratization and mandates around public health, activists backed such laws.[18]

Perhaps the primary legislative goal of the reformers was to raise the minimum marriageable age as well as the age below which a child required parental consent. If these were not raised, all the documentary proof was meaningless because many states still condoned the marriage of girls and boys at the common-law ages of twelve and fourteen, respectively, or some other combination only a couple of years above those ages. Politicians at the national level as well as reformers and state representatives all weighed in, advocating for higher marriage ages. Mary T. Norton, the fifth woman to serve in the U.S. House of Representatives, believed that women should support a ban on "May-December" marriages because it was a "peculiarly feminine problem." She argued that "every state should prohibit the marriage of girls under 18 years of age. Such a law would have made the disgusting Browning case impossible." Representatives Florence Kahn of California and Edith Nourse Rogers of Massachusetts echoed her sentiments.[19]

Mary Ellen Richmond (and her *Child Marriages* coauthor, Fred Hall) equivocated on the ideal minimum age, but largely because they believed that increasing the age too hastily in states with lower ages would lead to more legal evasion. They also believed that any state with a minimum age of sixteen or higher should permit exceptions for couples who would be better off married. They advocated for a gradual increase in marriage ages, especially in states that still abided by the common-law ages of twelve and fourteen. As they explained, "The evidence, we feel, points to 18 as the minimum toward which our cultural standards are likely to be advanced in time, but few states are ready for this as yet." As Richmond wrote to a colleague, "A clergyman's wife in New Hampshire succeeded practically single-handed in raising the minimum marriageable age for girls in her state to 18 last year. This is an age two years higher than the minimum in any other state in the Union, and it is a forward step that we ourselves would not have recommended with much more preparation." Richmond and Hall also pointed to what, for them, was a troubling truth about marriage law: many states had no straightforward minimums and/or absolute ages below which consent was required. Almost all statutes were worded differently, and some only stipulated an age below which a contracted marriage might be annulled or ages below which license issuers could be fined. At least one state put its minimum marriage ages in a statute regulating bigamy. This patchwork of awkwardly written laws constituted the minimums, not straightforwardly worded statutes declaring a "Minimum Age of Marriage in X State." All of this meant not only that marriage ages were inconsistent from state to state but that they were remarkably unclear in many.[20]

That said, Richmond, Hall, and others documented (in *Child Marriages* and elsewhere) what they took to be the minimum ages; these served as guides for reformers. Prodded by reformers, or acting on their own initiative and concerns, lawmakers in at least twelve states raised their marriage ages during the 1920s, either by instituting or raising the minimum marriageable age (Arizona, California, Connecticut, Delaware, Minnesota, New Mexico, New York, North Carolina, Pennsylvania, and Vermont) or changing the age below which a girl or boy needed parental consent (New Hampshire, Nebraska, and Ohio). Nebraska and Ohio simply equalized their age of majority, which had the effect of raising the age of consent for girls by three years because in both states "minors" required parental consent to marry. Some of these states— like Connecticut, Delaware, New Mexico, and Pennsylvania—were new to minimum age regulation, having previously mandated only parental consent below certain ages. Others, like California and New York, were long-time tinkerers with marriage laws. New York reformers, for instance, had been trying for years to institute minimum marriageable ages. Immediately after the Peaches and Daddy debacle, New York instituted minimum ages of fourteen and sixteen; in 1929, lawmakers legislated the extra consent (in addition to parental) of a children's court judge for the marriage of girls between fourteen and sixteen. In 1927, reformers also managed to make New York the first state to require all minors to submit documentary proof of age when applying for a marriage license.[21]

For every victory, however, there were usually multiple defeats, sometimes following swiftly on the heels of those victories, as laws passed one year were repealed the next. In 1923, bills aiming to raise the marriageable age to sixteen for girls and eighteen for boys failed in Indiana, Minnesota, and Montana. Reformers in Tennessee, which had abided by the common-law ages of twelve and fourteen since it entered the union, finally succeeded in raising the age below which children required parental consent in 1899 and again in 1919, only to have both ages (as well as waiting periods and other stipulations) repealed, some legislators bemoaning the financial losses of couples marrying in adjoining states, and others deriding what they saw as the overly protective and regulatory nature of the laws.[22]

HASTY AND HOT MARRIAGES

Although the campaigns to raise marriageable ages are the most obvious examples of the connections among age, marriage, and sexuality, waiting periods between application and issuance of license also demonstrate the linkage between what reformers saw as youthful people's propensity to misuse the institution of matrimony. These waiting periods were specifically designed to prevent what reformers called "hasty" or "hot" marriages because they believed that young people lacked the ability to think through the decision to marry and were much more likely to wed on a whim or under the influence of alcohol. If a waiting period were instituted, then there would be time either to sober up, rethink poor decisions, or alert parents to their children's proposed marriages. Yet the focus on hastiness must also be read not just in terms of perceptions about youthful folly but also for the ways that reformers understood the sex that young people were having more generally; they saw both marriage for sex and sex outside of marriage as impetuous and ill considered. Mary Richmond and Fred Hall documented a number of hasty marriages in their book. In one instance, "a girl of 15 in New York State went to the marriage license office with friends who were seeking a license. While there, she was dared to marry another friend of the bride and groom, a youth of 19. Taking the challenge, she was granted a license on the spot and married the same day." This case illustrated the idea of marriage on a lark, yet Richmond and Hall also included cases where a waiting period, they believed, would prevent sexual coercion and exploitation, instances where older men seduced teenage girls into marriage for sex, later abandoning them.[23]

Joanna Colcord, who worked with Richmond on the American Association for Organizing Charity committee and at Russell Sage, reported in 1920 that only the New England states, New Jersey, and Wisconsin had statutes that mandated waiting periods. Her article was meant as a call to arms and as a report on current activities spurred by the marriage committee. Bills proposed the previous year in California, Georgia, Illinois, Kentucky, Louisiana, and Maryland to institute a waiting period all failed. Richmond and Hall reported five years later that three additional states, Delaware, Georgia, and Nebraska, had instituted advance notice laws. As they explained, "Next to a minimum age law, the most important single legislative reform in connection with child marriage is the advance notice of intention to marry given to the license issuer some days (usually five) before the license can be issued. . . . It is a protection to children and to their parents." Arthur Towne, superintendent of the Brooklyn Society for the Prevention of Cruelty to Children, concurred. In a 1922 article he argued for a lapse of between ten and thirty days between application of license and issuance; this would permit both investigation into the "propriety" of the marriage and the couple to repent if they had been too "hasty." Mildred Mudgett, who taught social work at the University of Minnesota, explained that hasty marriages were "largely recruited from the ranks of youth." A waiting period was necessary, she continued, so that clerks might check on the applicants' eligibility to marry, combining both reasons in one measure: a waiting period would allow clerks to refuse an application, and it might give parents time to intervene because all applications would be printed in local newspapers.[24]

One reason that reformers were so intent on having all states institute advance notice bills was to cut down on what some called a "marriage-market town" or a "Gretna Green," so named for the border town in Scotland where many English youth married after the passage of a 1753 law mandating parental consent. Combined with age restrictions or residency requirements, the waiting period often meant that youth crossed state lines in search of a jurisdiction more amenable to their nuptial plans. And many towns were well aware of this, taking advantage of their location and a neighboring state's stricter laws in order to reap a profit not just in license fees but also for hotels, restaurants, florists, and jewelers. Colcord noted that an advance notice law passed in Nebraska was immediately repealed under pressure from the jewelers' association there, which saw part of its profits diverted to neighboring states if young people had to wait to marry. Only by all states adhering to similar laws, or by states mandating that out-of-state residents first prove they were eligible to marry in their own states, could this "marriage migration" be halted. Richmond and Hall, in their second coauthored book, *Marriage and the State*, found that in the twelve states that had advance notice laws in 1929, especially those that were contiguous, there simply were no marriage market towns. And all of this meant that those citizens that a state deemed ineligible for marriage, including those who were too youthful, remained unmarried.[25]

AMENDING THE CONSTITUTION

Some, of course, advocated for an amendment to the U.S. Constitution that would allow Congress to pass legislation aimed at creating uniformity between states. This approach—which had been advocated since the 1880s and which ultimately failed—mandated two steps: first, a constitutional amendment and, second, the actual legislation to regulate marriage. Although most of the attention to this amendment then and now focused on the supposed ability to prevent migratory divorce, the proposed amendments were usually worded explicitly to allow for the regulation of marriage as well. The federal oversight was particularly important for child marriage reformers who recognized that many young people simply crossed state lines to marry when they were denied the ability to wed at home. An amendment to the Constitution could prevent not just migratory divorce but also migratory marriage.[26]

Perhaps the most famous iteration of this was the Capper Amendment, so named for Republican senator from Kansas Arthur Capper, who sponsored the bill in 1921, 1923, 1925, 1927, and 1930. Mrs. Edward Franklin White, legislative secretary for the General Federation of Women's Clubs, helped Capper to draft it. The National Federation of Business and Professional Women's Clubs, the Daughters of the American Revolution, the National Congress of Mothers and Parent-Teachers Association, and the American Association of Home Economics all endorsed the bill. Following the necessary constitutional amendment, which he also sponsored, Capper's proposed bill would have raised the ages of consent to sixteen and eighteen, for girls and boys respectively; raised the ages below which consent was necessary to eighteen for girls and twenty-one for boys; and instituted a two-week waiting period, with a mandated public posting of the notice of the application. Although the bill was as concerned with divorce as it was with marriage, its sponsors regularly linked the two, arguing that if the wrong people were not able to marry, then they would not subsequently divorce. Because the bill's target was the varied marriage laws across the states, supporters like Capper often highlighted those variations. In the *Congressional Digest* in 1927, he explained, "Seventeen states fix no marriageable age—that is, an age at which young people may marry with consent of the parents. In nine of these, the common-law ages of 12 for girls and 14 for boys have been formally recognized." He went on to list the other almost-as-low combinations of ages that his bill would change. Boston judge Robert Grant explained, "While the divorce scandal is notorious and all know about it, heretofore only experts and students have realized how cruelly and ignorantly the young have been permitted to mismate. That hardy offshoot of liberty—the idea that marriage is nobody's business except the contracting parties—has offered constant encouragement to ill-considered or dangerous mating by neglecting to restrain the marriage of the very young, the feeble-minded, and the diseased."[27]

Many who agreed with Capper and his supporters about all of the problems of youthful marriage still opposed the amendment for a number of reasons, primarily centering their concerns around encroaching federal oversight of what many considered to be a matter for state legislators. Even among those in the anti-child-marriage movement there was a good deal of opposition to the Capper Amendment. Writing in 1925, for instance, Joanna Colcord argued against federal legislation until most states had come to what she considered reasonable marriage standards on their own. She feared that any federal legislation would inevitably reflect the greater number of states with lower ages of consent and no waiting periods, not those with new laws of which she approved. This was particularly so when reformers in various states worked hard at the state level to pass progressive legislation. Some reformers, and Mary Ellen Richmond was among them, feared that the same thing would simply repeat itself at the federal level and in the process cancel out the work of those states that had met with success.[28]

These legislative efforts reveal a tension between reformers' commitment to seeing young girls as victims and their sometime recognition that many of these marriages could not occur without the willing participation of both parties. After all, consent needed to be forged, ages needed to be fabricated, and state lines needed to be crossed, and it was not always possible to believe that girls were being abducted or were under the sway of particularly persuasive men. At times they blamed the impetuousness of youth itself—this is particularly evident in the critique of hasty marriages—but at others they seemed willfully blind to the ways that girls and some boys were choosing marriage. This stands in marked contrast to their indictment of youthful girls who chose to have sex outside of marriage. Progressives had hesitated little about condemning these choices, sometimes incarcerating girls in reformatories and institutions for the feeble-minded, where some were forcibly sterilized. Sexual activity trumped age in the case of premarital sex, branding girls as incorrigible in the eyes of reformers. They certainly had little trouble recognizing that single girls had *chosen* to have sex; that was precisely the problem. That choice seems to have prematurely aged them, their delinquency accelerating them on the road to adulthood in a way that made it difficult for reformers to think of them as children any longer. By contrast, when children married in a world that celebrated childhood innocence, witnesses saw a rupturing both of marriage and of childhood itself. This was because marriage was a legal and social signifier of *adulthood*. The two should have been fundamentally incompatible, but married children demonstrated that this was not so. Marriage was revealed as perhaps *not* being the meeting of romantic equals in its idealized form, and childhood was abruptly terminated both socially and legally. Despite this, the couple remained legally married, the child still biologically a child; this was what was so vexing for the reformers who sought to rescue child brides from their marriages.

CHILD MARRIAGE AND THE IMMIGRANT FAMILY

If reformers could not always fix the laws to prevent child marriages, many relied on their training as social workers and pointed to the family and improper parenting as the root cause of child marriage. As Arthur Towne, superintendent of the Brooklyn Society for the Prevention of Cruelty to Children, put it succinctly in 1922, "As a human problem, child marriage is one naturally belonging within the scope of social work." Towne continued, arguing against the common understanding about the source of child marriage: "Let us not imagine these marriages occur only among our immigrant population; they are probably about as prevalent among our native stock." Sociologists and some others in the social hygiene movement also noted that not only were immigrants' children less likely to marry early but they were less likely to marry at all. They could hardly be blamed for an increase in youthful marriage. Indeed, the highest rates of marriage—at any and all ages—were in rural America, especially the South (the subject of the next chapter). As sociologists pointed out, early marriage was more frequent among blacks than whites and more common among native-born whites than those whose parents had immigrated. Mary Richmond concurred. She had read the most recent census figures, and it was clear to her that the foreign born did not make up the majority of child brides. Indeed, the teaser on a mock-up of the cover for *Child Marriages* proclaimed: "More than two-thirds of a million people living in this country have been child brides or have been married to child brides. . . . Only a small minority of such brides are foreign; most of them are native white of native parentage." Implicit within this, of course, was the long-standing belief that "uncivilized" practices like youthful marriage were confined to other countries and their migrants. In the hierarchy of civilized cultures, with Anglo Saxons at the top, age of marriage was one of the proofs of that civilization. Nonwhite others, particularly those in hotter climates, were presumed to marry soon after puberty. Richmond's assertion that this was not the case for immigrants to the United States did not stop most reformers from

Table 7.1. Percentage of Married Girls in 1920 by Race and Nativity

Age	Native White— Native Parents	Native White— Foreign or Mixed Parents	Foreign-Born White	African American
15	1.5	0.4	1.4	2.5
16	4.7	1.3	3.9	7.4
17	10.8	3.8	9.5	16.9
18	20.5	9.4	19.5	30.5

Source: U.S. Census Bureau, *Fourteenth Census of the United States, 1920*, vol. 2, *Population*, 392–93.

focusing disproportionately on the issue, so convinced were they of the links between foreignness and child marriage.[29]

Not only were native white children of native white parents more likely to be married than first- or second-generation immigrants, but African American children were more likely to marry early than their white counterparts (tables 7.1 and 7.2). In both cases, these marriages of native-born children, white and black, were happening in rural America, particularly in the South (table 7.3). Reformers concerned about the welfare of white children and the future of white marriages paid little attention to the high rates of youthful marriage by blacks *or* whites in rural areas, even when those rates were sometimes triple those of the Northeast and Midwest, where many reformers made their homes.[30]

One way to track the growing importance of child marriage and its supposed connections to immigrants is to look at how one social service agency came to see it as a problem from the late nineteenth through the early twentieth centuries. This connection demonstrates that some reformers allowed ideology to trump evidence. Instead of focusing squarely on who was marrying at youthful ages, some reformers displaced their fears onto immigrants. The New York Society for the Prevention of Cruelty to Children published annual reports from 1875 through the 1930s. Along with statistics covering the number of complaints it received each year, the number of investigations, prosecutions, and convictions, each annual report included "highlights" of cases (sometimes with pictures) that the society found either particularly egregious or perhaps representative. On the rare occasion when a child marriage was highlighted, the focus was usually on an immigrant marriage. Indeed,

Table 7.2. Percentage of Married Boys in 1920 by Race and Nativity

Age	Native White— Native Parents	Native white— Foreign or Mixed Parents	Foreign-Born White	African American
15	0.2	0.1	0.3	0.2
16	0.3	0.2	0.4	0.6
17	0.9	0.3	0.6	1.6
18	3.0	0.8	1.3	5.2

Source: U.S. Census Bureau, *Fourteenth Census of the United States, 1920*, vol. 2, *Population*, 391–92.

Fred Hall complained privately in 1926 that the society had never made preventing child marriage a priority and that, in fact, "Chief Agent Pisar[r]a also, whose record is very bad in forcing young girls to marry, is quoted in a recent interview as favoring the child marriage bill." Hall meant that Pisarra (and perhaps others at the organization) until recently had seen youthful marriage as a *solution* to the problems of premarital sex and pregnancy, rather than as a problem in itself (as we saw, for instance, in the 1891 case quoted earlier). In the wake of the Peaches and Daddy scandal, the society had come out more publicly in advocating changes to the law to prevent minors from marrying. But that it had not seen child marriage as a problem until the second and third decades of the twentieth century indicates not so much that they were aware of the increase in underage marriage (which was occurring, though incrementally) as that they were worried about changes in marriage and, significantly, who was marrying. It is also telling which kinds of marriages the society chose to highlight in its annual reports: those where an older man (often an immigrant) coerced a younger girl (sometimes white) into marriage or a scheme where young immigrant girls were effectively sold into marriage. In other words, not only were these not statistically representative of the people who were marrying (even perhaps in New York City), but they tended to include the most extreme cases. Not represented were the far more typical cases of working-class girls (and sometimes boys) who chose to marry. This could be because the society wished to focus on cases involving obvious "cruelty"; and perhaps it was less wedded to the statistical methods of social science that guided organizations like the Russell Sage Foundation. Either way, it does indicate that for the New York Society for the Prevention of Cruelty to

**Table 7.3. Percentage of Married, Widowed, or Divorced
Boys and Girls Age Fifteen to Nineteen, 1910–1920**

Region	Boys 1910	Girls 1910	Boys 1920	Girls 1920
New England	0.7	6.0	1.1	6.3
Middle Atlantic	0.7	7.0	1.3	8.1
East North Central	0.7	8.5	1.6	10.3
West North Central	0.7	9.4	1.4	9.9
South Atlantic	2.0	15.6	3.3	17.5
East South Central	2.6	19.3	4.0	20.4
West South Central	1.9	19.7	3.2	19.8
Mountain	0.9	13.5	1.5	14.2
Pacific	0.6	9.9	1.3	12.4

Census divisions: New England (ME, NH, VT, MA, RI, CT); Middle Atlantic
(NY, NJ, PA); East North Central (OH, IN, IL, MI, WI); West North Central
(MN, IA, MO, ND, SD, NE, KS); South Atlantic (DE, MD, DC, VA, WV, NC, SC,
GA, FL); East South Central (KY, AL, TN), West South Central (AR, LA, OK,
TX); Mountain (MT, ID, WY, CO, NM, AZ, UT, NV); Pacific (WA, OR, CA).
Source: U.S. Census Bureau, *Fourteenth Census of the
United States, 1920*, vol. 2, *Population*, 400.

Children, youthful marriage *in itself*, though unfortunate, did not constitute a
form of child abuse.[31]

The New York Society for the Prevention of Cruelty to Children oper-
ated in a city teeming with immigrants at the turn of the century; it stands
to reason that its agents might focus on neglect and abuse among the poor
and newly arrived. But in so doing they contributed to the reputation of child
marriage being a problem among those same groups. In a rare case of child
marriage featured in an annual report from the nineteenth century, in 1889
the society detailed the case of fourteen-year-old Winnie, who "changed her
name to Mrs. K. Moto and became a Japanese by marriage." As even the report
admitted, "And had it been a home, it is not probable much would have been

said about the matter though she was under the age of consent. The place he took her to was, in fact, a pest-hole of Chinese, Japanese, and vile characters in Water Street." Investigation revealed that Moto treated Winnie with the "utmost consideration," that the marriage had not been consummated, and that she had married him because she had no home. Indeed, the society seems to have become involved in the matter only because someone had reported a white girl living with a Japanese man in a place the organization clearly did not consider to be "a home" by their middle-class, native-born standards. In a somewhat similar case, in 1920, the society reported on eleven-year-old Anna C. (presumably white), who had been "sold" by a white woman, her adoptive mother, to a "Chinaman." The white mother and her Chinese husband, who was "implicated in the opium traffic," were both prosecuted and deported.[32]

In another early case (1891), the society reported on an Italian girl named Maria Massa, who lived with her parents in Little Italy, "till they married her to Guiseppe [*sic*] de Paruolo. She was then only *thirteen* years old!" The trouble began when Maria fell in love with another man and left her husband; only when her parents and a judge effectively forced her back to her husband was the problem solved, especially so because "Maria's marriage relieved her parents of the expense of her support." Here mercenary Italian parents effectively made all the choices for their daughters, marrying them off at will, further cementing stereotypes about Italians and early marriage.[33]

Two 1920s studies sponsored by a children's aid society and a women's protective association made similar connections, even as they documented that immigrants were actually *not* more likely to marry than native-born girls. A study from Erie County, New York, for instance, explained that only 16.4 percent of the brides it studied were foreign born. The grooms, however, were another matter. The study documented much higher rates of foreign nativity: 47.6 percent. And the authors made it clear that even though the girls themselves might not be foreign born, their parents were: 62.3 percent were foreign born, 11.5 percent were a mix of foreign and native nativity, and only 24.6 percent were native born. Erie County, however, was anomalous in these proportions, studies of New York State and of course the national census itself documenting the opposite trends. A Cleveland Women's Protective Association study, *School-Girl Brides*, also noted that of the 643 couples in their study, 427 were both of American birth; the authors then spent a number of pages discussing the marriages of Austrian- and Italian-born girls. Focusing on foreign-born girls and men, even if they did not predominate, is hardly surprising for the 1920s and was a way of blaming something literally foreign for the institutional problems of marriage. Like the focus on children marrying, focusing on foreign children and their husbands allowed reformers to claim that marriage itself would be just fine if only the wrong people were not doing it.[34]

The connections that many drew between child marriage and foreign origins could have lent themselves well to a eugenic argument against early marriage: foreign brides having many babies because they began reproducing earlier, or young mothers giving birth to defective and feeble-minded children, for instance. Katherine Mayo made both of these arguments in *Mother India*, the best-selling 1927 screed against Indian self-rule and immigration to the United States. It was just the latest in a long line of American diatribes against Indian child marriage, and it would become crucial to arguments against American child marriage in the 1930s. Most reformers, however, seemed to see real differences in the child marriage Mayo described, which happened at much lower ages, and what was properly speaking usually adolescent marriage in the United States. That said, some, including Mary Ellen Richmond, did warn about the physiological harms of early marriage. The League of Women Voters, for instance, in a pamphlet designed to influence voters to enact progressive legislation on the issue, explained that "until a girl has passed her period of rapid growth and has also been able to store up a degree of vigor, she is not ready, physiologically speaking, for either marriage or child-bearing." The pamphlet even noted that in a warmer climate like Italy (where girls were presumed to mature more quickly), the marriage age was fifteen. But this stopped short of suggesting that early marriage produced defective offspring. Sociologist William F. Ogburn lamented that although "sex impulses become strong" and the capacity to reproduce develops shortly after puberty, most Americans did not wed in those years, postponing marriage till their late teens and twenties. But he also saw precisely why this happened: because men, especially, needed to "obtain an increased income" before they were ready for marriage.[35]

The difficulty with eugenic arguments was that they could be approached from both directions. Historians have tended to focus on negative eugenics— preventing or discouraging certain people from having children, one result of which was compulsory sterilization—yet many in the movement focused their energy on positive eugenics: encouraging the right sort of people to have children. And, at least when it came to age, the overwhelming message was that they should do so when still young. In *Modern Marriage* (1925), a guide for young men, Paul Popenoe, among the most famous eugenicists of his day, explained that "there is no reason why a woman should delay marriage; there are many why it is to her advantage to marry young." Among these, in his estimation, were the ability to have larger numbers of healthier children, all while maintaining the health of the mother herself: "The eugenic importance of having the first child soon after marriage lies in the fact that it tends to result in larger families. . . . Early marriage means healthy, vigorous children. There are fewer infant deaths among the offspring of young mothers." Popenoe did not set an absolute minimum in the book, but he did not see why a girl should wait much past eighteen or twenty, the former of which was generally the age at which she might choose marriage without parental consent. He was also writing for a particular audience—white, middle class, and educated—the very people he feared might be postponing marriage. Yet this was precisely the problem; in the realm of positive eugenics, it was difficult to make the argument that early marriage was good for some people but not others. Although the worries about youthful marriage were, no doubt, tinged with fears about "defective" offspring and immigrants who produced large families by starting too early, 1920s reformers were far more worried about the institution of marriage itself, as well as their own stated goal of child welfare, than they were about eugenic concerns.[36]

Foreign origins aside, it was difficult for reformers to separate child brides out from the families who supposedly forced their daughters into marriage or consented to their ruin. This had been true during the late nineteenth century as well. In 1898, the New York Society for the Prevention of Cruelty to Children reported on the case of a fifteen-year-old girl whose mother had consented to her marriage to an actor named Charles Felton, but only because she had been negligent in failing to prevent their having sex. The marriage ended tragically because Felton proved himself abusive to both his wife and their baby. Although the mother was condemned for not properly supervising her daughter (which had necessitated the marriage), many would have agreed that marriage was still the solution to the problem. By the 1920s, parents were coming in for more censure by reformers for believing what many themselves had formerly preached. Not only had reformers changed their attitude toward the powers of marriage to magically solve the problems of premarital sex, sometimes, of course, the reformers themselves were different people. Arthur Towne, in his 1921 address to the National Conference of Social Work, recommended, "Some governmental agency should look into each [marriage] application and act in the light of its findings. Experience shows that parents are often incapable of exercising prudent discretion in this matter. . . . Parents, even those of good character, are frequently unfit, especially in the midst of a tragic situation [presumably a pregnancy], to exercise sober judgment with respect to surrendering their daughters in marriage." He suggested that a juvenile or family court be appointed to investigate the license application of every girl between the minimum marriageable age and the age above which she would not need parental consent. A commentator in a reform journal called the *Family*, applauding the ability of judges to supersede parents' judgment, agreed: "Parents' consent to marriages for girls under sixteen augurs ignorance and lack of consideration for their daughters' welfare—in other words, unfit guardianship." Reformers looking for causes for child marriage sometimes documented the limited choices that working-class girls faced, but more often than not parents were held responsible. This was clearly in keeping with the Progressive Era turn toward demonizing the family that other historians have noted. Whereas such reformers tended to have different reactions to the girls themselves—incarcerating the single ones and attempting to "rescue" the married ones—parents could be blamed for both scenarios.[37]

PROTECTING THE INSTITUTION OF MARRIAGE

The supposedly adverse consequences of child marriage were a problem for reformers for the obvious and perfectly legitimate worries—poverty, single motherhood, sexual exploitation, and so forth—but the degree to which it upset them speaks to another concern. These reformers were worried about what the dissolution of "faulty" marriages, child marriages among them, meant for the future of marriage itself. If, as they believed, child marriages were more likely to end in divorce, and more quickly at that, marriage was revealed as impermanent and transitory. Of course they believed that people, husbands, wives, and their children, were better off in permanent marriages. But they also clearly believed that the good name of marriage itself suffered if married people did not take it seriously. In other words, righting the problem of child marriage was also a movement waged by marriage boosters intent on propping up its increasingly tarnished reputation. If marriages could be made permanent by safeguarding the entrance to marriage, rather than blocking its exit, then divorce itself would cease to be necessary and marriage would be understood once again as the permanent alliance it was meant to be.[38]

Marriage reformers were well aware that divorce was of great concern to Americans, and indeed to many of their fellow reformers, but they consistently asserted that to focus on divorce was to miss the point. Divorce could be prevented not just through different laws but through better marriages, and those marriages could only be better if qualified people entered into them after much forethought. As Mildred Mudgett of the University of Minnesota put it in 1925:

> Even the [social] worker in training is so submerged in the wreckage of human marriage that the most glaring headlines on divorce fail to shock her. [S]he is skeptical of the solution which is usually suggested, namely, some change in the divorce laws of her own state or of the country as a whole. Adjustment of divorce laws comes pretty nearly to being a case of "locking the barn after the horse is stolen"; or, to be more modern, installing a burglar alarm in the garage after the Ford is gone! The real tragedy has occurred long before the couple reaches the divorce court, and for that reason social workers are turning their attention more and more to a consideration of marriage reform.

Joanna Colcord, who worked as chairman of the Committee on Marriage Laws at the Russell Sage Foundation before moving to Minnesota to become general secretary of the Family Welfare Association there, agreed. She claimed straightforwardly that "at present the public mind is largely occupied with the question of divorce. It has not yet awakened to the fact that divorce could be lessened if unsuitable marriages were prevented." Colcord's aim was to target public attention away from divorce and its accessibility to marriage law itself; she believed that too much was focused on what she called the "shipwreck of families rather than upon their launching," which could of course prevent the shipwreck.[39]

And at least part of this was driven by a desire not just to eliminate the unhappiness caused by failed marriages but also to prevent failed marriages from making marriage itself seem unstable (as it was increasingly becoming by the 1920s). As Mary Richmond explained in a letter to a colleague in 1927 about what she saw as the fad of companionate marriage, "Why should such liaisons, whether temporary, or not, filch the honorable name of marriage? My friend, Mr. Joseph Lee, used to say that to call a cow's tail a leg did not put the cow in possession of five legs. It still had four and no more. To call arrangements such as I have just described 'marriages' is to debase our moral currency as surely as the circulation of two metals of unequal value at a parity debases a country's money." Richmond was offended by all marriages that did not take themselves as seriously as they should. Her worry about child marriage was thus twofold: that girls could be tricked into marriage and the ruin of their lives but also that child marriage was not good for the name of marriage itself. Richmond's colleague and protégée Joanna Colcord concurred on the subject of common-law marriage, another thorn in the side of marriage reformers, and its relation to sanctioned and licensed marriage: "According to Gresham's law, if two systems of currency of different basic value circulate in the same community at the same time, the baser of the two tends to drag the finer down to its own level. I think there is an analogy here!" Though Richmond and Colcord were speaking of two other forms of marriage that they decried, the principle remained the same: these were marriages that husbands and wives were more likely to exit, marriages that their participants did not take as seriously as they should, marriages that gave "real" marriages a bad name. This same belief applied to their fears about child marriage. A license issuer whom Richmond interviewed for *Child Marriages* explained it this way: "Very youthful marriages cheapen the relationship and detract from the solemnity of the association." The Women's Protective Association of Cleveland perhaps summed it up best: "To permit marriage to be entered into casually by immature young people who have no sense of its social responsibilities, its obligations, and but little training in the ideals of family life, is to weaken and cheapen the institution of marriage itself."[40]

A RETURN TO THE FEMINIST CASE AGAINST EARLY MARRIAGE

The anti-child-marriage movement of the 1920s worked toward the dual goals of child and marriage protection, but these were neither the only motives for limiting the marriage of minors nor the only set of reformers. In the wake of their victory in passing the Nineteenth Amendment, which guaranteed women the right to vote across the country, some feminists refocused their priorities toward equalizing a variety of laws that either discriminated against women or simply treated them differently from men. As the California Equal Suffrage Association had explained in the 1910s (before gaining suffrage) in a pamphlet called "Women under California Law," "A girl's minority ends at eighteen while a boy is a minor until he is twenty-one. This is unfair to the girl. The age of minority is a protection. It is no favor to remove this legal protection from girls three years earlier than it is ended for boys. The age of majority should be the same for both sexes." The National Woman's Party (NWP) took up this issue, in addition to arguing for the federal Equal Rights Amendment, and worked incrementally to change a variety of laws state by state. Among these were laws that allowed women to marry before men, with and without parental consent, and laws that stipulated a lower age of majority for women than men. The NWP was continuing in the tradition of women's rights advocates like Elizabeth Oakes Smith, though it was focusing much more on the law than she had done. While it sometimes shared similar goals to the social workers discussed above, the NWP was much less attached to notions of child protection, at times being willing to sacrifice the differential protections for girls (including around the age of consent to sex, statutory rape laws, and, most famously, gendered labor protections) in the name of sex equality. The party's vision for marriage was one where men and women did not perform different roles because they were husbands and wives. It was not, by and large, contesting the primacy of marriage; it just wanted unions to be more egalitarian. Part of this mandated equalizing the ages of marriage so that one party did not enter the marital union dependent on the other.[41]

The National Woman's Party did not always settle on one age at which it believed men and women should be eligible to marry. Instead members tried to work with whatever statutes a state had to raise the age at which girls could marry (with or without parental consent) to the age at which boys could already do so. This was both feminist and practical; the NWP seemed to believe that it would be easier to change one law instead of two. The NWP's model statute, "Age of Capacity to Contract Marriage," begins, "Any unmarried person of the age of ( ) years or upwards, and otherwise competent, is capable of contracting marriage, however, a marriage license shall not be issued where either party is under 21 years of age unless the previous consent of one of the parents, or guardians of such minor shall have been obtained." The first age was left blank so that members in any given state could fill in the age they thought best. The NWP was less concerned about child protection—it did not select an age at which a girl or boy really *was* capable of marriage—than it was about making the laws equal. As was noted in a draft bill proposed for Maryland, "Put in the age you think is best but have it the same for boys and girls."[42]

The NWP also focused on how marriage differentially affected men's and women's legal capabilities. Judges had generally held that marriage terminated the period of minority, turning minors into legal adults, and many states codified this explicitly, though sometimes only for girls (presumed to be more likely to marry before majority). These laws generally were designed to allow married children to assume control of inheritances and to legally contract as adults. This could mean that a married girl's property came under her husband's control, but it could also give a married girl control over her own property, especially following the passage of married women's property acts. The laws imbued people who were otherwise "underage" with legal personhood, and it did so through marriage. A memo to NWP members in Texas explains the problem with a bill that they might borrow from Arizona, where married minor girls became adults but married minor boys did not. The bill "gives a married woman whether she be over or under 21 years of age, the same rights as a man who is 21 years or over. Thus a married woman under 21 would have greater rights than a married man under 21." Similarly, party members opposed Alabama's law ending the minority of any girl over eighteen who got married: "It is no favor to have marriage end this legal protection three years earlier for a girl than it is ended for a boy." These two examples, which may have been written by different people (many memos are not signed), approach the significance of marriage and legal rights from opposite tacks: one sees early majority as a benefit, the other as a drawback. But both are agreed that it is unfair that the law should treat boys and girls differently. If marriage granted legal majority, then both husbands and wives should be eligible, or neither should.[43]

The NWP also believed that states should equalize the age of majority, which in many western and midwestern states was lower for girls than it was for boys (eighteen instead of twenty-one). It follows that, along with all the other laws the NWP was seeking to equalize, members would focus on differential ages of majority alongside the age of marriage. Even as the NWP objected to the use of the word "protection" when it referred to wives' legal subordination to their husbands—"Modern women do not wish 'protection' as inferior beings," party members wrote in relation to marriage laws in Michigan—it clearly saw the period of minority as one of protection and believed that if boys were minors until twenty-one, so too should girls be. In the same report on the legal status of women in Michigan, the authors noted that "since minority is meant as a protection to young people, the law should extend this protection to girls as long as boys." They included the varying ages of majority in digests of problematic laws in Idaho, Montana, Nevada, North Dakota, Oklahoma, Oregon, and others. As they wrote in a report entitled "Discriminations against Women in North Dakota Laws," "Minority and the protection that goes with it is shorter for girls than for boys." They noted also that the differential ages of majority meant that girls were not entitled to the support of their parents for the three years between the ages of eighteen and twenty-one that boys were. This was a consequence, of course, of the assumption that girls would be married earlier than their brothers. As they explained about a proposed bill in Ohio, "Since parents must support their *minor* children, it is only fair that girls should be provided for as long as boys."[44]

This issue would be the undoing of differential ages of majority by the Supreme Court in *Stanton v. Stanton*, though not until 1975. During the 1920s, however, the National Woman's Party met with some success not just in its attempts to change the ages at which boys and girls could contract marriage but also in the differential ages of majority. Between 1917 and 1930, a number of states that had differential ages of majority—California, Colorado, Iowa, Kansas, Missouri, Nebraska, Ohio, Vermont, and Washington, and one territory, Hawai'i—changed girls' age of majority to twenty-one (or twenty in the case of Hawai'i, where it matched that of boys). Although a lower age of majority might occasionally benefit an individual girl—if she were to inherit earlier or be able to escape an abusive home at a younger age—the National Woman's Party was determined to eliminate any laws that distinguished between men and women.[45]

The work of the National Woman's Party represents a different understanding of how reformers might approach the issue of marriage. Members believed, no matter what the consequences, that the age of majority and the ages of marriage should be equal, with the hope that once legally equal, men and women would have greater opportunity to *become* equal in their workplaces, homes, and marriages. While they met with almost no success in the realm of marriage—few states had equal marriage ages till the 1970s because male legislators continued to believe that girls would marry before boys—they certainly contributed to the discussion in raising girls' ages in some states, and they equalized the age of majority in many others.

Other feminists approached the issue differently. The League of Women Voters (LWV), which developed out of the somewhat more conservative National American Women Suffrage Association, believed that men and women were fundamentally different from one another and that the protections that women had gained as a result of earlier reforms—like limits on what kinds of jobs they could be made to perform or mothers' pensions for widowed women—would be lost if an Equal Rights Amendment were added to the Constitution. Like Mary Ellen Richmond, and for similar reasons, they opposed the amendment.[46]

In the realm of youthful matrimony, although they believed that the ages of marriage were generally too low, they did not advocate the equalizing of ages. The Program of the Legal Status Committee, adopted at the

1926 national convention, supported many of the goals (including waiting periods and methods to stem marriage migration) laid out by Mary Ellen Richmond in *Child Marriages* (indeed, they quote her) but settled on the different ages of eighteen (for girls) and twenty-one (for boys) as those below which they required parental consent for marriage. Although they did not say it explicitly, it seems that they believed that girls would want to marry earlier and that the law should allow them to do so without their parents' permission. In 1928, the California League of Women Voters also reported that it had helped to modify the civil code the year before to equalize the age of majority for girls (upward to twenty-one), with the proviso that a married girl between eighteen and twenty-one was an adult for the purposes of contract. Although age of marriage remained on their agenda at the national level and in various states through the early 1930s, the LWV claimed that the Uniform Marriage and Divorce Act was "not on our program," and indeed, it may have opposed the act for reasons similar to its opposition to the Equal Rights Amendment: the outcomes of federal legislation were unpredictable. In a flyer entitled "Look Twice at the 'Equal Rights' Amendment," the LWV posed a variety of questions about issues of marriage, divorce, child support, jury duty, and other issues germane to women. Among them: "In some States the legal age for marriage is lower for girls than for boys. Is this 'equal rights' or would the age have to be raised for girls or lowered for boys?" "In some States a woman reaches the age of majority at 18 years, a man at 21. Does the age for a man become 18 or that of a woman, 21, under 'equal rights'?" The answer to both questions, as it was to all questions in the advertisement, was *"Who knows? Nobody! Who must decide? The courts."* The point for the LWV was not only that it did not want the courts overburdened with litigation or having "Congress . . . take on the task of legislating in fields now reserved for the states," but also that it did not believe that "equal rights" were necessarily desirable if this meant there could be no legal distinction between men and women. It was for this reason that "equal rights" appeared in quotation marks. The LWV was in favor of advancing women's status in the wake of having won the vote, but it disagreed with the National Women's Party about what that looked like. The League of Women Voters, which had a demonstrable interest in protecting girls and raising the age of consent to sex, also clearly saw why girls might want to marry at younger ages than boys. The way its agenda differed from that of the National Women's Party, as well as from reformers who came from a social work background, highlights the different priorities that women (and some men) had in preventing children from marrying. Some wanted to protect children or the institution of marriage; the National Women's Party wanted to protect the rights of professional women and advance a futurist argument that looked forward to women's eventual equality; and still others, like the LWV, believed that women and girls were fundamentally different from men and boys because of sex, and should be protected because of it.[47]

Readers will probably not be shocked to learn that the union of Peaches and Daddy was not one of long standing. The two were in court in Westchester County (where they had married) within a year and were awarded a legal separation, though not an absolute divorce (unavailable in New York without proof of guilt, usually of adultery, which neither accused the other of having committed). In awarding the separation, Judge Albert Seeger excoriated Peaches not only for what he believed was her propensity to lie during the proceedings but also for her and her mother's behavior throughout the marriage. He clearly believed that the entire thing had been a sham from beginning to end and that Daddy had not mistreated Peaches in the least. He claimed that she had "enjoyed a life of ease and pleasure during her life with plaintiff [Browning], taking her breakfast in bed, and enjoying all the pleasures that money could buy and that the plaintiff could lavish upon her." Of Browning, the judge explained, "his intentions toward his wife were good. His treatment of the defendant and her mother was uniformly kind and considerate, but there was no limit to their demands." Browning was awarded a separation from bed and board; the judge also indicated that the law of New York entitled Peaches to sue for annulment but that this would make her legally ineligible to claim any of Browning's estate, an option she did not pursue.[48]

In the wake of the failed divorce, and because she was no longer being supported by Daddy, Peaches Browning signed a contract with a producer that would launch her on a traveling vaudeville career. She sued Daddy a few additional times in the late 1920s to establish her dower rights to his estate as his legal wife (successfully) and for divorce a second time, alleging infidelity (unsuccessfully). She remained married to Edward Browning until he died in 1934, when she inherited a share of his estate. Browning had written a will to ensure that she received no more than what New York State law mandated. Peaches Browning married an additional three times before dying in August 1956 after slipping in her bathroom and losing consciousness. Frances Belle Heenan Browning Hynes Civelli Willson, known to the world as Peaches, was forty-six years old.[49]

Whether Judge Albert Seeger was correct in his estimation that Peaches took advantage of Daddy (financially) and not the other way around (sexually), we cannot know definitively. Quite possibly both occurred. More important than determining guilt or innocence is the significance of the case for understandings of youthful marriage. Peaches and Daddy recast adult-child marriage as sexually suspect, even in the face of changing mores of assertive youthful sexuality, especially among the working class. Indeed, most reformers tended to ignore the motives of young people who married in favor of casting the marriages as exploitative by definition, even as they blamed single working-class girls who had sex outside of marriage. In both cases they also blamed parents, especially if they were poor or immigrant or both. They also fretted about the effects of young people marrying on the institution of marriage itself. While feminist reformers like the National Woman's Party single-mindedly pursued goals of sexual equality (sometimes at the expense of hard-fought protections for working women favored by the League of Women Voters), social workers seeking to eradicate child marriage always had mixed motives, working to protect children from what they believed were dangerous marriages, even as they sought to save the increasingly tarnished reputation of marriage itself.

Reform efforts around age of marriage tapered off in the late 1920s and early 1930s; Mary Ellen Richmond died in 1928, and she had been at the heart of the work. No one at the Russell Sage Foundation picked up where she had left off. Perhaps more important, the onset of the Great Depression, which made many young people postpone marriage indefinitely, prompted activists to turn to other concerns. Although some reformers managed to push through legislation during the early 1930s—Minnesota women finally passed a five-day waiting period bill in 1932—legislative action around youthful marriage waned in importance until the late 1930s, when a young Tennessee couple married, making headlines around the world.[50]

EIGHT

Marriage Comes Early in the Mountains

The Persistence of Child Marriage in the Rural South

On January 19, 1937, nine-year-old Eunice Winstead snuck away from her parents' three-room cabin in Treadway, Tennessee, a tiny hamlet tucked in the mountainous northeastern corner of the state, just below the Virginia state line. She was going to meet her neighbor, twenty-two-year-old Charlie Johns. They set off, clutching the marriage license that Charlie and his friend Sam Wolfe had gotten a week earlier at the courthouse in Sneedville, the county seat. They were looking for Walter Lamb, a Baptist preacher who lived in a hollow near the Clinch River. Wolfe, accompanying the couple, found Lamb at home and asked him to come up to the road, where Charlie and Eunice presented him with the marriage license. Lamb married them on the spot. Although the preacher said afterward that he thought Eunice looked a little young, the couple told him that if he didn't marry them, then someone else surely would. The marriage license said she was eighteen, and they gave him a dollar for his services. As he later explained, "I just stood in the middle of the road, said the marriage ceremony, and it was over." Charlie and Eunice were now husband and wife.[1]

When they found out about the wedding, the Winsteads and Johnses were not pleased, though Charlie's family seems to have been more upset. Although early marriage was common in Hancock County—indeed, Martha Winstead, Eunice's mother, had married at sixteen, and Eunice's sister Ina at thirteen—they all thought that nine was too young to be married. But both families resigned themselves to it quickly. They had known each other for years, and the Winsteads believed that Charlie was a good man who would take care of Eunice. The young couple could live with Charlie's parents until he had enough money to build a home; he was already farming forty acres of his own tobacco. And Eunice's mother was clear that the couple was not yet having sex. When asked if they lived together "as man and wife," she responded, "Course they don't. Eunice don't know nothin' and I am satisfied she is the same little girl she was when she left here that mornin' to git married." Though the bride might have been young, Eunice and Charlie had just done early what many thought they were likely to do eventually. They would grow into their marriage, and soon enough no one would even remember that it had begun so early.[2]

And that is probably what would have happened if someone in Treadway or Sneedville hadn't thought the marriage unusual, even for Hancock County, and told a reporter in Knoxville, about sixty miles away. The *Knoxville Journal* broke the story on January 30. By the next day it had been picked up by the Associated Press and was making major papers across the country, from the *New York Times* to the *Los Angeles Times*, and most papers geographically in between. Newspapers as far away as Singapore ran coverage, and reporters were soon on a quest to find more child brides across the United States. Within days Eunice and Charlie's story had by turns captivated and horrified the country, made headlines around the world, and led to an unprecedented nationwide conversation about child marriage.[3]

Of course, Eunice and Charlie were not typical, which is why they garnered so much attention. Although many girls in the United States married as legal minors, marrying at nine was extremely rare. Indeed, some accounts claimed that Eunice was the youngest bride on record (erroneously, as it turns out). Even though much of the reporting on Eunice, Charlie, and other child brides made it seem as if child marriage had reached epidemic proportions, the practice was actually on the wane. Rates of marriage and childbirth were both declining during the Great Depression: many people could not afford to marry, and the age of first marriage had risen since the 1920s. In one way, then, Eunice and Charlie were a distraction. As the Great Depression entered its eighth crippling year, many Americans were worried about the effects of sustained national poverty for families: postponed marriages, low birth rates, more premarital sex, and increases in marital desertion. Focusing on Eunice and Charlie allowed Americans to forget about the more widespread problems all around them.[4]

But even though early marriage had declined in most places, it remained common in the South. Rural southerners particularly were much more likely to marry at younger ages than those in other regions of the country, and southern states like Tennessee had laws that were most accommodating of early marriage with and without parents' permission. The national debate over Eunice and Charlie focused on that issue, with many declaring Tennessee "uncivilized" for allowing the marriage to occur. Most reporters did not bother to explore just why youthful marriage was more common in the South, but an investigation into conditions there demonstrates that the hallmarks of middle-class childhood were still lacking. Many rural southerners lived in communities where, for a variety of reasons, age was less engrained as being a fundamental way of understanding differences between people. As a result, childhood was not protected in the ways that middle-class Americans valued. If childhood was not strictly demarcated from adulthood, then some legal children were going to behave like adults. Child marriage was one result. Exploring the marriage of Eunice and Charlie in some depth allows us to investigate both the significance of this nationwide 1930s "child marriage scare" as well as the persistence of early marriage in the rural South.

AMERICA HAS ITS CHILD BRIDES

The Winstead and Johns families lived about half a mile from each other in Treadway and Eunice had known Charlie from a very young age. Her mother later told reporters that Eunice had idolized Charlie and had been sweet on him for some time: "We knew it was going to happen eventually because Eunice has been in love for the longest with Charlie and he has loved her since the first time he seen her." A year before the marriage Eunice had found Charlie with a picture of a woman from across the mountain and was so jealous that she had torn it up and put it under a rock. For his part, Charlie clearly also wanted to be with Eunice. One local reporter explained it this way: "They say the child bride is friendly and flirtatious, whereas the groom is shy and awkward and as one woman told me, 'He would go a mile out of his way to keep from speaking to a woman.'" The implication was that Eunice put him at ease, whereas grown women intimidated him. At some point Charlie must have gotten it into his head that the best way to be with Eunice forever was to marry her. A couple months earlier, Eunice's elder brother, Herbert, seventeen, had taken out a marriage license to marry Charlie's sister, Clara, who was twenty-four. Martha Winstead explained that a neighbor "put the peep on Herbie and Clarey," and their families stopped them from marrying. "Charlie was afeered we would do the same on Eunice." So Charlie made his move quickly, enlisting only his friend Sam in going with him to get the marriage license. When Eunice snuck out of her parents' home that day in January, it seems that she was unaware why Charlie wanted to meet with her secretly. But there was no indication that she was anything other than enthusiastic once Charlie told her the plan. The Reverend Lamb reported that she and Sam Wolfe did most of the talking when he met them on the road above his cabin, and she told many reporters later that "we slipped it over on the folks," referring to the adults who might have stopped the marriage.[5]

The first story to cover the marriage ran in the *Knoxville Journal* eleven days after they had married. It featured a picture of Eunice holding a bundle in her arms and looking upward at the camera; the photo was captioned, "Mrs. Charlie Johns. She plays with her doll and loves her husband." In fact the bundle was her sister's child, but most newspapers continued to report that it was a doll that Charlie had given Eunice as a wedding present, further infantilizing her. The initial stories largely treated the marriage as something of a joke and focused on the newlyweds' location in rural Appalachia. Clearly the backwardness of Treadway explained why one of its nine-year-olds had married. As concerned citizens called for an annulment, most papers explained in a cursory but accurate fashion why that was not possible: although the clerk should not have issued a marriage license for a girl below the common-law age of twelve, if neither Eunice and Charlie nor her parents sought to annul the marriage, officials were powerless to do so.[6]

The initial stories begat more stories, and soon Hancock County was besieged by photographers and reporters. Within days "five motorcars of news cameramen" were parked near the Johns home; with the photographers were reporters from Atlanta, Nashville, and New York. A group of neighbor men banded together outside the Johns cabin to protect Eunice, who remained in seclusion, "frightened by the strangers that have invaded the hills of Hancock County for a glimpse of the nation's youngest bride." By mid-February the *Knoxville Journal* explained that even though Charlie had gone back to farming his tobacco, strangers still came up to Treadway to see Eunice and that he and his neighbors had devised a system of signals to warn of strangers' approach so that Eunice could hide. *Time* ran columns on Eunice and Charlie throughout 1937, and *Life* sent a photographer for a full-page photo spread. Meanwhile the Johnses received hundreds of letters from across the country and were so inundated with offers for special features, radio and newsreel stories, movie deals, and vaudeville acts that Charlie hired a local attorney to manage the offers. It is unclear whether Charlie ever received any payment.[7]

Charlie and Eunice Johns. When Charlie Johns, twenty-two, and Eunice Winstead, nine, married in the hills of Hancock County, Tennessee, in 1937, they caused an international media sensation, which spurred Tennessee and a number of other states to update their marriage laws. This image is taken from the *Life* magazine photo spread that appeared in the February 15, 1937, issue.

While reporting on the marriage and the Tennessee legislature's plans to pass a new marriage law, reporters in upstate New York discovered another child bride: twelve-year-old Leona Roshia of Great Bend (near Watertown) had married nineteen-year-old Stanley Backus on January 15. On February 2, the *Watertown Daily Times* learned of the union and ran a story comparing it to the Winstead-Johns marriage, about which they had been reporting. Although both sets of parents claimed not to know about Leona and Stanley's plans before the wedding (falsely, as it turned out), they voiced their approval after the fact, perhaps because it would later be revealed that the two had had sex and Leona was pregnant. Indeed, Leona's mother placed a wedding announcement in the Watertown paper. The reporter for the *Watertown Times* alerted news outlets in New York City about the presence of a second child bride, and soon photographers and reporters for major news outlets arrived. The next day the story ran in the *New York Times*, and other major newspapers across the country picked it up, running the story in conjunction with the child marriage in Tennessee.[8]

The marriage of Eunice and Charlie had led some reporters to investigate the prevalence of child marriage in Tennessee, but the fact that a similar case could be found in New York, far removed from the hills of Appalachia, prompted reporters to write about the incidence of child marriage across the nation, both the numbers of underage brides reported in the census and the laws as they varied state by state. In a second day of coverage on the Roshia-Backus nuptials, many papers ran an Associated Press piece comparing state marriage laws and noting that Tennessee was unique in having no state statute governing age of marriage at all. As national papers increasingly reported on the two cases together, as well as their ensuing legal fates, the *Baltimore Sun* and the *Washington Post* both ran articles highlighting a new study by the American Youth Commission on child marriage in Maryland, which concluded that the Old Line State was not without its fair share of child brides. While some papers highlighted the incidence of child marriage in their own backyards, others made the case that the phenomenon was comparatively infrequent in their states. The *Washington Post* ran a story entitled "Tsk! Cradle Marriages Here? It Could Happen, Laws Reveal." The *Chicago Tribune*, by contrast, claimed that Illinois laws made child marriage rare, and ran pictures of Eunice and Charlie, Leona and Stanley, Mr. and Mrs. William Rudd of Vallejo, California (married at thirteen and twenty-two), and Mazie and Orville Bohannon of Gatlinburg, Tennessee (married at eleven and twenty-two). Throughout February and on into March, April, and beyond, local and national newspapers discovered child brides across the United States. In tallying up the year's most significant marriages, the *Boston Globe* listed the Johnses' union as second only to the nuptials of Edward VIII and Wallis Warfield Simpson.[9]

MOTHER INDIA'S RIVAL

The reporting about Eunice, Leona, and all the other child brides emphasized not only that child marriage was more common across the United States than people thought but also that the highest incidence was in the Southwest and Southeast, the latter the prime focus of their coverage. Reporters capitalized on a long tradition of depicting Appalachia and the Mountain South as backward in its extreme isolation. Instead of exploring the socioeconomic reasons for this, many reporters and commentators called the South "uncivilized" and made comparisons between Tennessee and countries they labeled "dark" or "heathen," particularly India. Ten years earlier, American journalist Katherine Mayo had published a scathing indictment of Indian culture in *Mother India*; child marriage had been a central theme, and newspapers and ordinary citizens eagerly equated Mayo's (disputed and sensationalized) findings with what had happened in Treadway. They used this language of "civilization" to indict Appalachian culture and to pressure Tennessee officials to either annul the marriage or change the law so that marriages like Eunice and Charlie's could not occur again.[10]

A *Los Angeles Times* story published shortly after the marriage—and before numerous other child marriages were found—explained, "One would have to go as far as India and its pagan people to find a modern counterpart of this unfortunate marriage. In that country weddings sometimes are solemnized in which the brides are mere infants in the view of the British law which seems powerless to prevent such marital alliances, while marriages of children of 8 to 12 years are by no means uncommon." Contrasting the presumably civilized British with the "pagan" Indians and highlighting the youth of Indian child brides made the point that civilization was tied to recognizing how childhood was different from adulthood. The *Chicago Times* ran a cartoon, clearly referencing various "dark" lands, of Eunice and Charlie getting married with the caption "In Darkest America." The *Chicago Tribune's* "America Has Its Child Brides" was subtitled: "Evil of India Repeated Here," and told readers that "tiny 9-year-old Eunice Winstead has directed nation-wide attention to the fact that mere children still are permitted to marry in this country. The pictures on this page of the child bride Eunice and the shockingly young mothers reveal that America cannot be too critical of India." This story used pictures of young white brides and mothers (posed with husbands or babies), much like Mayo's *Mother India*, to highlight the incongruity between youth and adulthood; it also emphasized that the shock was that the United States "still" permitted child marriage, as if the country had not yet escaped the uncivilized past where India remained trapped. Another newspaper interviewed the English sociologist Dame Rachel Crowdy, who "expressed surprise that the people of the United States considered themselves superior to Oriental countries in respect to child marriages. India, China, Turkey, and Japan, Dame Crowdy remarked, have introduced statutes limiting marriage to persons over fifteen or sixteen, whereas seven of the United States permit girls of twelve to marry." In an article called "Mother India's Rival," the *LA Times* explained: "Self-righteously superior to the 'barbaric custom' of child marriages in India has been this country." Until, of course, reporters revealed that "child marriage in America, is, after all, an established institution." "Mother India has made no pretenses. We have. The comparison does not do us much credit." A story published in the *Straits Times* in Singapore made note of just this disjuncture: "Civilised America was shocked to find that the backwoods law of Tennessee could permit the marriage of child brides. While the country seethed with indignation, enlightened New York discovered another child bride—aged 12—within the boundaries of its own State." While some in New York City might not have thought of upstate Watertown as so very different from Tennessee, the point was clear: even enlightened northerners shouldn't point fingers. Much closer to home, the *Knoxville Journal* published a letter to the editor: "Yours is the only state in the union that puts India in the shade." The writer explained that in the state where he or she lived "men are men and children are protected," highlighting what Tennessee could not do: differentiate adults from children and offer children the protection they deserved.[11]

Some newspapers also noted the connections between Tennessee as home to the infamous Scopes "monkey" trial on teaching evolution in schools. The *Chicago Tribune* led off with the comparison in its first story on the marriage. Observing the differences between Nashville and Knoxville, which were urban, and "up here in the hills that line the Clinch river," the reporter explained that Eunice's mother was opposed to annulling her daughter's marriage because she "bases her beliefs on the same fundamental religion— known in the mountains as 'hardshell'—that brought a $100 to $500 fine to John Scopes, who was tried and convicted of teaching evolution. The mountains resented it being said 'we come down from a passel of monkeys.'"

Herblock, "In a State Where You Can't Teach Evolution," February 3, 1937. Referencing
the 1925 Scopes trial, in which a Tennessee teacher was fined for teaching about
evolution, Herblock draws a parallel between a state where students are not educated in
science and the possibility of marrying at the age of nine. The cartoon is just one example
of the nationwide attention brought to Tennessee in the wake of the Winstead-Johns
marriage. A 1937 Herblock Cartoon © The Herb Block Foundation. Image courtesy of
the Prints & Photographs Division, Library of Congress, LC-DIG-hlb-01319.

Clarence Darrow, Scopes's attorney, weighed in, condemning the marriage. And famed cartoonist Herblock published a cartoon featuring the young couple under the caption: "In a State Where You Can't Teach Evolution." The critique works on three levels. Most straightforwardly, Tennesseans were portrayed as being so religious and uneducated that they could not appreciate the science behind evolution; they were, in a word, unenlightened. But the equation between the Scopes trial and child marriage also points to a connection between childhood, adulthood, and evolution: a state uncivilized enough not to believe in evolution also could not comprehend the developmental stages that separated a child from an adult. It was this fundamental confusion that allowed for the marriage in the first place. Last, the state of Tennessee itself could be seen as infantile because it had not yet advanced to the level of teaching evolution.[12]

It wasn't just reporters who were so upset about the marriage. Hundreds of ordinary citizens from across the country took it upon themselves to write to Tennessee governor Gordon Browning. Within a week of the news breaking, Browning claimed to have received more letters regarding the marriage than he had about the torrential rains that were flooding the Ohio and Mississippi Rivers and leaving hundreds of thousands homeless throughout January and February. Many letters highlighted the connection between child marriage and a lack of civilization in Tennessee. C. G. Johnstone, minister of the First Presbyterian Church in Harriman, Tennessee, for instance, explained that he thought

> of the millions of dollars that our church and your church have spent
> in civilizing the Indians here in America, and in sending missionaries
> to heathen India, China, Africa, and other land to lead these people
> out of these heathenish practices. And we do this not merely for
> spiritual reasons, but also with a view to change the social and moral
> life of those people, thus protecting little girls from physical and men-
> tal tortures which always result from child marriages. In other words
> we are lifting the standard of civilization in those dark, heathen lands,
> while here in Tennessee these standards are gradually being lowered.

H. J. Arnold, president of the Ohio Conference on Adult Education, also believed that the marriage had "outraged the ideals of childhood," expected that the governor must be revolted by "this reversion to barbarism, which is a blot upon the name of your fair state," and hoped that the marriage could be

annulled in order to prevent a recurrence of such "barbaric acts." Julia Wilson
of Mobile, Alabama, worried: "It looks like we are reverting to barbarism, but
I don't think even the savage braves took a little nine year old girl for a squaw."
These three letter writers all argued that it was possible to become less civilized and that Tennessee was clearly on that road.[13]

Some letter writers suggested that missionaries should be sent to Tennessee instead of to the countries where they had heretofore been doing most of
their work. One asked: "Can it be we have in our own nation uncivilized people, yea barbarians? Dare Christians send missionaries to foreign lands when
they are so *sorely* needed in these our own United States[?]" A transplanted
Tennessean writing from Washington, D.C., suggested that "Africa couldn't be
a worse example" and that "we should send the missionarys [*sic*] to the Rural
districts of Tennessee instead of Africa and other foreign countries as there[']s
plenty to be done here." Mr. and Mrs. Martin J. Krause of Saint Louis asked
the governor: "Why make up money to send missionaries to China, Africa,
and other foreign countries, when we have such urgent need of such teaching
in our own rural, outlying sections like this one?" These correspondents spent
little time considering what "civilization" meant exactly and why it might be
that Eunice and Charlie had married; they easily concluded that poor and
rural southerners were uncivilized, like those in dark and heathen lands, and
needed to be saved.[14]

Although most news stories did not explicitly address whether Charlie and Eunice were having sex, those that did so made it clear that Eunice's
mother believed they were not. As reassuring as this could have been to
those who worried about Eunice's safety—and many letter writers were not
convinced by Martha Winstead's claims—a marriage without consummation
also flew in the face of modern understandings of marriage that emphasized
sexual intimacy as key to marital fulfillment. It also more closely resembled
the arranged marriages of India and other "uncivilized" nations where some
couples consummated their marriages a number of years after entering them
when the brides and grooms reached puberty. I do not know when Eunice and
Charlie first had sex. But that Martha Winstead believed that a couple might
be married *without* having sex did little to assuage members of the public who
feared not just for Eunice's safety but also for the fate of matrimony itself.[15]

Noteworthy here, especially given the comparison to India, is that Eunice
and Charlie were white and, because of their location in Appalachia, most
likely descended from early English settlers. Eunice and Charlie notwithstanding, higher percentages of black girls in the United States married at

Table 8.1. Percentage of Married Girls in 1930 by Race and Age

Race	Age 14 and Under	Age 15	Age 16	Age 17
White	0.020	1.1	3.87	9.37
Black	0.053	2.8	8.3	17.5

Source: U.S. Census Bureau, *Fifteenth Census of the United States: 1930*, Population, vol. 2, 843–47.

young ages than did white girls (table 8.1), as did large numbers of girls in the Southwest, where Mexican Americans made their home. We know from their coverage of child marriage across the nation that reporters had been consulting the census, which means that they, too, must have been aware of this.[16]

But the newspaper coverage of child marriage, whether it mentioned Tennessee's lack of civilization or not, never discussed or pictured nonwhite child brides. Occasionally reporters would discuss the exalted Anglo-Saxon heritage of many in Appalachia, but race remained unspoken throughout the coverage, except in relation to those in "heathen" lands like India. Tennessee might be decried for its marital practices, but at least it was home to white girls in need of saving; the fate of brown and black girls was of less concern to reporters and observers of the controversy. Indeed, the discourse of civilization was a tool worth using only on behalf of those worth saving in the first place; had Americans cared to discover that there were large numbers of young African American and Mexican American girls in the South and Southwest who were also married, it probably would have confirmed that nonwhites in the United States were just as "uncivilized" as people of color were understood to be elsewhere. Observers cared about the issue, and the discourse of civilization was effective in inducing outrage and producing legislative change, precisely because Eunice and the other discovered child brides were white.[17]

Implicitly the fear was that the marriage of the Johnses and others like them might be leading to the degeneration of the white race. This was consistent with forcible sterilizations of young women in the rural South and elsewhere, a practice that increased markedly during the 1930s after the Supreme Court found the practice constitutional in 1927's *Buck v. Bell*. Eunice Winstead shared much demographically with those diagnosed as "feeble-minded" and then forcibly sterilized. She was young, white, female, and poor. In southern states during the 1930s, this was the typical victim of sterilization. Unlike

Eunice, the typical victim was also single and sexually active, that sexual activity seen as proof of her feeblemindedness and also a threat to the racial and gendered order of white supremacy, especially so in the face of African American efforts toward racial uplift and a politics of respectability. Eunice's youth also played into longstanding fears about the supposed propensity of the degenerate to bear many children, thus reproducing themselves many times over in the manner of the notorious Jukes and Kallikak families, made famous in two turn-of-the-century pseudoscientific studies about hereditary feeblemindedness.[18]

In a front-page story, the *Washington Post* published a statement from Katherine Mayo herself on the controversy that made these links explicit. Invoking eugenic themes from her book, Mayo explained that "child marriage is an offense against society, cruel to the child, and physically and mentally debasing to any race practicing it." She was grateful that in America, "it is a rarity, not a habit, resulting only from ignorance. Some backward States are without proper laws to control it. Other states are lax in enforcing the good laws they possess."[19] When national newspapers reported that New York quickly moved to prosecute Leona Roshia Backus's parents and husband, whereas Tennessee claimed to be powerless to do anything about the Winstead-Johns marriage, it only cemented the impression that northern states were, in fact, more civilized than those in the South.[20] That northern states already tended to have stricter laws regarding age of marriage was one way that reporters could both reveal child marriage to be everywhere and yet also focus on the South, invoking spatially delimited fears of racial degeneration.

THE EYES OF THE WORLD ARE ON TENNESSEE

All this talk of Tennessee's lack of civilization brought a good deal of embarrassment to the state and its residents. Tennessee legislators had long been resistant to regulating the marriage of minors, despite efforts by reformers. But the attention and embarrassment brought by Eunice and Charlie made legislators spring into action and serves as evidence of the power of the discourse of civilization. Throughout most of the nineteenth century, Tennessee was the only state with no statute governing either age of marriage or parental consent. At the very public urging of a group of women reformers, between 1899 and 1935, Tennessee legislators passed a number of laws that limited the ability of children to marry. These laws set ages below which children needed parental consent (sixteen in 1899, raised to eighteen in 1919); mandated a wait-ing period between issuance of license and actual marriage; necessitated that a clerk inform a girl's parents of her intention to marry by registered mail; and instituted fines for clerks who knowingly failed to comply with the rules (the last three all in 1929). Tennessee never set a minimum marriageable age, mean-ing that it continued to use the common-law ages of twelve and fourteen, but in conjunction with the necessity for parental consent below sixteen or eight-een. These laws were passed due to the tireless efforts of urban women who were largely aligned with the goals laid out by northern reformers like Mary Ellen Richmond, discussed in the previous chapter.[21]

By 1929, then, women's groups had convinced the legislature to make it more difficult for young people to marry in Tennessee than in any neigh-boring state. However, every year after the 1929 passage of what some called the "Woman's Bill," at least one member of the house or senate had proposed repeal. In 1935, the women lost their fight. Blaming the loss of "hundreds of thousands of dollars" in revenue on couples going to adjoining states to marry, the Tennessee legislature repealed the 1929 legislation. A casualty of this repeal was the requirement that minors gain parental consent. By the time Eunice and Charlie married two years later, Tennessee was again the only state that had neither a statutory minimum marriage age nor a law mandating parental consent.[22]

In the wake of the Winstead-Johns marriage, its attendant national con-troversy, and the negative attention directed at Tennessee, both reformers and lawmakers were eager to pass new legislation. As Ruth O'Dell, the only female member of the Tennessee legislature and a proponent of the earlier restrictive legislation, explained, "The people of Tennessee have again been humiliated and held up for scorn to the world, as objects of ignorance, depravity and of utter disregard of the sacred institution of marriage." State senator George Freeman, a sponsor of the new legislation, explained that the Winstead-Johns marriage "puts us in the attitude where we, as a state, are humiliated in the eyes of our sister states when we allow such things to take place within our borders." The *Knoxville Journal* concurred. In an editorial endorsing new laws, the paper explained that "the citizens of Tennessee would be grateful if the governor directs the enactment of laws to prevent such shocking marriages as that of the nine-year-old girl in Hancock county. The eyes of the world are on Tennessee." If marriage reform had been dismissed as simply a women's concern in the 1920s, now many more Tennesseans supported it. Such was the power of "civilization" and of the nation's scrutiny.[23]

The Tennessee assembly spent early February debating how to frame the new marriage bill, and by the middle of the month state senators passed a bill mandating fourteen as the minimum age for marriage. Ruth O'Dell then held public hearings on the bill. Following these, on February 23, the Tennessee house raised the minimum age from fourteen to sixteen in a unanimous vote. The senate approved the house bill, and on February 26, 1937, Governor Browning signed into law a bill that made sixteen the minimum age of marriage, instituted a three-day waiting period, and specified a fine of between $25 and $250 for any county clerk issuing a license in violation of the act. Most of that law remains on the books in Tennessee today and would not be there without Eunice and Charlie Johns and the agitation of citizens and reformers intent on restoring the state to "civilization." In the wake of the national conversation about the Winstead-Johns marriage, Minnesota, Rhode Island, and the District of Columbia also amended their marriage laws to make it more difficult for minors to marry, and other states came close to doing so. The year 1937 thus represents another turning point in the regulation of age of consent to marriage, not just in Tennessee, but across the country.[24]

LIFE AMONG THE BACK YONDER FOLK

Hollywood filmmakers also rushed to capitalize on the controversy: the result was *Child Bride*, released in 1938. Though clearly inspired by the previous year's events, it bears no resemblance to the marriage of Eunice and Charlie. *Child Bride* tells the tale of Miss Carol, a rural mountain woman who left her home to be educated and has returned as a schoolteacher trying to wean her people from the evils of child marriage. Among her students is Jennie, played by Shirley Mills, a happy-go-lucky girl who eventually will be sold into marriage by her mother, who is being blackmailed by her husband's murderer, Jake. Jake has not only killed the husband but threatens to lie and claim that the wife is really the murderer; marriage to Jennie is the price he is demanding. All the while, Miss Carol and her district attorney boyfriend attempt to convince the governor and the legislature to legally ban child marriage.[25]

The film was popular at the time, in part because it came quickly on the heels of the marriage of Eunice and Charlie, but also because it contained a voyeuristic nude swimming scene by twelve-year-old Mills. Like the newspaper coverage of the actual marriage, the film stereotypes the people of the fictional "Thunderhead Mountain." We can see this at work in the opening shot of the film, which is a message to the audience:

> Here is a page from the Book of Life . . .
> The characters are real people who live deep in the heart of Thunderhead Mountain.
> In dramatizing life among these "back yonder" folk ~ we aim neither to ridicule nor to defend their mode of living . . . and if our story will help to abolish Child Marriage ~ it will have served its purpose.

Contrary to the opening pledge, of course, the film takes great pains to ridicule the "back yonder folk." They all speak in a folksy dialect and wear soiled and ragged clothing; Jennie and Freddy play in the mud at one point. Most of them live in run-down shacks. They drink moonshine, engage in drunken midnight rampages, and kidnap Miss Carol; there is even a dwarf who engages in a particularly ridiculous fight sequence. In the wake of the Winstead-Johns marriage the previous year, the film's plot and opening message style themselves around trying to eradicate child marriage, and yet the Tennessee legislature had *already* legislated against child marriage by the time of the film's release.

The central drama of the film is whether Jennie will be forced to marry the evil Jake. In the film it is clear that Jennie should properly be with the equally youthful Freddy, though not until they grow up, of course. But because of Jake's machinations, Jennie will be forced into early marriage and sex wholly against her will. The wedding scene, in particular, emphasizes Jennie's youth and her terror at the prospect of what awaits her after the ceremony. The child bride of *Child Bride* is forced into marriage, unlike the child bride who inspired the movie, Eunice Winstead, who willingly married Charlie Johns. Like the newspaper coverage of Tennessee, condemnation of child marriage clearly worked best if children themselves did not choose marriage but instead had it forced on them and evil hillbillies were doing the forcing. That way the entire society could be condemned for its lack of civilization. But *Child Bride* goes one step further. In the guise of inciting its audience to anger about child marriage, which is staged as child abuse, *Child Bride* makes use of the nudity of a girl, whose character is supposedly in need of protection. It exploits in the name of banning exploitation, which is actually already legally banned. But it also clearly represents the changed attitudes of most Americans, even if exhibited in preposterous form: marriage itself was no longer capable of protecting young girls, who were presumed to be sexually vulnerable because of age, regardless of whether they were also wives.[26]

Missing from almost all accounts of the marriage, and certainly from those that focused on "civilization," was any discussion of why marriage was more common in rural and southern areas of the country. The numbers are clear (table 8.2). In 1930, the states of the Southeast had the highest rates of early marriage of any region, followed closely by the Southwest. New England ranked last. Tennessee was also impressive in its own right: 3 percent of fifteen-year-old girls were married; 8.5 percent of sixteen-year-old girls; and 17.3 percent of seventeen-year-old girls. Minnesota had the lowest figures: 0.1/0.8/1.7 percent, followed closely by Massachusetts. In terms of wives fourteen and under (for which the census does not give more precise age demarcations), the Southeast also made up the majority of the national total in 1930. Tennessee had 297 wives under fifteen, of a nationwide total of 4,506 (including widows and divorcées). Thus, Tennessee accounted for 6.6 percent of the country's total and yet had only 2.4 percent of its population fourteen and under. The percentages ten years later, though reduced, maintain the same regional differences.[27]

The numbers are impressive, and many newspapers at the time reported them faithfully, but none paused to consider the reasons behind them. As we learned in earlier chapters, childhood does not exist as an innate condition. It is constructed differently in varied societies. For children to be treated differently from adults, or adults from the elderly, societies must recognize age markers as culturally significant and then regulate people in ways that take those age markers or life stages into consideration. In all of the ways that societies tend to make age meaningful, the rural United States still lagged behind the rest of the country as late as the 1930s: less state bureaucracy to document births and ages, less contact with doctors or hospitals to gauge progress along a developmental scale, and less age-graded schooling to produce uniformity among same-age peers. Further, the Progressive Era innovations around childhood and adolescence—juvenile courts and reformatories, municipal curfews for minors, mandatory schooling, and bans on child labor—had made only minor inroads into less populated parts of the nation. Because of this, rural Americans were less likely to strictly cordon off childhood from adulthood. One consequence of this was that children and adolescents did things that others might consider adultlike—marriage, for instance—but that rural Americans

**Table 8.2. Number of Married, Widowed, or Divorced
Boys and Girls Age Fourteen and Under, 1930**

Region	Boys	Girls
New England	43	75
Middle Atlantic	127	245
East North Central	129	322
West North Central	71	247
South Atlantic	148	1,093
East South Central	106	1,311
West South Central	131	1,020
Mountain	30	98
Pacific	39	95

Census divisions: New England (ME, NH, VT, MA, RI, CT); Middle Atlantic
(NY, NJ, PA); East North Central (OH, IN, IL, MI, WI); West North Central
(MN, IA, MO, ND, SD, NE, KS); South Atlantic (DE, MD, DC, VA, WV, NC, SC,
GA, FL); East South Central (KY, AL, TN), West South Central (AR, LA, OK,
TX); Mountain (MT, ID, WY, CO, NM, AZ, UT, NV); Pacific (WA, OR, CA).
Source: U.S. Census Bureau, *Fifteenth Census of the United States: 1930*, Population, vol. 2, 925.

thought appropriate for young people, in part because those people's youth
was not as salient a characteristic as it was in the urban United States.[28]

We can see how Hancock County, Tennessee, and by extension many
other places in rural America, might have understood age differently than urban
Americans by considering some specific examples. School attendance, which
increased dramatically nationwide during the Depression, was still higher in cities than it was in rural areas. And it was higher among rural nonfarm children
than those in farming communities. Compared regionally, children in the South
were less likely to be in school than their peers in any other region. Because of
mandatory schooling laws, very high numbers of children aged seven to thirteen
did attend school nationwide—95.3 percent—but those rates decreased after
age thirteen, and they did so more quickly in the rural South than anywhere
else. Investigators for the Works Progress Administration, for instance, found
that more than half of out-of-school youth in the Appalachian counties they
studied had not gone beyond the sixth grade; only 7 percent had made it past
the eighth.[29]

Children in rural communities faced a number of obstacles to attending school. The first was the presence of a school. Because of poverty and low population density many communities did not have their own schools, meaning that children had to travel greater distances to be educated. Some schools in Appalachia could be reached only by traversing miles of mountain trails; the daily distance back and forth made them literally inaccessible for many would-be students. The second obstacle was that many parents could not afford their children's absence from farms, particularly in places like Hancock County, where 86 percent of its residents worked in agriculture. Many rural children attended school intermittently and some every other year. Some attended seasonally, missed enough classes that they were forced to redo a year's work, or simply stopped attending once they had grown to a certain size and become able farmworkers. As historian James Schmidt has noted for this region, many children were evaluated for labor based not on whether they were "old enough" but instead on whether they were "big enough." Chronological age was less important than physical size or ability. There were a number of reasons that children might leave school, but the end result was the same: young people who were not in school, or even those there intermittently, were less likely to be regarded as being fundamentally different from the older people living and working around them.[30]

Another factor encouraging age consciousness was age grading *within* schools themselves. More populous schools separated students from one another based on their date of birth, creating regimented grades that accorded with those students' ages. Smaller schools, like the two-room Fairmont School in Treadway that Eunice attended, did not have the space to separate students based on age. Students of many ages learned together. Because some students also attended school intermittently, there was no seamless correspondence between their age and the level of work they might be expected to perform; more advanced age did not necessarily accord with more advanced understanding or ability. Chronological age was less meaningful in this setting. It was not just that any individual student could not be identified by age based on grade in school, but also that in such an environment, attendance at school did not necessarily indicate particular ages; some families could afford to send their children to school for longer than others, and students did not all finish school at the same age. In places like Hancock County, Tennessee, with lower rates of school attendance and less age grading within those schools, chronological age was not really a fundamental category of identity the way that urban Americans had come to understand it.[31]

Many rural communities were also isolated. Hancock County, with its winding mountain trails far from any city, was cut off from many of the changes that had swept across the country from the early twentieth century onward. One observer writing in the *Woman's Law Journal* accounted for Eunice and Charlie's marriage by explaining that Hancock was the only county in Tennessee without "telephones, telegraph, or an inch of paved highway." These were the sorts of innovations on which people might have relayed middle-class ideals of childhood that discouraged the marriage of young girls. But Hancock County, and many parts of rural America, remained isolated from those norms.[32]

We have seen that early marriage was most common in the South; this was partially because much of the South remained rural. Works Progress Administration investigators noted that when girls left rural areas to move to cities, they tended to do so at earlier ages than young men; this increased the pressure on those girls who remained in rural areas to marry at even younger ages to the men who stayed behind. In her 1939 study of rural tenant farmwomen in the South, Margaret Jarman Hagood found that the mean age of marriage was 18.6 but that marriage much younger was not uncommon. "The most common reason given for the very early marriages was the death of one or both parents. One was afraid she would be an old maid and another just 'took the first chance she got,' at thirteen—she didn't know why." Marrying without the parental permission that was, in theory, necessary for girls below certain ages was referred to as "slipping off"; the practice was common enough that it had its own slang. As a teacher in the Appalachians put it during the 1920s, "as a rule marriage comes early in the mountains. A girl is a spinster at eighteen, and on the 'cull list' by twenty. The writer has had pupils leave school at twelve and thirteen to marry, although this is becoming less common every year." It may have been less common by the 1930s, but investigators confirmed that while the age of first marriage had gone up nationwide, rural Americans remained resistant to this trend, continuing to marry earlier than their urban counterparts. Residents of Hancock County did not believe in postponing what they saw as either inevitable or likely to happen eventually, simply because people were below what seemed to be arbitrary ages set by a government with which they might have little contact. In her accounting for the marriage, Martha Winstead clearly believed that although her daughter's marriage might have been a little early, it would have happened eventually anyway. It certainly wasn't disrupting any alternative plans she had for Eunice, including a life that was unlike that Martha Winstead herself was living. Eunice's age, in and of itself, was not enough to stand in the way of her marriage to Charlie, in large part because her age was less meaningful in a place like Treadway than it would have been in other parts of the country.[33]

WHAT DOES IT MEAN, A BIRTHDAY?

Race exacerbated all of these factors. Mexican Americans and African Americans who lived in rural areas of the South and Southwest—generally not the mountain homes made so famous during this controversy—were, as I have indicated, married young even more frequently than their white counterparts. Through midcentury, black youth particularly were more likely to be married than their white counterparts. In 1930, for instance, while 2.3 percent of white urban sixteen-year-old girls were married, 7.1 percent of black girls were. The numbers are much higher in rural areas: 5.6 percent of white rural sixteen-year-old girls on farms were wives, whereas 8.2 percent of black girls were. And whereas white rural nonfarm sixteen-year-old girls married at the same rate as their farm-based counterparts, black girls more than doubled their rate at 11.2 percent. Historian Sarah Deutsch has found that average ages of marriage for girls in the late-nineteenth- and early twentieth-century Mexican American villages she studied in the Southwest were between fifteen and twenty-one. During the 1880s, fully 25 percent of these girls married *below* fifteen, however, and this remained the case for more than 7 percent of girls as late as the first decade of the twentieth century. In large part, girls of color married for the same reasons that white girls did: they were poor, they labored at young ages, and they had little access to age-graded schooling or other institutions (pediatric medicine, state bureaucracy and compulsory birth registration) that tended to inculcate age consciousness. The problem was simply that all of these ills were worse for children of color in a segregated United States, where systemic racism and poverty structured life for many nonwhites no matter where they lived. As tenant farmers or migrant laborers, many southern African Americans relied on their children to contribute to the livelihood of their families. As one Shelby County, North Carolina, farmer and parent explained in the late 1930s, "The children need all the education they can get, but we need them to help on the farm. If you don't make your crop the white man will put somebody else there to do the work. The children go to school when there ain't no work for them in the fields, but when there is work, they has to stay home and do it." Most studies found that black children attended school fewer days than white children did, and though the largest proportion of out-of-school black youth had finished the fifth grade, many only went through the second.[34]

Poor and rural African Americans also tended to begin experimenting sexually at early ages, sometimes as young as seven or eight, though twelve and fourteen were the ages most frequently cited by studies at the time. Adults in small living quarters were often unable to shield children from sex, and one result was that children came to understand sex, even at young ages, as a routine part of daily life. With little access to contraception and early initiation into sex, rates of youthful pregnancy were also particularly high among rural blacks; pregnant girls also experienced little of the stigma that middle-class whites and blacks attached to premarital sex and pregnancy. Often these unplanned pregnancies simply led to marriage at young ages. This was especially the case because few marriages in rural African America were formally licensed. People married by moving in with each other and calling themselves married. Anthropologist Hortense Powdermaker found that in 1930s Indianola, Mississippi, only upper-class African Americans actually had licensed marriages; it was expensive enough that it was considered a status symbol. The majority of her poor and middle-class informants simply became married of their own volition, usually following sex. This type of union, called common-law marriage, was no less legal than formalized marriage, but it was unregulated, meaning that very youthful people could marry so long as they were able to live together.[35]

Writing in the same year as the Winstead-Johns marriage, Zora Neale Hurston identified two other reasons that black girls sometimes married early. In her novel *Their Eyes Were Watching God*, sixteen-year-old Janie Crawford is married off by her grandmother to Logan Killicks, an older, well-established widower. Janie herself is the product of her mother's rape by a schoolteacher at the age of seventeen, and when Janie's grandmother catches Janie kissing her friend Johnny Taylor, she fears that Janie, too, will be taken advantage of and effectively "ruined" before she can marry. In marrying Janie off to Logan, Nanny evinces an enormous faith in the institution of marriage; that Janie will have sex with her husband is expected, but the sex will be legitimate and Janie will presumably be protected within marriage. Janie marries Logan, Nanny dies, but Janie has almost immediately realized she cannot love Logan and elopes with Joe Starks within about a year (the timeline is sketchy), marrying two men (albeit one of them bigamously) before turning eighteen. (On meeting her soon-to-be-second-husband, he says, "You married? You ain't hardly old enough to be weaned." Nevertheless he himself marries her within a couple weeks.) In one case the marriage was effected as a means to prevent the rape to which so many black women and girls were subjected in the Jim Crow South; in the second, marriage was the same means of escape that so many other teenagers have seen it as being (albeit from a husband instead of parents).[36]

Early marriage among rural people, white, black, Mexican, or Indian, was also clearly linked to a lack of recognition of age itself. As one young man, a black migrant laborer named Albert who thought he was about eighteen, explained to a researcher: "What does it mean, a birthday? I don't have any, I really don't, not one that I know. I've been told I was born in May, but who can bother remembering the days? One day is like another. All days are the same. I have three children and I don't teach them their birthdays. I don't know their birthdays." In a life marked far more by the seasons than by demarcations of the Gregorian calendar or chronological age, Albert's age was far less meaningful to when he commenced doing just about anything than his size was, itself indicative of capacity to labor. Linking the timing of his marriage with the ability to work, he explained, "He was the one, the crew leader was, who told me I should pick a girl and stay with her and not go from one to the other. I was thirteen or fourteen, I don't know which. Maybe I was fifteen. What difference does it make, how old you call yourself? Here, out in the fields, you do the picking, no matter how old you are." This example dates from the mid-1960s, indicating that for the poorest of Americans in the rural South, chronological age was still of little importance past midcentury. Albert, who had married sometime in his midteens, still thought of age as something that "you call yourself," pointing out just how arbitrary it was to him, how very much *not* a part of his identity it was. Combined with the fact that he had received little schooling, had first had sex at age ten or eleven (he estimated), and had no hopes of any life beyond the one that he was currently living, there was simply no need to postpone marriage, no idea that postponing marriage was something that people did do. This was the situation for many poor rural Americans in the 1930s and 1940s; that Mexican and African Americans were much more likely to be poor than whites helps to explain why their rates of early marriage in rural America remained so high. It bears noting, for instance, that for all the uproar over Eunice's marriage, her parents were well aware of her birthday and age, her marriage to Charlie was licensed (albeit illegally), she was a regular student in an elementary school, and her parents were quite clear that she was still a virgin. Though the poverty of Eunice's community in Treadway partially accounted for why she married at age nine, that so many people cared about it also indicates her position of relative privilege vis-à-vis the thousands of poor African American and Mexican American girls who married as legal minors every year with no one caring at all. White girls like Eunice provoked outrage precisely because they were understood to possess the childhood innocence that scholar Robin Bernstein has demonstrated was denied to children of color well into the twentieth century.[37]

Three months after Eunice and Charlie were married, Homer Peel, thirty-two, and Geneva Hamby, variously reported as being nine, ten, eleven, and twelve years old, were married in Epperson, Tennessee, in the Cumberland Mountains of Monroe County, south of Knoxville. Homer had lied about Geneva's age to obtain the marriage license. Both Peel and the clerk for Monroe County were arrested, the first arrests under the law passed in February, but the chancellor for the county refused to annul the marriage even though they had violated the law. He said that the law could prevent marriages, not dissolve them once they had been solemnized. Besides, annulment would turn "Geneva out of house and home with no place to go." Homer and Geneva remained husband and wife. Like Eunice and Charlie, Homer and Geneva also lived in a rural area, where poverty was common, farming the primary occupation, and age-graded schooling less available, indeed where people were not always sure of their ages (perhaps the reason for confusion about Geneva's age in the press). And many young brides, like Geneva Hamby, whose mother had committed her to an orphanage because she was unable to raise her, may have chosen marriage because it seemed to offer them the security they desired. States could pass laws banning child marriage, but children still found their way around them to get married.[38]

In August 1937, Eunice returned to school but lasted only two days because her teacher switched her for what he called "general mischievousness" and "jumping around." Although Tennessee law mandated that all children attend school until the age of sixteen, the education commissioner ruled that "we will not take any action to compel a married child to attend school." Eunice never went back. Newspapers tended to check in with the couple on their anniversaries, and the Johnses always reported being content. Eunice gave birth to their first child when she was fifteen; the couple would have nine children altogether. There was a minor media blitz when Charlie tried, unsuccessfully, to annul the marriage of their first-born, Evelyn, who was seventeen when she secretly wed John Henry Antrican, twenty, without her parents' permission. The irony was not lost on those reporting the story. Eunice and Charlie remained married until Charlie's death in 1996. They lived near Treadway all their lives. Eunice died ten years after Charlie, in August 2006 at the age of seventy-eight, and is buried beside Charlie in the Johns family plot.[39]

NINE

Are They Marrying Too Young?

The Teenage Marriage "Crisis" of the Postwar Years

As a white, middle-class child in Oakland, California, in the 1950s and 1960s, Lucy Lang wanted nothing more than to grow up and escape the confines of home. Although Lang's parents seem not to have differed much from most parents at the time, she bridled at the restrictions they imposed on her. She also dreamed of love and fantasized about sex. As Lang would explain in the autobiography she wrote many years later, "I started seriously looking for a husband when I was twelve. I'd had enough of being a child, enough of being told what to do. I was unhappy at school; I resented homework; I didn't get along with my mother. . . . I wanted to be an adult, to be free, and to be loved." She felt that all of those things could be accomplished through marriage, and the sooner the better. Many of her friends were getting married during their teenage years and having children soon thereafter. If they could do it, so could she. Between the ages of twelve and fourteen, Lang auditioned a number of boys and men for the role. Premarital pregnancy was one possible route to marriage, and it fulfilled another of Lang's goals, motherhood, which she also equated with being an adult. She believed that her parents would have to consent to her marriage if she became pregnant. As she explained, "Sex and marriage, in that order, would be my ticket to freedom." She had sex for the first time, without contraception, at thirteen, but did not become pregnant.[1]

Although she soon parted from that particular boy, she met Mark Day not long thereafter and they quickly decided to marry. A few years her senior, he had recently dropped out of high school and was working as an apprentice cabinetmaker. Lang's parents wanted her to wait until she was sixteen, but she wheedled and threatened them—with pregnancy; she and Mark were already having sex—and they finally relented. There was, however, a hitch. When they went to the local license bureau (with Lang's parents in tow), they were informed that it was illegal for a girl to marry below the age of sixteen unless there were extenuating circumstances (usually a pregnancy). Not yet pregnant, they drove to Minden, Nevada, believing that it would be easier to marry in that state. There they were informed that not only was Lang too young to marry in Nevada as well, but so was Day. Regrouping, they realized that if they were going to achieve their goal, they would have to lie. Joined by Mark's parents in Reno, Lang and Day simply told the license bureau they were sixteen and eighteen (the required ages), their parents affirmed the lie, and they were married on September 8, 1962, just one week before Lang should have started ninth grade. Lucy Lang was fourteen, and Mark Day was seventeen. Lucy gave birth to their daughter, Liana, about nine months later. During that first year of marriage, the couple barely scraped by financially, sometimes depending on help from their parents. Partially as a result of this hardship, Lucy divorced Mark when she was sixteen but then, realizing that she could not live without him, remarried him at seventeen.[2]

This tale, filtered through Lucille Lang Day's eyes many years later in her 2012 memoir, *Married at Fourteen,* is perhaps most noteworthy for Day's characterization of her then teenage self as aware of what she believed marriage could get her and in her relentless pursuit of that goal in and of itself, sometimes in ways somewhat unrelated to the actual person who would join her in marriage. Although it at first appears extreme, the only real anomaly in Day's account is that she married the same man twice. In all other respects, her story serves as an example of precisely the kind of teenage marriage that both swept the nation from the 1940s through the 1960s and led to an enormous amount of handwringing by parents, teachers, reporters, and academics.

There is no question that there was a teenage marriage wave in the twenty years following World War II. Those doing the marrying were generally in their later teens, in contrast to the child brides who worried reformers in earlier moments. The median age of first marriage dipped to an all-time twentieth-century low of 20.1 and 22.5 for girls and boys, respectively, in 1956. During many years in the 1950s more girls married at eighteen than any other age, perhaps because this was the age at which they *could* marry without their parents' permission or because this was also when high school ended. And the numbers, both absolute and as a proportion of the population, for teenage marriages also rose exponentially. What some called a teenage or high school marriage crisis also attracted more attention to youthful marriage than perhaps any other time in the nation's history. As one anxious commentator explained in a 1961 *Coronet* article entitled "The Tragic Trap of Teenage Marriage," "Most of us think that too-early marriage is a custom that used to take place among remote native tribes. But the U.S. has become the early-marryingest country in the Western World." It is worth examining both of these issues—the actual increase and the attention it garnered—while recognizing that they were not the same thing. It is undeniable that more girls (and boys) married in their teenage years than they had previously, and there are real reasons why they did so, but the attention the phenomenon garnered was largely a function of which teenagers were doing the marrying.[3]

The explanation for why so many young people married is threefold: as other scholars have noted, there was an intense preoccupation with domesticity from the end of World War II through the early 1960s. This glorification of nuclear family life placed pressures on all Americans, including those in the teen years, to marry and raise families. Spinsterhood and bachelorhood were newly stigmatized. In this respect, teenage marriage had much in common with the marriage of those in their twenties and thirties (and many teenaged girls married men who were themselves somewhat older). Second, from the early twentieth century, standards of permissiveness around premarital sex had gradually been loosening, especially for middle-class girls. While men of all classes had long had sex before marriage (often with prostitutes, or sometimes middle-class men with working-class women), as the century wore on, it became increasingly acceptable for middle-class girls to experiment sexually with their dates, especially if they were "going steady" or engaged to be married. That said, in an era before the pill was widely available and when being prepared for sex with contraception might mark a girl as promiscuous, sex was often spontaneous and unprotected, and that sometimes resulted in pregnancy. So although pressure and desire for sex were both on the rise, as was a tacit acceptance of some sexual activity between committed couples, open conversations about and preparedness for sex were in their infancy. One result of this, in addition to unwed motherhood and secretive adoptions and abortions, was what people at the time called "forced marriage," so named because the pregnancy had necessitated a shotgun wedding. That marriage was still seen as the solution to premarital sex and pregnancy is also telling. Americans simultaneously believed that marrying as a teenager was too young, but if a girl was pregnant, then getting married was far better than having the child out of wedlock. Despite a growth in sensitivity to age since early in the century, which led many more to see adolescence as incompatible with marriage, that remained the preferred solution to premarital pregnancy. In midcentury America, fears about unregulated sex still clearly trumped the prolongation of childhood.[4]

Last, Lucy Lang Day makes it clear that one of her prime motives for marrying was the pursuit of adulthood. Though the existence of adolescent people was hardly novel in the United States, the teen culture that developed in the 1940s and 1950s was. Teenagers, and the term itself was relatively new, often found themselves caught between two worlds, treated on the one hand like children by their parents and on the other as proto-adults by the mass media (especially regarding sex). This was particularly so as the number of young people who were completing high school in the postwar era increased exponentially. As in earlier eras, some teens sought to cement their status as adults; they believed that marriage was one way to do this. They had varying degrees of parental support for this decision.[5]

Though the numbers of people under eighteen who married from the 1940s through the 1960s did increase, what caused the panic was which young people were doing the marrying. Rates of early marriage for rural people of all races and, in particular, for African American and Mexican American girls, remained relatively constant from 1900 through 1970. There were slight ups and downs, but the real increases during the postwar era were in the marriage of white girls, especially white girls in cities and suburbs. Early marriage was not seen as a problem, then, until white middle-class girls who were presumed to have futures started to squander them by marrying too young. Two of the major concerns of reporters and academics throughout the teenage marriage crisis, and they were legitimate concerns, were the high school dropout rate of youthful brides and pregnancy so soon after marrying. Most commentators stopped short of advocating that these girls should necessarily be going to college and finding careers—wife- and motherhood were certainly seen as their destiny—but they did worry about the effects for white families of "children raising children," especially if doing so while dependent on their parents because their youth made them unable to support their families. The related worry was about divorce. Most studies demonstrated that the divorce rate for those who married young was much higher than for those who married in their twenties (this remains the case). As divorce (or annulment in some circumstances) became increasingly available over the twentieth century, many lamented not just that teenage marriage was bad for teenagers but also that it was bad for marriage. Until the mid-1960s, however, the chief concern was over the divorce rate of whites, however, not that of African Americans. When evaluating the rise in teenage marriages of the 1950s and 1960s, then, we must bear in mind that its existence is statistically demonstrable, but that people cared about it as much as they did has everything to do with just who had produced it: white girls in suburbs and cities.

THE INCREASE IN EARLY MARRIAGE

The uptick in marriage and the decline in age at first marriage both began in the 1940s as the United States entered what would come to be known as World War II. As one sociologist explained at the time, the increase in marriages tracked consistently with events overseas, even before the United States had entered the war, though the highest jump occurred just after the Selective Service Act was passed. Rising from the late 1930s onward, the marriage rate reached a new high point at 12.6 per 1,000 people in 1941. Just as in the Great War, soldiers married to legalize their ties to sweethearts before they shipped out. And newspapers and government officials, when not worrying about prostitution and the spread of venereal disease, fretted that some girls made a habit of seeking out soldiers because they found them glamorous or as a way of "doing their part" for the war effort. Some of these unions ended in ill-planned marriages. In Elizabeth City, North Carolina, for instance, seventeen-year-old Wanda Whited received a three-year prison sentence after she successively married three enlisted men in six months; she had met all her husbands at the roller-skating rink in Norfolk, Virginia. Most marriages, of course, were monogamous, and with soldiers facing an uncertain fate, most Americans probably would have supported the right of couples to legalize their unions through marriage. Marriage would entitle a woman to survivor's benefits should her husband not return home, and many commentators believed that those who married in the early war years probably would have done so anyway; the war had simply accelerated their nuptials. People were looking to marriage for a sense of security in an uncertain world.[6]

Some of those marrying were doing so at young ages. As the chief of the Cook County Marriage License Bureau in Chicago reported in the early 1940s, "There are more sixteen and seventeen year old girls than ever before. Birth

**Table 9.1. Median Age at First Marriage
for Men and Women, 1920–1970**

Year	Male	Female
1920	24.6	21.2
1930	24.3	21.3
1940	24.3	21.5
1950	22.8	20.3
1960	22.8	20.3
1970	23.2	20.8

Source: U.S. Census Bureau, *Historical Statistics of the
United States: Colonial Times to 1970*, vol. 1, 19.

certificates are requested routinely now. Boys come from all over the country, many of them are under eighteen." But Chicago was not the only location to see an increase in early marriage, and it was one that would continue through the 1950s, peaking at the end of that decade before subsiding slowly through the 1960s (table 9.1). The median age of first marriage in 1940, for example, was 24.3 for men and 21.5 for women. By 1956, that hit an all-time low for the century of 22.5 for men and 20.1 for women. By 1970, the ages had started their rise, then at 23.2 for men and 20.8 for women, a rise that would continue till the present.

Most men and women marrying during this era were not minors, yet sizable proportions were marrying in their teens. If we look at those children aged fourteen and under, and fifteen through seventeen, who were married in four census years, beginning in 1940, we see that the percentages increase beginning in 1940 and then start to decline sometime after either 1950 or 1960, depending on the age category (table 9.2). Though absolute numbers of teenagers marrying increased in the 1960s (a result of the baby boom), the decline in the proportion that married is most obvious among girls, in part because the girls' increase is also the most notable.[7]

As in earlier eras, the highest proportions of married girls and boys were in primarily rural areas, and they were also concentrated in the South and West (which included the Southwest in the way the Census Bureau designated its regions). Although the numbers of those between the ages of fifteen and nineteen who were married increased nationwide during these years, the percentages were always significantly higher (often double) in certain

Table 9.2. Percentage of Married Boys and Girls, 1940–1970

Year	Boys Age 14	Girls Age 14	Boys Age 15–17	Girls Age 15–17
1940	0.10	0.28	0.38	4.55
1950	0.61	0.67	0.95	6.97
1960	0.55	1.06	1.13	6.64
1970	0.97	1.07	1.23	4.30

Sources: U.S. Census Bureau, *Sixteenth Census of the Population: 1940, Population*, vol. 4, *Characteristics by Age*, part 1, United States Summary, table 8, 22; U.S. Census Bureau, *1950 Census of the Population*, vol. 2, *Characteristics of the Population*, part 1, United States Summary, table 104, 182; U.S. Census Bureau, *Census of the Population: 1960*, vol. 1, *Characteristics of the Population*, part 1, United States Summary, table 176, 424–25; U.S. Census Bureau, *1970 Census of the Population*, vol. 1: *Characteristics of the Population*, part 1, United States Summary, section 2, table 203, 640.

regions (table 9.3). Girls remained far more likely to wed than boys, yet boys were more likely to show an increase in their propensity to marry than in earlier eras.

Almost all studies of the trend—sociological, governmental, and journalistic—emphasized, in contrast to the very young brides discussed in the previous chapter, that this was a phenomenon of teenage or high school marriage. Although the brides and grooms had sometimes dropped out of high school by the time of their unions, the vast majority of those minors who married during this era were in their later teens. In addition to the standard disclaimer that early marriage remained more popular among girls than boys, sociologists regularly reported that those girls who did marry were most likely to do so in their senior year of high school, and the phenomenon was decreasingly likely (though still not uncommon) through junior, sophomore, and freshman years. Studies of different schools and regions found rates of between 2.1 percent and 8.1 percent of senior girls marrying, down to variations between 1 percent and 3.3 percent of sophomore girls marrying. Most high school girls married out-of-school boys who were slightly older than they; the younger the girl, the larger the age difference. Marriages uniting a high school boy *and* girl remained in the minority.[8]

Both in demographics and in what it was called, the postwar furor over early marriage was really an instance of teen marriage, not child marriage. Whereas earlier reformers like Mary Ellen Richmond had concentrated

Table 9.3. Percentage of Married Teens Age Fifteen to Nineteen by Year, Sex, and Region, 1940–1960

Year/Sex	Northeast	North Central	South	West
1940				
Boys	0.7	1.3	2.9	1.4
Girls	5.1	9.5	18.6	13
1950				
Boys	1.9	2.9	4.5	3.7
Girls	8.6	14.8	23.7	20
1960				
Boys	2.5	3.5	4.9	4.5
Girls	10.2	14.7	20.3	18.4

Source: Taeuber and Taeuber, *People of the United States in the 20th Century,* table VII-5, 298.

the crusade against "child marriage" on those below the age of sixteen, here the focus was on those teens sixteen and above. Those who married at fourteen and fifteen (and below) certainly existed, yet they remained outside the norm, on the trailing edge of the much higher incidence of marriage at sixteen, seventeen, and eighteen. In other words, the furor over teen marriage occurred even though those marrying in large numbers were actually older than in previous periods of concern over youthful marriage. This is significant in large part because the numbers were not actually that different. Whereas proportionately more of each age of girl was marrying in 1950 than in 1920, sizable numbers of sixteen- and seventeen-year-olds did marry in the 1920s. But reformers like Richmond did not think them noteworthy because even twenty years after the "discovery" of adolescence at the turn of the century, it did not seem particularly inappropriate for a seventeen-year-old to marry. By the 1950s, however, following the marked rise in high school attendance during and after the Great Depression, seventeen had come to seem too young for marriage because any girl who married at that age should rightly have been in school. This remained most true for white and middle-class girls, but of course these were precisely the kinds of girls about whom people were worried when they chose to leave school to marry.[9]

The postwar period ushered in distinct changes to childhood as a stage of life, one of which was the elongation of the period of childhood and adolescence. Part of this was an adolescent culture of teenager-hood that lumped sixteen- and seventeen-year-olds in with their younger peers in ways that would have seemed strange in earlier eras. Although some teenagers were tempted by the possibilities of adulthood, at the same time far larger numbers of them were enjoying the middle-class benefits of a prolonged childhood. In other words, understandings of what it meant to be "too young to marry" had shifted upward since the early twentieth century. Had the same number of late teenagers marrying in the 1950s been doing so in the 1920s, it probably would not have caused nearly the same amount of concern.[10]

CAUSES OF EARLY MARRIAGE

The reasons for the uptick in teenage marriage are reflected in the reports given by teenage wives themselves. The first of these was pregnancy. A Minneapolis teenager who married at sixteen because she was pregnant explained to a newspaper reporter that she simply had not understood how easy it was to become pregnant: "My idea of pregnancy was that you had to plan carefully for a long time and have intercourse frequently before you could become pregnant." She had sex once with her boyfriend in a car on prom night "when they were allowed to be out late," and the resulting pregnancy prompted the marriage. She explained that she had never so much as petted before, and though she and her boyfriend knew about condoms, when they had sex, "it was a spur of the moment thing, and we weren't prepared." She tried to have an abortion and was unsuccessful. Instead she married her husband, and they lived first with his parents and then with hers. When neither of them could stand living with either set of in-laws, her husband dropped out of college so that he could work full-time and they moved into a place of their own. Unlike most who married while in high school, this girl did manage to graduate (largely thanks to a school specifically designed for pregnant girls), and she now made extra money by babysitting neighbor children while she looked after her own two children (they had a second child sixteen months after the first).[11]

If the data collected by sociologists studying teen marriage are in agreement about one thing, it is that large percentages of teenage brides married as the result of unplanned pregnancies. Because the studies are based on different towns and states, the numbers vary, but almost all investigators found a positive correlation between pregnancy and teenage marriage: the rates vary from approximately 31 percent to a high of 57 percent. Most investigators concurred that pregnancy was a more likely cause of teenage marriage the younger the girl and that premarital pregnancy was usually a factor when two high school students were marrying each other (one investigator found a causal rate of 87 percent for double teen marriages). Many girls, and especially those who dated young boys, were "forced" into marriage on discovering that they were pregnant. Looked at in the aggregate, nearly half of all 1950s teenagers who married were pregnant, and from the 1940s through 1960, the vast majority of pregnant teenagers (more than 85 percent) were married by the time they gave birth.[12]

This finding went hand in hand with another: that teenagers who started dating and going steady at younger ages were much more likely to marry at young ages. This was, in part, because they had simply begun the entire process of dating at earlier ages than their peers, but it was also that they were more likely, as a result of earlier dating, to have become sexually active at earlier ages. In the cases when that was not true, their earlier dating experience had led them to want to be sexually active and that had prompted an earlier marriage precisely so that they could have sex but do so legitimately. A girl named Jenny, for instance, started dating boys the summer she was fourteen. As she began her sophomore year, she started going steady with Jay, who was seventeen and worked at her uncle's service station. Jay asked her to marry him just after her fifteenth birthday. She told him that they would have to wait until she turned sixteen: "Not that Jay ever made it hard for me, but after all we were terribly in love and we wanted each other," she explained. "But I kept remembering that my mother had told me, 'Jenny, love is respect.' Oh, we got awfully tired of saying 'Better look at the picture' or 'Better go inside now,' but somehow we managed." Jenny and Jay were putting off sex because they believed that, as an unmarried couple, it was inappropriate for them to have intercourse. Following a brief break-up over Thanksgiving, Jenny realized that Jay "loved me more than he loved anybody else," and they drove to another state where a girl needed only to be fourteen to marry with a parent or guardian's consent (her aunt and uncle, with whom she lived, accompanied them). In addition to Jenny's realization that Jay loved her unconditionally, clearly one factor prompting the marriage was a desire to have sex but to do so "legitimately."[13]

In the late 1950s, Jenny was caught in a liminal moment where it was appropriate for a girl to neck and pet with her boyfriend but not to have intercourse before marriage. Many girls and boys broke these rules (hence the premarital pregnancies), but others did not. Jenny claimed to have heeded the words of her mother in realizing that if Jay truly loved her, he would not pressure her to have intercourse. The problem, of course, was that Jenny herself wanted to have sex, but the only way to do so legitimately was through marriage. In an era where some forms of sexual activity short of intercourse were permissible but where intercourse itself was reserved for marriage in the popular consciousness, wedlock was often seen as the only route to sexual fulfillment, itself also billed as the ultimate demonstration of true love. That more and more adolescents were going steady instead of dating multiple people also heightened the pressure, because the intimacy the couple experienced together had a much greater opportunity to develop. Going steady was much closer to marriage than dating had ever been. This, combined with the greater popular acceptance of what sociologists called "permissiveness with affection," led more and more couples further down a path toward sexual intercourse.[14]

Many of the sociologists who studied the early marriage trend during the 1950s and 1960s also believed that young people were marrying in such record numbers in order to become adults, though not necessarily in a legal sense (even if marriage did legally transform them in ways familiar from earlier eras). Instead, like Lucy Lang Day, these teenagers married and had children because these acts were symbolic of adulthood; achieving these milestones would, they believed, make them look and feel like adults. It would also remove them from the oversight and regulation of their parents. In one study, some high school principals claimed that they believed that there was "a greater desire for adult status among youth today," and that this partially accounted for their own married students. Another explained, "Just 'being married' gives the young people a feeling of status and recognition by their parents and other adults in the community." The study's authors linked this to the possession of a job by a husband and a baby by a wife, both of which would also "bring them respect and acceptance by adults." It was also the case that at high schools across the nation young people were taking marriage and family living classes, whose explicit goal was to prepare young people for becoming spouses and parents. Although it would be too much to argue that these classes outright sanctioned early marriage, by focusing so much attention on this as life's ultimate goal, the courses certainly gave marriage an authoritative stamp of approval and may well have encouraged young people to believe that they were more ready for marriage than those around them might have supposed.[15]

But there was also something far less practical about the connections between marriage and adulthood that lingered in the minds of teenagers. As a doctor and a minister affiliated with the Marriage Council of Philadelphia explained, "Marriage represents to many teen-agers a way of gaining adult status, of getting out from under, of being independent. It is almost as if they are saying, 'See, I am grown up. I really am an adult. I'm *married*!" A journalist for the *Ladies' Home Journal* subtitled her piece on teenage marriage, "In their rush to grow up, do teenagers see marriage as 'some sort of magic that will make them grown-up overnight?'" She answered, not surprisingly, in the affirmative. Lucy Lang Day described a series of actions she undertook in order to be more like an adult, all of which culminated in her marriage at fourteen. She took up smoking at age twelve: "I did it because it made me feel like an adult and because it was a way of being different from my parents, neither of whom smoked." Soon thereafter she ran away with a boy, and they checked into a motel in Los Angeles, the first time she had felt comfortable making out privately, out of a car, a shed, or someone else's home: "So this was what it was like for grown-ups. Well, they certainly had it good," she observed. Being an adult allowed one the freedom to do what one wanted when one wanted to do it. This included sex. Day explained that in almost all instances in which she was regulated, "I'd convinced myself that adults were no wiser than I was. . . . The adults also said that sex outside of marriage was wrong. This, I decided, was ridiculous." Meeting a boy who had dropped out of high school, she set her sights on him, partially because "he was part of the adult world I wanted so badly to enter myself." Although she did not end up having sex with this particular boy, once she had sex with her future husband, Mark Day, she explained, "Now that we'd made love, I felt fully connected to Mark. I also felt like an adult." Day described a scenario in which she felt that her parents' rules and regulations were a great burden to her. Her reaction to this was, in part, to question their authority as adults, to question the very wisdom that supposedly undergirded their authority. This sort of questioning of authority took more political forms, of course, later in the 1960s and 1970s, when young people rebelled against both their parents and older generations more generally. Instead, Day's reaction to what she perceived as her parents' overreliance on their status as adults to regulate her led her to want to join them in the ranks of adulthood herself. Marriage was her ticket there. She perceived it as both a rebellion against her parents' rules and a way to gain the very status that had allowed them to institute those rules in the first place. Instead of seeking to overthrow the power structure, she simply wanted access to it.[16]

By contrast, some commentary at the time, by journalists and academics, explored the nexus between early dating and the desire for adult status by faulting parents themselves for pushing their daughters into romance too early. Whereas 1920s reformers had blamed immigrant and working-class parents for early marriage, these reporters turned their attention to the middle class. Focusing on parental pressure, many explained that dating, going steady, and the accoutrements of both—including dances and makeup—were all increasingly the domain of the very young, including those who were not yet teenagers. Asking, "Are you pushing your daughter into too-early marriage?" *Good Housekeeping* noted that the ages for dances, dating, and going steady were moving ever lower and then indicted mothers for pushing their daughters (and sons) into these activities before they were ready. The author of this article noted that some mothers justified their attitudes toward early dating by explaining that it inculcated social poise and prepared their children for "real" dating, which would arrive in their teenage years; they would then have "a minimum of shyness and awkwardness" when it counted. Others simply blamed the fast pace of contemporary life, which accelerated children's social development. This author, however, believed that parents had their own motivations, varying from living vicariously through their daughters' social lives (because they either had or had not experienced dating fun of their own) to gaining social status and prestige through their socially successful children. Covering a 1962 Minnesota child welfare conference, one reporter summarized an overriding theme:

> To forestall teen-age marriage parents must stop pushing their children into intimate relationships with the opposite sex before they have a chance to enjoy childhood, an Iowa State University sociologist said Tuesday.
> Too many parents, said Dr. Lee G. Burchinal, encourage their youngsters to date, go steady, attend formal dances, and take part in other boy-girl activities, thereby forcing "heterosexual relationships" before the children are prepared for them.[17]

Although stories like this inevitably encouraged a certain amount of mother-blaming (itself epidemic during the 1950s and 1960s), they may contain a kernel of truth. No one was suggesting that parents encouraged early marriage (and indeed, almost all demonstrated that parents opposed their children marrying as teenagers, unless there was a pregnancy, and then they preferred marriage to an illegitimate child), but the implication here was that mothers who achieved status through their children were inadvertently encouraging early marriage. That children from higher socioeconomic brackets were more likely to date at earlier ages (even if they were less likely to marry at those ages) only confirmed the impression that middle-class mothers might be partially responsible for the teenage marriage trend. *Good Housekeeping*'s article closed with recommendations for parents to avoid a teenage marriage, one of which was to do everything possible to make a daughter happy and satisfied with her own age; this would discourage her from seeking status through imitating her elders.[18]

The emphasis by some parents on the social success of their daughters and sons may have had something to do with the culture of domesticity and family togetherness that historian Elaine Tyler May has demonstrated pervaded so much of the United States during the Cold War era. May argues that women who did not work outside the home were judged based on their success within homes: the décor and cleanliness of those homes, but also the successes of their residents, the children and husbands of these housewives. Seen in this light the social successes of one's children, including their popularity with the opposite sex, might well have reflected back on the mother who raised them. Given that many of these women, particularly if their children were in school, may have had time on their hands, their overinvestment in their daughters' dating lives may well have been a possibility. Certainly Betty Friedan thought so. Bemoaning the early marriage trend, Friedan cited a number of culprits, all of them loosely grouped into what she called the "feminine mystique," the belief that ultimate fulfillment would come to women through wife- and motherhood alone. While Friedan tended to indict "the young housewife sex-seekers" for using sex to "erase their lack of identity" and relying on marriage to give them an identity instead of facing the "responsibility of growing up alone," she also feared that mothers were pushing their daughters into sex and early marriage, encouraging them to emulate the (bad) choices they had already made. In the first chapter of *The Feminine Mystique*, Friedan noted the decreasing age of first marriage with horror, not so much because of what it meant for the institution of marriage or the children born of these unions (the fears of many others), but because of the opportunities lost by girls who wed too early.[19]

Like Friedan, some sociologists also looked to the affluence of the 1950s as an explanation for early marriage, noting that it was easier than ever for young men to find employment even without a high school education. In theory this abundance of jobs led to young people taking a chance on marriage because they would be able to afford to support a family on a husband's salary when in other eras they might not. The relative affluence of the 1950s and 1960s thus became one explanation for early marriage, even though most acknowledged that wealthier students were less likely to marry than poor students. But that working-class young men might be able to support wives was key to the explanation. Some commentators also noted that marriage for younger brides and grooms provided a sense of security that seemed lacking in a world beset by Cold War woes. As one sociologist summarized succinctly: "During periods of grave national unrest, the marriage rate tends to increase," and "Prosperity means that more young people can afford to get married." Overall, then, we can see a number of trends that animate discussions of gender, sexuality, and the family as explanations for why so many young people chose to marry during the 1950s and early 1960s. They dated and had sex at earlier ages; they sought adulthood that they thought marriage could provide for them; and they, no less than their parents, were living in a time when marriage and family living (on TV, in the news, in their schools) was billed as the apex of postwar American success.[20]

EARLY MARRIAGE AND THE LAW

Many, probably most, of the girls and boys who got married during the postwar period did so legally. A number of studies found that teenage marriages were quite likely to be celebrated both in the bride's home county and officiated over by ministers or other religious leaders. Family and friends attended the weddings, even if some were rather more rushed affairs than those not necessitated by an unplanned pregnancy. In order for teenagers to marry legally in most states, they required parental permission, which many clearly had if their parents were in attendance.[21]

Even though it was becoming increasingly difficult, some teenage brides and grooms continued to lie in order to marry. Sometimes these lies were to their own parents. In 1959, for instance, Clifford Turner convinced his father to consent to his marriage to Marcella Gilbert by claiming that they had already married in Tijuana and that he was the father of her unborn child, both of which were lies. Marcella was seven months' pregnant, but Clifford was not the father. When asked in court why he wanted to marry her, he explained, "Well, I liked her quite a bit then. I guess it was more that I felt sorry for her." Clifford's father took the couple to court, but only after the marriage had been solemnized. Other lies were to government officials. A central concern of reformers in earlier periods was that children were able to forge and lie their way into gaining marriage licenses. This was largely because license issuers were lax in following the rules (sometimes granting licenses by mail or to third parties sent to fetch the license on behalf of the couple) and because many counties did not require documentary proof of age in order to obtain a license. Not until after 1960, and in many cases 1970, did a majority of states require that applicants for a marriage license do anything other than swear to their stated age. By 1970, a growing number of states required that applicants actually produce documentary proof of age, often in the form of a birth certificate. Until that time, however, prospective brides and grooms could simply claim to be the ages they needed to be to obtain a license. This was clearly what Lucy Lang and Mark Day had done in order to marry in Reno. Bear in mind, however, that Lang and Day also had their parents lie on their behalf and, further, that in order to persuade a county official to issue them a license they had to physically pass for the ages they needed to be (in their case, sixteen and eighteen). But large numbers of teenagers were able to do just that. Comparing vital statistics records with the census (as one study has done) demonstrates significant statistical differences that only lying can explain. During the 1950s, the census records show more minor brides than marriage licenses do; this is because couples lied about their ages when getting married but no longer felt the need to lie when the census taker came to their door. By that point they were securely, legally married. This means that large numbers of people continued to lie about their ages during the 1950s in order to marry.[22]

The second (and sometimes overlapping) way to marry semi-legally was to go to another state where laws were more conducive to teenage marriage. Called migratory marriage, this had also long been a worry of marriage reformers. Lucy Lang and Mark Day had employed both strategies, of course, both lying *and* traveling to another state. Lang was young enough, and young-looking enough, that she needed to be married in a state with a lower minimum age than her fourteen-year-old self could physically approximate. Lang and Day were in good company; many other teens traveled to other states to marry. In May 1955, for instance, Virginia Gottardi, who had just turned fifteen, accompanied her thirty-year-old boyfriend, Lloyd Spencer, from their home in Pueblo, Colorado, to Ogden, Utah, to be married. At the time, Colorado had a minimum marriageable age of sixteen. When Spencer appeared in court defending himself on charges that he had contributed to the delinquency of a minor (his new wife), he was asked why he and Gottardi had gone to Utah to marry. He replied: "Because in the State of Utah when a girl is married at the age of fifteen nobody can annul the marriage but herself." It is unclear how Spencer had obtained a marriage license in Utah, which should have required parental consent for his bride, but obtain the license he did, perhaps through forging the consent. Asked by his parents-in-law's counsel, "Did you realize at the time it was illegal to marry Virginia Louise?" Spencer cagily replied, "In this State, yes." In addition to shoddy enforcement, age-of-marriage statutes were a patchwork of different minimum marriageable ages and ages below which parental consent was required. Those who could not marry in one state could simply travel to another that was more amenable.[23]

One study finds that during the 1950s and 1960s, before minimum marriage ages became more standardized among states, " 'marriage migration' appears to be regularly used as a way to avoid state age of marriage laws." That said, this migration was practiced by only somewhere between 1 and 3 percent of all younger married couples during this period. Recall that sociologists found that most high school marriages they studied took place in the brides' and grooms' home counties with parents present. Despite the panic over teenage marriage, then, most parents resigned themselves to their children's marriages, especially when a pregnancy was involved. This was not essentially a trend of elopement and secret weddings.[24]

And yet, secret weddings garnered a disproportionate amount of press, perhaps indicating that regardless of whether parents were eventually consenting to their children's marriages, they were none too pleased about it. As one reporter explained in *McCall's* in 1959,

> Many high school marriages are kept secret. The secret is usually
> poorly kept. The youngsters find it difficult not to talk about their
> fascinating new status and experiences, sexual and otherwise, and the
> marriage of a popular or outstanding high-school couple (football
> hero, cheerleader) often produces an imitative wave of from ten to
> twenty other marriages in the same school. It is also likely to cause
> an outbreak of such fringe phenomena as the wearing of dime-store
> wedding rings by many of the girls, who pretend to be married though
> they are not.

Here marriage is staged both as secret and as deeply gang-oriented: marriage was simply the thing to do at certain high schools. One of the more

scandalous tales in this regard was a 1960 *Good Housekeeping* story documenting a rash of secret marriages effected by Tucson, Arizona, teens who
married across the border in Nogales, Mexico. Journalist Betty Coe Spicer
was sure to explain that the epidemic in elopements came as a surprise to
the parents of Catalina High School students, known colloquially as "Blue
Blood High," both for its excellent scholastic record and for its location in
one of Tucson's best neighborhoods. Of course these parents "were aware of
the trend to youthful marriages," but "such stories always seemed to involve
'*other* teenagers. That small percentage of real juvenile delinquents who
are as much concern to good teenagers as they are to adults.'" This rash of
secret cross-border elopements now caused them great concern. The students Spicer interviewed explained that some married on a dare or under
the influence of alcohol, usually following a dance when they had permission to stay out late. It was unclear whether the marriages were legal because
few could remember where they had married or who had actually married
them, they lied about their ages, and they filled out forms in Spanish that
they did not understand. It was possible that the marriages were performed
by "'wildcatters'—unscrupulous operators selling black-market marriages
that were not marriages at all." Many of these students did not initially tell
anyone that they had married, making it impossible to calculate all those
involved, but Spicer relayed that the number of acknowledged married students attending the four city high schools was only twenty-five marriages out
of a total high school enrollment of nine thousand.[25]

Regardless of how teenagers were getting themselves married, some legislators attempted to transform the law to make it more difficult. In 1945, for
instance, North Carolina passed a bill mandating waiting periods in certain
counties between application for and issuance of license, largely to prevent
those from out of state entering North Carolina to obtain a marriage license;
over the next five years legislators considered making it a statewide policy but
do not seem to have done so. In 1955, Texas considered passing a bill that would
further punish clerks who issued marriage licenses to minors below the statutory ages because, as the bill's sponsor put it, "the fact that the present law does
not adequately safeguard against under-age marriages creates an emergency."
A number of other states, including Colorado, Kentucky, and Maryland, modified their ages somewhat, raising or instituting minimum marriageable ages
for girls or boys. In a trend that would become increasingly common in the
postwar period, however, Kentucky and Maryland made exceptions to the age
or consent requirements if the girl or boy could present a certificate from a

physician attesting to the prospective wife's pregnancy. As children had sex at earlier ages and as marriage law became increasingly difficult to break or evade, lawmakers built exceptions into the marriage laws themselves.[26]

Unlike earlier eras, there seems to have been little public interest in pushing for legal changes. Even the sociologists and commentators who reported on the teenage marriage crisis rarely focused on the law the way 1920s reformers (or even those of the 1930s) had done. Instead they looked to greater cultural and familial causes, employing the tools of social science to ask not *how* young people managed to marry but instead *why*. Feminists, who had previously been an important lobbying group on the issue, were also largely silent. In part this was because the organized feminist movement was close to dormant during the 1950s and did not revive until the mid-1960s, by which point the age of first marriage had begun to rise to prewar levels. But it was also the case that some organizations working on behalf of women actually saw women's lower statutory ages of marriage as an advantage not enjoyed by men. This belief may also explain why at least one state—South Carolina—actually lowered its minimum marriageable age for boys but not for girls.[27]

In 1950, for instance, Frieda S. Miller, director of the U.S. Women's Bureau at the Department of Labor, compiled a listing of what she called "State Laws of Special Interest to Women." She described this as "a simple digest . . . of significant State laws which have particular value for women." She divided each state's laws into those that benefited wives and mothers, widows, or working women. Varying state by state, the section for wives and mothers tended to describe some combination of a husband's support obligations, a wife's right in regard to her own earnings, and occasionally her right to live free from "dangerously violent conduct." For many states, among the advantages for women was that "legal age of consent to marriage [is] lower for females" and, in states where it remained true, "earlier age of majority for females." Chronicling the existing forty-eight states, the memos listed thirty with a lower age of consent to marriage for girls and seven with a lower age of majority. The memos, perhaps because they were based on inaccurate or incomplete sets of revised statutes, were actually undercounting, but the point is that Miller saw both lower ages as advantages for women and girls. By 1950, with the age of first marriage plummeting to an all-century low, the ability to marry at a younger age was cast as an advantage, not just by some individual girls who wanted that right, but by the U.S. Women's Bureau, an organization founded to advance the rights of working women. At a moment when marriage and family were meant to be the center of one's existence, and despite the hand-wringing of some academics and many reporters, there appeared to be little popular support for keeping young people away from the altar.[28]

In earlier eras married teenagers had often used their status to be excused from school, and courts had tended to support them. Some states even passed statutes explicitly excusing married students. Courts had also upheld the right of school boards to suspend or even expel married students because they were presumed either to pose a danger to their fellow students or to be a bad influence (a concern repeatedly raised in the sociological literature). These bans on married students were almost exclusively local (sometimes unwritten) school board policies, not state statutes; many courts explicitly cited the interest of school boards in their students when they affirmed the decisions to suspend married students. By the 1960s and early 1970s, however, some married students fought for, and won, the right to remain in school despite their marital status. They did so alongside pregnant girls who also achieved legal victories in their quest to be able to remain in school despite impending motherhood. Both trends are evidence of the increasing importance of education in the postwar period and an expression of children's own beliefs about their rights as young people. They also stand in contrast to girls like Lucy Lang Day who wanted to marry as a means of achieving adulthood. These students were calling on the state to protect the rights to which they believed themselves entitled, rights accorded to them by virtue of their ages. Enough teenagers were marrying in the postwar era that the trend itself held different meanings for a variety of its participants. Some saw marriage as incompatible with the rites of youth—and this was true economically for many who were forced to leave school in order to work—whereas others managed to combine marriage, and sometimes parenthood, with the completion of high school.[29]

State supreme courts upheld the students' rights to an education on a number of grounds, particularly equal protection and due process. They also noted that school boards instituting rules such as these were unable to justify them (the "bad influence" argument had little sway with many justices) and explained that the rules punished students who had married within the bounds of their state laws. These school board rules were not universal or uniform; some states did not have them, and they could vary considerably within a state. They were also not entirely new; the first case finding them unconstitutional dates from 1929. But in the wake of the teenage marriage crisis of the postwar years, increasing numbers of school boards had passed such rules to protect current students from an "unhealthy moral influence" and as a preventive measure to cut down on the drop-out rate (married students being more likely to do so). Some rules also barred students from extracurricular activities—particularly sports—so schools would not look as if they were countenancing the decisions of students to marry. In a series of decisions from the late 1960s through the mid-1970s, students won the right to attend school and to participate in all extracurricular offerings, no matter their marital status, demonstrating the liberationist mode that historian Michael Grossberg has argued characterized legal thinking around childhood in the period between World War II and the 1970s.[30]

Although married teenagers were increasingly being treated the same as their unmarried peers in terms of their legal right to an education, they continued to be treated differently by the juvenile justice system in some jurisdictions. As historian Carrie Hagan has demonstrated for the early 1960s, even though Los Angeles County juvenile courts had legal jurisdiction over minors whatever their marital status, judges tended to release or dismiss married girls from the courts. This follows the logic of the Colorado case discussed above, though the L.A. County cases target the behavior of the girls, not the husbands: those who had been charged or incarcerated for sexual delinquency were no longer delinquent if they were married. Though the teenagers in the education and delinquency cases were different people with varying claims, overall they had managed to retain the powers of marriage to protect them *from* something (in this case, punishment), even as they had successfully argued that their marriages could not deny them access *to* something (education). In both circumstances, children were claiming rights in a liberationist spirit.[31]

Increasingly pregnancy also allowed a back door into marriage below a state's minimum marriageable age. Some states had passed laws earlier in the twentieth century that allowed girls to marry below the minimum age if the prospective bride were pregnant; these laws became more common in the postwar era. In Ohio, for instance, the Juvenile Division of the Courts of Domestic Relations granted exceptions to its minimum marriageable age (sixteen) if girls had already had sex and become pregnant. In the 1956 case of fifteen-year-old Diana Whittington, a ward of the court by virtue of her delinquency, the court determined that she had already had sex with one George Frazier and, because she was two months' pregnant, granted her permission to marry. Although we cannot know how many teenagers made strategic use of these laws to gain access to marriage that they would have been denied absent a pregnancy, certainly this was the effect.[32]

UNDERSTANDING THE CRISIS

In contrast to previous uproars about underage marriage, this teenage marriage crisis caused an outcry because it spread to the sorts of girls and boys who normally postponed marriage. What bears noting, however, is that rates for Mexican American and African American girls, as well as those for rural white teenage girls (and some boys), remained relatively constant, though the media paid them little attention. This was at least partially similar to what occurred in the wake of the Winstead-Johns marriage. In that media frenzy, reporters and commentators certainly focused on the welfare of children in an area of the country—rural America—that has not always been of the greatest concern to urban dwellers. But they did so to the exclusion of its African American and Mexican American girls, both of whom had higher rates of child and adolescent marriage than white girls like Eunice Winstead. In the postwar years, teenagers of color, in rural and urban areas, continued to marry at rates comparable to earlier decades, but journalists, sociologists, and educators largely ignored them. The inquiry remained white, but it had turned inward.

From 1940 through 1960, the percentage of nonwhite girls (largely, but not exclusively, African American, and not including Latinas, whom the Census Bureau does not identify as a racial group), aged fifteen through seventeen, who were married rose from 8.5 percent in 1940 to 10 percent in 1950, and then decreased to 7.5 percent in 1960 (table 9.4). By contrast, the percentages of white girls in the same age bracket, though they also clearly increased (from 4 percent in 1940 to 6.5 percent in both 1950 and 1960), were still considerably lower than the rates for nonwhite girls. The rates for early marriage in rural America, which had always been higher than those of cities, remained relatively constant over this period, but the rates for urban and suburban girls increased dramatically (table 9.5), almost doubling in urban areas (which, by the 1940 census definition, would have included any area of more than 2,500 inhabitants). Even as the percentages of rural and nonwhite girls marrying remained the highest throughout the period, the *increases* were among white girls living in cities and suburbs, especially in the Northeast. The percentage of white urban married girls (aged fifteen to seventeen) rose from 2.6 percent in 1940 to 5.5 percent in 1950 to 6.3 percent in 1960. Although nonwhite urban girls also experienced an increase, it was much less dramatic because their rates were already so much higher than their white counterparts.[33]

Table 9.4. Percentage of Married Girls Age Fifteen to Seventeen by Race, 1940–1960

Year	Nonwhite Girls	White Girls
1940	8.51	4
1950	10.04	6.53
1960	7.46	6.53

Sources: U.S. Census Bureau, *Sixteenth Census of the Population: 1940, Population*, vol. 4, *Characteristics by Age*, part 1, United States Summary, table 8, 22–23; U.S. Census Bureau, *1950 Census of the Population*, vol. 2, *Characteristics of the Population*, part 1, United States Summary, table 104, 182–83, 185; U.S. Census Bureau, *Census of the Population: 1960*, vol. 1, *Characteristics of the Population*, part 1, United States Summary, table 176, 426–27.

The point, of course, is that early marriage became something approaching a crisis only when white, relatively affluent teenagers were marrying at ages that their elders found inappropriate. In articles published in *Good Housekeeping, Ladies' Home Journal, Reader's Digest, Coronet, McCall's,* and *Redbook,* among others, race is never mentioned, and the homes of the teenage brides they interview and the marriage scandals they investigate, when they are named, are in cities or suburbs. Perhaps the most telling evidence of a change from previous coverage of early marriage is that many of these stories in mainstream magazines conclude with recommendations to their readers on what they and all Americans can do to avoid the teenage marriage problem. Many of these are framed around what readers, as mothers, can do to discourage their daughters (and sometimes sons) from marrying while in high school. That the magazines acknowledge youthful marriage as a problem that its own readers might experience is far different from both the coverage and the work of reformers in the 1920s and 1930s, who were generally bent on eradicating child marriage in a population understood to be different from those doing the reporting and reforming. Teenage marriage mattered in the 1950s and 1960s precisely because it was white suburban girls who were doing the marrying.

Journalists were not alone in reporting on the phenomenon in this way. Sociologists, home economists, and family life educators, who began researching the issue in the 1950s, tended to focus on white teenagers because it was these young brides and grooms who had inspired the worries of their elders. As one 1970 study explained of the field, "The 'who' and 'why' of youthful marriages have received considerable attention from researchers and commentators on American life during the past decade. The trend of thought

**Table 9.5. Percentage of Married Boys and Girls Age Fifteen
to Seventeen by Year and Region, 1940–1960**

Sex and Year	Urban	Rural Non-Farm	Rural Farm
Boys 1940	.32	.39	.48
Girls 1940	2.98	6.04	6.47
Boys 1950	.97	.99	.88
Girls 1950	5.97	9.3	7.26
Boys 1960	1.11	1.18	1.09
Girls 1960	6.47	7.93	4.71

Sources: U.S. Census Bureau, *Sixteenth Census of the Population: 1940, Population*, vol. 4, *Characteristics by Age*, part 1, United States Summary, table 8, 22–24; U.S. Census Bureau, *1950 Census of the Population*, vol. 2, *Characteristics of the Population*, part 1, United States Summary, table 104, 184–87; U.S. Census Bureau, *Census of the Population: 1960*, vol. 1, *Characteristics of the Population*, part 1, United States Summary, table 176, 428–33.

passed through an initial stage of 'panic' at the first realization that many more young men and women were marrying in the 1950's as compared to the pre–World War II period." Like the journalists who covered the trend, and despite their commitment to objective reporting, most academics remained silent on race, though they were more likely to look at rural and urban differences. One Minnesota study, for instance, found that whereas 84 percent of high school principals in communities of under 2,500 could count at least one marriage in their schools, 52 percent of urban and suburban high school principals could say the same. Many early studies of the 1950s examined just one group of students, generally a group who lived relatively near the researcher. Early data came mostly from Iowa, Nebraska, and New Mexico, though there were also studies of California and Oregon. Because these researchers focused on one area, city, or racial group, that focus remained a constant, and they therefore found it difficult to make comparative analyses or even to comment on the significance of location or race. By the 1960s and certainly by the 1970s, as the teenage marriage trend was decreasing, researchers began to pay somewhat more attention to location and socioeconomic class. With some notable exceptions, they generally found that girls from poor or working-class backgrounds were more likely to marry in high school. A couple of articles that evaluated the differences and similarities among all previously published studies noted a somewhat greater likelihood of early marriage in rural areas, but the way the questions had been framed and the samples had been chosen made location difficult to assess.[34]

This should come as no great surprise, because the importance of place or race was never the chief concern of these studies. Much more interesting to these researchers was studying why contemporary American culture seemed to be encouraging large numbers of teenagers to choose marriage before they deemed it advisable. Indeed, a number of studies approach the problem from the perspective of a high school teacher or guidance counselor intent on guiding his or her students to a happy and successful life. The premise of such an article was that the teacher had noticed an increase in the number of female students who dropped out of high school before finishing, often because they had chosen to get married. A number of such studies appeared in the "Teacher Exchange for High School Family Life Educators" section of the journal *Marriage and Family Living*. But that there was an increase, and indeed that these writers worked at schools that had family life education classes or full-time guidance counselors, indicates a good deal about their students: likely urban or suburban, middle class, and white. If researchers who chose this topic were interested in the rise in the number of teen marriages (as opposed to consistency), the most significant rise was occurring among white teenagers outside of rural America. Thus it should come as no surprise that these teenagers were the primary focus of their research.[35]

By the late 1960s and 1970s, however, a couple of sociologists had at least begun to acknowledge race in their studies. Lee G. Burchinal, perhaps the most prolific author on the subject, began his academic career in the department of economics and sociology at Iowa State University before taking a post with the U.S. Office of Education. Although Burchinal's research was conducted in Iowa, an overwhelmingly white state at midcentury, by the early 1960s he had begun to incorporate census data into his studies and to publish longer articles summarizing the results of his colleagues nationwide. In one such article from 1960, Burchinal explained that among nonwhite females, increases in early marriage occurred between 1910 and 1930, with rates remaining relatively constant thereafter. By contrast, the big increases between 1940 and 1950 were among white females, with their rate remaining constant thereafter. As he put it in no uncertain terms, "The rise in youthful marriage rates in the 1940 to 1950 decade was limited largely to the white population of the United States." Five years later, he reiterated, "With few exceptions, young marriage rates among nonwhites were higher than and sometimes almost double those among whites."[36]

Lucy Lang Day's second marriage (to the same husband) went the way of the first, fulfilling the worst prophecies of reporters and sociologists writing about the teenage marriage boom of the 1950s and 1960s; indeed, her memoir is littered with the divorces of friends who also married as teenagers. Lucy and Mark were divorced (again) five months after their reunion. Day married, had a second child, and divorced a third time (in her twenties), then married a fourth time. As of the 2012 publication of her memoir, she was still married to her fourth husband. Contrary to sociologists' predictions, she graduated high school, attended UC-Berkeley with a small child, and went on to graduate school, earning a doctorate in science and mathematics education. She is also a published poet. Not just in these accomplishments is Day an exception to the rule. After all, she did marry and divorce the same man twice and have two subsequent husbands. And she began the whole process at the relatively young age of fourteen.[37]

But in other ways Day exemplifies the very trends that commentators wrote about. She was white and middle class, and she lived in a city. These were the reasons, of course, that many opposed the marriage of girls like Lucy Lang. It was easier to ignore or condemn those who married early if they lived outside the perceived mainstream. The marriage of rural Americans—white, black, and brown—continued throughout the 1950s and 1960s, their unions mired in the same poverty that made postponement seem beside the point. In some cases, like the African American tenant farmers of the previous chapter, they married because they lived in a world where age consciousness had gained little traction, in part because the revolution in access to education that had swept the nation at midcentury had bypassed poor black children.

When the furor over teenage marriage died down in the late 1960s and early 1970s, it was replaced by a crisis over teenage pregnancies occurring outside of marriage, and black teenagers would be at the center of that controversy. The 1950s and 1960s would be the last moment in which urban and suburban teens married at such high rates and indeed when the black marriage rate (for people of any age) would be so high.

TEN

There Was No Stopping Her

Teen Marriage Continues in Rural America

In 2004, Liset Rodriguez and James Linderos of Bellmead, a central Texas town of just under ten thousand people, were married. The two began dating when Liset was twelve and James sixteen. They married two years later, when Liset was fourteen, because the state of Texas was threatening a statutory rape charge. Liset was one of almost sixty Texas girls to wed at fourteen that year, all with parental permission and despite the state's mandate of sixteen as the minimum marriageable age. She gave birth to a daughter, Mersaydiz, soon thereafter. Liset's mother, Juana Rodriguez, who also married at fourteen in her native Mexico, explained of Liset's decision to marry James: "She is so stubborn. There was no stopping her." That may well have been true, but what bears noting is that Liset probably had few reasons *to stop*. Growing up poor in a working-class town just outside Waco, a conservative city with one of the highest teen pregnancy rates in the nation, Liset believed that she and James were going to marry at some point; with the law at their back and without plausible ambitions beyond Bellmead, there was no real reason *not* to marry.[1]

This has been, with minor variations, the story of teenage marriage in the United States in the late twentieth and early twenty-first centuries: poor and rural youth marrying because they were already having sex (or wanted to do so "legitimately"), some of them pregnant. And it is not at all uncommon, even though the age of first marriage has been on a steady increase from the 1960s and overall the rate of teen marriage has declined since its heyday in the 1950s. Those trends, however, are most notable among urban and suburban populations, and among those in the middle class and higher in any region. Among the rural working poor, early marriage remains common enough not to be abnormal. Two studies report that 6 and 9 percent, respectively, of contemporary American women of all ages have married below the age of eighteen, and the Centers for Disease Control reported in 2010 that in the prior five years, 4 percent of all women (and 1 percent of men) who married did so before legally becoming adults. So although early marriage is not statistically the norm, it is not that uncommon either. Because these studies confirm that teen marriage is largely a phenomenon of rural America, however, the practice has been particularly easy for more affluent urban and suburban Americans to ignore.[2]

Early marriage persists in rural America not for the same reason that sustained the practice in earlier eras: lack of age consciousness. First, although teens do continue to marry more in rural places, they do so at higher ages than their peers of fifty or one hundred years earlier. They also do so fully aware of their birthdays and ages, and cognizant of the norms that attend to certain ages. Indeed, state bureaucracy—in this case in the form of birth registration, birth certificates, and marriage licenses—has made such great inroads that it would be difficult for rural Americans to escape their own ages when seeking to marry. In some cases, age norms are simply different for rural Americans than they are for their urban peers; marriage in the teen years is more acceptable in rural locations, reinforcing the possibility of other teen marriages. Poverty does, however, remain a factor in early marriage today. In many places where education is poorly funded, where sex education is nonexistent, and where opportunities for young people, especially girls, seem limited to one's immediate environs, there are fewer reasons to believe that postponing marriage makes much sense. If more affluent girls wait to marry, especially in the wake of the second wave of the women's movement, it is generally because they believe that other opportunities await them with which marriage would interfere—finishing high school, going to college or graduate school, launching a career. In places where those opportunities seem more like fantasies, there is less reason to wait for marriage; indeed, marriage and child-rearing may be the things that seem most appealing and rewarding to poor girls without other opportunities. Postponing marriage requires a reason to do so; poor girls often do not have one.

Add to this the fact that rates of premarital pregnancy are higher among the poor—in part because of lack of access to contraception—and marriage comes to seem like a solution to pregnancy. If one grows up in areas of the country that are religiously conservative, areas that are themselves less likely to encourage contraception, open conversation about sex, or access to abortion, then marriage is even more likely to appeal. This is compounded by the fact that evangelical Christians tend to emphasize wife- and motherhood as the fulfillment of a woman's destiny, regardless. As teenagers have had sex at younger and younger ages over the course of the past fifty years, marriage has also been a "solution" to charges of statutory rape, as in the case of James and Liset Landeros. Many judges and prosecutors are willing to waive charges if a man takes responsibility for his actions by marrying the girl he has statutorily raped and impregnated; sometimes that "man" is really just a boy himself. If the girl and her family are amenable, youthful marriage seemingly solves a number of problems: illegitimacy, imprisonment of the husband, and, in theory, economic responsibility for the child. All of these issues, as I have indicated, are bound up in poverty but overlaid by region. There are poor and poorly educated children in cities, after all, but they are far less likely to marry at young ages than their rural peers; adherence to conservative moral values (often influenced by evangelical Christianity or Catholicism) accounts for this regional discrepancy.

THE DECLINE OF EARLY MARRIAGE AND THE RISE OF UNWED MOTHERHOOD

Beginning in the 1960s, the age of first marriage for both men and women began a steady climb that has continued through the early twenty-first century (table 10.1). At the same time, marriage itself has become decreasingly popular; it was during the postwar period, for instance, that the African American marriage rate began its steep decline. African Americans—who once accounted for a high proportion of youthful marriages—are now less likely to marry, at any age, than any other racial group in the United States. While most Americans will marry at least once in their lives, the proportion of single people, cohabitating non-married couples (of the same and different sexes), and alternative forms of family have all increased over the last fifty years.[3] The more affluent and better educated tend to marry later in life, but also to remain married, whereas the poor marry earlier and divorce more frequently. Despite the overall trend toward later marriage (or away from it altogether), teen marriage persists in this latter demographic segment, especially in rural America, the South particularly.[4]

Table 10.1. Median Age of First Marriage by Year, 1960–2010

Year	Men	Women
1960	22.8	20.3
1970	23.2	20.8
1980	24.7	22.0
1990	26.1	23.9
2000	26.8	25.1
2010	28.2	26.1

Source: U.S. Census Bureau, table MS-2, "Estimated Median Age at First Marriage, by Sex, 1890 to Present."

By 1970, the overall rate of teen marriage had subsided, especially among white suburban and urban teenage girls (table 10.2). The rates of teenage girls, aged fifteen to seventeen, who were wives during census years declined from a high of 6.8 percent for girls in 1960 to an estimated low of .44 percent in 2010. Black teenage marriage rates (especially in cities) fell the most precipitously and early marriage had returned to being the primarily rural phenomenon that it had been in the prewar years. It is most common among white and Latina teenagers and least common for African and Asian Americans.[5]

Because the rates of early marriage were indeed declining, journalists and academics also paid less attention. This was especially so because the marrying teens who had initially captured their attention—white and relatively affluent—were no longer doing so. In addition to this, the trend that now occupied reporters and academics who were prone to worry about or study teenagers was the birth rate for *unmarried* teenagers. Following the 1965 publication of Daniel Patrick Moynihan's *The Negro Family: The Case for National Action*, focus shifted to the large number of African American women with children who did *not* marry, rather than those who married too early. Of course, the Moynihan Report is significant not just for what it demonstrated statistically but also for its overblown rhetoric. It was the case, however, that black girls who stopped attending school were only half as likely to marry as were white girls from equivalent family backgrounds. As one sociologist explained, "Premarital conception among whites seems more often to lead to early marriage, but among blacks to 'illegitimate' births." A number of factors made this outcome more likely: aside from the fact that black girls were more likely to have supportive kin networks that would welcome them *and* their "illegitimate"

**Table 10.2. Percentage of Married Girls and Boys
Age Fifteen to Seventeen, 1960–2010**

Year	Girls	Boys
1960	6.64	1.13
1970	4.3	1.23
1980	3.12	0.76
1990	2.08	0.92
2000*	0.87	0.43
2010*†	0.44	0.31

* Also includes those separated, divorced, and widowed.
† These figures are estimates based on the American Community Survey.
Sources: U.S. Census Bureau, *Census of the Population, 1960,* vol. 1, *Characteristics
of the Population,* part 1, United States Summary, table 176, 424–25; U.S. Census
Bureau, *1970 Census of the Population,* vol. 1, *Characteristics of the Population,*
part 1, United States Summary, section 2, table 203, 640; U.S. Census Bureau,
1980 Census of Population, Detailed Population Characteristics, United States
Summary, section A, United States, table 264, 67–68; Carter et al., *Historical
Statistics of the United States,* vol. 1, 76, 81; U.S. Census Bureau, "Sex by Marital
Status by Age for the Population 15 Years and Over," 2000; U.S. Census Bureau,
"Sex by Marital Status for the Population 15 Years and Over," 2006–2010.

children, they also faced more restrictive housing options and were less likely
to receive parental support to establish independent households. Last, the
men they might potentially marry faced "astronomically high unemployment
rates." African Americans were on the leading edge of a growing disinclination
to marry (at any age), which in their case was fueled in part by poverty. In
addition, the importance of kin networks and the inability of black women to
find suitable husbands had slowly eroded the stigma against out-of-wedlock
pregnancy, negating one of the major reasons for youthful marriage in earlier
eras. The issues documented in the Moynihan Report had, in essence, also
manifested themselves in the decline in early marriage rates, and although
they had done so most dramatically among black girls, the trends were evident
for other racial groups as well.[6]

This focus on teen pregnancy persisted through the 1990s, with the publication of the Guttmacher Institute's highly publicized *Sex and America's Teenagers* in 1994. Even though the birth rate had actually declined since the 1950s
and 1960s, because more teenagers were having sex and were increasingly

disinclined to marry once pregnant, the proportion of births to single mothers was on the increase: from 15 percent in 1960 to 31 percent in 1970. It has continued to this day (the Centers for Disease Control reports a rate of 40.7 percent of births to unmarried women in 2012; the percentages vary by racial group). By the 1990s, even though the teenage pregnancy rate had *declined* and teens gave birth to only about 12 percent of the nation's children, teenage mothers accounted for about a third of all "illegitimate births." This fear about teenage pregnancy was compounded by Republicans' and Democrats' calls to "end welfare as we know it," where the "welfare queen" tended to be depicted as a single black woman who had begun to have children as a teenager. Whereas the 1950s and 1960s worries about teen marriage were directed toward the fate of teenagers themselves, and perhaps secondarily their offspring, by the 1980s and later, those fears had been eclipsed by a vision of teenagers as the cause of the nation's ills. Although the sexual practices of America's teens really did change over this period, and even though fears of an "epidemic" of teenage pregnancy were always overblown, the difference was clearly one of race. During the 1950s and 1960s, commentators had worried that white teens might be squandering their future through early marriage; by the 1980s, politicians tended to blame black teenagers for squandering the nation's future and its tax dollars. The debate about teenagers and sex, as well as the numbers themselves, had shifted. Commentators still believed that marriage could fix the problem of poverty—and indeed some governmental programs funded marriage education at the turn of the twenty-first century—but the main objects of concern, black teenagers, were decreasingly likely to marry, meaning that discussions of teenage marriage were rarely front and center in these debates.[7]

That teenage marriage rates had declined among middle-class white girls appears to explain why second-wave feminists, who were active beginning in the 1960s, did not make teenage marriage a focal point of their activism. Although Betty Friedan had highlighted early marriage as part of her larger indictment of the "problem that has no name" in 1963, the very people she had focused on—middle-class white girls and women—had ceased marrying in large numbers by the time that feminists began to organize in earnest in the late 1960s and early 1970s. Certainly many radical feminists took aim at the institution of marriage itself, attacking its legal strictures as well as the unequal relationships between husbands and wives, but few focused on age at marriage specifically. Explaining why is speculative, at best. In part many feminists may have wanted to target issues that were relevant to a preponderance of American women, not just a minority among them. The marital relation writ large was one such issue, but early marriage was not. Yet it also remains the case that among white, middle-class women who dominated the public discourse of both radical and liberal feminism, the practice of teenage marriage had already receded considerably. Black feminists, too, were unlikely to focus on ending a practice that had already fallen out of favor among African Americans. By contrast, Jennie Chávez of Las Chicanas noted in 1972 that Chicana feminists might be labeled "vendidos, sell-outs to the 'white ideas' of late marriage, postponing or not wanting children and desiring a vocation other than tortilla rolling," indicating that Chicana feminists did target early marriage in their activism. But many white feminists, though they certainly criticized marriage and implicitly or explicitly advocated against entering it too early, did not focus on "teen marriage" in its own right. Revolutions in birth control like the pill were becoming more available to middle-class girls by the 1970s, and sex and even childbirth outside of wedlock were increasingly destigmatized, all of which meant that shotgun pregnancies and forced marriages were no longer a great problem for the women that feminists targeted for revolution.[8]

EQUALIZING MARRIAGE LAW

Two legal changes are noteworthy during this period, one of which does stem in part from feminist organizing, if indirectly. First, during the 1960s and 1970s, almost all states equalized their ages of marriage and sometimes simultaneously their ages of majority, the two not unrelated. These changes were a result of shifting ideals of gender a long time in the making, whereby lawmakers realized they could no longer justify allowing (or encouraging) girls to marry before boys, which implicitly endorsed the idea that marriage was meant to be different for wives and husbands. Almost all of these states also equalized the age at which children needed parental consent, and some raised their minimum marriageable ages. Second, even though marriage ages were generally higher during this period than in earlier eras, many states increased the number of legal exceptions to their minimum marriageable ages. By the late twentieth century, then, whereas it was much more difficult to marry illegally and the minimum marriageable ages were generally higher than a century earlier, more states now made exceptions to their laws, especially when a girl was pregnant. For all that had changed in regard to attitudes toward sex and youth, and even as the divorce rate rose steadily higher, Americans and their elected representatives still placed undue faith in the abilities of the institution of marriage to contain and correct the problem of youthful sexuality.[9]

During the 1960s and especially the 1970s, most states equalized their marriage laws by sex, mandating the same minimum marriage ages for boys and girls (often sixteen, but sometimes fourteen, fifteen, or seventeen) and the same age below which boys and girls required parental consent (usually eighteen). They did so at a moment when almost all states were both lowering their age of majority (from twenty-one to eighteen) and revamping their statutes to eliminate gender-based distinctions. Setting eighteen—now the new age of majority in all states but Alabama, Nebraska, and Mississippi—as the age below which minors required consent to marry made sense. If people were adults at eighteen, they could decide to marry at that age as well, particularly because the age eligibility to marriage without parental consent had almost always been tied to age of majority (whether twenty-one or eighteen). Although a handful of states had previously mandated the same age for both sexes, by and large most had adopted differential ages for parental consent: twenty-one for boys and eighteen for girls. These distinctions in the age where children required parental consent went by the wayside in almost all states by the late 1970s, spurred in part by the lowering of the age of majority.[10]

Those states that had maintained differential ages of majority for men and women (recall that many had eliminated the distinction in the 1920s following the passage of the Nineteenth Amendment) simply had to lower one age, that of boys. And in 1975, the Supreme Court ruled in a Utah case adjudicating the right of minor boys to be eligible for child support longer than minor girls, *Stanton v. Stanton*, that differential ages of majority were unconstitutional. At the time some saw this as further proof that the law could not sustain gendered distinctions around marriage age. Today only a handful of states in one way or another maintain different minimum marriageable ages for boys and girls (Arkansas, Mississippi, New Hampshire, Ohio, and Rhode Island), and only two states require a higher age of parental consent than eighteen (Nebraska, whose age of majority is nineteen, and Mississippi, where it is twenty-one).[11]

At the same time that states were equalizing their marriage ages by sex, many built into their laws methods by which children could marry despite them. For instance, a state that set a minimum marriageable age of sixteen and required consent below eighteen could also mandate that a minor below sixteen might actually marry if she or he had parental permission (already required, regardless) *and* the permission of a judge, sometimes only if the bride were pregnant or had already given birth, or if the groom were the father of his bride's (unborn) child. Indiana, for instance, requires that those under eighteen need parental consent but set seventeen as the minimum marriageable age.

That said, Indiana makes exceptions for a girl or boy as young as fifteen if she is pregnant or a mother or he is the (expectant) father of his prospective bride's child. A court must also conduct a hearing about the marriage and inform the parents of the prospective spouses. These exceptions were not entirely new in the 1970s (some date from the 1910s and 1920s), though they became much more widespread in that decade. By the early 1980s, twenty-nine states had such exceptions; now almost all do.[12]

These exceptions were passed for a number of reasons. First, it was no longer possible for underage couples who wished to marry to do so illegally by lying about their ages or faking documentation or parental consent. The widespread availability of birth certificates by the 1970s for almost all Americans, including those in poor and rural areas, made this next to impossible, as did the increasing sophistication of state bureaucracy. In previous eras, people lied to get married. Even though state legislators had never encouraged the practice, lying did provide a back door to marriage. It was unnecessary to craft legal back doors to marriage when effective extralegal ones existed. By the later twentieth century it had also made far less sense—though it certainly still occurs—for couples to cross state lines in search of a jurisdiction that would allow them to marry at younger ages. Too many states mandated the same or very similar marriageable ages, making marriage migration far less appealing. Exceptions to minimum marriageable ages and parental consent laws, especially those around pregnancy, demonstrate lawmakers' belief that children should be born into marital relationships. The laws represent a belief that marriage will "solve" the problem of premarital teen pregnancy; they also evince a persistent belief that marriage is a social good to which all people, no matter their ages, should have access. It was these kinds of exceptions to the stated law that allowed James and Liset Linderos to marry. Sixteen is meant to be the minimum marriageable age in Texas, but by jumping through a variety of other judicial hoops, fourteen-year-old Liset Rodriguez became Liset Linderos.[13]

The law around age of marriage did not go uncontested by minors in the later twentieth century. Most challenges to marriage-age laws in earlier eras (like the cases from Chapters 3 and 6) involved the validity of the marriages of minors who had *already* managed to get married. Because marrying illegally was increasingly impossible, these cases have tended to center on the status of married minors and their entitlement to, or denial of, various benefits that generally accrue either to married people or to minors. One case from the early 1980s that made it all the way to the U.S. Court of Appeals for the Second

District, however, was a direct assault on the constitutionality of the right of states to regulate the age of marriage. In 1978, two New York teenagers aged thirteen and fifteen (called Maria Moe and Christina Coe in court documents) became pregnant and sought to marry the fathers of their unborn children. Both girls' mothers encouraged them to have abortions and refused to give their consent to the marriages, which was required under New York law. Moe and Coe brought suit, alleging that the marriage age and consent laws violated their constitutional right to marry, and also that the inability to be married subjected them to collateral effects, including loss of some state benefits, as well as the inability to legitimize their children. Both the district court and the appeals court affirmed New York's right to regulate marriage age on a number of grounds, among them a state's interest in "promoting the welfare of children by preventing unstable marriages." The declaration of a state's right to regulate marriage age, though rarely contested outright, affirms what most believe anyway: that children should not marry and that some laws should be in place to prevent the marriages. But because age is a blunt and arbitrary instrument for enforcing laws, and because many Americans remain attached to the notion that sex and pregnancy should occur within marriage, most states have crafted the various exceptions to their marriage laws that allow a state to discourage marriage for minors on the whole but allow those minors who have already had sex or become pregnant to enter the institution.[14]

By the early 1980s, it was clear that larger numbers of minors married in states with more lenient exceptions to their marriage age laws as well as in states that only required parental consent for minors (as opposed to also requiring judicial consent). Some of these minors had probably traveled in order to take advantage of the legal loopholes, but given the hoops they had to jump through (parental and judicial consent chief among them), it is more likely that minors marrying actually lived in the states with the more lenient laws. One 1984 study demonstrated that in a handful of states that allowed for minors to marry below statutory minimums if it was deemed in their "best interests," the percentages of those under eighteen marrying were 11 percent (girls) and 1.9 percent (boys). In two states without such exceptions the rates were much lower: 4.9 and 0.4 percent. The overall rates of minor marriage at the time were 7 percent of brides and 1 percent of grooms. Similarly, in five states that required parental and judicial consent to marry as a minor, 5.5 percent of brides and 0.7 percent of grooms were under the age of eighteen. By contrast, in four states and the District of Columbia that only required parental consent, 14.6 percent of brides and 2.9 percent of grooms were minors. In both comparisons there were much higher percentages of minors marrying when it was easier for them to do so.[15]

Accounting for causality here is tricky. Do minors marry simply because the law allows them to? Or are minors more likely to marry in states that themselves have more lenient age-of-marriage laws because the culture of those states is supportive of early marriage? Returning to the latter set of numbers is instructive. There was a great deal of variation in the rates of minor marriage in those states (Alabama, Kentucky, Massachusetts, Utah, and Washington, D.C.) that required only parental consent (the lenient states). Massachusetts boasted a rate of only 4.2 percent of minor brides—the same rate as the "strict" state, Minnesota, with the *lowest* rate. The District of Columbia had rates of 1.3 percent for brides and 0.1 percent for grooms, extremely low percentages, despite its leniency on consent. Although Alabama and Kentucky had quite high rates of minor marriages (21 percent and 24 percent, respectively, for brides, and 3.8 percent and 5.1 percent for grooms), it seems more likely that these rural southern states had high rates of minor marriage not just because of lenient consent laws but because Alabamians and Kentuckians believed, more than their northern and western neighbors, that marrying as a minor was perfectly acceptable. They crafted laws that allowed for it; Massachusetts had similar laws, but far fewer teens from the Bay State took advantage of them. Looking at the law in its cultural context allows us to understand why early marriage remains more appealing in some areas of the country than others. The law can certainly be read as an expression of the will of the people; whether minors take advantage of it has everything to do with the world around them.[16]

ACCOUNTING FOR EARLY MARRIAGE IN RURAL AMERICA

The frequency of early marriage is a matter of poverty and lack of incentives for delaying marriage and childrearing. No matter where they are, children and adolescents who grow up in homes planning for future schooling and careers do not tend to marry early. Teenage girls who have such plans also become pregnant at lower rates. These same girls then also have no need for shotgun weddings. But in some places in rural America, one can see how and why these trends might lead to early marriage: children born and raised in rural areas in impoverished or working-class families do not have the same incentives to postpone marriage that middle-class kids, intent on college and careers, do. Many poor children not only do not see those ambitions as realistic, indeed may not consider them at all, but their education has also not prepared them for such goals. And of course those who do see a future that demands a post-ponement of work, marriage, and childrearing tend to leave, no longer being rural Americans at all.

But poor children are born and raised in cities as well, children whose educational opportunities are just as influenced by badly funded schools and who are raised in communities blighted by a poverty that makes leaving those communities through education and the professions seem unlikely, if not impossible. Yet such urban teens remain less likely than their rural impover-ished peers to marry. Race remains a factor—whites and Latinos are much likelier to marry as teens, African Americans much less so—but the key indi-cator is location, itself overlaid by class (the two not unrelated). Why? The evidence points to two related factors: attitudes toward premarital sex and pregnancy, and conservative social values influenced by religiosity. Because of these cultural factors, rural poverty is different from its urban cousin.[17]

Teen pregnancy was a catalyst for marriage in rural *and* urban America through the 1960s, but that has largely ceased to be the case in cities. Teen pregnancy rates have fallen since the 1950s (though unmarried teen pregnancy rates have risen, as have unmarried pregnancy rates more generally) and were never as high as rhetoric about an "epidemic" of teen pregnancy during the 1980s and 1990s made them seem. A majority of current American teens have had sex, however, and large numbers of girls do become pregnant (about 615,000 per year).[18] Some of them marry. While some teens had already mar-ried *before* they became pregnant, sizable numbers still marry *after* pregnancy. This trend has become less common over the twentieth and twenty-first cen-turies as abortion became legal and as single motherhood has become more socially acceptable. That said, as recently as the 1990s, 15.5 percent of teen-age girls who found themselves single and pregnant decided to marry; this so-called solution to teenage pregnancy is most common among white and Latina teenagers and least common for African American girls. In addition to the desire to avoid giving birth out of wedlock, in some states marriage is also a way for men who are somewhat older than their pregnant brides to avoid prosecution for statutory rape. The laws are not written this way explicitly, but prosecutors can choose not to bring charges if a man marries his underage and pregnant girlfriend, and some statutes are written (just as when they were first passed) explicitly to exempt spouses from prosecution. A marriage can thus retroactively protect a man (or woman) who would otherwise be accused of statutory rape.[19]

Teenage pregnancy happens everywhere, but with some exceptions, rates of teen pregnancy tend to be higher in rural states than urban; the highest rates are in the South and Southwest. Teen pregnancy rates are also higher in more religiously conservative parts of the country, which themselves tend to be rural and southern, though not always both.[20] There are, of course, four possible outcomes for pregnant teenage girls (in addition to miscarriage): abortion, birth and subsequent adoption, single motherhood, and marriage. In 2010, 60 percent of teenage girls' pregnancies ended in birth, 26 percent in abortion, and the rest in miscarriage. The abortion rate for teenage girls is higher in urban states (primarily, but not exclusively, northeastern) than rural (of any region).[21] Relinquishment of a child for adoption has been declining rapidly since the mid-twentieth century but remains most likely among white girls with more education and future prospects; black girls and poor girls are least likely. Data by region are difficult to find.[22] Rates of single motherhood are high across the board but slightly higher in southern states.[23] And as we already know, the rate of early marriage is highest in rural states, particularly southern ones. So, to summarize, since the 1960s marriage has *not* been the most common outcome of teen premarital pregnancy in any area of the country, but it is *more* likely in rural areas than anywhere else. The initial phenomenon may be the same in many regions for many girls—unprotected sex at early ages, leading to pregnancy (both perhaps as a result of bad or nonexistent sex education, itself related to poverty)—but the outcomes are different. In urban America, single motherhood and abortion are the likelier results. In the 1984 study cited above, for instance, the flipside of Washington, D.C.'s very low rates of minor marriage were that the city had the highest rates of abortion and out-of-wedlock births in the country. The trend continues today, and although single motherhood is also the most likely outcome in rural America, pregnant girls there are proportionately more likely to marry than their urban counterparts when faced with an unplanned pregnancy. There are demonstrable racial differences in early marriage rates—particularly in African Americans' historical about-face in rejecting early marriage—but the real difference here is regional, with poverty remaining the constant.[24]

And the reason that rural teenage girls remain more likely to wed than their urban counterparts is some form of social conservatism inflected by a higher likelihood of religiosity (conservative Protestantism, Catholicism, or Mormonism) that both emphasizes marriage and shuns childbirth out of wedlock. Sex itself is more tied to the institution of marriage among those who are religiously conservative. In areas of the country where religious conservatives predominate, especially in districts that endorse abstinence-only education or that encourage virginity pledges, marriage is the only site sanctioned for sex. Teenage pregnancy is higher in those regions of the country, in part because teens are unprepared for what happens when they do have sex, but teen marriage (without pregnancy) may also be higher as a good-faith attempt to have sex only in sanctioned ways. That is, in order to have one of the perquisites of adulthood, sex, teenagers must enter one of its institutions, marriage. Studies show that those who take virginity pledges, themselves linked to conservative religiosity, are more likely to marry early, even if they have already broken the pledges. Fundamentalist religious beliefs and the social conservatism that leads to abstinence-only education are both found less in cities, where proportionately fewer teenage girls give birth *or* marry. It is helpful to think of these trends as a Venn diagram with four circles that overlap in the middle. The four circles represent rurality, southernness, religious conservatism, and impoverishment. Girls who are any one of those four things are more likely to wed at young ages; but when all four circles overlap, the odds increase substantially. This is why the rural South has the highest rates of early marriage: it is rural, southern, poor, and religiously conservative. These four factors combine and overlap to create a culture that is conducive to early marriage, both for its own sake and as a solution to unplanned pregnancies.[25]

As of 2015, Liset and James Linderos remain married. They have four children; the youngest, Alonzo, was born in November 2012. That year, their two older kids, Mersaydiz and James, were on the honor roll at La Vega Elementary School in Bellmead, Texas, where they all still live. Although most studies show that teenagers who marry are far more likely to divorce than those who marry in their twenties or thirties, there are, of course, exceptions and thus far the Linderoses are among them. Whether their marriage lasts is less significant (at least to this study) than the fact of its existence. Facing an unplanned pregnancy, as well as the possibility of a statutory rape prosecution, James and Liset Linderos, eighteen and fourteen, saw marriage as the solution to at least some of their problems. They made a decision that is now uncommon enough in urban and suburban areas that many Americans view teenage marriage as a relic of the past. But many thousands of American teenagers marry every year, most of them in the South and Southwest, the vast majority of them poor.[26]

Epilogue

Child marriage remains a persistent issue around the globe. The United Nations estimates that one in three girls in developing countries will marry before reaching the age of eighteen, one in nine by the age of fifteen. Approximately thirty-nine thousand girls marry every day. In 2010, there were more than sixty-seven million women between the ages of twenty and twenty-four who had been married as children. Half were in Asia, one fifth in Africa. Complications from childbirth and pregnancy are the main cause of death among adolescent girls between the ages of fifteen and nineteen in developing countries. Around the world, marriage as a child occurs primarily in rural areas where girls are poor.[1]

As in the United States, the majority of children who marry do so with the consent of their parents, many of whom believe that marriage is in their children's best interests. The similarities probably end there. Girls in developing countries often marry at much younger ages than American girls do, meaning that by contemporary standards it is much less likely that they were capable of exercising meaningful consent to the marriages. Indeed, many parents force their daughters into marriage as a means of cutting down on family expenditures or in exchange for a bride price. The number of child brides in the United States also pales in comparison to other countries, both in absolute numbers and on a per capita basis.[2]

The stipulations enshrined in a number of United Nations treaties—the Convention on the Rights of the Child and the Convention on Elimination of All Forms of Discrimination against Women—hold that those below the age of eighteen should not marry because they are presumed unable to freely and rationally consent to the decision. Not only does every state in the United States allow children below the age of eighteen to marry (with the consent of a parent or sometimes a judge), but the United States has not ratified either of the aforementioned conventions, largely because many conservatives do not want to bind the nation to treaties that would make us beholden to international standards. With few exceptions, when child marriage is discussed in the United States, it is done so as a problem located exclusively elsewhere. The United States holds itself up as a beacon for human rights, and yet American girls violate the dictates of human rights treaties that our government will not ratify.[3]

Although most teens in the United States who marry do so of their own volition, the practice should continue to give us pause for at least three reasons. The first is because of the consequences. Almost all studies of early marriage in this country demonstrate that girls who marry before adulthood suffer higher rates of medical problems, including depression, than do their peers who postpone marriage. They are less likely to become educated and more likely to live in poverty. They are also far more likely to divorce, and whereas divorce is, in all likelihood, in their own best interest, it was not their intention at the time of their marriage. Divorce itself has also been shown to disproportionately affect wives, who are more likely to be impoverished, especially if they are responsible for the care of children.[4]

Many of these harrowing truths are the consequence of poverty, not early marriage itself, though the marriage exacerbates matters. Rich girls do not marry at fifteen and sink into poverty. Instead, poor girls have sex without protection, become pregnant, and marry as a way to legitimate the child or because they lack access to abortion or simply because they see no other option. Marriage is not the cause of this problem, but as part of an ideological-economic constellation of beliefs and circumstances that includes poverty, abstinence-only education, and lack of access to contraception and abortion, it is the logical end. And even as one can see why girls choose early marriage, providing other options that might make it less appealing is certainly within our power.

The second reason to question youthful marriage stems from the first and is grounded in feminism. Marrying as a minor remains far more common for girls than it is for boys, which means that girls much more frequently suffer its unfortunate consequences than boys do. They are also more likely to be the primary custodial parent in the event of a divorce. Because more girls marry than boys do, it is also girls who are more likely to abandon the possibility of a life beyond motherhood and minimum-wage work. Early marriage cuts short girls' education and the possibility that they might combine a career with wife- and motherhood or forego marriage and motherhood altogether. Older men marrying girls also perpetuates the same patriarchal traditions that feminists have been fighting against for years, whereby the girl is valued for her appearance and reproductive capacity and the man for his abilities outside the home. May-December marriages, especially when the May is really February, throw into sharp relief the worst gendered expectations for asymmetrical power relations within the marital relationship. There is a reason, aside from sheer numbers and a sexual predilection for prepubescence, that polygamous members of fundamentalist religious sects marry girls: they are often young enough to be docile and compliant.

But a preference for marrying girls need not be so extreme. In a video leaked in 2013, Phil Robertson, star of *Duck Dynasty*, explained to a young man that "[girls] got to where they getting hard to find, mainly because these boys are waiting until they get to be about 20 years old before they marry 'em. Look, you wait 'til they get to be twenty years-old and the only picking that's going to take place is your pocket. You got to marry these girls when they're about fifteen or sixteen and they'll pick your ducks." Robertson married his own wife when she was sixteen and pregnant (he was twenty), meaning that he had committed statutory rape in Louisiana, where they lived. They had begun dating when she was fourteen. He also advised the young man he was counseling about any prospective bride: "Make sure that she can cook a meal. You need to eat some meals that she cooks, check that out. Make sure she carries her Bible. That'll save you a lot of trouble down the road." One presumes that Robertson mentions the Bible because he believes that it espouses wifely obedience. Robertson is advocating marrying a girl because she will be pliable and work to make her husband happy. Wait until she becomes a woman and she might gain a mind of her own. This is not at all unlike what Mayne Reid advocated in 1868's *The Child Wife* and what Elizabeth Oakes Smith so objected to in the 1850s: marrying a "baby-wife" before she grows up and decides she is no longer interested.[5]

The third reason to question the marriage of minors is because it plays into the fantasy that marriage itself is transformative and can fix the problem that has the minors (or their parents or lawmakers) considering it in the first place: desire for sex, past sex, or pregnancy. Marriage cannot solve these problems; indeed, most Americans no longer consider the first two to be problems at all. In a society that has largely eliminated the legal consequences of illegitimacy, bending our laws in order to allow pregnant teens to marry to legitimize a child makes little sense. Marriage cannot fix an unplanned pregnancy because marriage is, after all, just a contract between two people and the state. The institution of marriage will not make people capable parents; it cannot make them be kind to each other; it is unable to ensure that they are financially secure enough to rent an apartment or raise a child. A marriage is only as secure as the two people who happen to be in it, so pinning our hopes on marriage—which is expensive to leave and which has historically been the very least safe place for women—is more than a little delusional.

In this regard, it is worth pausing to examine the connections between the contemporary controversy over same-sex marriage and those about the marriage of children. Reformers from the late nineteenth century through the middle of the twentieth consistently used language that often belied their underlying concerns about "protecting" marriage itself. They worried that when children married, it besmirched marriage, sometimes *their* marriages. That connection lives on. Brigham Young University law professor Lynn Wardle, author of a lengthy 1984 law review article defending the right of states to bar children from marrying (discussed in Chapter 10) is also a longtime opponent of same-sex marriage, active in legal campaigns (including Proposition 8 in California) to bar same-sex couples from enjoying the same marriage rights that he does. In the wake of *Hollingsworth v. Perry*, *United States v. Windsor*, and *Obergefell v. Hodges*, Wardle has lost this fight. Although he qualified his opposition to young people marrying in terms of their own suffering and that of their children should they divorce, it is difficult not to see how his opposition was partially about different populations tarnishing the good name of marriage. Children who marry are more likely to divorce, but they are also less likely, one surmises, to take the institution as seriously as they should. Allowing gay people to marry not only treats them equally, it also upends a gendered version of marriage where men and women are presumed to have distinctly different roles, a version of marriage that enjoys considerable popularity among evangelical Protestants and Mormons.[6]

What unites the two is that marriage conveys the mantle of full adult citizenship on those who enter it. In opposing the issuance of marriage licenses to same-sex couples in the state of Pennsylvania (where a rogue county clerk began issuing them in the summer of 2013), Republican governor Tom Corbett made the comparison explicit. In a court filing claiming that the same-sex licenses had no "value or legitimacy," Corbett's administration asked, "Had the clerk issued marriage licenses to 12-year-olds in violation of state law, would anyone seriously contend that each 12-year-old . . . is entitled to a hearing on the validity of his 'license'?" Comparing gay people to children was a way of demonstrating how absurd it was that either should marry, but Corbett inadvertently called attention to what marriage does: it has the power, legally and symbolically, to make people into adults. Corbett sought to deny this to same-sex couples (he lost) and to children, to him the obvious point of comparison.[7]

One could certainly close by explaining that gay people above the age of eighteen are not children and thus deserve the right to marry alongside their heterosexual counterparts. The Supreme Court did just that, finally and decisively, in June 2015. It would be difficult to argue with the fairness of this (though clearly many do). Instead, what I find instructive about the child marriage controversies of the past is our misplaced faith in the institution of marriage itself. Marriage's luster is partially that it comes with certain legal benefits and obligations (which we could choose to apportion outside of its bounds), but I would argue that its real appeal lies in the power we have granted it to symbolically transform those who enter it. Many of us, even those opposed to its hegemony, recognize that marriage makes husbands and wives seem as if they are responsible, devoted, adultlike citizens. But rationally we all know that a marriage license does not make spouses devoted to each other, or sexually faithful, or any more responsible than the unmarried. Only actual people can do those things if they choose to do so every day; marriage itself cannot make them. We have allowed marriage to stand in for these traits for too long. Just as marriage has been incapable of socially or biologically transforming children into adults (despite its having done so in the realm of the law), so we must realize that marriage alone does not make our relationships any better than they were before marriage, and certainly no more deserving of respect or admiration or full adult citizenship. Such a transformation is fiction. This is just as true for husbands and wives as it is for husbands and husbands, wives and wives.

Notes

Abbreviations

In almost all cases the materials cited herein appear in the Bibliography. In an effort to save space, however, state session laws, codes, and revised statutes, both those published when they were passed and those assembled long after, do not. Readers will find complete citations for those in the notes. The notes also refer to the records of various state and federal court cases, as in "Record in *State v. Smith*." The full citations for those cases are in the bibliography under "Court Cases," and the records are listed by archive.

BJ	*Boston Journal*
CDT	*Chicago Daily Tribune*
CSA	Colorado State Archives
CSL	California State Library
CUA	Rare Books and Manuscripts Library, Columbia University Archives
DUA	David B. Rubenstein Library, Duke University Archives
HL	Huntington Library
KJ	*Knoxville Journal*
LAT	*Los Angeles Times*
LOC	Library of Congress
LWVP	League of Women Voters Papers
MA	Massachusetts Archives
MERP	Mary Ellen Richmond Papers
MSJCA	Massachusetts Supreme Judicial Court Archives
NCFRP	National Council on Family Relations Papers
NCSA	North Carolina State Archives
NWPP	National Woman's Party Papers
NYHS	New-York Historical Society
NYSA	New York State Archives

NYSPCC   New York Society for the Prevention of Cruelty to Children
NYT   *New York Times*
RAC   Rockefeller Archives Center
SFC   *San Francisco Call*
SWHA   Social Welfare History Archives, University of Minnesota
TSLA   Tennessee State Library and Archives
TSLAC   Texas State Library and Archives Commission
USCB   United States Census Bureau
WDT   *Watertown (N.Y.) Daily Times*
WP   *Washington Post*
WSA   Washington State Archives and Records Center

Introduction

1. Taylor, *Reminiscences*, 26, 39. For more on Taylor's neglect of the marriage in the narrative, see Rose, "Introduction," 13.

2. Lynn and Vecsey, *Loretta Lynn*, 1, 49–52; King and Schreiner, "Loretta Lynn." By 2002, she had changed her tune somewhat and was making it seem as if her marriage at thirteen (the age she was still claiming) was anomalous for her region of Kentucky and the South. See Lynn and Cox, *Still Woman Enough*, 23.

3. Carter et al., *Historical Statistics of the United States*, 77–78; Le Strat, Dubertret, and Le Foll, "Child Marriage," 524; Goodwin, McGill, and Chandra, "Who Marries and When?," 2.

4. Chudacoff, *How Old Are You?*, chap. 1; Field and Syrett, "Introduction." For an example of the notion of reaching certain age markers when "big enough," and not necessarily "old enough," see Schmidt, *Industrial Violence*, chap. 1. There is now a large and growing body of literature on the history of childhood in the United States and elsewhere. For some of the foundational texts see, e.g., Ariès, *Centuries of Childhood*; Kett, *Rites of Passage*; Zelizer, *Pricing the Priceless Child*; and Mintz, *Huck's Raft*. More recent scholarship that has been crucial to my thinking about the history of childhood and adolescence includes Robertson, *Crimes against Children*; Robertson, "Age of Consent Law"; Odem, *Delinquent Daughters*; Alexander, *"Girl Problem"*; Brewer, *By Birth or Consent*; Milanich, *Children of Fate*; and Schmidt, *Industrial Violence*.

5. The phrase appeared in Bulwer-Lytton, *Last of the Barons*. The earliest I have found the phrase "child bride" used in a newspaper in the United States is 1853; see Mrs. C. Lee Hentz, "The Hermit of Rockrest," *Kalamazoo (Mich.) Gazette*, April 29, 1853, 1. This was a reprint of a serialized chapter of a novel from *Godey's Lady's Book*. The first recording I have found to describe an actual married girl was from 1860; see "A Child Bride," *San Francisco Bulletin*, December 27, 1860, 1. "The Child-Wife," a poem by Constance Clanroland, makes an appearance in the Springfield, Mass., *Daily Republican* on May 9, 1851, page 1.

6. Coontz, *Marriage, a History*.

7. On the historical and contemporary differences in spousal marriage ages, see Chudacoff, *How Old Are You?*, 95–97; Elliott and Simmons, "Marital Events of

Americans: 2009," 14. On the significance (or lack thereof) of age for girls and women in the nineteenth century, see Field, *Struggle for Equal Adulthood.*

8. Ali and Minoui, *I Am Nujood*; Krakauer, *Under the Banner of Heaven*; Bramham, *Secret Lives of Saints.*

9. United Nations Population Fund, *Marrying Too Young*; Gorney, "Too Young To Wed"; "Why Won't America Ratify the UN Convention on Children's Rights?"; Terkel, "House Republicans Block Child Marriage Act"; de Silva-de Alwis, *Child Marriage and the Law.*

10. Ellis, *Sex in Relation to Society*, 194; Dubler, "Immoral Purposes," esp. 763, 765, 767–68, 776–78. Linda Gordon makes a similar point about what she calls the "fetishization of marriage" in her study of social workers and their regulation of the morality of their clients in *Heroes of Their Own Lives*, 102.

11. Women's Protective Association of Cleveland, *School-Girl Brides*, 37. On the connections between marriage and citizenship, see Cott, *Public Vows*; and Pascoe, *What Comes Naturally.* Also on the history of marriage, see May, *Great Expectations*; May, *Homeward Bound*; Riley, *Divorce*; Grossberg, *Governing the Hearth*; Basch, *Framing American Divorce*; Celello, *Making Marriage Work*; Coontz, *Marriage, a History*; Davis, *More Perfect Unions*; Hartog, *Man and Wife in America*; and Eby, *Until Choice Do Us Part.* Of the many trenchant critiques of marriage in the United States, I have been most influenced by Ettelbrick, "Since When Is Marriage a Path to Liberation?"; Fineman, *Neutered Mother*; Polikoff, *Beyond (Straight and Gay) Marriage*; Warner, *Trouble with Normal*; Duggan, "Holy Matrimony!"; and Geller, *Here Comes the Bride.*

12. For the persuasive argument that by the early modern period (and especially post-Revolution) within the realm of the law children were understood to lack the reason necessary for rational consent, see Brewer, *By Birth or Consent.*

13. For a brief summary of these advantages, see Syrett, " 'I Did and I Don't Regret It.' " And for a summary of the counterarguments, see Syrett, "Contested Meanings of Child Marriage."

14. For more on the history of consent, see Haag, *Consent.*

15. Brumberg, *Body Project*, 3–4, 23, and chap. 2.

16. Chambers-Schiller, *Liberty, a Better Husband*; Carter, *Southern Single Blessedness*; Israel, *Bachelor Girl.*

17. Le Strat, Dubertret, and Le Foll, "Child Marriage in the United States"; Mintz, *Prime of Life*, 145.

18. The Catholic Church, not the civil government, regulated marriage in French and Spanish colonies in early America, and I discuss this in some detail in Chapters 1 and 2. Once formerly French and Spanish territories entered the United States, however, marriage came under the jurisdiction of state or territorial governments. For an analysis of religion and marriage that incorporates U.S. law, see Botham, *Almighty God Created the Races*; and one that demonstrates the impact of religion on marital counseling, see Davis, *More Perfect Unions*, esp. chap. 5.

19. On Alabama, see Ala. Code § 26-1-1; on Nebraska, see Neb. Rev. Stats. 43-2101; on Mississippi, see Miss. Code § 1-3-27.

20. On legal personhood, see Welke, *Law and the Borders of Belonging*. On the contested meanings of adulthood, adolescence, and age in the law, see Zimring, *Changing Legal World of Adolescence*. And on the meanings we attach to particular ages, see Field and Syrett, "Introduction."

21. On the invention of adolescence, see Kett, *Rites of Passage*; Chinn, *Inventing Modern Adolescence*; and Baxter, *Modern Age*. On teenagers and youth, see Schrum, *Some Wore Bobby Sox*; Modell, *Into One's Own*; Palladino, *Teenagers*; Hine, *Rise and Fall of the American Teenager*; and Lesko, *Act Your Age!*

22. Milanich, *Children of Fate*, 27–28; Friedman, *Private Lives*, 96–97; Mason, *From Father's Property to Children's Rights*; Grossberg, "Children's Legal Rights?"; Grossberg, "Liberation and Caretaking."

23. Finstad, *Child Bride*.

24. For studies that do track marriages over a longer duration, see May, *Homeward Bound*; and Weiss, *To Have and to Hold*.

25. Taylor, *Reminiscences*; Rose, "Introduction."

26. Lynn and Vecsey, *Coal Miner's Daughter*; Lynn and Cox, *Still Woman Enough*; http://www.lorettalynn.com/50/?page_id=2.

27. Fraidy Reiss, "America's Child Bride Problem," *NYT*, October 13, 2015. My thanks to Holly Jackson and Corinne Field for sending me the story.

Chapter 1

1. "An Abstract of a letter from a Gentleman in N. Carolina to his friend in Maryland," June 7, 1762, Miscellaneous Papers, Series 1, vol. 1, 1755–1788, PC 21.2, NCSA. See also Clarke, *Arthur Dobbs*, 186–87.

2. Brewer, *By Birth or Consent*, chap. 8; Carr and Walsh, "Planter's Wife," 564–65; Gutiérrez, *When Jesus Came, the Corn Mothers Went Away*, chap. 9. For the situation in England, see Rickman, " 'He Would Never Consent in His Heart,' " 294–313.

3. Brewer, *By Birth or Consent*, intro., chap. 8. It is true that girls or boys who married above the age of seven but below the ages of twelve and fourteen, respectively, could generally have their marriages annulled at reaching those ages (as I detail below), but the same protection was not afforded children who married above twelve and fourteen. See ibid., 297, 299.

4. On common-law marriage as a legal doctrine, see Grossberg, *Governing the Hearth*, chap. 3; Grossman and Friedman, *Inside the Castle*, chap. 3; and Friedman, *Private Lives*, 17–27.

5. Blackstone, *Commentaries on the Laws of England*, 1:424–25; Brewer, *By Birth or Consent*, 297; Rickman, " 'He Would Never Consent in His Heart.' " On consent, see Blackstone, *Commentaries on the Laws of England*, 1:425. Blackstone is clear that there were statutes about parental permission in England—and Lord Hardwicke's 1753 law to prevent clandestine marriages was one of them—but that the common law had never required it.

6. Chudacoff, *How Old Are You?*, chap. 1; Field and Syrett, "Introduction."

7. Blackstone, *Commentaries*, 1:441. On the other ages and their arbitrariness, see also 451–52. See also Field and Syrett, "Introduction."

8. Blackstone, *Commentaries*, 1:424; Swinburne, *Treatise of Spousals*, 20.

9. Swinburne, *Treatise of Spousals*, 47.

10. Ibid., 48; Brumberg, *Body Project*, 3–4, 23, chap. 2.

11. David Pulsifer, ed., *Records of the Colony of New Plymouth in New England*, vol. 12: *Laws, 1623–1682* (1861; reprint, New York: AMS, 1968), 13, 29, 108, 190–91; John D. Cushing, ed., *The Laws of the Pilgrims: A Facsimile Edition of the Book of General Laws of the Inhabitants of the Jurisdiction of New-Plimouth, 1672 and 1685* (New York: Michael D. Glazier, 1977), 27–28 of 1671 facsimile, reiterated in 1685 facsimile, 47–48; *A Bibliographical Sketch of the Laws of the Massachusetts Colony from 1630 to 1686* (Boston: Rockwell and Churchill, 1890), 51; Brewer, *By Birth or Consent*, 312; *The Acts and Resolves, Public and Private, of the Province of the Massachusetts Bay*, vol. 1 (Boston: Wright and Potter, 1869), 61. The Massachusetts Body of Liberties remained in place until 1684, when it was revoked by Charles II. It was reinstated when the Massachusetts Colony was established (merging with Plymouth Bay) and then replaced by the Provincial Charter in 1691.

12. *The Code of 1650, Being a Compilation of the Earliest Laws and Orders of the General Court of Connecticut* (1821; reprint, Storrs, Conn.: Bibliopola, 1999), 68; *New-Haven's Settling in New-England. And Some Laws for Government: Published for the Use of the Colony* (London, 1656), reprinted in John D. Cushing, ed., *The Earliest Laws of the New Haven and Connecticut Colonies, 1639–1673* (Wilmington, Del.: Michael Glazier, 1977), 42; *The Book of the General Laws For the People within the Jurisdiction of Connecticut* (Cambridge: Samuel Green, 1673), reprinted in ibid., 120; *Proceedings of the First General Assembly of "The Incorporation of Providence Plantations," and The Code of Laws Adopted at That Assembly, in 1647*, reprinted in John D. Cushing, ed., *The Earliest Acts and Laws of the Colony of Rhode Island and Providence Plantations, 1647–1719* (Wilmington, Del.: Michael Glazier, 1977), 41–42. At some point Rhode Island also amended this act to make the children of a marriage so contracted illegitimate. See Cushing, *Earliest Acts*, 70, 148. John D. Cushing, ed., *Acts and Laws of New Hampshire, 1680–1726* (Wilmington, Del.: Michael Glazier, 1978). For marriage ceremonies in the colonies more generally, see Cook, "Marriage Celebration in the Colonies."

13. On the custody and control of children in the colonial era, see Mason, *From Father's Property to Children's Rights*, chap. 1.

14. Brewer, *By Birth or Consent*, 317–18; *Purdon's Digest: A Digest of the Laws of Pennsylvania, From the Year One Thousand Seven Hundred, to the Twenty-Second Day of April, One Thousand Eight-Hundred and Forty-Six*, 7th ed. (Philadelphia: James Kay Jr., and Brother, 1852), 794–95; *Laws of the Royal Colony of New Jersey, 1703–1745*, vol. 2 (Trenton: New Jersey State Library, 1977), 256–60.

15. William Walter Hening, *The Statutes at Large: Being a Collection of all the Laws of Virginia from the First Session of the Legislature, in the Year 1619*, 6 vols. (New York: R & W & G Bartow, 1819–23), 1:156–57, 433; 2:114, 281; 3:149–51, 441–46; 6:81–85. On these laws in England (1558), see Brewer, *By Birth or Consent*, 306–7, 310.

16. *The Statutes at Large of South Carolina; Edited, Under Authority of the Legislature, by Thomas Cooper*, vol. 2 (Columbia, S.C.: A. S. Johnston, 1837), 484–86. On English

antecedents, this from 1557, see John Raithby, ed., *The Statutes at Large, of England and Great Britain, from Magna Carta to the Union of the Kingdoms of Great Britain and Ireland,* 20 vols. (London: George Eyre and Andrew Strahan, 1811), 4:106.

17. On matrimonial investigations (*diligencias matrimoniales*) and Catholic marriage law in New Spain, see, e.g., Gutiérrez, *When Jesus Came, the Corn Mothers Went Away,* chaps. 8, 9, esp. 243–55, 271.

18. Thomas Herty, *A Digest of the Laws of Maryland, Being an Abridgment, Alphabetically Arranged, of all the public acts of assembly now in force, and of general use, from the first settlement of the state, to the end of November Session 1797, Inclusive, with References to the Acts at Large* (Baltimore: printed for the editor, 1799), 352; *Acts and Laws of the Commonwealth of Massachusetts* (Boston: Adams & Nourse, 1893), 7–8; *Laws of the State of Delaware, 1700–1797,* vol. 2 (New-Castle: Samuel and John Adams, 1797), 973–77; *Compilation of the Public Laws of the State of New Jersey* (Camden: J. Harrison, 1833), 223–24; *The Laws of the State of North Carolina, Enacted in the Year 1820* (Raleigh: Thomas Henderson, 1821), 11–12; "House of Commons," *Raleigh Register,* December 15, 1820, 2; "House of Commons," *Star and North-Carolina State Gazette,* December 15, 1820, 1; *Revised Code of North Carolina* (Boston: Little, Brown, 1855), 393; *Statutes at Large of Virginia, 1792–1806,* vol. 1 (Richmond: Samuel Shepherd, 1835), 134–35; *The Code of Virginia* (Richmond: William F. Ritchie, 1849), 472.

19. *Report of the Commissioners Appointed to Revise the Statute Laws of the State. Made to the Senate, November 2, 1827* (Albany, N.Y.: Croswell and Van Benthuysen, 1827), chap. 8, 1–2, NYSA; *The Revised Statutes of the State of New-York,* vol. 2 (Albany: Packard and Van Benthuysen, 1829), 138–39, 142.

20. *Laws of the State of New-York, Passed at the Fifty-Third Session of the Legislature* (Albany: E. Croswell, 1830), 391–92; "The Revised Statutes, No. X," *New York Commercial Advertiser,* December 16, 1829, 1; "The Revised Statutes, no. 10," *Saratoga Sentinel,* January 1, 1830, 1; "Law of Marriage," *New York Commercial Advertiser,* December 16, 1829, 2; "Amendment of the Marriage Law," *Schenectady Cabinet,* May 5, 1830, 3; "Laws Regulating Marriage," *Watch-Tower* (Cooperstown, N.Y.), May 10, 1830, 2; Kent, *Commentaries on American Law,* 13th ed., 95; David M'Adam, "Marriage of Minors," *NYT,* July 14, 1887. On the criminalization of marriage to a girl below fourteen, see "A Singular Divorce Case," *Albany Argus,* March 19, 1841, 1; "Report of the Committee on the Judiciary," S. Doc. No. 85, April 26, 1841, *New York Senate Documents,* 64th Sess., 1841, 2:1–4, NYSA; on the possibility of annulment, see *Laws of the State of New York Passed at the Sixty-Fourth Session* (Albany, N.Y.: Van Benthuysen, 1841), 234–35. Massachusetts, the first state to attempt to systematically record ages of marriage, noted three years into the experiment that "there seems to be a delicacy on the part of those authorized to solemnize marriages, as to obtaining some facts required by the present law, especially the ages of the parties." See *Third Annual Report to the Legislature Relating to the Registry and Returns of Births, Marriages, and Deaths in Massachusetts* (Boston: Dutton and Wentworth, 1845), xii.

21. *Revised Statutes of the State of New Hampshire, Passed December 23, 1842* (Concord: Carroll & Baker, 1843), 292; *General Statutes of the State of Connecticut* (New Haven: John H. Benham, 1866), 300.

22. Salmon P. Chase, ed., *The Statutes of Ohio and of the Northwestern Territory, Adopted or Enacted from 1788 to 1833 Inclusive, Together with the Ordinance of 1787* (Cincinnati: Corey and Fairbank, 1833), 101, 354; *The Laws of Indiana Territory, 1801–1809* (Springfield: Illinois State Historical Society, 1930), 67–68, 251; *Statutes of Illinois: 1818–1868* (Chicago: E. B. Myers, 1868), 436; *Statutes of the Territory of Wisconsin. Passed in 1838 and 1839* (Albany, N.Y.: Packard, Van Benthuysen, 1839), 139; *The Revised Statutes of the State of Wisconsin, Passed at the Second Session of the Legislature, Commencing January 10, 1849* (Southport: C. Latham Smoles, 1849), 391; *Revised Statutes of the Territory of Iowa* (Iowa City: Hughes and Williams, 1843), 434; *Code of Iowa, Passed at the General Assembly of 1850–51* (Iowa City: Palmer and Paul, 1851), 221; *The Public Statutes of the State of Minnesota, 1849–1858* (Saint Paul: Pioneer, 1859), 460; *Laws of the Territory of Michigan*, vol. 1 (Lansing: W. S. George, 1871), 646; *The Compiled Laws of the State of Michigan*, vol. 2 (Lansing: Hosmer and Kerr, 1857), 949; *Statutes of the Territory of Kansas* (Shawnee M. L. School: John T. Brady, 1855), 283, 488 (Kansas's ages of consent were in their bigamy statute); *The Compiled Laws of the State of Nevada, Embracing Statutes of 1861 to 1873, Inclusive*, vol. 1 (Carson City: Charles A. V. Putnam, 1873), 65; *Statutes of Oregon, Enacted and Continued in Force, by the Legislative Assembly, at the Fifth and Sixth Regular Sessions thereof* (Oregon: Asahel Bush, 1855), 536; *Laws of a Public and General Nature, of the District of Louisiana, of the Territory of Louisiana, of the Territory of Missouri, and the State of Missouri, Up to the Year 1824*, vol. 1 (Jefferson City: W. Lusk & Son, 1842), 65–66; *Laws of the State of Missouri*, vol. 2 (Saint Louis: E. Charless, 1825), 527.

23. *The Laws of the State of Vermont*, vol. 1 (Randolph: Sereno Wright, 1808), 264–65; *Revised Statutes of the State of Vermont, Passed November 19, 1839* (Burlington: Chauncey Goodrich, 1840), 319; *The Revised Statutes of the State of Maine, Passed October 22, 1840*, 2nd ed. (Hallowell: Glazier, Masters & Smith, 1847), 359; *Compilation of the Public Acts of the Legislative Council of the Territory of Florida, Passed Prior to 1840* (Tallahassee: Samuel S. Sibley, 1839), 88–89; *A Digest of the Laws of the State of Florida* (Tallahassee: Floridian Book and Job Office, 1881), 374; *Digest of the Statutory Laws of Kentucky of a Public and Permanent Nature* (Frankfort: Albert G. Hodges, 1834), 1154–58; *Revised Statutes of Kentucky* (Frankfort: A. G. Hodges, 1852), 384, 387. In 1852, Kentucky also allowed a next friend to sue for the annulment of a marriage if a boy below sixteen or a girl below fourteen married without parental permission. *A General Digest of the Acts of the Legislatures of the Late Territory of Orleans, and of the State of Louisiana*, vol. 3 (New Orleans: Peter K. Wagner, 1816), 22–28; *Civil Code of the State of Louisiana* (New Orleans: J. B. Steel, 1853), 14; *Statutes of the Mississippi Territory* (Natchez: Peter Isler, 1816), 329; *Digest of the Laws of Mississippi* (New York: Alexander S. Gould, 1839), 562–63; *The Laws of Texas, 1822–1897*, vol. 1 (Austin: Gammel, 1898), 1293–95; *The Code of West Virginia* (Wheeling: John Frew, 1868), 433–40; Harry Toulmin, Esq., *A Digest of the Laws of the State of Alabama* (Cahawba: Ginn and Curtis, 1823), 577; *The Code of Alabama* (Montgomery: Brittan and De Wolf, State Printers, 1852), 375, 562; *Laws of the Arkansas Territory* (Little Rock: J. Steele, 1835), 394; *Revised Statutes of the State of Arkansas* (Boston: Weeks, Jordan, 1838), 535, 538; *The Statutes of California, passed at the First Session of the*

Legislature, 15th December 1849–22nd April 1850 (San Jose: J. Winchester, State Printer, 1850), 424–25. In 1851, California also explicitly mandated that divorce was possible for a girl who had married below the age of fourteen without parental consent. See *The Statutes of California, Passed at the Second Session of the Legislature: Begun on the Sixth Day of January, 1851, and Ended on the First Day of May 1851 at the City of San Jose* (San Jose: Eugene Casserly, State Printer, 1851), 186.

24. See previous footnote for modifications to previous states. Kentucky also updated its statute somewhat in 1852 to give a girl some access to the profits from her estate during the period of her minority if she married below the age of sixteen without permission. *Public Laws of the State of Rhode-Island and Providence Plantations* (Providence: Miller & Hutchens, 1822), 367–74; *The Revised Code of the District of Columbia* (Washington: A. O. P. Nicholson, 1857), 291–92.

25. Blackstone, *Commentaries*, 1:451; James, "Age of Majority," 22–33. Maryland did not have a separate age of majority for girls but did pass legislation that allowed a girl to convey real estate before boys, at age eighteen. See Kent, *Commentaries on American Law*, rev. ed., 36. The states that modified the age of majority were Arkansas (in 1873: *A Digest of the Statutes of Arkansas* [Columbia, Mo.: E. W. Stephens, 1894], 874); California (in 1854: *The Statutes of California passed at the Fifth Session of the Legislature, January 4, 1854 to May 15, 1854* [Sacramento: B. B. Redding, State Printer, 1854], 44); Colorado (at least by 1867: *Revised Statutes of Colorado, Passed at the Seventh Session of the Legislative Assembly* [Central City: David C. Collier, 1868], 348); Hawai'i (by 1884, when still the Kingdom of Hawai'i, to eighteen and twenty: *Compiled Laws of the Hawaiian Kingdom* [Honolulu: Hawaiian Gazette, 1884], 483); Idaho (in 1864: *Laws of the Territory of Idaho, First Session* [Lewiston: James A. Glascock, 1864], 515); Illinois (probably in 1809: *The Statutes of Illinois: An Analytical Digest of all the General Laws of the State, In Force at the Present Time, 1818–1868* [Chicago: E. B. Myers, 1868], 332); Iowa (in 1839: *Revised Statutes of the Territory of Iowa* [Iowa City: Hughes and Williams, 1843], 432); Kansas (in 1868: *General Statutes of the State of Kansas* [Lawrence: John Speer, 1868], 580); Minnesota (at least by 1866: *The General Statutes of the State of Minnesota* [Saint Paul: Davidson & Hall, 1866], 399); Missouri (at least by 1879: *The Revised Statutes of the State of Missouri, 1889* [Jefferson City: Tribune Printing, 1889], 1274); Montana (at least by 1879: *The Revised Statutes of Montana* [Springfield, Ill.: H. W. Rokker, 1881], 554); Nebraska (at least by 1866 as a territory: *The Revised Statutes of the Territory of Nebraska* [Omaha: E. B. Taylor, 1866], 178); Nevada (in 1861: *The Compiled Laws of the State of Nevada, Statutes of 1861 to 1873, Inclusive* [Carson City: Charles A. V. Putnam, 1873], 105); North Dakota and South Dakota (at least by 1877 as Dakota Territory: *The Revised Codes of the Territory of Dakota, a.d. 1877* [Canton, D.T.: Sioux Valley News, 1883], 208; on the retention at statehood, see *The Revised Codes of the State of North Dakota, 1895* [Bismarck: Tribune, 1895], 606), and *The Revised Codes 1903, State of South Dakota* [Pierre: Ripple Printing, 1904], 593); Ohio (in 1834: *The Public Statutes at Large of the State of Ohio: From the Close of Chase's Statutes, February 1833, to the Present Time* [Cincinnati, 1853], 116); Oklahoma (in 1890: *The Statutes of Oklahoma, 1890* [Guthrie: State Capital Printing, 1891], 752);

Oregon (in 1864: *The Organic and Other General Laws of Oregon* [n.p.: Eugene Semple, 1874], 564); Utah (in 1852: *The Compiled Laws of the Territory of Utah, Containing All the General Statutes Now In Force* [Salt Lake City: Deseret News Steam, 1876], 345); Vermont (at least by 1839: *The Revised Statutes of the State of Vermont, Passed November 10, 1839* [Burlington: Chauncey Goodrich, 1840], 319, 331); and Washington (in 1866: *Code of Washington Containing All Acts of a General Nature* [Olympia: C. B. Bagley, 1881], 409).

26. *The Statutes of California, passed at the First Session of the Legislature* (San Jose: J. Winchester, State Printer, 1850), 424–25; *Statutes of California passed at the Fifth Session*, 44. Girls' indentures had traditionally ended earlier as well—at eighteen instead of twenty-one—and sometimes explicitly ended earlier in the case of marriage. See Mason, *From Father's Property to Children's Rights*, 33, 38.

27. *Public Statutes at Large of the State of Ohio*, 116; *Laws of the Territory of Idaho*, 515; *Revised Statutes of Montana*, 554; *Compiled Laws of the State of Nevada*, 105; *Statutes of Oklahoma*, 752; *Compiled Laws of the Territory of Utah*, 345; *Organic and Other General Laws of Oregon*, 564.

28. *Public Statutes of the State of Minnesota*, 399; *Digest of the Statutes of Arkansas*, 874; *Revised Statutes of the State of Missouri*, 1274; *Revised Statues of the Territory of Nebraska*, 178; *Statutes of Illinois*, 332; *Revised Statutes of Colorado*, 348; *Revised Statutes of the Territory of Iowa*, 432.

29. They did not match in Idaho, at least initially, where consent was necessary below twenty for a girl but age of majority was eighteen, and in Arkansas, but this was because Arkansas initially set only a minimum marriageable age and had no ages below which a girl or boy required parental consent to marry.

30. For making me think more about how age figured differently for men and women, I thank Corinne Field. See her *Struggle for Equal Adulthood*.

31. Clarke, *Arthur Dobbs*, 187–88, 200; later information on Justina Davis Dobbs Nash found at http://ncpedia.org/biography/davis-justina.

Chapter 2

1. Wright, *Yankee in Mexican California*, 84–85; Cleland, *Cattle on a Thousand Hills*, 184–87; Stamps, "Abel Stearns," 1; Bandini, *Description of California in 1828*, v–vii; *California Pioneer Register*, 50.

2. Abel Stearns to Narcisco Duran, April 29, 1841, SG box 61, Abel Stearns Papers, HL; Marriage Investigation Records of Abel Stearns and María Arcadia Bandini, 1841, ibid. Translations from the Spanish are by Haydée Noya. On the issue of Stearns being embarrassed by his own late marriage, and the couple postmarriage, see Wright, *Yankee in Mexican California*, 90–92. On mixed marriages during this period in Alta California, see Hurtado, *Intimate Frontiers*, chap. 2, esp. 25, 30; and Castañeda, "Engendering the History of Alta California," 241–45.

3. On marriage in this era, see D'Emilio and Freedman, *Intimate Matters*, 73–84; Coontz, *Marriage, a History*, chap. 10; and Lystra, *Searching the Heart*, chaps. 2, 3. On premarital pregnancy, see Smith and Hindus, "Premarital Pregnancy in America," 537–70.

4. On age consciousness and marriage, see Chudacoff, *How Old Are You?*, 22–23, and chap. 1 generally, 95–97.

5. Modell, Furstenberg, and Strong, "Timing of Marriage," esp. S123, S125; Monahan, *Pattern of Age at Marriage*; Mintz, *Prime of Life*, chap. 3, esp. 97–120.

6. On the labor of wives, see Boydston, *Home and Work*, chap. 4; and Cott, *Bonds of Womanhood*, chap. 2.

7. On the desire for children as being at one end of a spectrum of "natural" male desires in the antebellum period, see Stansell, *City of Women*, 183. On statutory rape laws, see Odem, *Delinquent Daughters*, 8–37.

8. Rowson, *Charlotte Temple*. For the reception of *Charlotte Temple*, see Rust, "Introduction," xi–xxx.

9. Reid, *Child Wife*, frontis. (1888); Meyers, *Edgar Allan Poe*, 142; Silverman, *Edgar A. Poe*, 107, 124, 347; Hutchisson, *Poe*, 36–37, 54–55; Reid, "Dead Man Defended," 22–28. My thanks to Renée Sentilles for telling me about Mayne Reid.

10. Reid, *Child Wife*, 102–4, 108–9 (emphasis his), 127.

11. Ibid., 249, 228, 379, 383, 391.

12. Reid and Coe, *Captain Mayne Reid*, 122, 124, 130–31, 134, chap. 11.

13. Chudacoff, *How Old Are You?*, chap. 2. On mostly failed efforts to collect vital statistics in North Carolina, e.g., see Johnson, *Ante-Bellum North Carolina*, 204.

14. *Third Annual Report to the Legislature, Relating to the Registry and Returns of Births, Marriages, and Deaths in Massachusetts* (Boston: Dutton and Wentworth, 1845), x, MA.

15. Mowatt, *Autobiography of an Actress*, 43–44, 49. On Mowatt, see Taylor, "Creation of a Public Persona," 65–80; Shapiro, "Anna Cora Mowatt," 85–95.

16. Mowatt, *Autobiography*, 55.

17. Devereux, *Plantation Sketches*.

18. DeCredico, *Mary Boykin Chesnut*, 12, 16; Bleser, *Hammonds of Redcliffe*, 4–5; Faust, *James Henry Hammond*, 58–61, 241–42; Herr, *Jessie Benton Fremont*, 58–64.

19. Jabour, *Scarlett's Sisters*, chap. 4, esp. 124, 128, 131–34, quotation on 131.

20. "Sketch of John Camm," 28–29; Spruill, *Women's Life and Work in the Southern Colonies*, 150; Martha Goosley to John Norton, August 5, 1769, John Norton and Sons Papers, MS 36.3, John D. Rockefeller Library Special Collections, Colonial Williamsburg Foundation, College of William and Mary. For another marriage, this between a sixty-four-year-old man and a sixteen-year-old girl (John Greenhow and Rebecca Harman, his third marriage), see *Virginia Gazette and American Advertiser*, March 22, 1786, abstracted in Headley, *Genealogical Abstracts*, 123; and Greenhow Family Bible, BX 5145 A4 1766, Colonial Williamsburg Foundation Special Collections Library, p. 3, available online: http://research.history.org/library/materials/manuscripts/view/index.cfm?id=GreenhowBible. My thanks to Lindsay Keiter for alerting me to both of these unions and for sending me the citations.

21. Scott, *Southern Lady*, 25; Censer, *North Carolina Planters*, 91–92, quotation on 92; Jabour, *Scarlett's Sisters*, 139, 154–61; Johnson, *Ante-Bellum North Carolina*, 200–201.

22. Schwartz, *Born in Bondage*, 179, chap. 7; King, *Stolen Childhood*, 143–50; Foster, *'Til Death or Distance Do Us Part*, chap. 1; Johnson, *Ante-Bellum North Carolina*, 535–37;

Stevenson, *Life in Black and White*, chap. 8; Fickling J. Glew to Mrs. E. Kane, September 22, 1825, Jared Irwin Papers, DUA; Edmonston, *Journal of a Secesh Lady*, 141.

23. "List of Slaves in the Plantation Purchased from I. C. Williams," n.d., Thomas Bibb Papers, DUA; Schwartz, *Born in Bondage*, 178–79, 187–89, 190–91; Rose Williams interview, *Born in Slavery*, 177; Fraser, *Courtship and Love*, 6, 40. On the denial of childhood to slaves and black children more generally, see Bernstein, *Racial Innocence*.

24. Stevenson, *Life in Black and White*, 246; Schwartz, *Born in Bondage*, 189.

25. "Negroe Ages" book, box 9, George Coke Dromgoole Papers, DUA; John Devereux Plantation Accounts Book, 1842–1863, box 3, Devereux Family Papers, DUA; "List of Negroes the property of W. Richard Corbin, March 28, 1859," box 2, Francis Porteous Corbin Papers, DUA; "List of Negroes the Property of Madame La Vicomtesse de Dampierre, March 1859," ibid.; Cornhill Plantation Book, 1827–1873, McDonald Furman Papers, DUA.

26. Cornhill Plantation Book; Plantation Book, box 2, Francis Wilkinson Pickens Papers, DUA.

27. Thornton, *American Indian Holocaust and Survival*, 43; see also chaps. 4, 5. On the legal interpretation of marriage according to Indian custom, see Pascoe, *What Comes Naturally*, 95–96; and *Annotated Statutes of the Indian Territory, Embracing All Laws of a General and Permanent Nature* (Saint Paul, Minn.: West, 1899), 12–13.

28. Hackel, *Children of Coyote*, 183–89; Fowler, *Wives and Husbands*, 45; Perdue, *Cherokee Women*, 43–45; Riley, *Building and Breaking Families*, 8, 26; Hurtado, *Intimate Frontiers*, 2–4; Spear, *Race, Sex, and Social Order*, 28–29; Fischer, *Suspect Relations*, 37–38, 72–73, 77; Stremlau, *Sustaining the Cherokee Family*, 121.

29. Boscana, *Chinigchinich*, 29, 31. See also Margolin, *Monterey in 1786*, 91–92; Heizer, *Indians of Los Angeles County*, 25–27.

30. Hebard, *Sacajawea*, 49–52; Colby, *Sacagawea's Child*, 42–43. On intermarriage between trappers and Indian women in the seventeenth and eighteenth centuries, see Faragher, "Custom of the Country"; Sleeper-Smith, *Indian Women and French Men*, 8, 23–28, chaps. 2, 3; and Spear, *Race, Sex, and Social Order*, chap. 1, esp. 21–28, 30–31, 37–41, 50–51. For the law of intermarriage between whites and Indians, see Pascoe, *What Comes Naturally*, 94–104; and Stremlau, *Sustaining the Cherokee Family*, 121. With a couple of notable exceptions, bans against white-Indian marriages were a product of the later nineteenth century.

31. Simmons, *Kit Carson and His Three Wives*, 7–29, 31–39. Simmons purports to walk the line between blatant celebrators of Carson and proponents of the new Western history that saw most white incursions into the West as imperialism. That said, and even though he admits that he has no actual evidence of how Carson behaved with any of his wives (it doesn't exist), he insists that all three were "love matches" whom Carson cared for deeply. We simply cannot know whether that was true or indeed whether that was even expected by any of the parties involved. Simmons is reading contemporary standards for marriage onto a past where they might not apply and seems just as enamored of Carson as those he criticizes. See also Johnson, "Writing Kit Carson in the Cold War."

32. Dunbar, *Journals and Letters of Major John Owen*, 188. On custom marriage, see Pascoe, *What Comes Naturally*, 95.

33. Cook, *Conflict between the California Indian and White Civilization*, 75–82; Hurtado, *Intimate Frontiers*, 41–44; Fischer, *Suspect Relations*, 73.

34. Simmons, *Kit Carson and His Three Wives*, 43, 52, 55–60; Stamatov, "Family, Kin, and Community," 86–90; Gutiérrez, *When Jesus Came, the Corn Mothers Went Away*, 244, 271–75, 315–16; Hurtado, *Intimate Frontiers*, 30; Castañeda, "Engendering," 243–44; Miranda, "Gente de Razón Marriage Patterns," 1–21.

35. Gutiérrez, *When Jesus Came, the Corn Mothers Went Away*, 315–16; Chávez-García, *Negotiating Conquest*, 32–34.

36. Stamatov, "Family, Kin, and Community," 92; Miranda, "Gente de Razón," 14–15; Hendricks and Colligan, *New Mexico Prenuptial Investigations*, 77.

37. Hendricks and Colligan, *New Mexico Prenuptial Investigations*, 46–47, 130.

38. Ibid., 176, 178, 148.

39. On the benefits to Stearns, see Moody, "De Baker, Doña Arcadia," 317. And on the benefits to Bandini and other Californianas, see Hurtado, *Intimate Frontiers*, 25; Miranda, "Gente de Razón," 8; and Castañeda, "Engendering," 241–42. Obviously specious claims to whiteness reveal that the racial category is socially constructed. In many ways, getting away with the claim was much more important than any proof of ancestry. But precisely because of this, marrying someone who was regarded as unequivocally white would have been helpful. While the law of community property remained in California (and other formerly Spanish territories) after U.S. annexation, much of the Californio elite lost their fortunes through new federal regulation. On this and the law of marital property, see Chávez-García, *Negotiating Conquest*, 53–55, 123–25.

40. Schlissel, *Women's Diaries*, 45, 151. Sometimes, of course, parents resisted their daughters' marriages at young ages because they were losing laborers. See Lucchetti, "*I Do!*," 98.

41. On common-law marriage, see Grossberg, *Governing the Hearth*, chap. 3; and Grossman and Friedman, *Inside the Castle*, chap. 3.

42. Ackley, *Crossing the Plains*, 232; Bethenia Owens-Adair quoted in Luchetti, "*I Do!*," 122, 125; Nutting (Woodson), *Sketch of the Life of Rebecca Hildreth Nutting Woodson*, 2, 4, 19–20.

43. Charlotte Matheny Kirkwood and Lucy Henderson Deady quoted in Schlissel, *Women's Diaries*, 45, 51. On the Kirkwoods and the Mathenys, see also http://genealogytrails.com/wash/spokane/matheny.htm.

44. Alice S. Walker, comp., "The Life Sketch of Amanda Mulvina Fisk Stout," HL.

45. Autobiography of Mary Minerva Dart Judd, HL; Autobiography of Lucy Hannah Flake, 1–2, 8, HL.

46. Compton, *In Sacred Loneliness*, 1, 11; Smith, *Nauvoo Polygamy*, 34, 36, 574–639.

47. Smith, *Nauvoo Polygamy*, xii; Compton, *In Sacred Loneliness*, 11.

48. Cott, *Public Vows*, 111–20; Alexander, "Wilford Woodruff," 20–38, quotation on 35. My thanks to Amanda Hendrix-Komoto for alerting me to the Mormon Reformation.

49. Terressa Artemesia Redd Romney, "Life Sketch of Sariah Louisa Chamberlain" (1935), 1–3, 6, HL; Biographical Sketch of Martha Cox, 1–2, 25, 122, 125, 135, 136, HL.

50. Biographical Sketch of Cox, 135–36.

51. Gene L. Gardner, "Biography of Mary Cox Lee" (1955), 13–15, 18, HL.

52. Cleland, *Cattle on a Thousand Hills*, 197; "Fair Flagmakers," August 19, 1889, *San Francisco Chronicle*, copy in Richard N. Schellens Papers, California Historical Society.

53. "Death of Abel Stearns," *Daily Alta California* (San Francisco), August 24, 1871, 2; Stamps, "Abel Stearns," 8; Starr, *Inventing the Dream*, 42; "Death Ends Long Coma of Rich Woman Pioneer," *SFC*, September 16, 1912, 5; "Many Claimants for Aged Woman's Estate," *SFC*, October 5, 1912, 9; "Heirs of Abel Stearns Fight for His Estate," *SFC*, July 11, 1913, 10.

Chapter 3

1. "Married," *Lynn (Mass.) News*, February 17, 1854, 3; "Married," *Salem (Mass.) Register*, February 20, 1854, 2; marriage record, Microfilm Record of Massachusetts Marriages, vol. 78, reel 8, p. 185, MA; "An Act for the Orderly Solemnization of Marriages," *Laws of the Commonwealth of Massachusetts, 1834–36* (Boston: Dutton and Wentworth, 1836), 252. This law updated a 1786 law that had set the ages at eighteen and twenty; see "An Act for the Orderly Solemnization of Marriages," passed June 22, 1786, *Acts and Laws of the Commonwealth of Massachusetts* (Boston: Adams and Nourse, 1893), 8. A few scholars have considered this case before. See esp. Grossberg, *Governing the Hearth*, 106–7; and Schmidt, "Ends of Innocence," 1029–31, who also notes its citations in legal journals and litigation.

2. The marriage license indicates that Sarah and Thomas were both born in Lynn. See marriage record, Microfilm Record of Massachusetts Marriages, vol. 78, reel 8, p. 185, MA. The record for their son Thomas's birth claims that Sarah was born in Baldwin, Maine. See Birth Records, reel 18, vol. 105, p. 275, MA.

3. Thomas Parton, Petition for Writ of Habeas Corpus, March 2, 1854; Affidavit of Susan Hervey, March 4, 1854, Supreme Judicial Court for Suffolk and Nantucket Counties, Record #847, record in *Parton v. Hervey*, MSJCA; DeBow, *Statistics View of the United States*, 366. Lynn had a population of 14,257.

4. "A Suit to Get Possession of a 'Wife,'" *Boston Courier*, March 6, 1854, 2. See also *National Era* (Washington, D.C.), March 7, 1854, 2; and *Parton v. Hervey*, 67 Mass. 119 (1854).

5. *Parton v. Hervey*; "The Lynn Marriage Case," *Daily Atlas* (Boston), March 9, 1854, 2; "Habeas Corpus," *Lynn (Mass.) News*, March 10, 1854, 2.

6. "Suit to Get Possession," 2. Pantalets were undergarments worn by young children from the early nineteenth century onward, usually under the white dresses that children below the age of seven or eight also wore. The reference to pantalets was designed to mark Sarah Hervey Parton as being particularly youthful, more youthful in fact than she was at age thirteen. See Paoletti, *Pink and Blue*, 32–33.

7. *Parton v. Hervey*; "Suit to Get Possession," 2.

8. Leloudis, *Schooling the New South*, 20–25; Chudacoff, *How Old Are You?*, 30–40; Schmidt, " 'Rendered More Useful.' "

9. *Third Annual Report to the Legislature Relating to the Registry and Returns of Births, Marriages, and Deaths in Massachusetts, for the Year Ending May 1st, 1844* (Boston: Wentworth and Dutton, 1845); *Fourth Annual Report to the Legislature Relating to the Registry and Returns of Births, Marriages and Deaths in Massachusetts, For the Year Ending April 30, 1845* (Boston: Dutton and Wentworth, 1845), 38–40; *Eighth Report to the Legislature of Massachusetts Relating to the Registry of Births, Marriages, and Deaths in the Commonwealth, From May 1, 1848 to Jan'y 1, 1850* (Boston: Dutton and Wentworth, 1851), 99–100. All reports in MA.

10. Record in *Shutt v. Carloss*, NCSA; *Laws of the State of North Carolina Enacted in the Year 1820* (Raleigh: Thomas Henderson, 1821), 11–12.

11. *Shutt v. Carloss*, 36 N.C. 232 (1840); record in *Shutt v. Carloss*.

12. Record in *Shutt v. Carloss*. On age consciousness in the Northeast, see Chudacoff, *How Old Are You?*, chap. 1; and Landrum, "From Family Bibles to Birth Certificates."

13. *Acts and Resolves Passed by the General Court of Massachusetts, In the Years 1843, 1844, 1845* (Boston: Dutton and Wentworth, 1845), 546; Petition of Daniel Nourse et al., February 25, 1852, Legislative Packet for Chapter 254, "Act in Addition to the Act to Punish Abduction," Acts of 1852, MA.

14. It is also possible that this refers to the necessity that a father himself exact revenge on the man who had stolen and married his daughter.

15. Petition of Nourse et al.; *Acts and Resolves of the General Court of Massachusetts in the Year 1850* (Boston: Dutton and Wentworth, 1850), 474.

16. "Massachusetts Legislature," *Boston Daily Advertiser*, February 28, 1852, 2; "Massachusetts Legislature," *Boston Daily Atlas*, February 28, 1852, 2; *Acts and Resolves Passed at the General Court of Massachusetts in the Year 1852* (Boston: White and Potter, 1852), 179.

17. *Hervey v. Moseley*, Record 232, in Superior Court/Essex Division Record Book, 1855, 122:147–48, MSJCA; "Court of Common Pleas," *Lynn (Mass.) News*, December 28, 1855, 2. Value of $5,000 in 2012 calculated at http://www.davemanuel.com/inflation-calculator .php. On men's wages, see Wilentz, *Chants Democratic*, 117.

18. *Hervey v. Moseley*, 122:148; "Court of Common Pleas," *Lynn (Mass.) News*, January 4, 1856, 2; *Hervey v. Moseley*, 73 Mass. 479 (1856); *Hervey v. Moseley*, Record 211, Supreme Judicial Court of Essex County Record Book, August 3, 1857, 382, MSJCA.

19. On wrongful death suits, see Zelizer, *Pricing the Priceless Child*, 142–43. Zelizer notes that when these suits were allowed—and state governments did go back and forth over the century about their legitimacy—damages were awarded based on simple calculations about the wages that a child might be expected to earn. Household work was valued. And working-class parents, who most suffered the loss of their children's services, were more likely to bring such suits and to be awarded damages. On seduction suits, see Freedman, *Redefining Rape*, 38–41.

20. *Goodwin v. Thompson*, 2 Greene 329 (Iowa 1849).

21. *Stansbury v. Bertron*, 7 Watts & Serg. 362 (Pennsylvania 1844); *Robinson v. English*, 34 Pa. 324 (1859). Michael Grossberg cites two of the three preceding cases and discusses the issue from the perspective of judges in *Governing the Hearth*, 78, 330n40, 339n8. See also *Cotten v. Rutledge*, 33 Ala. 110 (1858).

22. Testimony of Jane Milam Hunter in *Hunter v. Milam*, 111. Cal. 261 (1896), Transcript upon appeal, p. 50, CSL; *Stansbury v. Bertron*. On young women and work at midcentury, see Kessler-Harris, *Out to Work*, chaps. 2, 3; and Stansell, *City of Women*, esp. chap. 6. On prostitution, see Stansell, *City of Women*, 173–80; Gilfoyle, *City of Eros*, 59–66; and Cohen, *Murder of Helen Jewett*, chap. 6.

23. *Wood and Wife v. Henderson*, 3 Miss. 893 (1838). While Mississippi was the first state to pass a married woman's property law, it did so in 1839, the year after this case was decided, meaning that at least at the moment Frances Nixon Wood married her husband, she would have understood that he would control her estate, even if she continued to own any real property like land (as the common law mandated).

24. Tyler, *Commentaries on the Law of Infancy*, 135–36; and Keezer, *Law of Marriage and Divorce*, 21, summarize judicial interpretation on age-of-consent statutes and minors who married; *Goodwin v. Thompson*; Grossberg, *Governing the Hearth*, 95–96, 106–7.

25. Grossberg, *Governing the Hearth*, 104. On divorce, see Cott, *Public Vows*, 49–52; Riley, *Divorce*, chap. 2; and Basch, *Framing American Divorce*, chap. 2.

26. *Parton v. Hervey*; Grossberg, *Governing the Hearth*, 69, 73–75, 76, 78, 96, 106–7, 143–44, who also quotes part of the same passage from *Parton v. Hervey*; for discussion of other cases that cite it, see Schmidt, "Ends of Innocence," 1030; and for treatises that did so, see, e.g., Reeve, *Law of Baron and Femme*, 313n1; Tyler, *Commentaries on the Law of Infancy*, 136; and Keezer, *Law of Marriage and Divorce*, 21.

27. Birth Records, reel 18, vol. 105, p. 275, MA; *Parton v. Parton*, Record 637, Essex County Supreme Judicial Court Record Book for April 1862–November 1865, 373, MSJCA; "Supreme Judicial Court," *Salem (Mass.) Register*, April 27, 1865, 2; Marriage Records, reel 20, vol. 189, MA. On the grounds for divorce in Massachusetts, see Phillips, *Untying the Knot*, 141.

28. 1865 Massachusetts State Census, family 659, line 30, microfilm 09545601870 (accessed through www.familysearch.org); 1870 United States Census, p. 208, family 1224, NARA microfilm publication M593, FHL microfilm 0552141 (accessed through www.familysearch.org); 1880 United States Census, citing sheet 118D, family 5, NARA microfilm T9-0554 (accessed through www.familysearch.org); Massachusetts Marriage Records, reel 43, vol. 354, p. 51, MA; Massachusetts Births, reel 17, vol. 155, p. 170 (Mollie), reel 57, vol. 387, p. 59 (Sadie), and reel 60, vol. 405, p. 22 (Nellie), all in MA; "7 Pemberton Square, Boston," *Boston Daily Advertiser*, March 29, 1888, 5; "Liquor under the Carpet," *Boston Herald*, November 11, 1888, 6; "Suburban News," *Boston Daily Advertiser*, July 1, 1887, 5; "Sentenced to Three Months," *BJ*, September 20, 1888, 1.

29. "Hotels and Stores Burned," *New York Herald*, May 8, 1890, 3; Massachusetts Deaths, reel 87, vol. 411, p. 98 (Nellie), p. 119 (Mollie), and vol. 465, p. 550 (Mary), all in MA; "A West End Investment," *Boston Herald*, September 30, 1896, 5.

30. "The Glen Hotel Fire," *Boston Herald,* June 1, 1891, 2; "Glen House Burned in East Watertown," *BJ,* May 7, 1890, 4; "Watertown," *BJ,* April 27, 1883, 1; "Watertown," *BJ,* April 26, 1887, 1; "Watertown," *BJ,* June 30, 1887, 1; "Accidents," *BJ,* July 6, 1888, 3; "Suburban Liquor Raids," *Boston Daily Advertiser,* May 30, 1887, 8; "War on Liquor Dealers," *Boston Herald,* May 30, 1887, 8; "Watertown," *BJ,* June 3, 1889, 1.

Chapter 4

1. Elizabeth Oakes Smith, "A Human Life. Being the Autobiography of Elizabeth Oakes Smith," 250, 251, 252, 243, ms. copy, microfilm reel 1, New York Public Library.

2. Scherman, "Elizabeth Oakes Smith"; Wiltenburg, "Excerpts from the Diary of Elizabeth Oakes Smith," 534–36; Rickels and Rickels, *Seba Smith,* 22–23.

3. On the early women's rights advocates' focus on marriage, see Cott, *Public Vows,* 64–67; and for a slightly later period (mostly the 1870s), see Leach, *True Love and Perfect Union.*

4. Address of Mrs. Abby Price, *Proceedings of the 1850 Woman's Rights Convention Held at Worcester,* 34–35, 29, 23. On the connections between marriage and economic prospects for women, see Basch, *In the Eyes of the Law,* 177–78.

5. Abby Kelly Foster speaking at the 1851 Woman's Rights Convention in Worcester: http://www1.assumption.edu/WHW/old/AKFos_ter_1851_speech; *Proceedings of the National Woman's Rights Convention, Held at Cleveland, Ohio,* 109.

6. *Proceedings of the Ohio Women's Convention, Held at Salem,* 20–21.

7. Blackwell, *Laws of Life,* 127, 135, 140–41. For more on the age of adolescence and girls' puberty, see DeLuzio, *Female Adolescence in American Scientific Thought,* 10–11, 16, 92. Feminists would take up the physiological arguments in much more detail in regards to sex and marriage by the 1870s. See Leach, *True Love and Perfect Union,* chaps. 1, 2.

8. Antoinette Brown Blackwell quoted in Stanton, Anthony, and Gage, *History of Woman Suffrage,* 728.

9. *Proceedings of the Woman's Rights Convention … Held at Cleveland,* 50, 51, 52. Writing fifty years later, Cyrus Edson concluded that, unlike in Europe, the availability of work for women in the United States meant that they were not forced into early marriages, which would clearly have compromised their offspring. See Edson, "Evils of Early Marriages," 230–34.

10. For more on the emergence of this literature, see Horowitz, *Rereading Sex,* esp. chap. 5.

11. Lewis, *Chastity,* 19, 50, 51, 55 (italics his). For more on ideas about "civilization," which was usually constructed through gender and race, see Bederman, *Manliness and Civilization,* intro.

12. Alcott, *Moral Philosophy of Courtship,* 49, 59, 66; Alcott, *Physiology of Marriage,* 21, 24–25.

13. On phrenology, see Horowitz, *Rereading Sex,* 115–18.

14. Hazen, *Courtship Made Easy,* 6; Fowler, *Fowler on Matrimony,* 65; Fowler, *Marriage,* 127. See also Caswall, *Young Ladies and Gentlemen's Hymeneal Instructor,* 7, 9; and Foote, *Medical Common Sense,* 361.

15. Smith, *Woman and Her Needs*; Scherman, "Elizabeth Oakes Smith."

16. E. Oakes Smith, "Woman and Her Needs," no. 10, *New-York Daily Tribune*, June 19, 1851.

17. E. Oakes Smith, "Woman and Her Needs," no. 4, *New-York Daily Tribune*, January 23, 1851, 7; Smith, "Woman and Her Needs," no. 6, *New-York Daily Tribune*, March 21, 1851.

18. Smith, "Woman and Her Needs," no. 6; Smith, *Woman and Her Needs*, 67.

19. Smith, "Woman and Her Needs," no. 6; Smith, *Sanctity of Marriage.*

20. E. Oakes Smith, "Woman and Her Needs," no. 5, *New-York Daily Tribune*, March 4, 1851, 3; Brewer, *By Birth or Consent*, esp. chap. 8, 291.

21. Smith, "Woman and Her Needs," no. 5, 3.

22. Blackstone, *Commentaries on the Laws of England*, 1:424. For one commentator's discussion on the distinction between the contracts, see Smith, *Cases on Selected Topics in the Law of Persons*, 140–41. For the problems of marriage and age to contract theory, see Brewer, *By Birth or Consent*, 291, 325–37. On the spread of age consciousness in this era, see Chudacoff, *How Old Are You?*, chap. 2. On boys and military service, see Cox, "Boy Soldiers of the American Revolution," esp. 26. My thanks to Frances Clarke for pointing out the ways in which minor boys were bound by their service even when they were legally too young to serve.

23. Schouler, *Treatise on the Law of Husband and Wife*, 19; E. Oakes Smith, "Woman and Her Needs," no. 7, *New-York Daily Tribune*, April 24, 1851; Stanton, letter to the *Tribune*, May 30, 1860, quoted in Stanton, Anthony, and Gage, *History of Woman Suffrage*, 738. On coverture, see Blackstone, *Commentaries*, 1:430; Cott, *Public Vows*, 11–12; Basch, *In the Eyes of the Law*, 17; and Salmon, *Women and the Law of Property*, xv.

24. On Woodhull and free love, see Horowitz, *Rereading Sex*, 347–49. On Smith and divorce, see Smith, "Woman and Her Needs," no. 7; Basch, *Framing American Divorce*, 74.

25. Gabriel, *Notorious Victoria*, 9–10, 12–13; Goldsmith, *Other Powers*, 52, 63; Johnston, *Mrs. Satan*, 25–27; Woodhull in *Woodhull and Claflin's Weekly*, October 8, 1873, 12, quoted in Gabriel, *Notorious Victoria*, 13–14; Woodhull, " 'And the Truth Shall Make You Free,' " 23, 17 (italics hers).

26. Smith, "Woman and Her Needs," no. 7; Smith, "Human Life," 255.

Chapter 5

1. "Gen. Clay's Wedding," *Wheeling Register*, November 15, 1894, 1; "Clay's Child Bride," *Minneapolis Journal*, October 22, 1897, 6; "Clay Seeks Divorce," *Columbus Daily Enquirer*, August 30, 1898, 5; "Child Wearies of Patriarch," *Daily Olympian* (Washington), November 23, 1897, 1; Richardson, *Cassius Marcellus Clay*, 129–31. At the time, the statutory age of marriage in Kentucky for girls was twelve, though they required parental consent below the age of twenty-one. Richardson's parents were both dead, so presumably she had her relatives' consent to the marriage. See *General Statutes of the Commonwealth of Kentucky* (Frankfort: Kentucky Yeoman Press, 1873), 515–17.

2. Grossberg, "Guarding the Altar."

3. "Reform in Divorce," *New York Herald*, February 22, 1895, 4. This article, which covered the meeting of the National Woman's Council, called the age of consent to marriage

"a minor point," but their agenda included it nevertheless. On the changes in childhood in this era, see Zelizer, *Pricing the Priceless Child*, 11; Mintz, *Huck's Raft*, esp. chap. 4. On the changes in marriage and divorce, see Cott, *Public Vows*; Riley, *Divorce*, chaps. 3, 5; and Basch, *Framing American Divorce*, chap. 3.

4. "A California Bride," *Daily Picayune* (New Orleans, La.), July 17, 1872, 2; "A Child-Bride," *Albany Argus*, November 29, 1873, 3; "She Is a Beautiful Child," *St. Louis Republic*, April 16, 1897, 7; "13-Year-Old Girl Weds in Gotham," *Duluth News Tribune*, September 14, 1905, 4; "Bride of 13 Accuses Child Wife in Her Divorce Petition," *Wilkes-Barre Times*, May 14, 1908, 13; "Child Bride in Honeymoon," *Tucson Citizen*, December 18, 1908, 1. For more on short dresses, see "Child Bride Eloped with Horse Trainer," *Pawtucket (R.I.) Evening Times*, May 17, 1901, 3; "Girl of 11 Wedded to Boy of 17," *Pawtucket (R.I.) Evening Times*, November 9, 1901, 9; "Child Bride Asks Divorce," *Anaconda (Mont.) Standard*, November 11, 1902, 11; "A Baby Bride Seeks Divorce," *Olympia Record*, April 14, 1904; "Court Frees Veteran from Child-Bride," *Philadelphia Inquirer*, October 12, 1905, 3; and "Handel Reunited with Child Bride," *Philadelphia Inquirer*, February 6, 1905, 7. On the significance of graduating from short dresses to a longer dress, see Paoletti, *Pink and Blue*, chap. 2. On the penny press, see Schudson, *Discovering the News*, 27.

5. "Little Girl Killed by Child Bride," *San Jose Mercury News*, May 2, 1908, 4; "Child-Bride Clings to Dolls," *Bellingham Herald*, August 14, 1909, 7; "Takes a 15-Year-Old Bride after Five Years' Romance," *Philadelphia Inquirer*, June 30, 1904, 2.

6. See esp. "Child Brides in Massachusetts," *CDT*, January 13, 1894, 7.

7. On the 1885 English scandal, see Walkowitz, *City of Dreadful Delight*, chap. 3. On the purity campaigns in the United States, see Pivar, *Purity Crusade*, esp. chap. 4; Odem, *Delinquent Daughters*, 12–17; Cocca, *Jailbait*, chap. 1, esp. 12–16; Freedman, *Redefining Rape*, chap. 7; Feimster, *Southern Horrors*, 68–74; Dunlap, "Reform of Rape Law"; Wood, *Freedom of the Streets*, chap. 6; and Larson, " 'Even a Worm Will Turn at Last.' " See also "Shame of America."

8. *Laws of the State of New York Passed at the One Hundred Eighteenth Session of the Legislature*, vol. 1 (Albany: James B. Lyon, 1895), 281. On the acceptance of marital sex with minors (but not premarital), see Cocca, *Jailbait*, 2, 9, 15.

9. Gardener, "What Shall the Age of Consent Be?," 196. For an example of one reformer who connected the two ages of consent, see M.T.H., "Michigan," 214. For those who placed too much stock in the ability of parental consent laws to prevent early marriage see, e.g., Blackwell, "Another Physician Speaks," 212–13; and Spencer, "Age of Consent," esp. 413. On the related seduction laws, see Freedman, *Redefining Rape*, chap. 2.

10. Campbell, "Why an Age of Consent?," 287. Lewis also makes the same point in "The Primary Source of Age-of-Consent Legislation," 206: "It is not enough that the age of consent be 'raised.' *It must be erased.* It is unchristian; it ought to be un-American. It is a shame and crime against manhood and a triple crime against girlhood. It outrages motherhood."

11. Holly, " 'Age of Consent,' in Colorado," 5.

12. There are exceptions to this last statement. Some women's rights activists did write, often obliquely, about the possibility of marital rape. See Freedman, *Redefining Rape*, 54–55, 67–68.

13. Cott, *Public Vows*, 109–11; Riley, *Divorce*, chaps. 3, 5; Basch, *Framing American Divorce*, chap. 3. For a variety of perspectives on the issue from the period, see the forum "Is Divorce Wrong?," 513–38.

14. Wright, *Report on Marriage and Divorce in the United States, 1867–1886*; Department of Commerce and Labor, Bureau of the Census, *Special Reports: Marriage and Divorce, 1867–1906*. For more on the impact of the first report, see Dike, "Statistics of Marriage and Divorce."

15. Davis, "Marriage and Divorce," 32; Robinson, "Diagnostics of Divorce," 149.

16. Jacques, "Preface," vi. On the issue of variety in laws, see Dike, "Statistics," 596–99. Some noted, however, that what statistics did exist seemed to indicate that differential laws themselves could not account for the rise in divorce and that migratory divorce was not nearly as significant a phenomenon as many feared it to be. See Dike, "Condition and Needs of Statistics," 514; Dike, "Statistics of Marriage and Divorce," 609–11; and "Marriage and Divorce Laws," *New York Tribune*, January 1, 1898, 7.

17. See, for the 1880s and 1890s, 17 Cong. Rec. 433 (1886); 19 Cong. Rec. 33 (1888); 21 Cong. Rec. 528 (1889); 23 Cong. Rec. 790–93 (1891); 26 Cong. Rec. 3688 (1893); 33 Cong. Rec. 6121 (1899); 34 Cong. Rec. 188 (1900); 35 Cong. Rec. 57 (1901); Riley, *Divorce*, 119–21, 134–35; "For Uniform State Laws," *NYT*, January 31, 1895, 16; Bennett, "Uniformity in Marriage and Divorce Laws," 223; *Report of the National Divorce Reform League for the Year Ending December 31, 1896*, 8; and Grossman and Friedman, *Inside the Castle*, 48.

18. *The General Statutes of the State of Kansas* (Lawrence: John Speer, 1868), 560–62; *General Laws of the State of Texas* (Austin: By Authority, 1866), 990; *Revision of the Statutes of New Jersey* (Trenton: John L Murphy, 1877), 632; *The Civil Code of the State of California*, vol. 1 (San Francisco: A. L. Bancroft, 1874), 29, 32; *The Code of Georgia*, 2nd ed. (Macon: J. W. Burke, 1873), 295; *The Revised Statutes of Indiana* (Chicago: E. B. Myers, 1881), 1154; *Revised Statutes of the State of Missouri*, vol. 1 (Jefferson City: Tribune Printing, 1889), 907; *Compiled Laws of New Mexico* (Topeka, Kans.: Geo. W. Crane, 1884), 518; *Battle's Revisal of the Public Statutes of North Carolina* (Raleigh: Edwards, Broughton, 1873), 587–88; *Compiled Laws of the Hawaiian Kingdom* (Honolulu: Hawaiian Gazette, 1884), 423; *Revised Statutes of Arizona* (Prescott: Prescott Courier Print, 1887), 371; *Compiled and Revised Laws of the Territory of Idaho* (Boise City: Milton Kelly, 1875), 643–44; *Laws of the State of New Hampshire, Passed June Session 1887* (Concord: Josiah Sanborn, 1887), 482; *Laws of the State of New York Passed at the One Hundred and Tenth Session of the Legislature* (Albany: Banks & Brothers, 1887), 25–26; *Revised Statutes and Other Acts of a General Nature of the State of Ohio in Force January 1, 1880* (Columbus: H. W. Derby, 1879), 1528; *Compiled Laws of the State of Michigan, 1897*, vol. 3 (Lansing: Robert Smith, 1899), 2649; *Revised Codes of the State of North Dakota, 1895* (Bismarck: Tribune, 1895), 608; *Compiled Laws of the State of North Dakota, 1913* (Rochester, N.Y.: Lawyers Co-Operative, 1914), 1044; *General Laws of the State of Rhode Island and Providence Plantations* (Providence:

E. L. Freeman & Son, 1896), 623; *Laws Passed at the First Session of the Legislature of the State of South Dakota* (Pierre: State Bindery, 1890), 257; *Acts of Tennessee Passed by the Fifty-First General Assembly* (Nashville: Marshall and Bruce, 1899), 36; *The Revised Statutes of the State of Utah in Force January 1, 1898* (N.p., 1898), 330; *Official Code of West Virginia* (N.p., 1931), 1170; *The Compiled Statutes of the District of Columbia* (Washington: Government Printing Office, 1894), 273. See also Grossberg, "Guarding the Altar."

19. "Civil Code," *Sacramento Daily Union*, November 18, 1871, 4; "Our New Civil Code: Some of Its Defects—Interesting Revelations," *Daily Alta California* (San Francisco), November 16, 1872, 1. See also "Our Shameful Code," ibid., November 22, 1872, 2.

20. The states in the 1900s were Arizona (in 1901: *The Revised Statutes of Arizona Territory* [Columbia, Mo.: E. W. Stephens, 1901], 809); Oklahoma (in 1907: *Compiled Laws of Oklahoma* [Kansas City, Mo.: Pipes-Reed, 1909], 995); Massachusetts (in 1902: *The Revised Laws of the Commonwealth of Massachusetts*, vol. 2 [Boston: Potter & Wright, 1902], 1348); New York (in 1907: *Laws of the State of New York, Passed at the One Hundred and Thirtieth Session of the Legislature*, vol. 1 [Albany: J. B. Lyon, 1907], 1749); Illinois (in 1905: *Revised Statutes of the State of Illinois* [Chicago: Callaghan, 1935], 2044); Kansas (in 1905: *General Statutes of Kansas, 1905* [Topeka: Crane, 1906], 884 [though Kansas was inconsistent, keeping its previous ages of fifteen and twelve in its divorce statute but changing them upward to seventeen and fifteen in its marriage statute]); Montana (at least by 1907: *The Revised Codes of Montana of 1907*, vol. 2 [Helena: State Publishing, 1908], 1064); Washington (in 1909: *Session Laws of the State of Washington Passed at the Extraordinary Session, Convened June 23, Adjourned August 21, 1909* [Olympia: E. L. Boardman, Public Printer, 1909, 54]. The states in the 1910s were Arizona (in 1913: *The Revised Statutes of Arizona, 1913: Civil Code* (Phoenix: McNeil, 1913], 1309); Kansas (in 1913: *Revised Statutes of Kansas* [Topeka: Kansas State Printing Plant, 1923], 451–52); South Carolina (in 1911: *Code of Laws of South Carolina*, vol. 1 [Charlottesville, Va.: Michie, 1912], 1040); Tennessee (in 1919: *Public Acts of the State of Tennessee Passed by the Sixty-First General Assembly* [Jackson, Tenn.: McCourt, Mercer, 1919], 595); and Hawai'i (in 1913: *Revised Laws of Hawaii* [Honolulu: Honolulu Star-Bulletin, 1915], 1100). I have been unable to determine in which decade Missouri once again updated its law, but it was in either 1909 or 1919; see *The Revised Statutes of the State of Missouri*, vol. 1 (Jefferson City: Hugh Stephens, 1919), 1203. Maryland had raised its age of consent for girls to eighteen, at least by 1920. See *The Annotated Code of the Public General Laws of Maryland*, vol. 2 (Baltimore, 1924), 2132.

21. *Laws of the State of New York Passed at the One Hundred and Tenth Session of the Legislature*, 25–26; "Marriage of Young People," *New York Herald*, July 19, 1887, 4; *Laws of the State of New York Passed at the One Hundred and Nineteenth Session of the Legislature*, vol. 1 (Albany: James B. Lyon, 1896), 216, 235.

22. *Laws of the State of New York, Passed at the One Hundred and Thirtieth Session of the Legislature*, 1749; *Laws of the State of New York Passed at the Hundred and Twenty-Sixth Session of the Legislature*, vol. 1 (Albany: J. B. Lyon, 1903), 610; *Laws of the State of New York Passed at the Hundred and Thirty-Fifth Session of the Legislature* (Albany: J. B. Lyon,

1912), 459; *Laws of the State of New York Passed at the Hundred and Thirty-Ninth Session of the Legislature* (Albany: J. B. Lyon, 1916), 2002. On the support of ministers, see "New Marriage Law," *Northern Christian Advocate* (Auburn, N.Y.), February 14, 1907, 104; and "The New Marriage Law," ibid., January 16, 1908, 4. New York was also anomalous in having such a strict divorce statute that annulments were relatively common in the state as a backdoor to divorce. See Friedman, *Private Lives*, 69–70.

23. Whereas the files from some North Carolina counties include both consents and denials of consent, by contrast, the files that made their way to the Ohio State Archives contain only consents, and these are largely given through forms where parents filled in the information required of them. It is unclear whether Ohio county clerks simply did not keep the denials of consent or whether they did not receive them in the same way that North Carolina clerks did. See, e.g., Delaware County Probate Court, Consent to Marry Certificates for minors and marriage returns, 1910–1952, State Archives Series 4960; and Franklin County Probate Court, Marriage Consents, 1882–1931, microfilm reel GR 3910, both in Ohio History Center, State Library and Archives.

24. Joseph Campbell to Register of Deeds of Lincoln County, January 16, 1914 [though almost certainly 1913, given the response and the other correspondence in the folder]; W. H. Sigmon, Register of Deeds for Lincoln County, to Joseph Campbell, January 17, 1913; and Campbell to Sigmon, n.d., all in folder marked "Marriage records concerning parental consent," Lincoln County Miscellaneous Records, CR 060.928.4, NCSA. On the laws, *Revised Code of North Carolina, 1854* (Boston: Little, Brown, 1855), 393; and *Revisal of 1905 of North Carolina*, vol. 1 (Raleigh: E. M. Uzzell, 1905), 998. The minimum ages had been fourteen and sixteen since 1850; parental consent had been mandated since 1873.

25. J. C. Capel to Register of Deeds of Montgomery County, November 24, 1902; and J. M. Vanhoy to same, July 23, 1906, both in folder marked "Marriage Permissions," Montgomery County Miscellaneous Records, CR 067.928.2, NCSA; Livvie Burns to J. C. Williams, April 3, 1912, folder marked "Marriage Licenses," in Halifax County Miscellaneous Records, 1761–1927, CR 047.928.5, NCSA.

26. A. M. Lutz to Register of Deeds for Lincoln County, December 11, 1914; C. A. Spencer to W. H. Sigmon, July 26, 1912; and Notice from S. R. Beam, June 23, 1917, all in Lincoln County Miscellaneous Records.

27. Mrs. L. B. Conrad to Register of Deeds of Lincoln County, March 13, 1913; and J. A. Bowman to Register, December 24, 1914, both in Lincoln County Miscellaneous Records; J. B. Stowe to Register of Deeds, March 16, 1912, Halifax County Miscellaneous Records; V. Cobb to Register of Deeds, January 21, 1913, Lincoln County Miscellaneous Records.

28. F. L. Little to Register of Deeds, n.d., Lincoln County Miscellaneous Records. On the age of consent in South Carolina, see *Code of Laws of South Carolina*, 1040; and Hall and Brooke, *American Marriage Laws*, 114.

29. The letters of consent outnumber the denials, but it may be that some registers of deeds only kept the consents. Only a handful of counties kept consents or denials that made their way to the state archives at all. The youngest consent I have found is for a girl

"not quite 15 years": John Pemberton, marked as colored, to P. H. Morris, April 17, 1878, Montgomery County Miscellaneous Records. Pemberton signed with an *X*.

30. See, e.g., Statement of W. L. Gilbert, May 12, 1915; C. C. Lowe to Register of Deeds for Lincoln County, July 15, 1914, Lincoln County Miscellaneous Records.

31. "At Last," *Mt. Sterling (Ky.) Advocate*, October 11, 1898, 3; "And Dora Is Married Again," *Guthrie (Okla.) Daily Leader*, October 8, 1898, 1; "Clay Seeks Divorce," *Columbus Daily Enquirer*, August 30, 1898, 5.

Chapter 6

1. "Runaways Are Home," *Morning Olympian* (Washington), July 12, 1908, 1. Details of their courtship and marriage are drawn from record in *In re Hollopeter*, 52 Wash. 41 (1909), folder 7754, box 859, Washington State Supreme Court Records, WSA.

2. Record in *In re Hollopeter*: Grover on 3–6, Eugene Hollopeter on 23–27, Clara Hollopeter on 29–34 of transcript.

3. Ibid.: Nat Glenn on 10 of transcript.

4. Odem, *Delinquent Daughters*, 15; *In re Hollopeter*; "Ex Parte Hollopeter," 159–62. In Washington, the age of majority, eighteen for girls and twenty-one for boys, was equalized to twenty-one for men and women in 1923; see *West's Revised Code of Washington, Annotated*, volume for Titles 26 & 27 (Saint Paul, Minn.: West, 2005), 58; "Imogene Glenn Is Taken to Seattle," *Olympia Record*, September 28, 1908, 1; "Grover Hollopeter Is Given Child Wife," *Morning Olympian* (Washington), March 2, 1909, 1; US Department of Commerce and Labor, Bureau of the Census, *Special Reports, Marriage and Divorce: 1867–1906. Part I*, 188; Blackstone, *Commentaries on the Laws of England*, 1:424–25.

5. On the emergence of adolescence and the codification and glorification of childhood during this period, see Hall, *Adolescence*; Kett, *Rites of Passage*, chaps. 8, 9; Odem, *Delinquent Daughters*, chap. 1; Zelizer, *Pricing the Priceless Child*; Chudacoff, *How Old Are You?*, chaps. 3, 4; and Mintz, *Huck's Raft*, 156, 168, 172–78, 180–83. On curfews, see Lucius Cannon, "Curfew: Texts of the Ordinances of Some of the Cities of the United States," *Saint Louis Public Library Monthly Bulletin*, August 1919, copy in box 210, folder 1, American Social Health Association Papers, SW 45, SWHA.

6. On the ways that adolescence prolonged childhood, see Kett, *Rites of Passage*, chap. 8, esp. 217, 238; and Mintz, *Huck's Raft*, 196–98. For the canonical text of the movement, see Hall, *Adolescence*. The on-off switch argument is in Zimring, *Changing Legal World of Adolescence*, 105.

7. On the history of early marriage in the South, see Brewer, *By Birth or Consent*, 309–11, 313–14; Grossberg, *Governing the Hearth*, 106. For the actual numbers see, e.g., Bureau of the Census, *Fourteenth Census of the United States*, vol. 2: *Population*, table 10, p. 400 (covering 1910 and 1920). On the South and rural areas more generally as lagging behind more industrialized and northern areas in terms of norms for childhood, see Mintz, *Huck's Raft*, 135, 146–51, 182.

8. Chudacoff, *How Old Are You?*, 129.

9. Bureau of the Census, *Twelfth Census of the United States, Census Reports*, vol. 2: *Population, Part II*, lxxxix, 255; Bureau of the Census, *Sixteenth Census of the United States*, vol. 4: *Characteristics by Age, Part I: US Summary*, 21.

10. *Kruger v. Kruger*, 64 Misc. 382 (New York County, 1909); *Kellogg v. Kellogg*, 122 Misc. 734 (New York County, 1924).

11. Grossberg, *Governing the Hearth*, 69, 74, 76, 79, 88, 96. See the notes on cases under "Minimum Age" and "Parental Consent" for each state in May, *Marriage Laws and Decisions*.

12. For cases affirming the ability of the underaged party to sue for annulment, see *Owen v. Coffey*, 201 Ala. 531 (1918); *Taub v. Taub*, 87 N.J. Eq. 624 (1917), Record in *West v. West*, 62 Cal. App. 541 (1923), CSL. For those denying that right to the party who was already an adult, see *Fodor v. Kunie*, 92 N.J. Eq. 301 (1920); and *Baker v. Baker*, 112 Neb. 738 (1924).

13. *Cushman v. Cushman*, 80 Wash. 615 (1914).

14. For cases holding that cohabitation past the age of consent constituted affirmation of marriage, see *Garner v. State*, 9 Ala. App. 60 (1913); *State v. Parker*, 106 N.C. 711 (1890); *Jimenez v. Jimenez*, 93 N.J. Eq. 257 (1922); and *May v. Meade*, 236 Mich. 109 (1926). For lack of cohabitation allowing for annulment, see *Griffin v. Griffin*, 225 Mich. 253 (1923). For those denying the ability of parents to sue for annulment, see *Niland v. Niland*, 96 N.J. Eq. 438 (1924) and others discussed in this chapter.

15. See, e.g., *Johnson v. Alexander*, 39 Cal. App. 177 (1918). Some judges denied the annulment suits of those who had married below the age of consent precisely because they had knowingly committed fraud in so doing. See *Smith v. Smith*, 205 Ala. 502 (1921); and *Gibbs v. Gibbs*, 92 N.J. Eq. 542 (1921).

16. *People v. Beevers*, 99 Cal. 286 (1893); *State v. Bittick*, 103 Mo. 183 (1890).

17. "Owen Palmer's Wife," *St. Louis Republic*, March 22, 1890, 1; *Cochran v. State*, 91 Ga. 763 (1892).

18. *Gibbs v. Brown*, 68 Ga. 803 (1882); *Little v. Holmes et al.*, 181 N.C. 413 (1921). See also *Aldrich v. Bennet*, 63 N.H. 415 (1885).

19. *Little v. Holmes.*

20. *Holland v. Beard*, 59 Miss. 161 (1881).

21. Record for *Ex Parte Nolte*, Case No. 7312, Court of Civil Appeals, Fourth Supreme Judicial District of Texas, TSLAC.

22. "She Loves Scott," *Minneapolis Journal*, October 21, 1899, 4; "Wins His Child Bride," *Duluth News Tribune*, November 28, 1899, 1; "State ex. Rel. Scott v. Lowell et al.," 877.

23. "Youthful Hubby Gets His Wife," *Morning Olympian* (Washington), December 26, 1909, 4. For similar cases, see "Wants His Child Bride," *Omaha World Herald*, July 17, 1896, 5; and "Groom, 18, Accuses Parents of Wife, 15," *Philadelphia Inquirer*, July 25, 1911, 3.

24. *Marone v. Marone*, 105 Misc. 371 (New York County, 1918).

25. *Herrman v. Herrman*, 93 Misc. 315 (New York County, 1916). Transcript is in *New York Supreme Court Cases and Briefs*, 176 App. Div., NYSA; quotation on 28–29.

26. *State v. DeMarco*, 20 Ala. 52 (1924). Not all were so successful. See *State ex rel. Foot v. District Court*, 77 Mont. 290 (1926).

27. *People v. Pizzura*, 211 Mich. 71 (1920).

28. "Wade the Ohio to Elope," *Anaconda (Mont.) Standard*, September 16, 1902, 5; "Fifteen and Thirteen Elope and Are Married," ibid., October 20, 1906, 13; "Child Bride Will Go to Husband's Parents," *BJ*, March 1, 1906, 6; "Weds Girls of 15," *Morning Oregonian* (Portland), April 11, 1907, 14.

29. "Married at Thirteen," *Kansas City Evening Star*, November 3, 1884, 3; "The Bride Too Young," *Los Angeles Herald*, August 9, 1891, 1; "An Unnatural Alliance," ibid., February 13, 1897, 5; "A Baby Bride Seeks Divorce," *Olympia Record*, April 14, 1904, 1. See also "Child-Wife of Chinese Granted Divorce Decree," *Los Angeles Herald*, July 28, 1910, 6; and NYSPCC, *Sixteenth Annual Report*, December 31, 1890, Case No. 49,682, 30–32, NYHS.

30. "Money Value of a Squaw," *St. Louis Republic*, November 2, 1894, 9; "Indian Girls of Beauty, Grace and Presentation," *State* (Columbia, S.C.), March 8, 1901, 6; "An Error Corrected," *Cleveland Gazette*, September 9, 1899, 1; Stremlau, "Allotment, Sexuality, and the State," 17. See also "Sought Indian Girls for Wives," *San Francisco Chronicle*, September 11, 1897, 5; "After Indian Wives," *Jackson (Mich.) Citizen Patriot*, September 30, 1897, 5. My thanks to Rose Stremlau for alerting me to this phenomenon.

31. "Bride Won at Pistol's Muzzle," *Bellingham (Wash.) Herald*, January 19, 1909, 2; "Child Bride Freed of Forced Marriage," *Trenton Evening Times*, September 17, 1904, 1; "Lustrous Eyes Cause Trouble," *SFC*, October 9, 1910, 33. For a discussion of polygamous and perhaps coerced marriages to underage brides in a Chicago church during the 1920s, see Chatelain, *South Side Girls*, 88–89.

32. Brooklyn Society for the Prevention of Cruelty to Children, *Eleventh Annual Report* (Brooklyn, N.Y.: Standard Union Job Printing, 1891), "Case No. 9641," between 16 and 17, Brooklyn Collection, Brooklyn Public Library; NYSPCC, *Sixteenth Annual Report*, December 31, 1890, 24–25, NYHS; "Bar Young Chinese Bride from Spouse; Tong War Feared," *SFC*, November 25, 1913, 9. For more on Italians importing girls into the United States for marriage or other sexual services, see NYSPCC, *Eighteenth Annual Report*, December 31, 1892, Case No. 69,057, 42, NYHS. For more on SPCCs, see Gordon, *Heroes of Their Own Lives*; and Pearson, *Rights of the Defenseless*; on Cameron and her rescue mission, see Pascoe, *Relations of Rescue*.

33. "Shot Child Bride," *Grand Rapids Press*, January 2, 1906, 1; "Murdered His Wife," *Jonesboro (Ark.) Evening Sun*, October 9, 1907, 1; "Chinese Girl Wife Is Found Slain," *SFC*, March 8, 1911, 18.

34. Robertson, *Crimes against Children*, 99, chap. 5; Freedman, *Redefining Rape*, 46; "A Balloonist's Luck," *Los Angeles Herald*, September 21, 1897, 5–6. See also Odem, *Delinquent Daughters*, chap. 2.

35. Record in *People v. Souleotes*, 26 Cal. App. 309 (1915), CSL. See pp. 13, 14 for a discussion about the misrepresentation of Mabel's age.

36. For more on judges disallowing the annulment of minor marriages, even when statutory law allowed for it, and the ways this reflected a concern about preserving marriage for the good of society, see Kuby, "Till Disinterest Do Us Part," 386, 399–410.

37. "Cupid Still Having Woes," *Morning Olympian* (Washington), August 26, 1909, 1; "Hollopeter Divorces Bride of Elopement," *Olympia Record*, November 14, 1912, 1; "Dream of Wedded Bliss Flitted On before Says Girl," *Morning Olympian* (Washington), October 17, 1912, 1; "Elopement Romance Has Its End in Divorce Court," ibid., November 15, 1912, 1; "Grover Hollopeter Weds Miss Lucy Robinson," *Olympia Record*, December 29, 1913, 3; Marriage Record for Imogene Glenn and Harry Hontchens, March 17, 1915, *Washington, Marriage Records, 1865–2004*, accessed online through ancestry.com; Death Certificate for Grover Ezra Hollopeter, March 2, 1947, *Washington, Deaths, 1883–1960*, accessed online through ancestry.com; "Grover Ezra Hollopeter" at http://www.findagrave.com/cgi-bin/fg.cgi?page=gr&GRid=11268079.

Chapter 7

1. "Browning May Wed New Cinderella, 15," *NYT*, April 1, 1926, 26; "Browning, 51, Weds Heenan Girl of 15; Her Parents Assent," *NYT*, April 11, 1926, 1; "Children's Society in Browning Case," *NYT*, April 2, 1926, 3; "Plans Court Action in 'Cinderella' Case," *NYT*, April 6, 1926, 31; "Heenan Girl Too Ill to Appear in Court," *NYT*, April 9, 1926, 6. On marriage ages in New York, which had changed a good deal over time, see Chapter 5; and "State Moves to Curb Child Marriages," *NYT*, August 10, 1924, XX4. See also Greenburg, *Peaches and Daddy*.

2. On the enormous transformations in youth and sexuality, see, among others, Fass, *Damned and the Beautiful*; White, *First Sexual Revolution*; D'Emilio and Freedman, *Intimate Matters*, chap. 11; Clement, *Love for Sale*, chap. 4; Alexander, *"Girl Problem"*; and Myers, *Caught*.

3. See, e.g., Simmons, *Making Marriage Modern*.

4. "Browning, 51"; "Browning May Wed."

5. On the changes in youthful sexuality during this decade, see n. 2, above.

6. De Block and Adriaens, "Pathologizing Sexual Deviance"; Sacco, *Unspeakable*, 106, 115; Freedman, "'Uncontrolled Desires'"; Foucault, *History of Sexuality*, 43, 153–54.

7. On Browning's first divorce, see Greenburg, *Peaches and Daddy*, chap. 4, and, for the quotation by Adele Browning, 65.

8. Adoption ad and Mary Louise Spas in the *New York Daily Mirror* quoted in ibid., 68, 92–93. See also chaps. 5 and 6.

9. "Charlie Chaplin Weds Lita Grey in Mexico," *NYT*, November 26, 1924, 1; Louvish, *Chaplin*, 135, 197, 291. Much the same could be said for Jerry Lee Lewis, who married his thirteen-year-old first cousin once-removed in 1957 when he was twenty-two. The marriage and its attendant publicity seriously impacted his career in the United States. See Tosches, *Hellfire*, 76–77, 79, 82, 139–40, 152–64.

10. Mary E. Richmond to Mrs. Louis F. Slade, March 21, 1925, folder 214, box 11, MERP, CUA; John Glenn, press release on death of Mary Richmond, September 14, 1928, folder 114, box 13, series 3, Russell Sage Foundation Collection, RAC. On Richmond's work in the realm of marriage law, see Agnew, *From Charity to Social Work*, 185–93.

11. Letters from various charity organizations to Helen Kempton, Associate Secretary for American Association for Organizing Charity, August 1918, folder 38, box 13, Family Service Association of America Papers, SWHA; John Glenn, press release on death of Mary Richmond. See also May, *Marriage Laws and Decisions*; Richmond and Hall, *Child Marriages*; and Richmond and Hall, *Marriage and the State*.

12. Mary E. Richmond, "Child Marriages in New York State," December 4, 1925, folder 113, box 13, series 3, Russell Sage Foundation Collection, RAC; *Laws of the State of New York, Passed at the One Hundred and Thirtieth Session of the Legislature*, vol. 1 (Albany: J. B. Lyon, 1907), 1749; Agnew, *From Charity to Social Work*, 188.

13. Record in *Kruger v. Kruger* (1909), New York County Supreme Court, New York County Clerk's Archives; Brief of Appellant, 31, in record of *Thomas J. Cushman v. Merrill Cushman*, case 11846, box 1442, Washington State Supreme Court Records, WSA. On the annulment of youthful marriages, see also Kuby, "Till Disinterest Do Us Part"; and Grossman and Guthrie, "Road Less Taken," 307–30.

14. NYSPCC, *Seventeenth Annual Report*, December 31, 1891, 18, NYHS.

15. Towne, "Community Program," 69–70; Colcord, "What Has Social Work to Do," 254; Jane Deeter Rippin in "Informal Discussion," 129. On marriage "righting the ruin" of a pregnancy, see Robertson, *Crimes against Children*, chap. 6.

16. Richmond and Hall, *Child Marriages*, 59, 70–71, 76–79; Reuter and Runner, *Family*, 209 (statistics were from the Census Bureau). On legal infancy and annulment, see also Grossman and Guthrie, "Road Less Taken," 315–18.

17. Odem, *Delinquent Daughters*, chap. 4; Clement, *Love for Sale*, chap. 4; Alexander, *"Girl Problem"*; Myers, *Caught*; Schlossman and Turner, "Status Offenders, Criminal Offenders," esp. 43–44; Agnew, *From Charity to Social Work*, 190–93.

18. NYSPCC, *Fifteenth Annual Report*, December 31, 1889, 52, NYHS; record in *Territory of New Mexico v. Thomas Harwood*, 1909, pp. 17–21 of original testimony, folder 1298, New Mexico Supreme Court Records, New Mexico State Library and Archives; *Territory of New Mexico v. Harwood*, 15 N.M. 424 (1909). On falsifying age, see also Dunham, "Child Marriages in Pennsylvania," 281. On the rise of birth certificates, see Landrum, "From Bibles to Birth Certificates"; and Pearson, " 'Age Ought to Be a Fact.' "

19. "Women Urge May-December Marriage Ban," news clipping, *Star*, February 4, n.d. [1926 or 1927], folder 118, box 7, part 2, MERP, CUA.

20. Richmond and Hall, *Child Marriages*, 52–53; Mary Ellen Richmond to Jeffrey Brackett, November 23, 1924, folder 213, box 11, part 2, MERP, CUA. Richmond was partially inaccurate in her evaluation of the success in New Hampshire; it appears that the age below which a girl needed consent was raised to eighteen, but she was still free to marry under certain circumstances (including parental permission) at thirteen or above. See *Laws of the State of New Hampshire, Passed January Session, 1923* (Concord: n.p., 1923), 128; May, *Marriage Laws and Decisions*, 264. The state with the minimum marriageable age in its bigamy statute was Kansas; see *General Statutes of the State of Kansas* (Lawrence: John Speer, 1868), 368.

21. *Arizona Code 1939*, vol. 5 (Indianapolis: Bobbs Merrill, 1939), 2; *Statutes of California* (San Francisco: Bancroft-Whitney, 1921), 333–34; on Connecticut, see May, *Marriage*

Laws and Decisions, 78; on Delaware, see ibid., 85; *Mason's Minnesota Statutes, 1927* (Saint Paul: Citer-Digest, 1927), 1704; *Compiled States of Nebraska, 1929* (Lincoln: State Journal, 1929), 956, 1032; *Laws of the State of New Hampshire, Passed January Session, 1923*, 128; *New Mexico Statutes Annotated, 1929 Compilation* (Denver: W. H. Courtwright, 1929), 1137; *Laws of the State of New York, Passed at the One Hundred and Forty-Ninth Session of the Legislature* (Albany: J. P. Lyon, 1926), 1056–57; *Laws of the State of New York Passed at the One Hundred and Fiftieth Session of the Legislature* (Albany: J. P. Lyon, 1927), 1325–27; *Laws of the State of New York Passed at the Hundred and Fifty-Second Session of the Legislature* (Albany: J. P. Lyon, 1929), 1495; *Public Acts of the State of Tennessee, Passed by the Sixty-Sixth General Assembly* (Kingsport, Tenn.: n.p., 1929), 13–15; *State of North Carolina, Public Laws and Resolutions, 1923* (Raleigh: Commercial Printing, 1923), 249; *Throckmorton's 1930 Annotated Code of Ohio* (Cleveland: Baldwin, 1930), 1919 of Remedial; *1928 Cumulative Supplement to Digest of Pennsylvania Statute Law of 1920* (Saint Paul: West, 1928), 621. On New York's efforts to raise the minimum ages, see "New York State Legislature Raises Marriage Age," 99; and "New York's Child Marriage Law," 427–28. The North Carolina law ostensibly raised the marriageable age from fourteen to sixteen, but because marriage between fourteen and sixteen was still possible with parental consent (which was required below eighteen anyway), not much had changed. See Colcord, "Marriage Legislation, 1923," 14–15; and the law cited above.

22. Colcord, "Marriage Legislation, 1923," 15; *Acts of Tennessee Passed by the Fifty-First General Assembly* (Nashville: Marshall and Bruce, 1899), 36; *Public Acts of the State of Tennessee Passed by the Sixty-First General Assembly* (Jackson: McCourt, Mercer, 1919), 595; "Horton Signs Marriage Bill," *Nashville Banner*, April 13, 1929, 1; *Public Acts of the State of Tennessee, Passed by the Sixty-Sixth General Assembly* (Kingsport, Tenn.: Southern, 1929), 13–15.

23. Richmond, "Child Marriages in New York State"; Richmond and Hall, *Child Marriages*, 66, 65. Common law marriage was also outlawed in some states precisely because reformers believed that young people were able to marry without permission. See Grossman and Friedman, *Inside the Castle*, 87.

24. Colcord, "Attacking Our Marriage Laws," 1920, folder 116, box 7, MERP, CUA; Richmond and Hall, *Child Marriages*, 67, 146; Towne, "Young Girl Marriages," 302; Mudgett, "When People Apply at a Marriage License Bureau," 285–86; "Monogamy in Peril, Rector Tells Club," *NYT*, February 28, 1925, 28; "Marriage Bills," 239. See also Colcord, "Why Marriage Bills Fail Which Provide for Advance Notice," reprint from *Family*, June 1922, folder 116, box 7, MERP, CUA.

25. Colcord, "To Put 'Marriage-Market' Towns Out of Business," 26–27; Richmond and Hall, *Marriage and the State*, 174–80, chap. 9; Colcord, "What Has Social Work," 256; Colcord, "Why Marriage Bills Fail"; Reuter and Runner, *Family*, 205. On Gretna Greens, see Colcord, "What Has Social Work," 254.

26. For a version of the bill that includes marriage as well as divorce, see Hearings before the Judiciary Committee, 67th Cong., 2d Sess., on H. J. Res. 83, January 26, 1922. See also Stein, "Past and Present Proposed Amendments."

27. Capper Amendment detailed in *Congressional Digest* 6, nos. 6–7 (June–July 1927): 185; Capper quoted on 195, Grant quoted on 201, folder marked "Legal Status of Women: Marriage and Divorce," box 103, LWVP, LOC. Articles that explicitly discuss the age provisions of the Capper bill from the *Woman Patriot*, the *New York Times*, and a letter in the *Washington Post* from lawyer Iredell Meares were included in 69 Cong. Rec. 10064–69 (1928).

28. Colcord, "What Has Social Work," 254–55. See also Colcord, "Why Marriage Bills Fail."

29. Cover mockup in folder 213, box 11, MERP, CUA; Towne, "Girl Marriages," 292; Ogburn, "Factors Affecting Marital Status," 191; Ogburn, "Eleven Questions concerning American Marriage," 188; Hall, *Adolescence*, 1:474–78; Dunham, "Child Marriages in Pennsylvania," 282–83. For a helpful analysis of other child-saving programs tinged by efforts to "civilize" children, see Bullard, *Civilizing the Child*.

30. To be fair, laws passed at the state level would have applied equally to children of all races and ethnicities, but it is striking the degree to which white girls, of a variety of ethnicities, were singled out as being at risk for early marriage. Some sociologists, who looked at the same numbers I have just presented, did comment on the fact that "Negroes" married earlier than whites, primarily in rural America. See Ogburn, "Eleven Questions," 189. See also "Child Marriages in Kentucky," 369–70.

31. Hall quoted in Mary Ellen Richmond to Joanna C. Colcord, May 7, 1926, folder 212, box 11, MERP, CUA.

32. NYSPCC, *Fifteenth Annual Report*, 50–52; NYSPCC, "Eleven Years Old, Sold to Chinaman as Bride," *Forty-Sixth Annual Report*, December 31, 1920, 21; see also "Child Bride' Victim of Ex-Convict," ibid., 22; and NYSPCC, Case No. 222,348, *Thirty-Fourth Annual Report*, December 31, 1908, 19, all in NYHS.

33. NYSPCC, Case No. 54,787, *Seventeenth Annual Report*, December 31, 1891, 19, NYHS.

34. Towne, "Girl Marriages," 299; Richmond, "Child Marriages in New York State"; Children's Aid Society for the Prevention of Cruelty to Children of Erie County, N.Y., *Child Marriages in Erie County*, pts. 1, 3; Women's Protective Association, *School-Girl Brides*, 23–24; "Child Marriages in Kentucky," 370. See also Richmond and Hall, *Child Marriages*, 67; and *School-Girl Brides*, 20–22, 24.

35. Agnew, *From Charity to Social Work*, 187; "Child Marriages," November 1926, in folder: "Legal Status of Women: Marriage and Divorce," box 103, LWVP, LOC; Ogburn, "Eleven Questions," 187–88.

36. Popenoe, *Modern Marriage*, 49–59, quotations on 49, 51, 53. In a later (1943) edition, Popenoe argues that age itself is a poor measure of intelligence and capacity for marriage. Noting the numbers of children below fourteen who were married at the time of the 1930 census, he claims that although everyone denounces them, "it would be even more profitable to denounce the vastly more numerous marriages in which the partners are able to vote but intellectually have the minds of children—imbeciles who perhaps have less real intelligence than an average child in the first grade at school. The 'child bride' may grow

up some day; the imbecile never will!" Popenoe, *Modern Marriage: A Handbook for Men*,
6. An extended 1913 pamphlet from the Eugenics Record Office documenting marriage
laws related to eugenics does not even mention the age of marriage. See Davenport, *State
Laws Limiting Marriage Selection Examined in the Light of Eugenics*. G. Stanley Hall also
weighed in on marriage age, and his primary concern was the *delay* of marriage and childbirth by educated women, not precocious marriage, though he did discuss it; see Hall,
Adolescence, 2:592–98. For more on eugenics, particularly Paul Popenoe and the positive
school, see Kline, *Building a Better Race*, chap. 5; and Davis, *More Perfect Unions*.

37. NYSPCC, Case No. 113,625, *Twenty-Fourth Annual Report*, December 31, 1898, 27–28,
NYHS; Towne, "Young Girl Marriages," 301; "New York's Child Marriage Law," 428. On
the question of Progressive Era social workers and the family, see Gordon, *Heroes of Their
Own Lives*; Alexander, *"Girl Problem."*

38. For a similar argument, see Kuby, "Till Disinterest Do Us Part."

39. Mudgett, "When People Apply at a Marriage License Bureau," 284; Colcord, "What
Has Social Work," 254.

40. Mary Richmond to Worth M. Tippy, December 18, 1927, folder 114, box 13, Russell
Sage Foundation Collection, RAC; Colcord, "What Has Social Work," 253; Richmond
and Hall, *Child Marriages*, 48; *School-Girl Brides*, 37; Agnew, *From Charity to Social Work*,
190–93. On companionate marriages, see also Davis, " 'Not Marriage at All.' "

41. Alice L. Park, "Women under California Law," n.d., folder 2, box 17, Harbert Collection, HL. My thanks to Corinne T. Field for this source. See also Freedman, *Redefining
Rape*, chap. 11; and Cott, *Grounding of Modern Feminism*.

42. Legal Research Department, National Woman's Party, "Age of Capacity to Contract
Marriage," folder 12, box 200, group 2, NWPP, LOC; "A Bill Entitled AN ACT to add a
new section … ," folder 13, box 201, ibid.

43. "Explanatory Matter Relative to Bills #1 to #26 Inclusive, Attached Hereto," 1, folder
14, box 201, NWPP, LOC; "The Legal Position of Women in Alabama, 1921," 2, folder 15,
ibid. See also Katz, Schroeder, and Sidman, "Emancipating Our Children," esp. 217, 237;
"Parent and Child," 295; "Does Marriage Alone Emancipate a Male Minor?"

44. "Michigan Laws Discriminating against Women," 1922, 2, 8, folder 20, box 203,
NWPP, LOC; "The Legal Position of Women in Idaho," 2, folder 18, box 202, ibid.; "The
Status of Women under the Laws of Montana, 1927," 2, folder 2, box 203, ibid.; "The Legal
Position of Women in Nevada," 2, ibid.; "The Legal Position of Women in North Dakota,
1924," 2, folder 4, box 204, ibid.; "How Women Are Discriminated against in Oklahoma," 1,
folder 5, ibid.; "The Legal Position of Women in Oregon, 1926," 2, ibid.; "Discriminations
against Women in North Dakota Laws, 1930," 3, folder 4, ibid.; "*Statement*" about their
proposal to amend Section 8023 of the General Code of Ohio, folder 14, box 201, ibid.

45. California (1927): *Statutes of California, 1927* (Sacramento: California State Printing
Office, 1927), 1119; Colorado (1919): *Laws Passed at the Twenty-second Session of the
General Assembly of the State of Colorado* (Denver: American, 1919), 406; Hawaiʻi (1919):
Revised Laws of Hawaii, 1925 (Honolulu: *Star-Bulletin*, 1925), 1080; Iowa (by 1927): *Code
of Iowa, 1927* (n.p.: State of Iowa, 1927), 1342; Kansas (1917): *Revised Statues of Kansas,*

1923 (Topeka: Kansas State Printing Plant, 1923), 582; Missouri (1919): *Revised Statutes of the State of Missouri, 1929* (n.p.: Published by Authority, 1929), 273; Nebraska (1921): *Compiled Statutes of Nebraska, 1929* (Lincoln: State of Nebraska, 1930), 956; Ohio (1923): *Throckmorton's Annotated 1930 Code of Ohio* (Cleveland: Baldwin Law, 1930), 592; Vermont (1929): *The Vermont Statutes, Revision of 1947* (Montpelier: Published by Authority, 1947), 75; Washington (1923): *Session Laws of the State of Washington, Eighteenth Session* (Olympia: Frank M. Lamborn, 1923), 222–23. Nebraska later lowered its age of majority to nineteen for both sexes; see *Revised Statutes of Nebraska* (2008) § 43-2101. On possible benefits of lower majority, see Syrett, "Statutory Marriage Ages," 120–23.

46. Agnew, *From Charity to Social Work,* 188–89.

47. "An Explanation of the Program of the Legal Status of Women Committee, Adopted by the 1926 Convention of the National League of Women Voters," 6, folder: "Legal Status of Women: Marriage and Divorce," box 103, series 2, LWVP, LOC; California Response to Questionnaire from Committee on the Legal Status of Women, April 14, 1928, folder: "Legal Status," ibid.; Office Manager to Mrs. Edwin L. Goss, October 14, 1927, folder: "Committee on Legal Status, General Correspondence, 1927–28," ibid.; "Look Twice at the 'Equal Rights' Amendment," flyer, folder on Equal Rights Amendment, reel 36, National American Women's Suffrage Association Papers, LOC.

48. Judge Seeger quoted in Greenburg, *Peaches and Daddy,* 288–90.

49. Ibid., 302-3, 315, 318, chaps. 27, 28; "Peaches Browning Is Dead at 46; Child-Bride Symbol of Twenties," *NYT,* August 24, 1956, 19.

50. On Minnesota's five-day waiting period triumph, see materials in Minnesota folder, box 198, LWVP, LOC. On the gradual decline in the importance of marriage legislation in the League of Women Voters, see the state files in boxes 195–200, LWVP, LOC, which contain states' agendas for the early 1930s. Mary Ellen Richmond died on September 13, 1928; see September 14 press release by John Glenn.

Chapter 8

1. Marriage license for Eunice Winstead and Charlie Johns, January 12, 1937, reel A-2346, vol. E, Hancock County Marriage Records, TSLA; "What God Hath Joined," *Time,* February 15, 1937, 41; Mrs. Fred. J. Sheets, " 'Marryin' Parson' Talks about Child Wedding," *Rogersville (Tenn.) Review,* February 11, 1937, 1; "Charles and Eunice Winstead Johns," 217.

2. Eleanor Sheets, "Nine-Year-Old Bride's Mother Talks Freely to a Review Representative," *Rogersville (Tenn.) Review,* February 4, 1937, 1; "Charles and Eunice Winstead Johns," 217.

3. John Thompson, " 'I Love Charlie,' 9-Year Old Bride Says of Her Six-Foot Tall Mountain Husband, 22," *KJ,* January 30, 1937, 16; "Child Bride Happy in Play with Doll," *NYT,* January 31, 1937, 40; "Child Bride and Her Husband," *LAT,* January 31, 1937, 2; "What God Hath Joined," *Time,* February 15, 1937, 41–42; "Life on the American Newsfront: The Case of the Child Bride," *Life,* February 15, 1937, 15; "Nine-Year-Old Girl Married in America," *Straits Times* (Singapore), February 14, 1937, 4.

4. On marriage, divorce, and childbirth during the Great Depression, see May, *Homeward Bound*, 32–33; and Lynd and Lynd, *Middletown in Transition*, 149–50, 166–67.

5. Sheets, "Nine-Year-Old Bride's Mother," 1; "Charles and Eunice Winstead Johns," 217; Sheets, " 'Marryin' Parson,' " 1; marriage license for Herbert Winstead and Clara Johns, issued December 31, 1936, reel A-2346, vol. E, Hancock County Marriage Records, TSLA; "Takes Bride, 9," *CDT*, January 31, 1937, 11.

6. Thompson, " 'I Love Charlie,' " 16; "Groom, 22, Buys Bride, 9, Doll as Nuptial Gift," *Nashville Tennessean*, January 30, 1937, 3; "Nine-Year Old Girl's Wedding Stirs Protests," *Chicago Tribune*, February 2, 1937, 3; "Fan Mail Swamps Charlie, Eunice," *KJ*, February 5, 1937, 2; "Child Marriage Stirs Protests," *LAT*, February 2, 1937, 2. Tennessee had no minimum marriage age, which meant the common law governed marriage. Between the ages of seven and twelve, Eunice and Charlie's marriage was considered "imperfect" or "inchoate"; if neither disavowed the marriage, then it stood.

7. "Nine Is Early, Preacher Says," *KJ*, February 3, 1937, 12; "Neighbors Help Protect 9-Year-Old Bride from Eyes of Curious World," *KJ*, February 4, 1937, 1; "Reporters and Photographers Swarm Hancock for Stories and Pictures of Young Bride," *Rogersville (Tenn.) Review*, February 4, 1937, 1, 8; "Young Bride Kept Hidden," *KJ*, February 14, 1937, 1; "Miscellany," *Time*, February 8, 1937, 42; "What God Hath Joined," 41–42; "Married," *Time*, May 31, 1937, 56; "Exempt Bride," *Time*, August 23, 1937, 31; "Life on the American Newsfront," 15; "Private Lives," *Life*, August 23, 1937, 65; "Fan Mail Swamps Charlie, Eunice," *KJ*, February 5, 1937, 1; "Charlie Gets a Lawyer and May Accept Offers," *KJ*, February 7, 1937, 1; "Movies Open to Eunice; Money Offers Pour In," *KJ*, February 8, 1937, 1; "Checkered Frock of Gingham, Size 9, Is Promised Bride," *Memphis Commercial Appeal*, February 5, 1937, 5; "Charlie Johns' Attorney Raps Senate Resolution," *KJ*, February 10, 1937, 1. Another posed photo spread appeared in a number of publications; see, e.g., "How a Nine-Year-Old Bride Keeps House," *Morristown (Tenn.) Gazette*, February 15, 1937, 1.

8. "Girl, 12, Is Bride of Man, 19, at Carthage," *WDT*, February 2, 1937, 22, 12; "Marriage of Girl, 9, Stirs Angry Protests," *Watertown (N.Y.) Daily News*, February 1, 1937, 1, 18; "Miss Leona E. Roshia Is Wed to Stanley S. Backus," *WDT*, January 16, 1937, 8; "News Writers See Child Bride," *Watertown (N.Y.) Daily News*, February 3, 1937, 16; "Girl 12, Man 19, Wed," *NYT*, February 3, 1937, 9; "Factory-Hand Husband of 12-Year-Old Girl Arrested," *LAT*, February 4, 1937, 2; "12-Year-Old Girl Married to Youth of 19 in New York," *WP*, February 3, 1937, 1; "Girl of 12 Weds Youth of 19 with Mother's Sanction," *Hartford Courant*, February 3, 1937, 1.

9. William O. Varn, "Marriage Laws Vary by State," *WDT*, February 3, 1937, 18; "10-Year-Old Maryland Bride Revealed by Youth Study," *Baltimore Sun*, February 5, 1937, 1; "Maryland Data Disclose Many Wedded Young," *WP*, February 5, 1937, 1; "Child Marriages Not Rare in Nation"; "Discover 5,000 Child Brides in U.S. under 15"; "Census Lists 5,000 Girl Brides under 15, Thousands Just Over," *WP*, February 7, 1937, 1; "Child Bride No Stranger to America," *KJ*, February 6, 1937, 7; "America Has Its Child Brides," *CDT*, February 14, 1937, E7; "Child Marriages Difficult under Law of Illinois" *CDT*, February 10, 1937, 5;

"Tsk! Cradle Marriages Here? It Could Happen, Laws Reveal," *WP*, February 12, 1937, 17; "Windsor's Marriage Tops of '37 Weddings in News," *Boston Globe*, December 19, 1937, A37.

10. Mayo, *Mother India*. On the language of civilization, especially as a means to make arguments about childhood, race, and gender, see Bederman, *Manliness and Civilization*; Bullard, *Civilizing the Child*, esp. chap. 3; Brumberg, "Zenanas and Girlless Villages," esp. 363, 385, 367–71; Schmidt, *Industrial Violence and the Legal Origins of Child Labor*, 58, 61. On representations of Appalachia and the rural South as uncivilized, see Campbell, *Southern Highlander and His Homeland*, 20–21; Whisnant, *All That Is Native and Fine*; Rice, "Introduction"; and Blackwell, "Female Stereotypes and the Creation of Appalachia." On the significance of *Mother India*, see Pande, "Coming of Age," esp. 211–12; and Sinha, "Introduction."

11. "Child Marriages," *LAT*, February 3, 1937, A4; "In Darkest America," *Chicago Daily Times*, February 3, 1937, 21, copy in folder 4, reel 1, Gordon Browning Papers, TSLA; "Recent Child Marriage Emphasizes Problem in Limiting These Unions," news clipping, May 3, 1937, folder 16, box 1, part 3, MERP, CUA; "Mother India's Rival," *LAT*, February 23, 1937, A4; "Nine-Year-Old Girl Married in America," 4; "Girl Marriage Shocks Former Native of State," *KJ*, February 6, 1937, 3.

12. "Nine Year Old Girls' Wedding Stirs Protests," *Chicago Tribune*, February 2, 1937, 3; "'Terrible Burden' for Child So Young, 'Monkey Trial' Lawyer Says of Eunice," *KJ*, February 5, 1937, 1; Herblock, "In a State Where You Can't Teach Evolution," Newspaper Enterprise Association Service, February 3, 1937, accessible online at http://www.loc .gov/pictures/item/2009632462/.

13. "Child Marriage Bill Quickly Passes Senate," *Morristown (Tenn.) Gazette*, February 6, 1937, 1; C. G. Johnstone to Governor Gordon Browning, February 1, 1937; H. J. Arnold to Browning, January 31, 1937; and Julia Wilson to Browning, January 31, 1937, all in folder 3, reel 1, Gordon Browning Papers. On discourses of reversion to barbarism and the continuum of civilization, especially in the works of G. Stanley Hall, see Bederman, *Manliness and Civilization*, chap. 3.

14. Robert Helmuth Brackett to Browning, February 7, 1937; Bertha L. Spori to Browning, February 2, 1937; Mr. and Mrs. Martin J. Krause to Browning, n.d., all in folder 3, reel 1, Gordon Browning Papers.

15. On the issue of consummation not following immediately upon marriage in India, see Pande, "Coming of Age," 207–10.

16. Bureau of the Census, *Fifteenth Census of the United States: 1930, Population*, 2:843–47. While Mexican Americans are not singled out because of the way the Census Bureau defined race, rates were similarly high in Arizona, New Mexico, and Texas. See ibid., 923–94.

17. See also Melvin and Smith, *Rural Youth*, 63. For a similar situation in terms of the representation of child labor, see Sallee, *Whiteness of Child Labor Reform*; and Bullard, *Civilizing the Child*, 6.

18. On eugenics, see Cahn, *Sexual Reckonings*, 160, chap. 6; and Kline, *Building a Better Race*, 25, 106–7, chap. 4. On black racial uplift, see Gilmore, *Gender and Jim Crow*; and Wolcott, *Remaking Respectability*.

19. " 'Mother India' Author Lashes Child Marriage," *WP*, February 6, 1937, 1.

20. New York could take legal action against Backus and the Roshias for several reasons. First, New York did have a statutory marriage age for girls (fourteen), whereas Tennessee did not. Although both grooms had clearly lied about their brides' ages, in New York the law was much clearer that the couple was violating a minimum age. Leona's husband and parents were also charged with perjury for falsifying a birth certificate alleging that Leona was eighteen, the means of attaining the marriage license. They continued to insist she was eighteen even when state officials produced a record of her birth twelve years earlier. The parents were also charged with obstructing justice. Finally, it became clear soon after the Roshia-Backus nuptials that Leona was pregnant and authorities were able to arrest Stanley on second-degree criminal assault (statutory rape) charges; they alleged that the couple had had sex before the marriage. None of these circumstances existed in Tennessee, however, where Eunice's and Charlie's parents were unaware of the marriage until after it had taken place, no birth certificate was faked, and no one alleged that Eunice had had sex either before *or after* the marriage itself. See "Bride's Mother Says Child Is 18," *Daily Boston Globe*, February 7, 1937, A11; "Arrest the Parents of Watertown Bride," *NYT*, February 9, 1937, 3; "Child Bride's Parents Held," *LAT*, February 9, 1937, 3; "Bride, 12, Taken from Husband, 18," *WDT*, February 2, 1937, 18, 20; "Husband of Girl Bride Is Jailed," *WDT*, February 4, 1937, 24; "Perjury Case against Roshia," *WDT*, February 20, 1937, 22, 13.

21. *Acts of Tennessee Passed by the Fifty-First General Assembly* (Nashville: Marshall and Bruce, 1899), 36; *Public Acts of the State of Tennessee Passed by the Sixty-First General Assembly* (Jackson: McCourt, Mercer, 1919), 595; "Horton Signs Marriage Bill," *Nashville Banner*, April 13, 1929, 1; *Public Acts of the State of Tennessee, Passed by the Sixty-Sixth General Assembly* (Kingsport, Tenn.: Southern Publishers, 1929), 13–15. See also Michael Grossberg, "Guarding the Altar."

22. *Public Acts of the State of Tennessee, Passed by the Sixty-Ninth General Assembly* (Clarksville, Tenn.: Star, 1935), 214–15; "Senate Votes Out 5-Day Marriage License Law," *Memphis Commercial Appeal*, April 16, 1935, 13; "Senators Rally to Cupid and Pass Bill Repealing 5-Day Marriage Law," *Nashville Tennessean*, April 16, 1935, 4. For more on the repeal of the minimum marriage ages, which is not made explicit in the bill itself, see "Child's Marriage Termed 'Tragedy'; New Law Talked," *Nashville Banner*, February 1, 1937, 3; "Moves to Prohibit Child Marriages," *Baltimore Sun*, February 2, 1937, 8; "Child Wife's Marriage Legal, Tennessee Law Books Reveal," *Memphis Commercial Appeal*, February 2, 1937, 3.

23. "Only Woman Legislator to Be Honored Saturday," *Press-Scimitar* (Memphis), March 31, 1937, folder 8, Sophie Friedman Papers, Sophia Smith Collection, Smith College; "Legislators of Tennessee Rap Child Wedding," *CDT*, February 9, 1937, 1; "Assembly Condemns Mate of Child Bride," *Memphis Commercial Appeal*, February 9, 1937, 2; "Child Wedding Ban Is Sought," *KJ*, February 2, 1937, 2; "Governor Browning's Duty," *KJ*, February 3, 1937, 1.

24. *Public Acts of the State of Tennessee Passed by the Seventieth General Assembly* (Nashville: Printing Department, Tennessee Industrial School, 1937), 262–65; "House for

16, Senate for 14 as Age to Wed for Tennesseans," *CDT*, February 24, 1937, 8; "Tennessee House Passes Marriage Minimum of 16," *LAT*, February 24, 1937, 12; "Tennessee Senate Passes Marriage Bill," *LAT*, February 26, 1937, 5; "Child Marriage Bill Approved by House, 91–0," *Nashville Journal*, February 23, 1937, 1; "Marriage Age Fixed at 16 in Tennessee," *Daily Boston Globe*, February 27, 1937, 15. Sixteen remains the age of consent for marriage in Tennessee; those above sixteen but below eighteen must have parental consent to marry. See *Tennessee Annotated Code*, § 36-3-105, § 36-3-106. The three-day waiting period also remains, though it may be waived by a judge, and an individual below eighteen may also petition to have the age requirement to marriage removed, effectively making it possible for those below sixteen to marry. See ibid., § 36-3-107. Other states: *Session Laws of the State of Minnesota, Passed during the Fiftieth Session of the State Legislature, At the Session Commencing January 5, 1937* (Saint Paul: Mike Kolm, Secretary of State, 1937), 583–84; *Rhode Island General Laws of 1938* (Providence: Thompson and Thompson, 1938), 809–10; *District of Columbia Code, 1951 Edition (Annotated)*, 2 vols. (Washington: Government Printing Office, 1952), 2:944; and Bill file for H.B. No. 1168, box 4-19/172, Records of the Texas Legislature, TSLAC.

25. *Child Bride.*

26. Ibid.

27. Bureau of the Census, *Fifteenth Census of the United States: 1930, Population*, vol. 3: 566, 642, 843–45, 914–16, 922, 919, 925; Moore, "Present Status and Future Trends," 408. Texas had the most wives under fifteen, with 393, or 8.7 percent of the total. See also "Texas Leads All States in Child Brides with 393 upon Census Rolls," *Houston Post*, February 7, 1937, 1. For 1940, see Bureau of the Census, *Sixteenth Census of the United States: 1940, Population*, vol. 4, pt. 1: 109–11, vol. 4, pt. 4: 441. For a longer discussion, see also Melvin and Smith, *Rural Youth*, chap. 4.

28. On the significance of these institutions and their relative lack in the rural South, see Schmidt, *Industrial Violence*, 22, 51, 167; Mintz, *Huck's Raft*, 135, 181; Chudacoff, *How Old Are You?*, 34–40, 59–62; and Lassonde, *Learning to Forget*, chap. 2.

29. Bureau of the Census, *Fifteenth Census: 1930, Population*, vol. 2: 1096–101, 1104, 1219–20; Melvin and Smith, *Rural Youth*, 50, 47.

30. Bureau of the Census, *Fifteenth Census: 1930, Population*, vol. 3, pt. 2: 908; Schmidt, *Industrial Violence*, chap. 8, esp. 18, 23; Campbell, *Southern Highlander*, 264, 268, 289.

31. "Child Bride Switched," *NYT*, August 9, 1937, 3.

32. Palmer, "Child Marriage," 49.

33. Bureau of the Census, *Fifteenth Census: 1930, Population*, vol. 2: 848; Melvin and Smith, *Rural Youth*, 59, 64; Hagood, *Mothers of the South*, 109, 167–68, 206; Campbell, *Southern Highlander*, 132.

34. Melvin and Smith, *Rural Youth*, 63; Johnson, *Growing Up in the Black Belt*, 109, 113, 131–32; Reid, *In a Minor Key*, 30–31; Deutsch, *No Separate Refuge*, 44, 228n15. On compulsory birth registration, see Landrum, "From Bibles to Birth Certificates"; and Pearson, " 'Age Ought to Be a Fact.' "

35. Johnson, *Growing Up in the Black Belt*, 225–26, 232–33; Powdermaker, *After Freedom*, 149, 153, 158–59, 205. Rose Stremlau found similar patterns of common-law marriage among Cherokees in Oklahoma around the turn of the century. See *Sustaining the Cherokee Family*, 53–54, 121–22.

36. Hurston, *Their Eyes Were Watching God*, 11–13, 15, 17, 19–26, 28–29, 32–33.

37. Coles, *Migrants, Sharecroppers, Mountaineers*, 542–43, 544, 546; Bernstein, *Racial Innocence*.

38. "Child Bride's Age in Doubt," *LAT*, April 19, 1937, 3; "Child Bride's Mate Arrested," *LAT*, April 23, 1937, 9; "14-Year-Old Wife Asks Divorce, Custody of Her Child, Alimony," *Atlanta Constitution*, June 29, 1937, 1.

39. "Bride, 9, Whipped in School, Waives Right to 'Larnin,'" *WP*, August 10, 1937, 1; "Exempt Bride," *Time*, August 23, 1937, 31; "It's Different for Daughter," *CDT*, September 12, 1960, 1; "Eunice Blanche Johns," Obituaries, *Middleboro (Tenn.) Daily News*, September 12, 2006.

Chapter 9

1. Day, *Married at Fourteen*, 5, 17, 34, 48, 50–51, 56, 60, 67, 69, 77.

2. Ibid., 75–79, 83, 89–90, 97, 139, 145.

3. Bureau of the Census, *Historical Statistics of the United States*, 1:19; David Landman, "Tragic Trap of Teenage Marriage," *Coronet*, February 1961, 119, copy in folder 9, box 4, NCFRP, SWHA. Julie Solow Stein also writes on the postwar teenage marriage boom and, using many of the same materials, we have come to similar conclusions about the meanings of the "crisis." See "Early to Wed."

4. On marriage, domesticity, and sexuality in this era, see May, *Homeward Bound*; Bailey, *From Front Porch to Back Seat*; Weiss, *To Have and To Hold*, esp. chap. 1; and Ehrmann, *Premarital Dating Behavior*.

5. On teenagers, see Schrum, *Some Wore Bobby Sox*; Modell, *Into One's Own*; and Cahn, *Sexual Reckonings*, chap. 8. The *Oxford English Dictionary* dates the origins of "teen-ager," as a noun, to 1941 in the United States.

6. Panunzio, "War and Marriage," 443–44; Duvall, "Marriage in War Time," 74; Sundal and McCormick, "Age at Marriage and Mate Selection," 38; "Solicitor Plans Marriage Probe," *Raleigh News and Observer*, August 16, 1944, 3; Weiss, *To Have and to Hold*, 21–23.

7. Duvall, "Marriage in War Time," 74; Sundal and McCormick, "Age at Marriage," 40–41. The percentages are even higher if one counts teenagers who were "ever married," which included the divorced. See Department of Health, Education, and Welfare, *Teenagers*, 2. Bear in mind also that the overall *number* of teenagers marrying is actually increasing, but as a proportion of their age cohort, their numbers are in decline.

8. Burchinal, "Research on Young Marriage, 6–12.

9. Snyder, *120 Years of American Education*, 6–7; Stein, "Early to Wed," 363.

10. On changes in childhood in the postwar period, see Fass and Grossberg, *Reinventing Childhood after World War II*; Mintz, *Huck's Raft*, chap. 14.

11. Jane E. Brody, "Teen-Age Mom: My Kids Will Get Sex Information," *Minneapolis Tribune*, October 12, 1965, 9, copy in folder 9, box 41, NCFRP, SWHA. Many newspaper accounts of teenage marriage included interviews with teen wives and husbands. Although I recognize that these interviews are filtered through the lenses of reporters and editors who were interested in constructing particular kinds of stories, these accounts still remain a valuable source for understanding the motivations of teens who married and did not necessarily end up in court as a result of their marriages. In addition, many of the reporters who covered this phenomenon seem deliberately to have chosen "ordinary" girls and boys as a way of making the story seem as relatable as possible. That the social science data backs up the particulars makes them also seem more credible.

12. Moss and Gingles, "The Relationship of Personality to the Incidence of Early Marriage," 377 (31 percent); Burchinal, "Adolescent Role Deprivation," 381 (39.6 percent); Burchinal, "Trends and Prospects for Young Marriages in the United States," 248 (33–50 percent); Burchinal, "Research on Young Marriage," 9; Burchinal, "School Policies," 45 (57 percent); Ivins, "Student Marriages in New Mexico," 72; Inselberg, "Marital Problems and Satisfaction," 76 (43 percent); Furstenberg, *Destinies of the Disadvantaged*, 9; Stein, "Early to Wed," 368.

13. Story of Jenny in Parton, "Why Do They Marry So Young?," 172. Lee G. Burchinal, "Does Early Dating Lead to School-Age Marriage?" *Iowa Farm Science* 13, no. 8 (1959), copy in folder 6, box 41, NCFRP, SWHA; David R. Mace, "A Marriage Counselor Looks at Teen-Age Marriage," 5–7, speech delivered to the Minnesota Council on Family Life and the Community Health and Welfare Council of Hennepin County, 1961, copy in ibid.; Bayer, "Early Dating and Early Marriage," 631; Burchinal, "Adolescent Role Deprivation," 382; Burchinal, "Trends and Prospects," 246–47; Burchinal, "Research on Young Marriage," 9; Paget, *Facts about Teenage Marriages in San Bernardino County*, 7.

14. Parton, "Why Do They Marry So Young?," 172. On changes in sex and dating practices during this era, see May, *Homeward Bound*, chap. 5; Bailey, *From Front Porch to Back Seat*; Cole, "American Youth Goes Monogamous," 29–33; Ehrmann, *Premarital Dating Behavior*; Cahn, *Sexual Reckonings*, chap. 8.

15. Duvall, "Research Finds," 76; Landis and Kidd, "Attitudes and Policies," 130; Burchinal, "Adolescent Role Deprivation," 378; Moss and Gingles, "Teen-Age Marriage," 188. On marriage and family living classes themselves, see Bailey, *From Front Porch to Back Seat*, 119–37; Cahn, *Sexual Reckonings*, 220, 236–37; and materials collected in folders 4–7, box 82; folder 8, box 81; folders 4, 13, box 176; folders 1, 4, 6, 8, box 84; and folder 22, box 193, American Social Health Association Records, SWHA.

16. Mudd and Hey, "When the Young Marry Too Young," 25; Spicer, "Teenage Secret Marriage Epidemic," 74; Day, *Married at Fourteen*, 17, 26, 34, 44, 65.

17. David, "Are You Pushing Your Daughter into Too-Early MARRIAGE?," 216, 221; Sam Newlund, "Expert Says Parents Spur Teen Marriage," *Minneapolis Evening Tribune*, March 21, 1962, 18, copy in folder 10, box 41, NCFRP, SWHA. See also Mace, "Marriage Counselor Looks at Teen-Age Marriage," 3–7.

18. David, "Are You Pushing Your Daughter," 221.

19. May, *Homeward Bound*, chap. 7; Friedan, *Feminine Mystique*, 16, 276–77, 280, 301.

20. Landis and Kidd, "Attitudes and Policies," 129–130; Moss, "Teenage Marriage," 111; Burchinal, "Trends and Prospects," 245; Stephanie Brown, "Are They Too Young To Wed?," *Minneapolis Sunday Tribune*, June 22, 1958, 1, copy in folder 9, box 41, NCFRP, SWHA; Landman, "Tragic Trap," 119; Grafton, "Why Teen-Age Marriages"; Avery, "Toward Understanding," 30.

21. Data on parental attitudes or attendance at weddings is, of course, not systematic, but a number of sociologists reported that parents initially opposed to weddings eventually became supportive. See De Lissovoy, "High School Marriages," 252; and Lee G. Burchinal, "Comparisons of Factors Related to Adjustment in Pregnancy-Provoked and Nonpregnancy Provoked Youthful Marriages," *Midwest Sociologist* 21 (July 1959): 9, typescript in folder 9, box 41, NCFRP, SWHA.

22. Record in *Turner v. Turner*, 167 Cal. App. 2d 636 (1959), quotation on 6, CSL; Blank, Charles, and Sallee, "Do State Laws Affect the Age of Marriage?," 16–17, 2, 12–13.

23. Record in *Spencer v. People, in Interest of Spencer*, 14–15, 29, 31–32, Case 17791, June Term, 1955, CSA. Virginia and Lloyd lost their suit in the lower court, but the Supreme Court reversed the decision on appeal, ruling that Colorado honored the marriages of other states, which meant that the couple remained married, and that marriage did not constitute one of the qualifications of delinquency, meaning that Lloyd could not have been guilty of contributing to Virginia's designation as a delinquent, because legally she was not one.

24. Blank, Charles, and Sallee, "Do State Laws Affect the Age of Marriage?," 20.

25. Samuel Grafton, "Why Teen-Age Marriages Are Falling Apart," *McCall's*, November 1959, copy in folder 9, box 41, NCFRP, SWHA; Spicer, "Teenage Secret Marriage Epidemic," 74–75, 155, 156.

26. "Marriages," *Raleigh News and Observer*, December 5, 1944, 1; "Marriage Bill," *Raleigh News and Observer*, March 21, 1945, 2; "Here's How to Get a Marriage License," ibid., May 9, 1945, 12; "Group Would Strengthen Divorce, Marriage Laws," ibid., February 21, 1948, 5; S. B. No. 80, 54th Legislative Session, 1955, State of Texas, box 100-77, Texas Bill Files, TSLAC; *Colorado Revised Statutes 1953*, vol. 4 (Chicago: Callaghan, 1954), 618; *The Annotated Code of the Public General Laws of Maryland*, vol. 2 (Baltimore: King Brothers, 1951), 2845; *Commonwealth of Kentucky Revised Statutes, 1962*, vol. 2 (Frankfort: Legislative Research Commission, 1962), 2.

27. *Code of Laws of South Carolina, 1952, 1960 Cumulative Supplement* (Columbia: R. L. Bryan, 1960), 152.

28. Frieda S. Miller and Maurice J. Tobin, "State Laws of Special Interest to Women," January 1, 1950, folder 4, box 210, group 2, NWPP, LOC.

29. On school board policies, see Burchinal, "Trends and Prospects," 253; Burchinal, "School Policies," 43–7; Burchinal, "Research on Young Marriage," 12–14; Landis and Kidd, "Attitudes and Policies," 130–32; Cavan and Beling, "Study of High School Marriages," 293–95; Ivins, "Student Marriages in New Mexico Secondary Schools," 73; Landis, "High School Student Marriages," 272–73; Avery, "Toward Understanding," 27; "Rulings Issued on State Laws," *Raleigh News and Observer*, September 12, 1945, 5.

30. Matthews, "Courts and Married Students"; Snyder, *120 Years of American Education*, 1–6; Seger, "Wellsand v. Valparaiso Community School Corporation"; "Case Note: Constitutional Law—Married High School Students"; *Holt v. Shelton*, Civ. No. 833 (U.S. District Court for the Middle District of Tennessee, 1972); Price, "Marriage vs. Education," 248–60. Vladimir De Lissovoy reported in 1973 that "school boards throughout the country have become much more liberal in permitting young marrieds to remain until graduation or to return to school in order to finish work for a high school diploma." See De Lissovoy, "High School Marriages," 253–54. Grossberg, "Liberation and Caretaking," 21; Grossberg, "Children's Legal Rights?"

31. Hagan, "Girls, Sex, and Juvenile Delinquency," 123, chap 6, esp. 303–4.

32. *Throckmorton's Annotated Code of Ohio, 1930* (Cleveland: Baldwin Law, 1930), 193; consent for Diana Whittington, June 18, 1956, Franklin County Probate Court Marriage Consents & Misc. Papers 1955–1957, microfilm reel GR 2710, Ohio History Center, State Library and Archives.

33. Bureau of the Census, *1940 Census*, Population, vol. 4, pt. 1: table 8, 22–23; Bureau of the Census, *1950 Census*, vol. 2, pt. 1: table 104, 182–83, 185; Bureau of the Census, *1960 Census*, vol. 1, pt. 1: table 176, 426, 428, 429–30.

34. Anderson and Letts, "High School Marriages and School Policies in Minnesota," 267. See also De Lissovoy and Hitchcock, "High School Marriages in Pennsylvania," 263–65; Ivins, "Student Marriages in New Mexico Secondary Schools," 72; Bartz and Nye, "Early Marriage," 258; Burchinal, "School Policies and School Age Marriages," 45; and Carson, "Family Background, School and Early Marriage," 348–49, 351.

35. On the teacher–guidance counselor approach, see Moss and Gingles, "Teen-Age Marriage"; Ivins, "Student Marriages in New Mexico Secondary Schools"; and Inselberg, "Marital Problems and Satisfaction in High School Marriages."

36. Burchinal, "Research on Young Marriage," 7; Burchinal, "Trends and Prospects," 243–44. A 1962 study by Kingston and Gentry examining principals' reports of behavioral problems with married students in Georgia high schools discussed both white and black students but made no claims as to enumerating the percentages of students from either race who were married. See "Married High School Students and Problem Behavior," 284–88.

37. Day, *Married at Fourteen*, 145, 205, 213, 333.

Chapter 10

1. Paul Salopek, "From Child to Bride: Early Marriage Survives in the U.S.," *Chicago Tribune*, December 12, 2004; *Vernon's Texas Annotated Codes*, Family Code, Sections 1.001 to 5 (Austin: West, 2005), 53–54.

2. Le Strat, Dubertret, and Le Foll, "Child Marriage in the United States," 524; Goodwin, McGill, and Chandra, "Who Marries and When?," 2. Both of these studies use random samples to determine the number of women in their sample who *had married* by age 18. By contrast, the CDC found that between 2006 and 2010, 4 percent of American women who married did so below the age of eighteen *in that five-year period*, and 1

percent of men had done so. See Copen, Daniels, Vesper, and Mosher, "First Marriages in the United States," 5–6.

3. Bureau of the Census, "Households and Families, 2010," 15; Willoughby, Hall, and Luczak, "Marital Paradigms," 2–3; Coontz, *Marriage, a History*, chap. 16; Mintz, *Prime of Life*, 105; Banks, *Is Marriage for White People?*, 2–3.

4. Le Strat, Dubertret, and Le Foll, "Child Marriage in the United States"; Uecker, "Early Marriage in the United States," chap. 2, esp. 18; Glass and Levchak, "Red States, Blue States, and Divorce"; Grossman and Friedman, *Inside the Castle*, 52–56; Mintz, *Prime of Life*, 131.

5. Le Strat, Dubertret, and Le Foll, "Child Marriage in the United States"; Goodwin, McGill, and Chandra, "Who Marries and When?"; Copen, Daniels, Vespa, and Mosher, "First Marriages in the United States."

6. U.S. Department of Labor, Office of Policy Planning and Research, *Negro Family*; Carlson, "Family Background, School and Early Marriage," 348–50. On single motherhood and pregnancy among white and black girls, see also Solinger, *Wake Up Little Susie*; Furstenberg, *Destinies of the Disadvantaged*, 11–15, chap. 1; and Modell, *Into One's Own*, 43, 48–50. On marriage patterns by race, see Grossman and Friedman, *Inside the Castle*, 54–56.

7. Alan Guttmacher Institute, *Sex and America's Teenagers*; Reed and Spurlock, "Young and Pregnant," 39–42; Furstenberg, *Destinies*, 21–23, chap. 5; Quadagno, *Color of Welfare*; CDC data are at http://www.cdc.gov/nchs/fastats/unmarried-childbearing.htm.

8. Chávez, "Women of the Mexican American Movement," 38.

9. In addition to these two major changes, some jurisdictions continued to institute various hoops through which minors needed to jump in order to obtain a marriage license, largely as an effort to prevent divorce. See Elkin, "Premarital Counseling for Minors."

10. Wardle, "Rethinking Marital Age Restrictions," 9–11.

11. *Stanton v. Stanton*, 421 U.S. 7 (1975); Warren Weaver, Jr., "Justices Void Law on Majority Ages," *NYT*, April 16, 1975, 21; "Court Decision Might Control Marriage Age," *Farmington (N.Mex.) Daily Times*, April 16, 1975, 4A. The case before the court concerned child support and the differential ages until which a Utah father was obligated to support a son versus a daughter. Although the court limited its opinion to the issue of support, Justice Blackmun was also clear that different societal expectations for girls and boys could not be a rational reason for treating them differently (by age) under the law. See Arkansas Code § 9-11-102 (sixteen and seventeen; consent below eighteen); Mississippi Code § 93-1-5 (fifteen/seventeen; extra stipulations below twenty-one/twenty-one); Nebraska Revised Statutes § 42-102 (seventeen/seventeen; consent below nineteen/nineteen); New Hampshire Revised Statutes, § 457:4-5 (thirteen/fourteen, consent below eighteen/eighteen); Ohio Revised Code § 3101.01 (sixteen/eighteen; consent below eighteen for girl); Rhode Island Laws § 15-2-11 (sixteen/eighteen; consent below eighteen for girl).

12. Wardle, "Rethinking," 11–12; Cornell University Law School, "Marriage Laws of the Fifty States, District of Columbia and Puerto Rico," http://www.law.cornell.edu/wex/

table_marriage; U.S. Department of Health, Education, and Welfare, *Teenagers*, 13; *West's Indiana Code* (2008): 166–68; Grossman and Friedman, *Inside the Castle*, 44–45.

13. On the decrease in marital migration, see Blank, Charles, and Sallee, "Do State Laws Affect the Age of Marriage?," 2. On the persistence of the phenomenon in the 1970s, see Wardle, "Rethinking," 45.

14. *Moe v. Dinkins*, 669 F. 2d 67 (2d Cir. 1982); *Moe v. Dinkins*, 533 F. Supp. 623 (1981 U.S. Dist. LEXIS 13974); "Conditional Cross Petition for a Writ of Certiorari to the United States Court of Appeals for the Second District," 8–11, NYSA; for commentary on *Moe v. Dinkins*, see also Wardle, "Rethinking," 1–4; and Grossman and Friedman, *Inside the Castle*, 44.

15. Wardle, "Rethinking," 41–44. Similarly, *Teenagers*, 13, found that those states that lowered their minimum marriageable age during the 1960s saw an increase in teenage marriage and those that raised their age saw a decrease, sometimes with corresponding elevation in neighboring states.

16. Wardle, "Rethinking," 41–44.

17. Goodwin, McGill, and Chandra, "Who Marries and When?," 3; Seiler, "Is Teen Marriage a Solution?," 3–4; Furstenberg, *Destinies*, 99.

18. Cocca, " '16 Will Get You 20,' " 26–27. As of 2013, 71 percent of male and female nineteen-year-old teens have had sex; see Guttmacher Institute, "Fact Sheet: American Teens' Sexual and Reproductive Health," May 2014, at http://www.guttmacher.org/pubs/FB-ATSRH.html#1.

19. Bachu, "Trends in Premarital Childbearing: 1930 to 1994," 5; Furstenberg, *Destinies*, 108.

20. Guttmacher Institute, "Fact Sheet"; Strayhorn and Strayhorn, "Religiosity and Teen Birth in the United States," 1–7. Three states that are both rural *and* have low rates of teen pregnancy are Maine, Vermont, and New Hampshire.

21. Guttmacher Institute, "Fact Sheet"; Kost and Henshaw, "U.S. Teenage Pregnancies, Births, and Abortions, 2010," 4, 17. This is partially because abortion is more easily available in urban than rural states, but also because of attitudes toward the termination of pregnancies.

22. Department of Health and Human Services, Administration for Children and Families, "Voluntary Relinquishment for Adoption," 1–2; Chandra, Abma, Mazza, and Bachrach, "Adoption, Adoption Seeking, and Relinquishment for Adoption in the United States," 9.

23. Data on unwed motherhood by state is from the Annie E. Casey Foundation based on data from the CDC's National Center for Health Statistics. See here for a chart from 2009 to 2013: http://datacenter.kidscount.org/data/tables/106-children-in-single-parent-families#detailed/2/2–52/false/36,868,867,133,38/any/429,430.

24. Wardle, "Rethinking," 43–44. Hispanic women have the highest probability of marriage by eighteen (10 percent), followed by non-Hispanic white women (6 percent),

and non-Hispanic black women (3 percent). See Goodwin, McGill, and Chandra, "Who Marries and When?," 3. These numbers, however, are not broken down by region.

25. Uecker, "Early Marriage in the United States," 19–20; Uecker and Stokes, "Early Marriage in the United States"; Brückner and Bearman, "After the Promise," 275; Lehrer, "Role of Religion in Union Formation," 180–81; Xu, Hudspeth, and Bartkowski, "Timing of First Marriage"; Glass and Levchak, "Red States"; Hammond, Cole, and Beck, "Religious Heritage and Teenage Marriage."

26. https://www.facebook.com/liset.j.landeros; *Bellmead Bulletin*, August 2012, 11 (accessed online August 11, 2014).

Epilogue

1. United Nations Population Fund, *Marrying Too Young*, 5; Gorney, "Too Young To Wed."

2. United Nations Population Fund, *Marrying Too Young*; Gorney, "Too Young to Wed."

3. United Nations Population Fund, *Marrying Too Young*, 10; "Why Won't America Ratify the UN Convention on Children's Rights?" For a critique of relying on the supposedly universal category of age alone in order to determine marriage law internationally, see Pande, "Coming of Age," 18–19.

4. Le Strat, Dubertret, and Le Foll, "Child Marriage in the United States"; Seiler, "Is Teen Marriage a Solution?"; Dahl, "Early Teen Marriage and Future Poverty."

5. Coates, "Myth of Western Civilization"; my thanks to Jan Ellen Lewis for sending me this; "How Duck Dynasty's Phil Robertson Avoided Prison for Breaking Statutory Rape Laws."

6. Wardle, "Rethinking Marital Age Restrictions"; Lisa Leff and Paul Elias, "California Court Weighs Same-Sex Marriage Ban," *Deseret News* (Salt Lake City, Utah), March 6, 2009; *Hollingsworth v. Perry*, 570 U.S. ___ (2013); *United States v. Windsor*, 570 U.S. ___ (2013); *Obergefell v. Hodges*, 576 U.S. ___ (2015).

7. "Pennsylvania Governor: Gay Couples Barred from Marriage 'Like 12-Year-Olds,'" *Guardian*, August 29, 2013. My thanks to Renée Sentilles for alerting me to this story.

Bibliography

PRIMARY SOURCES

Archives

Albany, N.Y.

New York State Library and Archives

Record in *Hermann v. Hermann*

Record in *Moe v. Dinkins*

Report of the Commissioners Appointed to Revise the Statute Laws of the State. Made to the Senate, November 2, 1827. Albany: Croswell and Van Benthuysen, 1827.

"Report of the Committee on the Judiciary," S. Doc. No. 85, April 26, 1841, *New York Senate Documents*, 64th Sess., 1841, vol. 2.

Report of the Secretary of State, of the Number of Births, Marriages and Deaths, for the Year 1847, S. Rep. No. 73, April 12, 1848.

Report of the Secretary of State, of the Number of Births, Marriages and Deaths, for the Year 1848, S. Rep. No. 86, April 10, 1849.

Austin, Texas

Texas State Library and Archives

Record in *Ex Parte Nolte*

Records of the Texas Legislature

Boston, Mass.

Massachusetts Archives

Petition of Daniel Nourse, et al., February 25, 1852, Legislative Packet for Chapter 254, "Act in Addition to the Act to Punish Abduction," Acts of 1852

Records of Massachusetts Births

Records of Massachusetts Deaths

Records of Massachusetts Marriages

Reports to the Legislature of Massachusetts Relating to the Registry and Return of Births,
   Marriages, and Deaths, in the Commonwealth of Massachusetts
Massachusetts Supreme Judicial Court Archives
   Record in *Hervey v. Moseley*
   Record in *Parton v. Hervey*
   Record in *Parton v. Parton*
Brooklyn, N.Y.
   Brooklyn Collection, Brooklyn Public Library
   Annual Reports of the Brooklyn Society for the Prevention of Cruelty to Children
Columbus, Ohio
   Ohio History Center
      Delaware County Probate Court, Consent to Marry Certificates for Minors and
         Marriage Returns, 1910–1952
      Franklin County Probate Court, Marriage Consents and Miscellaneous Papers
Denver, Colo.
   Colorado State Archives
      Record in *Spencer v. People, in the Interest of Virginia Louise Spencer*
Durham, N.C.
   David M. Rubenstein Library, Duke University
      Devereux Family Papers
      Francis Porteous Corbin Papers
      Francis Wilkinson Pickens Papers
      George Coke Dromgoole Papers
      Jared Irwin Papers
      McDonald Forman Papers
      Thomas Bibb Papers
Minneapolis, Minn.
   Social Welfare History Archives, University of Minnesota
      American Social Health Association Papers
      Family Service Association of America Papers
      National Council on Family Relations Papers
Nashville, Tenn.
   Tennessee State Library and Archives
      Governor Gordon Browning Papers
      Hancock County Marriage Records
New York, N.Y.
   New York County Clerk's Office
      Record in *Kruger v. Kruger*
   New-York Historical Society
      Annual reports of the New York Society for the Prevention of Cruelty to Children
   New York Public Library

Elizabeth Oakes Smith, "A Human Life: Being the Autobiography of Elizabeth Oakes Smith"
Rare Books and Manuscripts Library, Columbia University
    Mary Ellen Richmond Papers
Northampton, Mass.
  Sophia Smith Collection, Smith College Archives
    Sophie Friedman Papers
Olympia, Wash.
  Washington State Archives
    Record in *Cushman v. Cushman*
    Record in *In re Hollopeter*
Raleigh, N.C.
  North Carolina State Archives
    "An Abstract of a letter from a Gentleman in N. Carolina to his friend in Maryland," June 7, 1762
    Halifax County Miscellaneous Records
    Lincoln County Miscellaneous Records
    Montgomery County Miscellaneous Records
    Record in *Shutt v. Carloss*
Sacramento, Calif.
  California State Archives
    Record in *Hunter v. Milam*
    Record in *People v. Souleotes*
    Record in *Turner v. Turner*
    Record in *West v. West*
Santa Fe, N.Mex.
  New Mexico State Library and Archives
    Record in *Territory of New Mexico v. Harwood*
San Francisco, Calif.
  California History Museum
    Richard N. Schellens Papers
San Marino, Calif.
  Huntington Library
    Abel Stearns Papers
    Autobiography of Lucy Hannah Flake
    Autobiography of Mary Minerva Dart Judd
    Biographical Sketch of Martha Cox
    Gene L. Gardner, Biography of Mary Cox Lee
    Harbert Collection
    Life Sketch of Amanda Mulvina Fisk Stout
    Terressa Artemesia Redd Romney, Life Sketch of Sariah Louisa Chamberlain

Sleepy Hollow, N.Y.
   Rockefeller Archive Center
      Russell Sage Foundation Collection
Washington, D.C.
   Library of Congress
      League of Women Voters Papers
      National American Women's Suffrage Association Papers
      National Woman's Party Papers
Williamsburg, Va.
   John D. Rockefeller Library Special Collections, College of William and Mary
      Greenhow Family Bible
      John Norton and Sons Papers

Newspapers

Albany Argus
Anaconda (Mont.) Standard
Atlanta Constitution
Baltimore Sun
Bellingham (Wash.) Herald
Boston Courier
Boston Daily Advertiser
Boston Daily Atlas
Boston Herald
Boston Journal
Chicago Daily Times
Chicago Daily Tribune
Cleveland Gazette
Columbus Daily Enquirer
Daily Alta California (San Francisco)
Daily Atlas (Boston)
Daily Olympian (Washington)
Daily Picayune (New Orleans, La.)
Daily Republican (Springfield, Mass.)
Deseret News (Salt Lake City, Utah)
Duluth (Minn.) News Tribune
Farmington (N.Mex.) Daily Times
Grand Rapids Press
Guthrie (Okla.) Daily Leader
Hartford Courant
Jackson (Mich.) Citizen Patriot
Jonesboro (Ark.) Evening Sun
Kalamazoo (Mich.) Gazette

Kansas City Evening Star
Knoxville Journal
Los Angeles Herald
Los Angeles Times
Lynn (Mass.) News
Memphis Commercial Appeal
Middleboro (Tenn.) Daily News
Minneapolis Journal
Mt. Sterling (Ky.) Advocate
Morning Olympian (Washington)
Morning Oregonian (Portland)
Morristown (Tenn.) Gazette
Nashville Banner
Nashville Tennessean
National Era (Washington, D.C.)
New York Commercial Advertiser
New York Herald
New York Times
New York Tribune
Northern Christian Advocate (Auburn, N.Y.)
Olympia Record
Omaha World Herald
Pawtucket (R.I.) Evening Times
Philadelphia Inquirer
Press-Scimitar (Memphis)
Raleigh Register
Raleigh News and Observer
Rogersville (Tenn.) Review
Sacramento Daily Union
Salem (Mass.) Register
San Francisco Bulletin
San Francisco Call
San Francisco Chronicle
San Jose Mercury News
Saratoga Sentinel
Schenectady Cabinet
St. Louis Republic
Star and North-Carolina State Gazette
State (Columbia, S.C.)
Straits Times (Singapore)
Trenton Evening Times
Tucson Citizen

Washington Post
Watch-Tower (Cooperstown, N.Y.)
Watertown (N.Y.) Daily News
Watertown (N.Y.) Daily Times
Wheeling Register
Wilkes-Barre Times

Court Cases

Aldrich v. Bennet, 63 N.H. 415 (1885)

Baker v. Baker, 112 Neb. 738 (1924)

Cochran v. State, 91 Ga. 763 (1892)

Cotten v. Rutledge, 33 Ala. 110 (1858)

Cushman v. Cushman, 80 Wash. 615 (1914)

Ex Parte Nolte, 296 S.W. 906 (Tex. Civ. App. 1925)

Fodor v. Kunie, 92 N.J. Eq. 301 (1920)

Garner v. State, 9 Ala. App. 60 (1913)

Gibbs v. Brown, 68 Ga. 803 (1882)

Gibbs v. Gibbs, 92 N.J. Eq. 542 (1921)

Goodwin v. Thompson, 2 Greene 329 (Iowa 1849)

Griffin v. Griffin, 225 Mich. 253 (1923)

Herrman v. Herrman, 93 Misc. 315 (New York County, 1916)

Hervey v. Moseley, 73 Mass. 479 (1856)

Holland v. Beard, 59 Miss. 161 (1881)

Hollingsworth v. Perry, 570 U.S. ___ (2013)

Holt v. Shelton, Civ. No. 833 (U.S. District Court for the Middle District of Tennessee, 1972)

Hunter v. Milam, 111 Cal. 261 (1896)

In re Hollopeter, 52 Wash. 41 (1909)

Jimenez v. Jimenez, 93 N.J. Eq. 257 (1922)

Johnson v. Alexander, 39 Cal. App. 177 (1918)

Kellogg v. Kellogg, 122 Misc. 734 (New York County, 1924)

Kruger v. Kruger, 64 Misc. 382 (New York County, 1909)

Little v. Holmes et al., 181 N. C. 413 (1921)

Marone v. Marone, 105 Misc. 371 (New York County, 1918)

May v. Meade, 236 Mich. 109 (1926)

Moe v. Dinkins, 669 F.2d 67 (2d Cir. 1982)

Moe v. Dinkins, 533 F. Supp. 623 (1981 U.S. Dist. LEXIS 13974)

Niland v. Niland, 96 N.J. Eq. 438 (1924)

Obergefell v. Hodges, 576 U.S. ___ (2015)

Owen v. Coffey, 201 Ala. 531 (1918)

Parton v. Hervey, 67 Mass. 119 (1854)

Parton v. Parton (Essex County Supreme Judicial Court, Mass., 1865)

People v. Beevers, 99 Cal. 286 (1893)

People v. Pizzura, 211 Mich. 71 (1920)

People v. Souleotes, 26 Cal. App. 309 (1915)

Robinson v. English, 34 Pa. 324 (1859)

Shutt v. Carloss, 36 N.C. 232 (1840)

Smith v. Smith, 205 Ala. 502 (1921)

Spencer v. People in Interest of Virginia Spencer, 292 P.2d 971, 133 Colo. 196 (1955)

Stansbury v. Bertron, 7 Watts & Serg. 362 (Pennsylvania 1844)

Stanton v. Stanton, 421 U.S. 7 (1975)

State ex rel. Foot v. District Court, 77 Mont. 290 (1926)

State v. Bittick, 103 Mo. 183 (1890)

State v. DeMarco, 20 Ala. 52 (1924)

State v. Parker, 106 N.C. 711 (1890)

Taub v. Taub, 87 N. J. Eq. 624 (1917)

Territory of New Mexico v. Harwood, 15 N.M. 424 (1909)

Turner v. Turner, 167 Cal. App. 2d 636 (1959)

United States v. Windsor, 570 U.S. ___ (2013)

West v. West, 62 Cal. App. 541 (1923)

Wood and Wife v. Henderson, 3 Miss. 893 (1838)

Government Documents

Bachu, Amara. "Trends in Premarital Childbearing: 1930 to 1994." *Current Population Reports*, P23-197. Washington: U.S. Census Bureau, 1999.

Carter, Susan, Scott Sigmund Gartner, Michael R. Haines, Alan L. Olmstead, Richard Sutch, and Gavin Wright, eds. *Historical Statistics of the United States: Earliest Times to the Present, Millennial Edition*. Vol. 1. New York: Cambridge University Press, 2006.

Copen, Casey E., Kimberly Daniels, Jonathan Vespa, and William Mosher. "First Marriages in the United States: Data from the 2006–2010 National Survey of Family Growth." *National Health Statistics Reports*, no. 49. Washington: National Center for Health Statistics, 2012.

DeBow, J. D. B. *Statistics View of the United States . . . Being a Compendium of the Seventh Census*. Washington: Beverley Tucker, Senate Printer, 1854.

Department of Health and Human Services, Administration for Children and Families. "Voluntary Relinquishment for Adoption." Washington: Administration for Children and Families, 2005.

De Silva-de-Alwis, Rangita. *Child Marriage and the Law*. New York: UNICEF, 2008.

Elliott, Diana B., and Tavia Simmons. "Marital Events of Americans: 2009." *American Community Survey Reports*, ACS-13. Washington: U.S. Census Bureau, 2011.

Goodwin, Paula, Brittany McGill, and Anjani Chandra. "Who Marries and When? Age at First Marriage in the United States: 2002." *NCHS Data Brief*, no. 19. Hyattsville, Md.: National Center for Health Statistics, 2009.

Hearings before the Judiciary Committee, 67th Cong., 2d Sess., on H. J. Res. 83, Jan. 26, 1922. Washington: Government Printing Office, 1922.

Melvin, Bruce L., and Elna N. Smith. *Rural Youth: Their Situation and Prospects.*
    Washington: Government Printing Office, 1938.
Snyder, Thomas D., ed. *120 Years of American Education: A Statistical Portrait.*
    Washington: National Center for Educational Statistics, U.S. Department of
    Education, Office of Educational Research and Improvement, 1993.
Taeuber, Irene B., and Conrad Taeuber. *People of the United States in the 20th Century.*
    Washington: Government Printing Office, 1971.
United Nations Population Fund. *Marrying Too Young: End Child Marriage.* New York:
    United Nations Population Fund, 2012.
U.S. Bureau of the Census. *Eighteenth Census of the United States: Population.* 3 vols.
    Washington: Government Printing Office, 1961.
———. *Fifteenth Census of the United States: Population.* 6 vols. Washington: Government
    Printing Office, 1932.
———. *Fourteenth Census of the United States: Population.* 4 vols. Washington:
    Government Printing Office, 1922.
———. *Historical Statistics of the United States: Colonial Times to 1970,* pt. 1. Washington:
    Government Printing Office, 1975.
———. "Households and Families, 2010." *U.S. Census Briefs,* April 2012.
———. *Nineteenth Census of the United States: Population.* 2 vols. Washington:
    Government Printing Office, 1973.
———. *Seventeenth Census of the United States: Population.* 4 vols. Washington:
    Government Printing Office, 1952.
———. "Sex by Marital Status by Age for the Population 15 Years and Over." Census 2000
    Summary File 3, accessed online at American Fact Finder (census.gov).
———. "Sex by Marital Status for the Population 15 Years and Over." 2006–2010
    American Community Survey Selected Population Tables, accessed online at
    American Fact Finder (census.gov).
———. *Sixteenth Census of the United States: Population.* 4 vols. Washington:
    Government Printing Office, 1943.
———. *Special Reports: Marriage and Divorce, 1867–1906.* Washington: Government
    Printing Office, 1909.
———. "Table MS-2. Estimated Median Age at First Marriage, by Sex: 1890 to Present."
    Internet release date September 15, 2004, https://www.census.gov/population/
    socdemo/hh-fam/tabMS-2.pdf.
———. *Twelfth Census of the United States: Population.* 2 vols. Washington: Government
    Printing Office, 1902.
———. *Twentieth Census of the United States: Population,* Detailed Population
    Characteristics, United States Summary, Section A: United States. Washington:
    Government Printing Office, 1984.
———. *Twenty-First Census of the United States: Population,* General Population
    Characteristics, 1990 CP-1-1. Washington: Government Printing Office, 1992.

U.S. Department of Health, Education, and Welfare. *Teenagers: Marriages, Divorces, Parenthood, and Mortality*. Rockford, Md.: National Center for Health Statistics, 1973.

U.S. Department of Labor. Office of Policy Planning and Research. *The Negro Family: The Case for National Action*. Washington: Office of Policy Planning and Research, 1965.

Wright, Carroll Davidson. *A Report on Marriage and Divorce in the United States, 1867–1886: Including an Appendix Relating to Marriage and Divorce in Certain Countries in Europe*. Washington: Government Printing Office, 1889.

PUBLISHED PRIMARY SOURCES

Ackley, Mary E. *Crossing the Plains and Early Days in California: Memories of Girlhood Days in California's Golden Age*. San Francisco, 1928. Reprinted in *Let Them Speak for Themselves: Women in the American West, 1849–1900*, edited by Christiane Fischer, 229–35. Hamden, Conn.: Archon, 1977.

Alcott, William. *The Moral Philosophy of Courtship and Marriage*. Boston: John P. Jewett, 1857.

———. *The Physiology of Marriage*. 1866. Reprint, New York: Arno, 1972.

Ali, Nujood, with Delphine Minoui. *I Am Nujood, Age 10 and Divorced*. Translated by Linda Coverdale. New York: Broadway Books, 2010.

Anderson, Wayne J., and Sander M. Letts. "High School Marriages and School Policies in Minnesota." *Journal of Marriage and the Family* 27, no. 2 (May 1965): 266–70.

Avery, Curtis E. "Toward Understanding the Problems of Early Marriage." *Family Life Coordinator* 9 (April 1961): 27–34.

Bandini, José. *A Description of California in 1828*. Translated by Doris Marion Wright. Berkeley, Calif.: Friends of the Bancroft Library, 1951.

Bartz, Karen Winch, and F. Ivan Nye. "Early Marriage: A Propositional Formulation." *Journal of Marriage and the Family* 32, no. 2 (May 1970): 258–68.

Bayer, Alan E. "Early Dating and Early Marriage." *Journal of Marriage and the Family* 30, no. 4 (1968): 628–32.

Bennett, Edmund. "Uniformity in Marriage and Divorce Laws." *American Law Register and Review* 44, no. 4 (April 1896): 221–31.

Blackstone, William. *Commentaries on the Laws of England*. 4 vols. Oxford: Clarendon, 1765–69.

Blackwell, Elizabeth. *The Laws of Life, with Special Reference to the Physical Education of Girls*. 1852. Reprint, London: Sampson Low, Son, 1859.

Blackwell, Emily, M.D. "Another Physician Speaks." *Arena* 11 (1895): 212–15.

Born in Slavery: Slave Narratives from the Federal Writers' Project, 1936–1938. Texas Narratives, vol. 16, pt. 4. Washington: Library of Congress, 1941.

Boscana, Friar Geronimo. *Chinigchinich: A Historical Account of the Origin, Customs, and Traditions of the Indians at the Missionary Establishment of St. Juan Capistrano, Alta-California*. Translated by Alfred Robinson. Oakland, Calif.: BioBooks, 1947.

Bulwer-Lytton, Edward. *The Last of the Barons.* 3 vols. London: Saunders and Otley, 1843.

Burchinal, Lee G. "Adolescent Role Deprivation and High School Age Marriage." *Marriage and Family Living* 21, no. 4 (November 1959): 378–84.

———. "Research on Young Marriage: Implications for Family Life Education." *Family Life Coordinator* 9 (September–December 1960): 6–24.

———. "School Policies and School Age Marriages." *Family Life Coordinator* 8, no. 3 (March 1960): 43–48.

———. "Trends and Prospects for Young Marriages in the United States." *Journal of Marriage and the Family* 27, no. 2 (May 1965): 243–354.

Campbell, Vie H. "Why an Age of Consent?" *Arena* 12 (1895): 285–88.

Carlson, Elwood. "Family Background, School and Early Marriage." *Journal of Marriage and the Family* 41, no. 2 (May 1979): 341–53.

Caswall, Edward. *The Young Ladies and Gentlemen's Hymeneal Instructor: Or, the Philosophy of Love, Courtship and Marriage.* New York: John Nicholson, 1847.

Cavan, Ruth Shonle, and Grace Beling. "A Study of High School Marriages." *Marriage and Family Living* 20, no. 3 (August 1958): 293–95.

Chávez, Jennie V. "Women of the Mexican American Movement." In *Chicana Feminist Thought: The Basic Historical Writings*, edited by Alma M. García, 36–39. New York: Routledge, 1997.

Child Bride. Directed by Harry Revier. 1938. Narberth, Pa.: Alpha Video, 2004. DVD.

"Child Marriages in Kentucky." *Journal of Social Hygiene* 12, no. 6 (1926): 369–70.

Children's Aid Society for the Prevention of Cruelty to Children of Erie County, N.Y. *Child Marriages in Erie County: A Study by the Juvenile Protective Department of the Children's Aid Society, Buffalo, N.Y.* Buffalo, N.Y.: Children's Aid Society, 1927.

Colcord, Joanna C. "Marriage Legislation, 1923—Successful and Unsuccessful." *Family* 5, no. 1 (March 1924): 14–17.

———. "To Put 'Marriage-Market' Towns Out of Business." *Literary Digest*, March 12, 1929.

———. "What Has Social Work to Do with the Founding of New Families?" *Official Proceedings of the Annual Meeting of the National Conference on Social Welfare* (1926): 251–59.

Cole, Charles W. "American Youth Goes Monogamous." *Harper's Magazine*, March 1957, 29–33.

Coles, Robert. *Migrants, Sharecroppers, Mountaineers.* Boston: Little, Brown, 1967.

Davenport, Charles B. *State Laws Limiting Marriage Selection Examined in the Light of Eugenics.* Bulletin no. 9. Cold Spring Harbor, N.Y.: Eugenics Records Office, 1913.

David, Lester. "Are You Pushing Your Daughter into Too-Early MARRIAGE?" *Good Housekeeping*, October 1961, 80–81, 216–21.

Davis, Noah. "Marriage and Divorce." *North American Review* 139 (July 1884): 30–41.

Day, Lucille Lang. *Married at Fourteen: A True Story.* Berkeley, Calif.: Heyday, 2012.

De Lissovoy, Vladimir. "High School Marriages: A Longitudinal Study." *Journal of Marriage and the Family* 35, no. 2 (May 1973): 245–55.

De Lissovoy, Vladimir, and Mary Ellen Hitchcock. "High School Marriages in Pennsylvania." *Journal of Marriage and the Family* 27, no. 2 (May 1965): 263–65.

Devereux, Margaret. *Plantation Sketches*. Cambridge, Mass.: Riverside, 1906.

Dike, Samuel. "The Condition and Needs of Statistics of Marriage and Divorce." *Publications of the American Statistical Association* 3, no. 24 (December 1893): 513–18.

————. "Statistics of Marriage and Divorce." *Political Science Quarterly* 4, no. 4 (December 1889): 592–614.

Dunbar, Seymour, ed. *The Journals and Letters of Major John Owen, Pioneer of the Northwest, 1850–1871*. Vol. 1. New York: Edward Eberstadt, 1927.

Dunham, Arthur. "Child Marriages in Pennsylvania." *Family* 7, no. 9 (January 1927): 280–83.

Duvall, Evelyn Millis. "Marriage in War Time." *Marriage and Family Living* 4, no. 4 (November 1942): 73–76.

————. "Research Finds: Student Marriages." *Marriage and Family Living* 22 (February 1960): 76–77.

Edmonston, Catherine Ann Devereux. *"Journal of a Secesh Lady": The Diary of Catherine Ann Devereux Edmonston, 1860–1866*. Edited by Beth G. Crabtree and James W. Patton. Raleigh, N.C.: Division of Archives and History, Department of Cultural Resources, 1979.

Edson, Cyrus. "The Evils of Early Marriages." *North American Review* 158 (February 1894): 230–34.

Elkin, Meyer. "Premarital Counseling for Minors: The Los Angeles Experience." *Family Coordinator* 26, no. 4 (October 1977): 429–43.

Ellis, Havelock. *Sex in Relation to Society*. Vol. 6 of *Studies in the Psychology of Sex*. Philadelphia: F. A. Davis, 1920.

"Exempt Bride." *Time*, August 23, 1937, 31.

"Ex Parte Hollopeter." *Pacific Reporter* (March 19–May 9, 1909): 159–62.

Finstad, Suzanne. *Child Bride: The Untold Story of Priscilla Beaulieu Presley*. New York: Harmony, 1997.

Foote, Edward B., M.D. *Medical Common Sense; Applied to Causes, Prevention and Cure of Chronic Diseases and Unhappiness in Marriage*. New York, 1863.

Fowler, L. N. *Marriage: Its History and Ceremonies; With a Phrenological and Physiological Exposition of the Functions and Qualifications for Happy Marriages*. 19th ed. New York: Fowler and Wells, 1848.

Fowler, O. S. *Fowler on Matrimony: Or, Phrenology and Physiology Applied to the Congenial Companions for Life*. New York: O. S. and L. N. Fowler, 1842.

Friedan, Betty. *The Feminine Mystique*. New York: W. W. Norton, 1963.

Gardener, Helen H. "What Shall the Age of Consent Be?" *Arena* 11 (1895): 196–98.

Hagood, Margaret Jarman. *Mothers of the South: Portraiture of the White Tenant Farm Woman*. 1939. Reprint, New York: W. W. Norton, 1977.

Hall, Fred S., and Elisabeth W. Brooke. *American Marriage Laws in Their Social Aspects: A Digest*. New York: Russell Sage Foundation, 1919.

Hall, G. Stanley. *Adolescence: Its Psychology and Its Relations to Physiology, Anthropology, Sociology, Sex, Crime, Religion, and Education.* 2 vols. New York: D. Appleton, 1904.

Hazen, Harry, Jr. *Courtship Made Easy: Or the Mysteries of Making Love Fully Explained.* New York: Dick and Fitzgerald, 1858.

Heizer, Robert F., ed. *The Indians of Los Angeles County: Hugo Reid's Letters of 1852.* Highland Park, Calif.: Southwest Museum, 1968.

Hendricks, Rick, ed., and John B. Colligan, comp. *New Mexico Prenuptial Investigations from the Archivos Históricos del Arzobispado de Durango, 1800–1893.* Las Cruces: New Mexico State University Library, Rio Grande Historical Collections, 2000.

Herblock. "In a State Where You Can't Teach Evolution." Newspaper Enterprise Association Service, February 3, 1937. http://www.loc.gov/pictures/item/2009632462/.

Holly, Carrie Clyde. "'Age of Consent,' in Colorado." *Arena* 14 (September 1895): 3–16.

Hurston, Zora Neale. *Their Eyes Were Watching God.* 1937. Reprint, New York: Perennial, 1990.

"Informal Discussion." *Official Proceedings of the Annual Meeting of the National Conference on Social Welfare* (1918): 128–32.

Inselberg, Rachel M. "Marital Problems and Satisfaction in High School Marriages." *Marriage and Family Living* 24, no. 1 (February 1962): 74–77.

"Is Divorce Wrong?" *North American Review* 149 (November 1889): 513–38.

Ivins, Wilson. "Student Marriages in New Mexico Secondary Schools: Practices and Policies." *Marriage and Family Living* 22, no. 1 (February 1960): 71–74.

Jacques, D. R. Preface to *A Compendium and Comparative View of the Thirty-Eight State Laws of Marriage and Divorce in the United States (in 1882),* by Charles Noble, v–vii. New York: Baker, Voorhis, 1882.

Johnson, Charles S. *Growing Up in the Black Belt: Negro Youth in the Rural South.* New York: Schocken, 1941.

Keezer, Frank. *The Law of Marriage and Divorce.* Boston: William J. Nagel, 1906.

Kent, James. *Commentaries on American Law.* Vol. 2. 13th ed. Edited by Charles M. Barnes. Boston: Little, Brown, 1884.

———. *Commentaries on American Law.* Vol. 2. Rev. ed. Edited by William M. Lacy. Philadelphia: Blackstone, 1889.

King, Caitlin R., and Bruce Schreiner. "Loretta Lynn: Turns Out She Married at 15, Not 13." *Associated Press,* May 20, 2012.

Kingston, Albert, and Harold Gentry. "Married High School Students and Problem Behavior." *Journal of Educational Sociology* 35, no. 6 (February 1962): 284–88.

Landis, Judson T. "High School Student Marriages, School Policy, and Family Life Education in California." *Journal of Marriage and the Family* 27, no. 2 (May 1965): 271–76.

Landis, Judson T., and Kenneth C. Kidd. "Attitudes and Policies concerning Marriages among High School Students." *Marriage and Family Living* 18, no. 2 (May 1956): 128–36.

Lewis, A. H., D.D. "The Primary Source of Age-of-Consent Legislation." *Arena* 11 (1895): 202–6.

Lewis, Dio. *Chastity; Or, Our Secret Sins.* 1874. Reprint, New York: Arno, 1974.

"Life on the American Newsfront: The Case of the Child Bride." *Life*, February 15, 1937, 15.

Lynn, Loretta, with Patsi Bale Cox. *Still Woman Enough.* New York: Hyperion, 2002.

Lynn, Loretta, with George Vecsey. *Loretta Lynn: Coalminer's Daughter.* Chicago: Henry Regnery, 1976.

M.T.H. "Michigan." *Arena* 14 (1895): 213–18.

"Marriage Bills." *Journal of Social Hygiene* 12, no. 4 (April 1926): 239.

"Married." *Time*, May 31, 1937, 56.

May, Geoffrey L. *Marriage Laws and Decisions in the United States: A Digest.* New York: Russell Sage Foundation, 1929.

Mayo, Katherine. *Mother India.* New York: Harcourt Brace, 1927.

"Miscellany." *Time*, February 8, 1937, 42.

Monterey in 1786, Life in a California Mission: The Journals of Jean François de la Pérouse. Edited by Malcolm Margolin. Berkeley, Calif.: Heyday Books, 1989.

Moss, J. Joel. "Teenage Marriage: Crossnational Trends and Sociological Factors in the Decision of When to Marry," *Acta Sociologica* 8, nos. 1–2 (1964): 98–117.

Moss, J. Joel, and Ruby Gingles. "The Relationship of Personality to the Incidence of Early Marriage." *Marriage and Family Living* 21, no. 4 (November 1959): 373–77.

———. "Teen-Age Marriage—The Teacher's Challenge!" *Marriage and Family Living* 23, no. 2 (May 1961): 187–90.

Mowatt, Anna Cora. *Autobiography of an Actress; Or, Eight Years on the Stage.* Boston: Ticknor and Fields, 1854.

Mudd, Emily H., and Richard N. Hey. "When the Young Marry Too Young." *National Parent-Teacher*, September 1960.

Mudgett, Mildred. "When People Apply at a Marriage License Bureau." *Official Proceedings of the Annual Meeting of the National Conference of Social Welfare* (1925): 284–90.

"New York's Child Marriage Law." *Journal of Social Hygiene* 15, no. 7 (October 1929): 427–28.

"New York State Legislature Raises Marriage Age from 12 to 14 Years!" *Survey*, April 15, 1927, 99.

Ogburn, William Fielding. "Eleven Questions concerning American Marriage." In *The Family: Source Materials for the Study of Family and Personality*, edited by Edward Byron Reuter and Jessie Ridgway Runner, 183–91. New York: McGraw-Hill, 1931.

———. "Factors Affecting Marital Status." In *The Family: Source Materials for the Study of Family and Personality*, edited by Edward Byron Reuter and Jessie Ridgway Runner, 191–200. New York: McGraw-Hill, 1931.

Paget, Norman W. *Facts about Teenage Marriages in San Bernardino County.* San Bernardino, Calif.: Family Service Agency, 1959.

Palmer, Hazel. "Child Marriage." *Women Lawyers' Journal* 25 (1938–39): 49–51.

Panunzio, Constantine. "War and Marriage." *Social Forces* 21, no. 4 (May 1943): 442–45.

Parton, Margaret. "Why Do They Marry So Young?" *Ladies' Home Journal*, November 1958, 163–65, 172–76.

Popenoe, Paul. *Modern Marriage*. New York: Grosset and Dunlap, 1925.

———. *Modern Marriage: A Handbook for Men*. 2nd ed. New York: Macmillan, 1943.

"Private Lives." *Life*, August 23, 1937, 65.

Proceedings of the 1850 Woman's Rights Convention Held at Worcester, October 23rd and 24th, 1850. Boston: Prentiss and Sawyer, 1851.

Proceedings of the National Woman's Rights Convention, Held at Cleveland, Ohio on Wednesday, Thursday, and Friday, October 5th, 6th, and 7th, 1853. Cleveland: Gray, Beardsley, Spear, 1854.

Proceedings of the Ohio Women's Convention, Held at Salem, April 19th and 20th, 1850. Cleveland: Smead and Cowles, 1850.

Reeve, Tapping. *The Law of Baron and Femme*. 3rd ed. 1862. Reprint, Union, N.J.: Lawbook Exchange, 1998.

Reid, Captain Mayne. *The Child Wife*. 1868. Reprint, New York: E. P. Dutton, 1905.

———. "A Dead Man Defended, Being Some Reminiscences of the Poet Poe." In *Captain Mayne Reid: His Life and Adventures*, by Elizabeth Reid, assisted by Charles H. Coe, 22–28. London: Greening, 1900.

Reid, Elizabeth, assisted by Charles H. Coe. *Captain Mayne Reid: His Life and Adventures*. London: Greening, 1900.

Reid, Ira De Augustine. *In a Minor Key: Negro Youth in Story and in Fact*. Westport, Conn.: Greenwood, 1940.

Report of the National Divorce Reform League for the Year Ending December 31, 1896. Boston: Everett, 1897.

Reuter, Edward Byron, and Jessie Ridgway Runner, eds. *The Family: Source Materials for the Study of Family and Personality*. New York: McGraw-Hill, 1931.

Richmond, Mary, and Fred S. Hall. *Child Marriages*. New York: Russell Sage Foundation, 1925.

———. *Marriage and the State: Based upon Field Studies of the Present Day Administration of Marriage Laws in the United States*. New York: Russell Sage Foundation, 1929.

Robinson, William C. "The Diagnostics of Divorce." *Journal of Social Science* 1, no. 14 (1881): 136–51.

Rowson, Susanna. *Charlotte Temple*. Edited by Marion L. Rust. 1791. Reprint, New York: W. W. Norton, 2011.

Schouler, James. *A Treatise on the Law of Husband and Wife*. Boston: Little, Brown, 1882.

"The Shame of America—The Age of Consent Laws in the United States: A Symposium." *Arena* 11 (1895): 192–215.

Smith, Elizabeth Oakes. *The Sanctity of Marriage*. Woman's Rights Tracts, no. 5. In *Woman's Rights Commensurate with Her Capacities and Obligations: A Series of Tracts*,

Comprising Sixteen Articles: Essays, Addresses, or Letters of the Prominent Advocates of Woman's Larger Sphere of Action, 1–8. Syracuse, N.Y.: Lathrop's, 1853.

———. *Woman and Her Needs.* New York: Fowlers and Wells, 1851.

Smith, Jeremiah. *Cases on Selected Topics in the Law of Persons.* Cambridge, Mass.: Riverside, 1898.

Spencer, Anna Garlin. "The Age of Consent—Its Significance." *Forum* 44 (1913): 406–20.

Spicer, Betty Coe. "Teenage Secret Marriage Epidemic." *Ladies' Home Journal,* March 1960, 74–75, 155–57.

Stanton, Elizabeth Cady, Susan B. Anthony, and Matilda Joslyn Gage, eds. *History of Woman Suffrage.* Vol. 1. Rochester, N.Y.: Charles Mann, 1889.

"State ex. Rel. Scott v. Lowell et al." *Northwestern Reporter* 80 (October 7–December 30, 1899): 877–78.

Sundal, A. Philip, and Thomas C. McCormick. "Age at Marriage and Mate Selection: Madison, Wisconsin, 1937–1943." *American Sociological Review* 16, no. 1 (February 1951): 37–48.

Swinburne, Henry. *A Treatise of Spousals or Matrimonial Contracts: Wherein all the Questions Relating to That Subject Are ingeniously Debated and Resolved.* London: S. Roycroft, 1686.

Taylor, Susie King. *Reminiscences of My Life in Camp, with the 33d United States Colored Troops Late 1st S. C. Volunteers.* Edited by Patricia W. Romero. 1902. Reprint, New York: Markus Wiener, 1988.

Terkel, Amanda. "House Republicans Block Child Marriage Act." *Huffington Post,* December 17, 2010, http://www.huffingtonpost.com/2010/12/17/house-republicans-block-child-marriage-prevention-act_n_798382.html.

Towne, Arthur. "A Community Program for Protective Work with Girls." *Journal of Social Hygiene* 6, no. 1 (1920): 57–71.

———. "Young Girl Marriages in Criminal and Juvenile Courts." *Journal of Social Hygiene* 8, no. 3 (July 1922): 287–305.

Tyler, Ransom H. *Commentaries on the Law of Infancy.* Albany, N.Y.: William Gould and Son, 1882.

"What God Hath Joined." *Time,* February 15, 1937, 41–42.

"Why Won't America Ratify the UN Convention on Children's Rights?" *Economist,* October 6, 2013.

Women's Protective Association of Cleveland. *School-Girl Brides.* Cleveland, Ohio: Women's Protective Association, 1926.

Woodhull, Victoria. "'And the Truth Shall Make You Free': A Speech on the Principles of Social Freedom Delivered in Steinway Hall, Monday, November 20, 1871." New York: Woodhull and Claflin, 1871.

Woodson, Rebecca Hildreth Nutting. *A Sketch of the Life of Rebecca Hildreth Nutting Woodson.* Typescript in *American Women's Diaries (Western Women)* (Readex Film Products), microfilm reel 14.

SECONDARY SOURCES

Books

Agnew, Elizabeth N. *From Charity to Social Work: Mary E. Richmond and the Creation of an American Profession.* Urbana: University of Illinois Press, 2004.

Alan Guttmacher Institute. *Sex and America's Teenagers.* New York: Alan Guttmacher Institute, 1994.

Alexander, Ruth. *The "Girl Problem": Female Sexual Delinquency in New York, 1900–1930.* Ithaca, N.Y.: Cornell University Press, 1998.

Ariès, Philippe. *Centuries of Childhood: A Social History of Family Life.* Translated by Robert Baldick. New York: Vintage, 1965.

Bailey, Beth. *From Front Porch to Back Seat: Courtship in Twentieth-Century America.* Baltimore: Johns Hopkins University Press, 1989.

Banks, Ralph Richard. *Is Marriage for White People? How the African American Marriage Decline Affects Everyone.* New York: Dutton, 2011.

Basch, Norma. *Framing American Divorce: From the Revolutionary Generation to the Victorians.* Berkeley: University of California Press, 2001.

———. *In the Eyes of the Law: Women, Marriage, and Property in Nineteenth-Century New York.* Ithaca, N.Y.: Cornell University Press, 1982.

Baxter, Kent. *The Modern Age: Turn-of-the-Century Culture and the Invention of Adolescence.* Tuscaloosa: University of Alabama Press, 2008.

Bederman, Gail. *Manliness and Civilization: A Cultural History of Race and Gender in the United States, 1880 to 1917.* Chicago: University of Chicago Press, 1995.

Bernstein, Robin. *Racial Innocence: Performing American Childhood from Slavery to Civil Rights.* New York: New York University Press, 2011.

Bleser, Carol, ed. *The Hammonds of Redcliffe.* New York: Oxford University Press, 1981.

Botham, Fay. *Almighty God Created the Races: Christianity, Interracial Marriage, and American Law.* Chapel Hill: University of North Carolina Press, 2009.

Boydston, Jeanne. *Home and Work: Housework, Wages, and the Ideology of Labor in the Early Republic.* New York: Oxford University Press, 1994.

Bramham, Daphne. *The Secret Lives of Saints: Child Brides and Lost Boys in Canada's Polygamous Mormon Sect.* Toronto: Random House Canada, 2008.

Brewer, Holly. *By Birth or Consent: Children, the Law, and the Anglo-American Revolution in Authority.* Chapel Hill: University of North Carolina Press for the Omohundro Institute of Early American Culture and History, 2007.

Brumberg, Joan Jacobs. *The Body Project: An Intimate History of American Girls.* New York: Random House, 1997.

Bullard, Katharine S. *Civilizing the Child: Discourses of Race, Nation, and Child Welfare in America.* Lanham, Md.: Lexington Books, 2014.

Cahn, Susan K. *Sexual Reckonings: Southern Girls in a Troubling Age.* Cambridge, Mass.: Harvard University Press, 2007.

California Pioneer Register and Index, 1542–1848. Baltimore: Regional, 1964.

Campbell, John C. *The Southern Highlander and His Homeland*. New York: Russell Sage, 1921.

Carter, Christine Jacobson. *Southern Single Blessedness: Unmarried Women in the Urban South, 1800–1860*. Urbana: University of Illinois Press, 2009.

Celello, Kristin. *Making Marriage Work: A History of Marriage and Divorce in the Twentieth-Century United States*. Chapel Hill: University of North Carolina Press, 2009.

Censer, Jane Turner. *North Carolina Planters and Their Children, 1800–1860*. Baton Rouge: Louisiana State University Press, 1984.

Chambers-Schiller, Lee Virginia. *Liberty, a Better Husband: Single Women in America: The Generations of 1780–1840*. New Haven, Conn.: Yale University Press, 1984.

Chatelain, Marcia. *South Side Girls: Growing Up in the Great Migration*. Durham, N.C.: Duke University Press, 2015.

Chávez-García, Miroslava. *Negotiating Conquest: Gender and Power in California, 1770s to 1880s*. Tucson: University of Arizona Press, 2004.

Chinn, Sarah E. *Inventing Modern Adolescence: The Children of Immigrants in Turn-of-the-Century America*. New Brunswick, N.J.: Rutgers University Press, 2008.

Chudacoff, Howard. *How Old Are You? Age Consciousness in American Culture*. Princeton, N.J.: Princeton University Press, 1989.

Clarke, Desmond. *Arthur Dobbs, Esquire, 1689–1765: Surveyor-General of Ireland and Governor of North Carolina*. Chapel Hill: University of North Carolina Press, 1957.

Cleland, Robert Glass. *The Cattle on a Thousand Hills: Southern California, 1850–1880*. San Marino, Calif.: Huntington Library, 1951.

Clement, Elizabeth Alice. *Love for Sale: Courting, Treating, and Prostitution in New York City, 1900–1945*. Chapel Hill: University of North Carolina Press, 2006.

Cocca, Carolyn E. *Jailbait: The Politics of Statutory Rape Laws in the United States*. Albany: State University of New York Press, 2004.

Cohen, Patricia Cline. *The Murder of Helen Jewett: The Life and Death of a Prostitute in Nineteenth-Century New York*. New York: Alfred A. Knopf, 1998.

Colby, Susan M. *Sacagawea's Child: The Life and Times of Jean-Baptiste (Pomp) Charbonneau*. Spokane, Wash.: Arthur H. Clark, 2005.

Compton, Todd. *In Sacred Loneliness: The Plural Wives of Joseph Smith*. Salt Lake City, Utah: Signature Books, 1997.

Cook, S. F. *The Conflict between the California Indian and White Civilization, III: The American Invasion, 1848–1870*. Berkeley: University of California Press, 1943.

Coontz, Stephanie. *Marriage, a History: From Obedience to Intimacy, or How Love Conquered Marriage*. New York: Viking, 2005.

Cott, Nancy F. *The Bonds of Womanhood: "Woman's Sphere" in New England, 1780–1835*. New Haven, Conn.: Yale University Press, 1977.

———. *The Grounding of Modern Feminism*. New Haven, Conn.: Yale University Press, 1989.

———. *Public Vows: A History of Marriage and the Nation*. Cambridge, Mass.: Harvard University Press, 2000.

Davis, Rebecca L. *More Perfect Unions: The American Search for Marital Bliss.* Cambridge, Mass.: Harvard University Press, 2010.

DeCredico, Mary A. *Mary Boykin Chesnut: A Confederate Woman's Life.* Madison, Wis.: Madison House, 1996.

DeLuzio, Crista. *Female Adolescence in American Scientific Thought, 1830–1930.* Baltimore: Johns Hopkins University Press, 2007.

D'Emilio, John, and Estelle B. Freedman. *Intimate Matters: A History of Sexuality in America.* New York: Harper and Row, 1988.

Deutsch, Sarah. *No Separate Refuge: Culture, Class, and Gender on the Anglo-Hispanic Frontier in the American Southwest, 1880–1940.* New York: Oxford University Press, 1987.

Eby, Clare Virginia. *Until Choice Do Us Part: Marriage Reform in the Progressive Era.* Chicago: University of Chicago Press, 2014.

Ehrmann, Winston. *Premarital Dating Behavior.* New York: Henry Holt, 1959.

Fass, Paula S. *The Damned and the Beautiful: American Youth in the 1920's.* New York: Oxford University Press, 1979.

Fass, Paula S., and Michael Grossberg, eds. *Reinventing Childhood after World War II.* Philadelphia: University of Pennsylvania Press, 2012.

Faust, Drew Gilpin. *James Henry Hammond and the Old South: A Design for Mastery.* Baton Rouge: Louisiana State University Press, 1982.

Feimster, Crystal N. *Southern Horrors: Women and the Politics of Rape and Lynching.* Cambridge, Mass.: Harvard University Press, 2009.

Field, Corinne T. *The Struggle for Equal Adulthood: Gender, Race, Age, and the Fight for Citizenship in Antebellum America.* Chapel Hill: University of North Carolina Press, 2014.

Field, Corinne T., and Nicholas L. Syrett, eds. *Age in America: The Colonial Era to the Present.* New York: New York University Press, 2015.

Fineman, Martha Albertson. *The Neutered Mother, the Sexual Family, and Other Twentieth-Century Tragedies.* New York: Routledge, 1995.

Fischer, Kirsten. *Suspect Relations: Sex, Race, and Resistance in Colonial North Carolina.* Ithaca, N.Y.: Cornell University Press, 2001.

Foster, Frances Smith. *'Til Death or Distance Do Us Part: Love and Marriage in African America.* New York: Oxford University Press, 2010.

Foucault, Michel. *The History of Sexuality.* Vol. 1: *An Introduction.* Translated by Robert Hurley. New York: Vintage, 1978.

Fowler, Loretta. *Wives and Husbands: Gender and Age in Southern Arapaho History.* Norman: University of Oklahoma Press, 2010.

Fraser, Rebecca J. *Courtship and Love amongst the Enslaved in North Carolina.* Jackson: University Press of Mississippi, 2007.

Freedman, Estelle B. *Redefining Rape: Sexual Violence in the Era of Suffrage and Segregation.* Cambridge, Mass.: Harvard University Press, 2013.

Friedman, Lawrence. *Private Lives: Families, Individuals, and the Law.* Cambridge, Mass.: Harvard University Press, 2004.

Furstenberg, Frank. *Destinies of the Disadvantaged: The Politics of Teenage Childbearing.* New York: Russell Sage, 2007.

Gabriel, Mary. *Notorious Victoria: The Life of Victoria Woodhull Uncensored.* Chapel Hill, N.C.: Algonquin Books, 1998.

Geller, Jaclyn. *Here Comes the Bride: Women, Weddings, and the Marriage Mystique.* New York: Seal, 2001.

Gilfoyle, Timothy J. *City of Eros: New York City, Prostitution, and the Commercialization of Sex, 1790–1920.* New York: W. W. Norton, 1994.

Gilmore, Glenda Elizabeth. *Gender and Jim Crow: Women and the Politics of White Supremacy in North Carolina, 1896–1920.* Chapel Hill: University of North Carolina Press, 1996.

Goldsmith, Barbara. *Other Powers: The Age of Suffrage, Spiritualism, and the Scandalous Victoria Woodhull.* New York: Alfred A. Knopf, 1998.

Gordon, Linda. *Heroes of Their Own Lives: The Politics and History of Family Violence, Boston, 1880–1960.* 1988. Reprint, Urbana: University of Illinois Press, 2002.

Greenburg, Michael. *Peaches and Daddy: A Story of the Roaring 20s, the Birth of Tabloid Media, and the Courtship That Captured the Hearts and Imaginations of the American Public.* Woodstock, N.Y.: Overlook, 2008.

Grossberg, Michael. *Governing the Hearth: Law and Family in Nineteenth-Century America.* Chapel Hill: University of North Carolina Press, 1985.

Grossman, Joanna L., and Lawrence M. Friedman. *Inside the Castle: Law and the Family in 20th Century America.* Princeton, N.J.: Princeton University Press, 2011.

Gutiérrez, Ramón A. *When Jesus Came, the Corn Mothers Went Away: Marriage, Sexuality, and Power in New Mexico, 1500–1846.* Stanford, Calif.: Stanford University Press, 1991.

Haag, Pamela. *Consent: Sexual Rights and the Transformation of American Liberalism.* Ithaca, N.Y.: Cornell University Press, 1999.

Hackel, Steven W. *Children of Coyote, Missionaries of Saint Francis: Indian-Spanish Relations in Colonial California, 1769–1850.* Chapel Hill: University of North Carolina Press, 2005.

Hartog, Hendrik. *Man and Wife in America: A History.* Cambridge, Mass.: Harvard University Press, 2000.

Headley, Robert K., ed. *Genealogical Abstracts from 18th-Century Virginia Newspapers.* Baltimore: Genealogical Publishing, 1987.

Hebard, Grace Raymond. *Sacajawea: Guide and Interpreter of Lewis and Clark.* 1932. Reprint, New York: Dover, 2002.

Herr, Pamela. *Jessie Benton Fremont: A Biography.* New York: Franklin Watts, 1987.

Hine, Thomas. *The Rise and Fall of the American Teenager.* New York: William Morrow, 1999.

Horowitz, Helen Lefkowitz. *Rereading Sex: Battles over Sexual Knowledge and Suppression in Nineteenth-Century America.* New York: Vintage, 2002.

Hurtado, Albert L. *Intimate Frontiers: Sex, Gender, and Culture in Old California.* Albuquerque: University of New Mexico Press, 1999.

Hutchisson, James M. *Poe*. Jackson: University Press of Mississippi, 2005.

Israel, Betsy. *Bachelor Girl: 100 Years of Breaking the Rules—A Social History of Living Single*. New York: William Morrow, 2003.

Jabour, Anya. *Scarlett's Sisters: Young Women in the Old South*. Chapel Hill: University of North Carolina Press, 2007.

Johnson, Guion Griffis. *Ante-Bellum North Carolina: A Social History*. Chapel Hill: University of North Carolina Press, 1937.

Johnston, Joanna. *Mrs. Satan: The Incredible Saga of Victoria C. Woodhull*. New York: G. P. Putnam's Sons, 1967.

Kessler-Harris, Alice. *Out to Work: A History of Wage-Earning Women in the United States*. New York: Oxford University Press, 1982.

Kett, Joseph. *Rites of Passage: Adolescence in America, 1790 to the Present*. New York: Basic, 1977.

King, Wilma. *Stolen Childhood: Slave Youth in Nineteenth-Century America*. 2nd ed. Bloomington: Indiana University Press, 2011.

Kline, Wendy. *Building a Better Race: Gender, Sexuality, and Eugenics from the Turn of the Century to the Baby Boom*. Berkeley: University of California Press, 2001.

Krakauer, Jon. *Under the Banner of Heaven: A Story of Violent Faith*. New York: Doubleday, 2003.

Lassonde, Stephen. *Learning to Forget: Schooling and Family Life in New Haven's Working Class, 1870–1940*. New Haven, Conn.: Yale University Press, 2005.

Leach, William. *True Love and Perfect Union: The Feminist Reform of Sex and Society*. New York: Basic, 1980.

Leloudis, James L. *Schooling the New South: Pedagogy, Self, and Society in North Carolina, 1880–1920*. Chapel Hill: University of North Carolina Press, 1996.

Lesko, Nancy. *Act Your Age! A Cultural Construction of Adolescence*. 2nd ed. New York: Routledge, 2012.

Louvish, Simon. *Chaplin: The Tramp's Odyssey*. New York: Thomas Dunne, 2009.

Lucchetti, Cathy. *"I Do!": Courtship, Love, and Marriage on the American Frontier*. New York: Crown, 1996.

Lynd, Robert S., and Helen Merrell Lynd. *Middletown in Transition: A Study in Cultural Conflicts*. New York: Harcourt Brace, 1937.

Lystra, Karen. *Searching the Heart: Women, Men, and Romantic Love in Nineteenth-Century America*. New York: Oxford University Press, 1989.

Mason, Mary Ann. *From Father's Property to Children's Rights: The History of Child Custody in the United States*. New York: Columbia University Press, 1994.

May, Elaine Tyler. *Great Expectations: Marriage and Divorce in Post-Victorian America*. Chicago: University of Chicago Press, 1980.

———. *Homeward Bound: American Families in the Cold War Era*. New York: Basic, 1988.

Meyers, Jeffrey. *Edgar Allan Poe: His Life and Legacy*. New York: Cooper Square, 2000.

Milanich, Nara B. *Children of Fate: Childhood, Class, and the State in Chile, 1850–1930*. Durham, N.C.: Duke University Press, 2009.

Mintz, Steven. *Huck's Raft: A History of American Childhood*. Cambridge, Mass.: Belknap Press of Harvard University Press, 2004.

———. *The Prime of Life: A History of Modern Adulthood*. Cambridge, Mass.: Belknap Press of Harvard University Press, 2015.

Modell, John. *Into One's Own: From Youth to Adulthood in the United States, 1920–1975*. Berkeley: University of California Press, 1991.

Monahan, Thomas P. *The Pattern of Age at Marriage in the United States*. 2 vols. Philadelphia: Stephenson-Brothers, 1951.

Myers, Tamara. *Caught: Montreal's Modern Girls and the Law, 1869–1945*. Toronto: University of Toronto Press, 2006.

Odem, Mary E. *Delinquent Daughters: Protecting and Policing Adolescent Female Sexuality in the United States, 1885–1920*. Chapel Hill: University of North Carolina Press, 1995.

Palladino, Grace. *Teenagers: An American History*. New York: Basic, 1997.

Paoletti, Jo B. *Pink and Blue: Telling the Boys from the Girls in America*. Bloomington: Indiana University Press, 2012.

Pascoe, Peggy. *Relations of Rescue: The Search for Female Moral Authority in the American West, 1874–1939*. New York: Oxford University Press, 1990.

———. *What Comes Naturally: Miscegenation Law and the Making of Race in America*. New York: Oxford University Press, 2009.

Pearson, Susan J. *The Rights of the Defenseless: Protecting Animals and Children in Gilded Age America*. Chicago: University of Chicago Press, 2011.

Perdue, Theda. *Cherokee Women: Gender and Culture Change, 1700–1835*. Lincoln: University of Nebraska Press, 1999.

Phillips, Roderick. *Untying the Knot: A Short History of Divorce*. New York: Cambridge University Press, 1991.

Pivar, David. *Purity Crusade: Sexual Morality and Social Control, 1868–1900*. Westport, Conn.: Greenwood, 1973.

Polikoff, Nancy D. *Beyond (Straight and Gay) Marriage: Valuing All Families under the Law*. Boston: Beacon, 2008.

Powdermaker, Hortense. *After Freedom: A Cultural Study in the Deep South*. 1939. Reprint, New York: Atheneum, 1968.

Quadagno, Jill. *The Color of Welfare: How Racism Undermined the War on Poverty*. New York: Oxford University Press, 1994.

Rickels, Patricia, and Milton Rickels. *Seba Smith*. Boston: Twayne, 1977.

Riley, Denise. *Building and Breaking Families in the American West*. Albuquerque: University of New Mexico Press, 1996.

———. *Divorce: An American Tradition*. New York: Oxford University Press, 1992.

Robertson, Stephen. *Crimes against Children: Sexual Violence and Legal Culture in New York City, 1880–1960*. Chapel Hill: University of North Carolina Press, 2005.

Richardson, H. Edward. *Cassius Marcellus Clay: Firebrand of Freedom*. Lexington: University Press of Kentucky, 1976.

Sacco, Lynn. *Unspeakable: Father-Daughter Incest in American History.* Baltimore: Johns
   Hopkins University Press, 2009.
Sallee, Shelley. *The Whiteness of Child Labor Reform in the New South.* Athens: University
   of Georgia Press, 2004.
Salmon, Marylynn. *Women and the Law of Property in Early America.* Chapel Hill:
   University of North Carolina Press, 1986.
Schlissel, Lillian. *Women's Diaries of the Westward Journey.* New York: Schocken, 2004.
Schmidt, James D. *Industrial Violence and the Legal Origins of Child Labor.* New York:
   Cambridge University Press, 2010.
Schrum, Kelly. *Some Wore Bobby Sox: The Emergence of Teenage Girls' Culture, 1920–1945.*
   New York: Palgrave MacMillan, 2004.
Schudson, Michael. *Discovering the News: A Social History of American Newspapers.*
   New York: Basic Books, 1978.
Schwartz, Marie Jenkins. *Born in Bondage: Growing Up Enslaved in the Antebellum South.*
   Cambridge, Mass.: Harvard University Press, 2000.
Scott, Anne Firor. *The Southern Lady: From Pedestal to Politics.* Chicago: University of
   Chicago Press, 1970.
Silverman, Kenneth. *Edgar A. Poe: Mournful and Never-Ending Remembrance.* New York:
   Harper Perennial, 1991.
Simmons, Christina. *Making Marriage Modern: Women's Sexuality from the Progressive Era
   to World War II.* New York: Oxford University Press, 2011.
Simmons, Marc. *Kit Carson and His Three Wives: A Family History.* Albuquerque:
   University of New Mexico Press, 2003.
Sleeper-Smith, Susan. *Indian Women and French Men: Rethinking Cultural Encounters in
   the Western Great Lakes.* Amherst: University of Massachusetts Press, 2001.
Smith, George D. *Nauvoo Polygamy: "But We Called It Celestial Marriage."* Salt Lake City,
   Utah: Signature Books, 2008.
Solinger, Rickie. *Wake Up Little Susie: Single Pregnancy and Race before* Roe v. Wade.
   New York: Routledge, 1992.
Spear, Jennifer M. *Race, Sex, and Social Order in Early New Orleans.* Baltimore: Johns
   Hopkins University Press, 2009.
Spruill, Julia Cherry. *Women's Life and Work in the Southern Colonies.* New York: W. W.
   Norton, 1998.
Stansell, Christine. *City of Women: Sex and Class in New York, 1780–1860.* New York:
   Alfred A. Knopf, 1986.
Starr, Kevin. *Inventing the Dream: California through the Progressive Era.* New York:
   Oxford University Press, 1986.
Stevenson, Brenda E. *Life in Black and White: Family and Community in the Slave South.*
   New York: Oxford University Press, 1996.
Stremlau, Rose. *Sustaining the Cherokee Family: Kinship and the Allotment of an Indigenous
   Nation.* Chapel Hill: University of North Carolina Press, 2011.

Thornton, Russell. *American Indian Holocaust and Survival: A Population History since 1492.* Norman: University of Oklahoma Press, 1987.

Tosches, Nick. *Hellfire: The Jerry Lee Lewis Story.* New York: Dell, 1982.

Walkowitz, Judith. *City of Dreadful Delight: Narratives of Sexual Danger in Late Victorian London.* Chicago: University of Chicago Press, 1992.

Warner, Michael. *The Trouble with Normal: Sex, Politics, and the Ethics of Queer Life.* New York: Free Press, 1999.

Weiss, Jessica. *To Have and to Hold: Marriage, the Baby Boom, and Social Change.* Chicago: University of Chicago Press, 2000.

Welke, Barbara Young. *Law and the Borders of Belonging in the Long Nineteenth Century United States.* New York: Cambridge University Press, 2010.

Whisnant, David E. *All That Is Native and Fine: The Politics and Culture of an American Region.* Chapel Hill: University of North Carolina Press, 1983.

White, Kevin. *The First Sexual Revolution: The Emergence of Male Heterosexuality in Modern America.* New York: New York University Press, 1992.

Wilentz, Sean. *Chants Democratic: New York City and the Rise of the American Working Class, 1788–1850.* New York: Oxford University Press, 1984.

Wolcott, Victoria. *Remaking Respectability: African American Women in Interwar Detroit.* Chapel Hill: University of North Carolina Press, 2001.

Wood, Sharon E. *The Freedom of the Streets: Work, Citizenship, and Sexuality in a Gilded Age City.* Chapel Hill: University of North Carolina Press, 2005.

Wright, Doris Marion. *A Yankee in Mexican California: Abel Stearns, 1798–1848.* Santa Barbara, Calif.: Walter Hebberd, 1977.

Zelizer, Viviana. *Pricing the Priceless Child: The Changing Social Value of Children.* 1985. Reprint, Princeton, N.J.: Princeton University Press, 1994.

Zimring, Franklin. *The Changing Legal World of Adolescence.* New York: Free Press, 1982.

Articles and Book Chapters

Alexander, Thomas G. "Wilford Woodruff and the Mormon Reformation of 1855–57." *Dialogue: A Journal of Mormon Thought* 15 (Summer 1992): 20–38.

Associated Press. "Pennsylvania Governor: Gay Couples Barred from Marriage 'Like 12-Year-Olds.'" *Guardian,* August 29, 2013.

Blackwell, Deborah L. "Female Stereotypes and the Creation of Appalachia, 1870–1940." In *Women of the Mountain South: Identity, Work, and Activism,* edited by Connie Park Rice and Marie Tedesco, 74–94. Athens: Ohio University Press, 2015.

Blank, Rebecca M., Kerwin Kofi Charles, and James M. Sallee. "Do State Laws Affect the Age of Marriage? A Cautionary Tale about Avoidance Behavior." Working Paper 13667, National Bureau of Economic Research, 2007.

Brückner, Hannah, and Peter Bearman. "After the Promise: The STD consequences of Adolescent Virginity Pledges." *Journal of Adolescent Health* 36, no. 4 (April 2005): 271–78.

Brumberg, Joan Jacobs. "Zenanas and Girlless Villages: The Ethnology of American
    Evangelical Women, 1870–1910." *Journal of American History* 69 (September 1982):
    347–71.
Carr, Lois Green, and Lorena S. Walsh. "The Planter's Wife: The Experience of White
    Women in Seventeenth-Century Maryland." *William and Mary Quarterly*, 3rd ser., 34,
    no. 4 (October 1977): 542–71.
"Case Note: Constitutional Law—Married High School Students—Participation in
    Extracurricular Activities." *Tennessee Law Review* 40 (Winter 1973): 268–75.
Castañeda, Antonia I. "Engendering the History of Alta California, 1769–1848: Gender,
    Sexuality, and the Family." In *Contested Eden: California before the Gold Rush*, edited
    by Ramón A. Gutiérrez and Richard J. Orsi, 230–59. Berkeley: University of California
    Press, 1998.
Chandra, Anjani, Joyce Abma, Penelope Mazza, and Christine Bachrach. "Adoption,
    Adoption Seeking, and Relinquishment for Adoption in the United States." *Advance
    Data*, no. 306, May 11, 1999.
"Charles and Eunice Winstead Johns." In *Hancock County, Tennessee and Its People,
    1844–2003*, vol. 3, 217. Sneedville, Tenn.: Hancock County Historical and Genealogical
    Society, 2004.
Coates, Ta-Nehisi. "The Myth of Western Civilization." *Atlantic*, December 31, 2013.
Cocca, Carolyn. "'16 Will Get You 20': Adolescent Sexuality and Statutory Rape Laws."
    In *Adolescent Sexuality: A Historical Handbook and Guide*, edited by Carolyn Cocca,
    15–29. Westport, Conn.: Praeger, 2006.
Cook, Frank Gaylord. "The Marriage Celebration in the Colonies." *Atlantic Monthly*,
    March 1888, 350–62.
Cox, Caroline. "Boy Soldiers of the American Revolution: The Effects of War on Society."
    In *Children and Youth in a New Nation*, edited by James Marten, 13–28. New York:
    New York University Press, 2009.
Dahl, Gordon B. "Early Teen Marriage and Future Poverty." *Demography* 47, no. 3
    (August 2010): 689–718.
Davis, Rebecca L. "'Not Marriage at All, but Simple Harlotry': The Companionate
    Marriage Controversy." *Journal of American History* 94, no. 4 (March 2008): 1137–63.
De Block, Andreas, and Pieter R. Adriaens. "Pathologizing Sexual Deviance: A History."
    Journal of Sex Research 50, nos. 3–4 (2013): 276–98.
"Does Marriage Alone Emancipate a Male Minor?" *Yale Law Journal* 22, no. 4 (February
    1913): 338–43.
Dubler, Ariela R. "Immoral Purposes: Marriage and the Genus of Illicit Sex." *Yale Law
    Journal* 115, no. 4 (January 2006): 756–812.
Duggan, Lisa. "Holy Matrimony!" *Nation*, March 15, 2004, 14, 16–18.
Dunlap, Leslie K. "The Reform of Rape Law and the Problem of White Men:
    Age-of-Consent Campaigns in the South, 1885–1910." In *Sex, Love, Race: Crossing
    Boundaries in North American History*, edited by Martha Hodes, 352–72. New York:
    New York University Press, 1999.

Ettelbrick, Paula. "Since When Is Marriage a Path to Liberation?" In *Same-Sex Marriage: Pro and Con*, edited by Andrew Sullivan, 122–28. New York: Vintage, 2004.

Faragher, John Mack. "The Custom of the Country: Cross-Cultural Marriage in the Far Western Fur Trade." In *Western Women: Their Land, Their Lives*, edited by Lillian Schlissel, Vicki L. Ruiz, and Janice Monk, 199–215. Albuquerque: University of New Mexico Press, 1988.

Field, Corinne T., and Nicholas L. Syrett. "Introduction." In *Age in America: The Colonial Era to the Present*, edited by Corinne T. Field and Nicholas L. Syrett, 1–20. New York: New York University Press, 2015.

Freedman, Estelle B. "'Uncontrolled Desires': The Response to the Sexual Psychopath, 1920–1960." *Journal of American History* 74, no. 1 (June 1987): 83–106.

Glass, Jennifer, and Philip Levchak. "Red States, Blue States, and Divorce: Understanding the Impact of Conservative Protestantism on Regional Variation in Divorce Rates." *American Journal of Sociology* 119, no. 4 (January 2014): 1002–46.

Gorney, Cynthia. "Too Young to Wed: The Secret World of Child Brides." *National Geographic*, June 2011, 79–99.

Grossberg, Michael. "Children's Legal Rights? A Historical Look at a Legal Paradox." In *Children at Risk in America: History, Concepts, and Public Policy*, edited by Roberta Wollons, 111–40. Albany: State University of New York Press, 1993.

———. "Guarding the Altar: Physiological Restrictions and the Rise of State Intervention in Matrimony." *American Journal of Legal History* 26, no. 3 (July 1982): 197–226.

———. "Liberation and Caretaking: Fighting over Children's Rights in Postwar America." In *Reinventing Childhood after World War II*, edited by Paula S. Fass and Michael Grossberg, 19–37. Philadelphia: University of Pennsylvania Press, 2012.

Grossman, Joanna, and Chris Guthrie. "The Road Less Taken: Annulment at the Turn of the Century." *American Journal of Legal History* 40, no. 3 (July 1996): 307–30.

Guttmacher Institute, "Fact Sheet: American Teens' Sexual and Reproductive Health." May 2014. http://www.guttmacher.org/pubs/FB-ATSRH.html#1.

Hammond, Judith A., Bettie S. Cole, and Scott H. Beck. "Religious Heritage and Teenage Marriage." *Review of Religious Research* 35, no. 2 (December 1993): 117–33.

"How Duck Dynasty's Phil Robertson Avoided Prison for Breaking Statutory Rape Laws." *Political Blindspot*, January 16, 2014. http://politicalblindspot.com/how-duck-dynastys-phil-avoided-prison/.

James, T. E. "The Age of Majority." *American Journal of Legal History* 4 (1960): 22–33.

Johnson, Susan Lee. "Writing Kit Carson in the Cold War: 'The Family,' 'The West,' and Their Chroniclers." In *On the Borders of Love and Power: Families and Kinship in the Intercultural American Southwest*, edited by David Wallace Adams and Crista DeLuzio, 278–318. Berkeley: University of California Press, 2012.

Katz, Sanford N., William A. Schroeder, and Lawrence R. Sidman. "Emancipating Our Children—Coming of Legal Age in America." *Family Law Quarterly* 7, no. 3 (Fall 1973): 211–41.

Kost, Kathryn, and Stanley Henshaw. "U.S. Teenage Pregnancies, Births, and Abortions, 2010: National and State Trends by Age, Race, and Ethnicity." Washington: Guttmacher Institute, May 2014.

Kuby, William. "Till Disinterest Do Us Part: Trial Marriage, Public Policy, and the Fear of Familial Decay in the United States, 1900–1930." *Journal of the History of Sexuality* 23, no. 3 (September 2014): 383–414.

Landrum, Shane. "From Family Bibles to Birth Certificates: Young People, Proof of Age, and American Political Cultures, 1820–1915." In *Age in America: The Colonial Era to the Present*, edited by Corinne T. Field and Nicholas L. Syrett, 124–47. New York: New York University Press, 2015.

Larson, Jane E. "'Even a Worm Will Turn at Last': Rape Reform in Late Nineteenth-Century America." *Yale Journal of Law and the Humanities* 9, no. 1 (1997): 1–71.

Lehrer, Evelyn L. "The Role of Religion in Union Formation: An Economic Perspective." *Population Research and Policy Review* 23, no. 2 (April 2004): 161–85.

Le Strat, Yann, Caroline Dubertret, and Bernard Le Foll. "Child Marriage in the United States and Its Association with Mental Health in Women." *Pediatrics* 128, no. 3 (September 2011): 524–30.

Matthews, Howard A. "The Courts and Married Students." *School Life* 44 (November–December 1961): 5–9.

Miranda, Gloria E. "Gente de Razón Marriage Patterns in Spanish and Mexican California: A Case Study of Santa Barbara and Los Angeles." *Southern California Quarterly* 63, no. 1 (Spring 1981): 1–21.

Modell, John, Frank F. Furstenberg, Jr., and Douglas Strong. "The Timing of Marriage in the Transition to Adulthood: Continuity and Change, 1860–1975." *American Journal of Sociology* 84: Suppl. (1978): S120–S150.

Moody, Charles Amadon. "De Baker, Doña Arcadia." *Out West* 30, no. 4 (April 1909): 317.

Moore, Bernice Milburn. "Present Status and Future Trends in the Southern White Family." *Social Forces* 16, no. 3 (March 1938): 406–10.

Pande, Ishita. "Coming of Age: Law, Sex and Childhood in Late Colonial India." *Gender and History* 24, no. 1 (April 2012): 205–30.

"Parent and Child: Whether Marriage of an Infant Emancipates Him." *Harvard Law Review* 25, no. 3 (January 1912): 295.

Pearson, Susan. "'Age Ought to Be a Fact': The Campaign against Child Labor and the Rise of the Birth Certificate." *Journal of American History* 101, no. 4 (March 2015): 97–121.

Price, John P. "Marriage vs. Education: A Constitutional Conflict." *Mississippi Law Journal* 44, no. 2 (1973): 248–60.

Reed, James W., and John C. Spurlock. "Young and Pregnant: Teenager Pregnancies in the United States." In *Adolescent Sexuality: A Historical Handbook and Guide*, edited by Carolyn Cocca, 31–44. Westport, Conn.: Praeger, 2006.

Rice, Connie Park. "Introduction: A Tapestry of Voices: Women's History in the Mountain South." In *Women of the Mountain South: Identity, Work, and Activism*, edited by Connie Park Rice and Marie Tedesco, 1–20. Athens: Ohio University Press, 2015.

Rickman, Johanna. "'He Would Never Consent in His Heart': Child Marriages in Early Modern England." *Journal of the History of Childhood and Youth* 6, no. 2 (Spring 2013): 294–313.

Robertson, Stephen. "Age of Consent Law and the Making of Modern Childhood in New York City, 1886–1921." *Journal of Social History* 35, no. 4 (Summer 2002): 781–98.

Rose, Willie Lee. Introduction to *Reminiscences of My Life in Camp*, by Susie King Taylor, 7–17. 1902. Reprint, New York: Markus Wiener, 1988.

Rust, Marion. Introduction to *Charlotte Temple*, by Susanna Rowson, xi–xxx. 1791. Reprint, New York: W. W. Norton, 2011.

Scherman, Timothy. "Elizabeth Oakes Smith." In *Dictionary of Literary Biography 235: American Women Prose Writers, 1820–1870*, 222–30. Detroit, Mich.: Gale Research, 2000.

Schlossman, Steven, and Susan Turner. "Status Offenders, Criminal Offenders, and Children: 'At Risk' in Early Twentieth-Century Juvenile Court." In *Children at Risk in America: History, Concepts, and Public Policy*, edited by Roberta Wollons, 32–57. Albany: State University of New York Press, 1993.

Schmidt, James D. "The Ends of Innocence: Age as a Mode of Inquiry in Sociolegal Studies." *Law and Social Inquiry* 32, no. 4 (Fall 2007): 1027–57.

———. "'Rendered More Useful': Child Labor and Age Consciousness in the Long Nineteenth Century." In *Age in America: Colonial Era to the Present*, edited by Corinne T. Field and Nicholas L. Syrett, 148–65. New York: New York University Press, 2015.

Seger, Randolph L. "Wellsand v. Valparaiso Community School Corporation: Equal Protection for the Married Football Player." *Indiana Law Journal* 47, no. 2 (1972): 378–92.

Seiler, Naomi. "Is Teen Marriage a Solution?" Washington: Center for Law and Social Policy, 2002.

Shapiro, Marilyn. "Anna Cora Mowatt: Forgotten Dramatist and Actress." In *Women's Contributions to Nineteenth-Century American Theatre*, edited by Miriam López Rodríguez and María Dolores Narbona Carrión, 85–95. Valencia, Spain: University of Valencia Library, 2004.

Sinha, Mrinalini. "Introduction." In Katherine Mayo, *Mother India: Selections from the Controversial 1927 Text*, edited by Mrinalini Sinha, 1–62. Ann Arbor: University of Michigan Press, 2000.

"Sketch of John Camm." *William and Mary Quarterly* 19, no. 1 (July 1910): 28–30.

Smith, Daniel Scott, and Michael Hindus. "Premarital Pregnancy in America, 1640–1971: An Overview and an Interpretation." *Journal of Interdisciplinary History* 5 (1975): 537–70.

Stamps, Pearl Pauline. "Abel Stearns, California Pioneer." *Grizzly Bear*, May 1926, 1–2, 4, 8, 12.

Stein, Edward. "Past and Present Proposed Amendments to the United States Constitution Regarding Marriage." *Washington University Law Quarterly* 82, no. 3 (2004): 611–85.

Stein, Julie Solow. "Early to Wed: Teenage Marriage in Postwar America." *Journal of the History of Childhood and Youth* 6, no. 2 (Spring 2013): 359–82.

Strayhorn, Joseph, and Jillian C. Strayhorn. "Religiosity and Teen Birth in the United States." *Reproductive Health* 6, no. 14 (2009): 1–7.

Syrett, Nicholas L. "The Contested Meanings of Child Marriage in the Turn-of-the-Century United States." In *Children and Youth during the Gilded Age and Progressive Era*, edited by James Marten, 145–65. New York: New York University Press, 2014.

———. "'I Did and I Don't Regret It': Child Marriage and the Contestation of Childhood in the United States, 1880–1925." *Journal of the History of Childhood and Youth* 36, no. 2 (Spring 2013): 314–31.

———. "Statutory Marriage Ages and the Gendered Construction of Adulthood in the Nineteenth Century." In *Age in America: The Colonial Era to the Present*, edited by Corinne T. Field and Nicholas L. Syrett, 103–23. New York: New York University Press, 2015.

Taylor, Kelly S. "The Creation of a Public Persona in the Poetry of Anna Cora Mowatt." *American Periodicals* 11 (2001): 65–80.

Uecker, Jeremy E., and Charles E. Stokes. "Early Marriage in the United States." *Journal of Marriage and the Family* 70, no. 4 (November 2008): 835–46.

Wardle, Lynn D. "Rethinking Marital Age Restrictions." *Journal of Family Law* 22, no. 1 (1983–84): 1–57.

Willoughby, Brian J., Scott S. Hall, and Heather P. Luczak. "Marital Paradigms: A Conceptual Framework for Marital Attitudes, Values, and Beliefs." *Journal of Family Issues* (2013): 188–211.

Wiltenburg, Joy. "Excerpts from the Diary of Elizabeth Oakes Smith." *Signs: Journal of Women in Culture and Society* 9, no. 3 (1984): 534–48.

Xu, Xiaohe, Clark D. Hudspeth, and John P. Bartkowski. "The Timing of First Marriage: Are There Religious Variations?" *Journal of Family Issues* 26, no. 5 (July 2005): 584–618.

UNPUBLISHED PAPERS AND DISSERTATIONS

Hagan, Carrie Settle. "Girls, Sex, and Juvenile Delinquency in Post–World War II Los Angeles." Ph.D. diss., Carnegie Mellon University, 2012.

Stamatov, Suzanne. "Family, Kin, and Community in Colonial New Mexico, 1694–1800." Ph.D. diss., University of New Mexico, 2003.

Stremlau, Rose. "Allotment, Sexuality, and the State: Reconceptualizing the Privatization of Land and the Politicization of Indigenous Bodies in the South." Unpublished paper in possession of the author.

Uecker, Jeremy. "Early Marriage in the United States: Why Some Marry Young, Why Many Don't, and What Difference It Makes." Ph.D. diss., University of Texas at Austin, 2010.

Index

Page numbers in italics indicate figures or tables.

Abandonment, fear of, 46–47

Abduction: charges of, 153; petition regarding, 85–87

Abortion, 228, 234, 254, 261, 263–64, 268

Ackley, Mary, 69

Adolescence, 20, 44, 46, 58, 145–46, 163, 218, 229, 233–34

Adolescence (Hall), 145

Adulthood, 162; age of majority as, 17, 34–37, 113, 259; childhood and, 3, 5, 22, 70, 122, 124, 140, 144, 145, 146, 185, 204, 208–9, 211, 218–19; desire for, 145, 226, 229, 236–37, 245; legal transformation into via marriage, 4, 9, 17, 27, 89, 126, 131, 133, 144, 148–56, 162, 164, 177, 196, 197, 199; privileges of, 4, 16, 21, 36, 117, 122, 145, 162, 234, 236–37, 265; responsibilities of, 8, 10, 16, 58, 65, 102, 105, 114, 141; for slaves, 58, 60; symbols of, 7–8, 185, 236, 270–71

African Americans, 1, 14, 214, 222; age-consciousness of, 222–25; as feminists, 258; marriage decline of, 254, 264; marriage as minors by, 57–60, 187–88, 213, 229, 247–48; poverty of, 222–25, 251, 254, 263, 264; pregnancy rates for, 223, 251; rape of, 223–24; as slaves, 17, 57–60; unwed motherhood of, 255–56, 263

Age: in common law, 19–22; of puberty, 22; significance of, 3, 84–85, 143, 144, 145, 163, 177, 220. *See also* Adolescence; Adulthood; Childhood

Age, minimum marriageable: migratory marriage due to, 129, 184, 241–42; reformers of, in 1920s, 179–81; in the South, 215–16; state equalizing of, 258; state statutes regarding, 23–34, 130–33, 244–45, 259–62. *See also entries for individual states*

Age consciousness, 20, 43, 44, 51, 102, 113, 146, 253; absence of, 83–85, 219–20, 222–25, 251; inculcation of, 82–83, 102, 220, 222; in Massachusetts, 78, 81–83; in New York, 131–33; in rural America, 140, 224, 253; among slaves, 58–59

Age of majority: as adulthood, 12, 19, 22, 34–35, 113, 144; equalization of, 181, 195–98, 199, 259; gender distinctions in, 17, 34–37, 114–15, 195–98, 244; lowering of, 259; for property management, 20–21, 35; service to parents until, 19, 88–89

Alabama, 212; age of majority in, 12, 197, 259; marriage law in, 31, 32, 33, 134, 262; marriage of minors in, 154, 262; reformers in, 197

Alaska, marriage law in, 135

Albany Argus, 122

Alcott, William, 108–9

Alexander, Thomas, 73

Allen, William, 150

Alta California, 39–42, 61–62, 65–67, 75–76

American Academy of Pediatrics, 2–3

343